Doll Values

EDITION

=━ ANTIQUE TO MODERN ━=

OUR #1
BESTSELLING
DOLL
BOOK!

COLLECTOR BOOKS
A Division of Schroeder Publishing Co., Inc.

Linda
Edward

Front cover: Three small pictures from top to bottom: 12" composition Kewpie, $190.00. Photo courtesy of Withington Auction, Inc. 18" Izannah Walker doll with wardrobe and provenance, sold for $41,000.00 at auction. Photo courtesy of Withington Auction, Inc. 20" Gibson Girl, $2,100.00. Photo courtesy of Withington Auction, Inc. Large picture: 12" character child, mold 206, $9,000.00. Photo courtesy of James D. Julia, Inc.

Back cover: 10" Parian-type, fancy hair, glass eyes, decorated shoulderplate, all original, $1,500.00. Doll from private collection.

Cover design by Christen Byrd
Book design by Beth Ray

COLLECTOR BOOKS
P.O. Box 3009
Paducah, Kentucky 42002-3009

www.collectorbooks.com

Copyright © 2011 Linda Edward

The current values in this book should be used only as a guide. They are not intended to set prices, which vary from one section of the country to another. Auction prices as well as dealer prices vary greatly and are affected by condition as well as demand. Neither the author nor the publisher assumes responsibility for any losses that might be incurred as a result of consulting this guide.

Proudly printed and bound in the
United States of America

ACKNOWLEDGMENTS

Thank you to the following collectors and auction houses for sharing their dolls and those of their friends for this edition of *Doll Values*: Alderfer Auction & Appraisal, Virginia Aris, Patty Asker, Carol Barboza, Zendelle Bouchard, Joe Bucchi, Pat Buckley, Steve Carissimo, Ben Cassara, Ruth Cayton, Cybermogul Dolls, Lucy DiTerlizzi, Dolls and Lace, Dollsantique, Dollhappy, Dollyology Vintage Dolls, The Doll Works, Emmie's Antique Doll Castle, Shirley Fisher, Fourty Fifty Sixty, Glenda Antique Dolls & Collectables, Gloria's Antique Dolls, Valerie Gomes, Joan Gourgas, Jean Grout, Virginia Heyerdahl, Elaine Holda, Susan Holeman, William J. Jenack Estate Appraisers & Auctioneers, James D. Julia, Inc., Joan & Lynette Antique Dolls and Accessories, Joy's Antique Dolls, Doris Lechler, Ann Lloyd Antique Dolls, Joy Macielle/Quality Vintage Doll Patterns, Judy Masters, McMasters Harris Auction Co., Memories of Things Past, Ursula Mertz, Morphy Auctions, My Dear Dolly, My Dolly Dearest, Marie Novocin, Cathy Ellis O'Brien, Glenda O'Connor, George & Cynthia Orgeron, Dominique Perrin, Louise Scala, Sharing My Dolls 'N Stuff, Skinner, Inc., Patricia Snyder, Sweetbriar Auctions, Turn of the Century Antiques, Patricia Vaillancourt, Suzanne Vlach, Helen Welsh, and Withington Auction, Inc.

I would also like to thank all doll researchers and collectors who have generously shared their dolls and knowledge through the many fine reference books, articles, seminars, special exhibits, and doll club programs. Without this constant exchange of information we would all be searching in the dark for answers.

Finally, I must thank my husband, Al Edward, for his encouragement, support, and belief in me and the work I pursue.

HOW TO USE THIS BOOK

This book is a tool for the collector, a place to start on a journey of study that can enrich a lifetime. The best piece of advice this collector ever received was "buy every doll reference book you can find." Each volume, be it old or new, contains some piece of information that will be of aid to the collector. Building a reference library of your own will pay you back many times over in the knowledge it will bring you, knowledge which will ultimately allow you to make better decisions when purchasing a doll for your own collection. In addition to building a reference library, I would also suggest that you take every opportunity to look at dolls wherever you go. Nothing beats first-hand examination. Visit every doll museum and special display you can find, go to shows and really look at the dolls that interest you most. Join a doll club to learn more and share your discoveries with others. All of these experiences will put you in a better position to understand and evaluate a doll when you are considering a purchase.

The question of course is, how much is a doll worth? It is the question we contend with when buying our dolls, inheriting our dolls, insuring our dolls, and in deciding to sell our dolls. In

How to Use This Book

value speaks to how important an item is to us and to the world in general. Does an item teach us something about the past, is it significant to some particular event or person, does an item have special sentimental value to us personally? This type of value, although important, is not always reflected in an item's monetary value. Monetary value or market value relates to how much it would cost to go out and purchase any particular item at the present time. Market value is collector-driven. Demand for particular items, combined with the current economic climate, determine the market value of a doll. In other words, a perfectly wonderful example of any given doll will vary in market value during differing economic conditions. This makes certain times good "selling times" and other times good "buying times." This book can be a guide to helping collectors make wise decisions in regard to their collecting actions.

When evaluating any doll there are several questions to ask oneself. These relate to identification, quality, originality, condition, rarity, and value. Each component is important to the overall picture of any doll. All dolls should be thoroughly examined before making a purchase.

Identification. What is this doll? A doll is classified by the material from which its head is made. Therefore, a doll with a composition head on a cloth body will be considered a composition doll, or a doll with a papier-mâché head on a leather body will be considered a papier-mâché doll, and so on. Look for and learn about makers' marks. These will be of invaluable aid in identifying the doll at which you are looking. Many manufacturers marked their dolls on the back of the head or on the torso. An appendix of makers' initials and an appendix of known mold numbers are included in the back of this book to assist you.

Quality. As stated by Patsy Moyer in the first edition of this book, "all dolls are not created equal." Any model of doll made by any particular manufacturer can range vastly in quality depending on the conditions on the day it was made. Remember, these dolls were produced in factories which in many cases turned out thousands of dolls a year. How worn was the mold when this doll was poured, what weather conditions affected the materials it was made from, how tired was the worker who cleaned or painted a particular doll that day? If you line up six AM 390s you will be looking at six different degrees of quality of finish. Therefore, when preparing to make a purchase, consider each example of doll carefully from a standpoint of quality. A sharply molded, evenly textured, well painted doll will always be of more value than an example of the same doll with blurry molding, uneven texture, or poor quality painting.

Originality is another important component of a doll evaluation. Does the doll have the correct eyes, wig, body type, and clothing? Each of these parts adds value to the doll and dolls on incorrect bodies or with replaced clothing or wigs should not bring the same amount in the marketplace as examples in all-original condition.

Condition. What is the overall condition of the doll? Check carefully to look for damage or repair to the doll. In most cases a damaged or repaired doll will not be worth as much as a perfect example.

Rarity is perhaps one of the most important aspects of doll evaluation. How unusual is this doll? How many were made and survive? How difficult would it be to find another example of this doll today? Sometimes rarity can cause us to forgive problems of originality or condition that would, in a more common doll, deter us from adding a particular example to our collection.

Value takes into account all of the aforementioned qualifications we have discussed and combines them with somewhat more elusive components such as collector demand and trends.

How to Use This Book

At various points in time collectors tend to favor certain dolls. A good example of this can be seen in the value of the Bye-Lo Baby. Every generation of collectors tends to start out collecting the dolls they had or wanted as children. In the 1950s and 1960s many adult collectors eagerly sought the Bye-Lo Baby from the 1920s and the dolls achieved a comparatively high market price. In the past 20 years the value of the Bye-Lo has changed very little compared to other antique dolls because collector demand for them has quieted down.

After evaluating each of the aforementioned aspects of any doll, this book will assist you in figuring out the current market value of the doll. Unless otherwise noted, the values stated in this volume represent dolls in good overall condition with original or appropriate clothing. When looking at the values presented here, gage the particular doll you are considering accordingly. Allow a lower value for dolls which do not meet the standard for the values listed here. This is especially important in judging vintage collectible or modern dolls. These must be in perfect and completely original condition with appropriate hang tags to attain the values listed in this guide. For example, an all-original #3 Barbie doll in good condition will bring approximately half the price of the same doll mint-in-box.

This book is laid out in alphabetical order. You will notice that it is not divided into "antique" and "modern" sections as some other books are. The reason for this choice is threefold. Firstly, the line between antique and modern is not as clear cut in doll collecting as it is in other areas. In furniture, for instance, a piece must be at least 100 years old to be considered antique, whereas in car collecting a vehicle that is 25 years old is considered antique. In doll collecting the line is blurry, although it generally falls somewhere in the neighborhood of 75 years. Dolls 30 to 75 years old are most often referred to as "collectible vintage," and dolls 30 years old or less are usually referred to as "modern." Secondly, many doll-making companies were in business for such long periods of time that they produced dolls which would now be considered antique as well as dolls that fall into the collectible vintage and modern categories. Thirdly, it is the belief of this author that by not creating barriers between dolls of different ages we see a more complete picture of the doll world and promote a better understanding of the history of the dolls we love and of our fellow collectors.

As stated previously, this book is laid out in an alphabetical order by the manufacturer's name or by general type. Most dolls are marked in some way which indicates their maker. Wherever possible those markings have been included for reference. The general type headings include dolls made of like materials. Under these headings you will find dolls made by small companies, or about which little is known as well as unmarked, and as yet unattributable dolls.

The values listed in this book are compiled from several sources including auction prices, online auction prices, dealer asking prices, dealer prices realized, as well as other sources. These values are then compiled, analyzed, and averaged. Although the collecting world is now much more global than it was even just a few years ago, there are still some regional differences in value which are generated by collector interest and doll availability in certain areas. This book is meant as a guide and is not the "definitive" word on doll values. Ultimately a doll is worth whatever a particular collector wishes to pay for it. Neither this author nor the publisher of this book takes any responsibility for any decision or action taken by an individual on the basis of the information presented here. As stated earlier, this book is one more tool for collectors to use in their decision-making processes.

How to Use This Book

Finally I will say that study, evaluation, and value, although important, are not the bottom line in doll collecting. Ultimately we each need to "follow our bliss" as it were, and buy dolls that mean something to us and enrich our lives and collections.

Collectors seeking to learn more about dolls and exchange doll knowledge can turn to a national organization whose goals are education, research, preservation, and enjoyment of dolls. The United Federation of Doll Clubs can tell you if a doll club in your area is accepting members or tell you how to become a member-at-large. You may write for more information at:

United Federation of Doll Clubs, Inc.
10900 North Pomona Avenue
Kansas City, MO 64153
Phone: 816-891-7040
Fax: 816-891-8360
Email: info@ufdc.org
www.ufdc.org

CODES

GOLD (All Caps)	MAIN CATEGORY EX: ADVERTISING DOLLS
Red (Roman)	First subcategory, usually a name of the doll, company, or material ex: Gerber Baby
Green (Italic)	Second subcategory ex: *1979 – 1985*
Black (Roman)	Third subcategory ex: Talker
Black (Indented-Italic)	Fourth subcategory ex: *Hard plastic head*
* at auction	

ADVERTISING DOLLS

Dolls of various materials, made by a variety of manufacturers, to promote commercial brands or specific products. Doll in good condition with original clothing and accessories.

Cream of Wheat, Rastus, uncut panel of cut-and-sew cloth, ca. 1929, $100.00. *Photo courtesy of Memories of Things Past.*

Aunt Jemima, cloth, Aunt Jemima, Uncle Moses, Diana, and Wade Davis
    16".................. $95.00 – 105.00
Buster Brown Shoes, composition head, cloth body, tag reads "Buster Brown Shoes"
    15"................. $250.00 – 300.00
Button Nose, 1947, for Dan River sheets, cloth mask face
    23"..................... $30.00 – 35.00
Clicquot Club Eskimo, 1939, Reliable Doll Co., composition, painted eyes, plush snowsuit
    14"................. $225.00 – 275.00
Colgate Fab Soap Princess Doll, ca. 1951
    5½".................... $12.00 – 18.00
Cream of Wheat, Rastus, printed cloth doll
    16".................. $90.00 – 100.00
Gerber Baby, 1936 to present. An advertising and trademark doll for Gerber Products, a baby food manufacturer located in Fremont, Michigan. More for black or special sets with accessories.
1936, cloth one-piece doll, printed girl or boy, holds can

    8".................. $450.00 – 500.00
1955 – 1958, Sun Rubber Company, designed by Bernard Lipfert, vinyl
    12" – 18".......... $90.00 – 110.00
1965, Arrow Rubber & Plastic Co., vinyl
    14".................. $125.00 – 150.00
1972 – 1973, Amsco, Milton Bradley, vinyl
    10"..................... $55.00 – 70.00
    14" – 18"............. $35.00 – 45.00
1979 – 1985, Atlanta Novelty, vinyl, flirty eyes, cloth body
    17"..................... $70.00 – 90.00
Talker
    17"................... $80.00 – 100.00
Collector Doll, christening gown, basket
    12"..................... $75.00 – 90.00
Porcelain, limited edition
    17"................. $275.00 – 325.00
1989 – 1992, Lucky Ltd., vinyl
    6"....................... $12.00 – 18.00
    11"..................... $35.00 – 40.00
    14 – 16"............. $35.00 – 40.00
1994 –1996, Toy Biz, Inc., vinyl
    8"....................... $12.00 – 15.00
    15"..................... $20.00 – 25.00
Battery operated
    12 – 13".............. $20.00 – 25.00
Talker
    14"..................... $35.00 – 40.00
    17"..................... $45.00 – 50.00
Green Giant, Sprout, 1973
    10½" .... $18.00 – 25.00
Hotpoint Devil, 1930s, designed by Josef Kallus,

24" Polly Ponds bride for Ponds Cold Cream, soft vinyl doll, $125.00. *Photo courtesy of Zendelle Bouchard.*

composition head, wooden segmented body
16"................ $550.00 – 600.00
Jolly Joan, Portland, Oregon, restaurant
11"................ $100.00 – 125.00
Kellogg's cereals
Corn Flakes, Red Riding Hood, printed cloth
13½".............. $125.00 – 150.00
Goldilocks & Three Bears, set of four, printed cloth
12" – 15"........ $240.00 – 265.00
Korn Krisp cereal
Miss Korn-Krisp, ca. 1900, cloth marked body
24"................ $180.00 – 205.00
Little Debbie, 1972, made by Horsman, all
vinyl with rooted hair
11" .... $28.00 – 32.00
Miss Addie, Ad Detergent, 1950s, hard plastic
doll by Arranbee, wigged, sleep eyes
11"................ $100.00 – 130.00
Mr. Peanut, 1940s, segmented, wooden
9".................... $125.00 – 150.00
Prince Macaroni, mail-in premium dolls, vinyl,
dressed in costumes from the provinces of Italy
6¼".................... $15.00 – 20.00
Sunbeam Bread
Miss Sunbeam, by Horsman, all vinyl, rooted hair
14"..................... $20.00 – 25.00
Swiss Miss Hot Chocolate, 1977, cloth doll,
painted features, yarn hair
16"....................... $8.00 – 10.00
"The Selling Fool," 1926, made by Cameo,

15" Uneeda Biscuit boy, composition, $450.00. *Photo courtesy of Alderfer Auction & Appraisal.*

wood segmented body, hat represents radio tube,
composition advertising doll for RCA Radiotrons
16".............. $900.00 – 1,100.00
Too few in database for a reliable range.
Uneeda Biscuit Boy, 1914, made by Ideal
15"................ $425.00 – 475.00
Zu Zu Kid, 1916, composition doll made by
Ideal kid to advertise gingersnaps made by
the National Biscuit Co.
14"................ $225.00 – 275.00

ALABAMA BABY

1900 – 1925, Roanoke, Alabama. Ella
Gauntt Smith, cloth over plaster doll, stitched
on skull cap, painted features. Tab jointed
at shoulders and hips, painted feet may be
bare with stitched toes or have shoes painted
in pink, blue, black, brown, or yellow.

17½" Alabama baby, earlier model with applied ears, sold for $1,500.00. *Photo courtesy of McMasters Harris Auction Co.*

Earlier model with applied ears
11" – 14".. $1,600.00 – 2,200.00
18" – 24".. $2,500.00 – 3,200.00
Black
14" – 18".. $5,500.00 – 6,000.00
20" – 22".. $6,200.00 – 6,800.00
Wigged
24"........... $2,700.00 – 3,300.00
Later model with molded ears, bobbed hairstyle
14" – 16".. $1,800.00 – 1,900.00
18" – 22".. $1,900.00 – 2,100.00
Black
14" – 18".. $2,800.00 – 3,000.00

20" – 22".. $3,800.00 – 5,800.00
Wigged
30" $1,000.00

MADAME ALEXANDER

1912 – present, New York City. In 1912 in New York City, Beatrice and Rose Alexander, known for making doll costumes, began the Alexander Doll Co. They began using the "Madame Alexander" trademark in 1928. Beatrice Alexander Behrman became a legend in the doll world with her long reign as head of the Alexander Doll Company. Alexander made cloth, composition, and wooden dolls, and eventually made the transition to hard plastic and vinyl. Dolls are listed by subcategories of the material of which the head is made. With Madame Alexander dolls, especially those made from 1950 on, condition as it relates to value is extremely important. **For the values listed here the doll must be in perfect condition with complete original clothing and tags. Dolls with incomplete or soiled costumes will bring one fourth to one third of the value of perfect examples.** Unusual dolls with presentation cases, trousseaux, or rare costumes may bring much more.

Cloth, 1930 – 1950 on
All-cloth head and body, mohair wig, flat or molded mask face, painted side-glancing eyes
Storybook characters such as Little Women, Dickens characters, Edith, and others
16" .... $750.00 – 900.00
Set of four Little Women MIB
$7,000.00*
Alice in Wonderland
Flat face .... $800.00 – 900.00
Mask face,
14" – 16" .... $700.00 – 800.00
Animals, such as March Hare, etc.

15" – 16" .... $300.00 – 600.00
Baby
13" .... $325.00 – 375.00
17" .... $500.00 – 550.00
24" .... $575.00 – 625.00
Funny, 1963 – 1977
18" .... $65.00 – 70.00
Little Shaver, 1940 – 1944, yarn hair
7" .... $450.00 – 525.00
10" .... $450.00 – 500.00
15" .... $575.00 – 675.00
22" .... $700.00 – 800.00
Muffin, ca. 1963 – 1977
14" .... $65.00 – 75.00
So Lite Baby or Toddler, 1930s – 1940s
20" .... $375.00 – 425.00
Suzie Q, 1940 – 1942
16" .... $700.00 – 800.00
Teeny Twinkle, 1946, disc floating eyes
15" .... $475.00 – 550.00
Dionne Quintuplets, various materials
Cloth, 1935 – 1936
16" .... $850.00 – 950.00
24" .... $1,600.00 – 1,800.00
Composition, 1935 – 1945, all-composition, swivel head, jointed toddler or baby body, molded and painted hair or wigged, sleep or painted eyes. Outfit colors: Annette, yellow; Cecile, green; Emilie, lavender; Marie, blue; Yvonne, pink. Add more for extra accessories or in layette.

11" Dionne quintuplets, $2,200.00. *Photo courtesy of Morphy Auctions.*

Baby

8" .... $200.00 – 250.00
Complete set.. $1,300.00 – 1,400.00
Set of five with wooden nursery furniture
8" .... $2,600.00 – 3,000.00

Toddler

8" .... $250.00 – 300.00
Complete set .. $1,400.00 – 1,600.00
11" .... $350.00 – 400.00
Complete set .. $2,000.00 – 2,200.00
14" .... $425.00 – 475.00
Complete set .. $2,700.00 – 3,000.00
16" .... $600.00 – 650.00
Complete set. $3,600.00 – 4,000.00
20" .... $600.00 – 700.00
Complete set.. $3,900.00 – 4,200.00
On cloth body
22" .... $650.00 – 750.00
Complete set . $3,400.00 – 3,700.00

Vinyl, 8", in carousel, 1998, 75th
anniversary set.. $350.00 – 400.00

Dr. Dafoe, 1937 – 1939
14" .... $1,250.00 – 1,350.00

Nurse

13" – 15" .... $900.00 – 975.00

Composition, 1930 – 1950
Babies, cloth body, sleep eyes, marked "Alexander," dolls such as Baby Genius, Butch, Baby McGuffy, Pinky, and others
10" – 12" .... $175.00 – 350.00
14" – 16" .... $200.00 – 275.00
18" – 20" .... $350.00 – 400.00

Baby Jane, 1935
16" .... $900.00 – 1,100.00

Child

Alice in Wonderland, 1930s, swivel waist
7" – 9" .... $375.00 – 425.00
11" – 14" .... $425.00 – 600.00
18" – 21" .... $700.00 – 950.00

Babs Skater, 1948, marked "ALEX" on head, clover tag
18" .... $1,200.00 – 1,350.00

Carmen (Miranda), 1942, black hair

9" – 11" .... $300.00 – 375.00
14" – 17" .... $450.00 – 650.00
21" .... $1,400.00 – 1,800.00

Fairy Queen, ca. 1939 – 1946, clover wrist tag, tagged gown
15" – 18" .... $600.00 – 700.00
21" – 22" .... $850.00 – 900.00

Flora McFlimsey, 1938, freckles, marked "Princess Elizabeth"
14" – 17" .... $400.00 – 500.00
22" .... $650.00 – 750.00

Jane Withers, 1937 – 1939, green sleep eyes, open mouth, brown mohair wig
12" – 13½" .. $1,500.00 – 2,000.00
15" – 17" .. $1,000.00 – 1,300.00
18" – 19" .. $1,500.00 – 1,600.00
20" – 22" .. $1,700.00 – 1,800.00

Jeannie Walker, tagged dress, closed mouth, mohair wig
13" – 14" .... $675.00 – 750.00
14" MIB $2,200.00*
18" .... $800.00 – 1,000.00

Judy, original box, wrist tag, Wendy Ann face, eyeshadow
21" .... $3,200.00 – 3,400.00

Karen Ballerina, blue sleep eyes, closed mouth, "Alexander" on head
15" .... $950.00 – 1,000.00
18" .... $1,300.00 – 1,400.00

Kate Greenaway, yellow wig, marked "Princess Elizabeth"

20" Jane Withers, 1937, $1,200.00. *Photo courtesy of Joan & Lynette Antique Dolls and Accessories.*

13" – 15"........ $750.00 – 800.00
18"................. $850.00 – 900.00
24".............. $950.00 – 1,050.00
Little Betty, 1939 – 1943, side-glancing painted eyes
9" – 11".......... $250.00 – 375.00
Little Colonel
Closed mouth
11" – 15"........ $625.00 – 850.00
Open mouth
14" – 17"........ $650.00 – 700.00
23" – 26"..... $850.00 – 1,000.00
Little Genius, blue sleep eyes, cloth body, closed mouth, clover tag
12" – 14"........ $225.00 – 250.00
16" – 20"........ $250.00 – 275.00
Little Women, Meg, Jo, Amy, Beth
Set of four
7"........................... $375.00 each
9"........................... $350.00 each
13" – 15".$350.00 – 375.00 each
Madelaine DuBain, 1937 – 1944
14"................. $550.00 – 600.00
17"................. $650.00 – 700.00
Marcella, 1936, open mouth, wig, sleep eyes
17" – 24" .... $650.00 – 900.00
Margaret O'Brien, 1946 – 1948
14" – 17"........ $800.00 – 900.00
19" – 24".. $1,100.00 – 1,400.00
Marionettes by Tony Sarg

13" Princess Elizabeth, open mouth, $400.00. *Photo courtesy of McMasters Harris Auction Co.*

12"................. $450.00 – 550.00
McGuffey Ana, 1935 – 1937, sleep eyes, open mouth, tagged dress
11" – 13"........ $600.00 – 700.00
14" – 16"........ $600.00 – 825.00
17" – 20"........ $700.00 – 900.00
21" – 25"..... $775.00 – 1,500.00
28"........... $1,000.00 – 1,400.00
Painted eyes
9" .... $250.00 – 300.00
Portraits, 1941 – 1947, Wendy Ann face,
20" – 22".. $1,800.00 – 2,000.00
Princess Elizabeth, 1937 – 1941
Closed mouth
13"................. $500.00 – 600.00
Open mouth
13" – 16"........ $500.00 – 600.00
18" – 24"........ $600.00 – 800.00
28".............. $900.00 – 1,000.00

14" hard plastic Jo of Little Women, ca. 1950, $400.00. *Photo courtesy of Morphy Auctions.*

18" Scarlett O'Hara, composition, $700.00. *Photo courtesy of Sweetbriar Auctions.*

Madame Alexander

Scarlett, 1937 – 1946, add more for rare costume
> 11"................. $500.00 – 700.00
> 14"................. $600.00 – 900.00
> 18".............. $700.00 – 1,100.00
> 21"........... $1,400.00 – 1,500.00

Snow White, 1939 – 1942, marked "Princess Elizabeth"
> 13"................. $450.00 – 500.00
> 16" – 18"........ $550.00 – 750.00

Sonja Henie, 1939 – 1942, open mouth, sleep eyes
> 13" – 15"........ $650.00 – 800.00
> 17" – 18"...... $675.00 –1,100.00
> 20" – 23"..... $900.00 – 1,200.00

Three Little Pigs, 1938 – 1939
> 12".........$600.00 – 750.00 each
> Set of 3 ..... $2,500.00 – 2,600.00

Tiny Betty, 1934 – 1943, side-glancing painted eyes, elaborate or rare costumes bring high end of range
> 7".................... $200.00 – 400.00

W.A.A.C. (Army), W.A.A.F. (Air Force), W.A.V.E. (Navy), ca. 1943 – 1944
> 14"................. $700.00 – 750.00

Wendy Ann, 1935 – 1948, more for special outfit
> 11" – 15"........ $400.00 – 550.00
> 17" – 21"........ $600.00 – 800.00
> *Painted eyes*
> 9" .... $250.00 – 325.00

Swivel waist, molded hair or wig
> 14" .... $400.00 – 450.00

Hard Plastic and Vinyl, 1948 on. MIB will bring double.

Alexander-kins, 1953 on

1953, 7½" – 8", straight-leg nonwalker
> Nude .... $350.00 – 375.00
> Dressed .... $550.00 – 750.00

1954 – 1955, straight-leg walker
> Nude .... $250.00 – 300.00
> Dressed .... $500.00 – 700.00
> Tagged Madeline, ca. 1950, for FAO Schwarz $1,300.00*

1956 – 1965, bent-knee walker, after 1963 marked "Alex"
> Nude .... $150.00 – 200.00
> Dressed .... $400.00 – 550.00

1965 – 1972, bent-knee nonwalker, price depends on costume
> Nude .... $75.00 – 95.00
> Dressed .... $200.00 – 450.00

1973 – 1976, straight-leg nonwalker, marked "Alex" on back of torso, price depends on costume
> Dressed .... $50.00 – 150.00

1976 – 1994, straight-leg nonwalker, marked "Alexander" on back of torso
> Dressed .... $40.00 – 75.00

Babies

Baby Brother or Sister, 1977 – 1982, vinyl
> 14"..................... $65.00 – 80.00

Baby Ellen, 1965 – 1972, vinyl, rigid vinyl body, marked "Alexander 1965"
> 14"................. $100.00 – 125.00

Baby Genius, 1956 – 1962, hard plastic and vinyl, price depends on costume
> 8".................... $150.00 – 300.00

Baby McGuffy, 1974 – 1976, vinyl, cloth body
> 21"................................$100.00

Bonnie, 1954 – 1955, vinyl
> 19" .... $55.00 – 65.00

Happy, 1970 only, vinyl
> 20"................. $175.00 – 200.00

14" W.A.V.E. $650.00. *Photo courtesy of Cybermogul Dolls.*

Madame Alexander

15" Kathy Cry, ca. 1957, $85.00. *Photo courtesy of My Dolly Dearest.*

Hello Baby, 1962 only
    22"................ $150.00 – 175.00
Honeybun, 1951, vinyl
    18" – 19"........ $200.00 – 225.00
Huggums
    Big, 1963 – 1979
    25".................. $85.00 – 100.00
    Little, rooted hair, 1963 – 1988
    12"..................... $40.00 – 50.00
Kathy Baby, 1954 – 1956, vinyl
    13" – 15"............ $60.00 – 85.00
Kathy Cry, 1957 – 1958, vinyl, nurser
    11" – 15"............ $60.00 – 85.00
    18" – 25"........ $110.00 – 160.00
Kitten, 1962 – 1963, vinyl, cloth body
    14" – 18".......... $35.00 – 100.00
    24", ca. 1961 ... $65.00 – 150.00
Little Angel, 1950 – 1957, vinyl head, latex body
    9".................... $100.00 – 125.00
Little Bitsey, 1967 – 1968, all-vinyl
    9".................... $130.00 – 150.00
Littlest Kitten, vinyl
    8".................... $125.00 – 175.00
Lively Kitten, 1962, vinyl, cloth body, knob makes head and limbs move
    14"................ $225.00 – 275.00
Mary Cassatt, 1969 – 1970, vinyl
    14".................. $75.00 – 125.00
    20"................ $200.00 – 250.00
Pussy Cat, 1965 – 1985, vinyl

    14"..................... $45.00 – 55.00
    18", 1989 – 1993. $90.00 – 140.00
    Black, 1970 – 1976
    14".................. $75.00 – 150.00
Sweet Tears, 1965 – 1974
    9"...................... $75.00 – 90.00
    With layette
    1965 – 1973... $150.00 – 175.00
Victoria, baby, 1967 – 1989
    20"..................... $70.00 – 85.00
Bible Character Dolls, 1954 only, hard plastic, original box made like Bible
    8"............................ $8,500.00+
Cissette, 1957 on 10", hard plastic head, synthetic wig, pierced ears, closed mouth, seven-piece adult body, jointed elbows and knees, high-heeled feet, mold later used for other dolls. Marks: None on body, clothes tagged "Cissette." Doll's listed are in good condition with original clothing. Value can be doubled for mint-in-box.
Basic doll
    In undergarments.. $150.00 – 175.00
    In street dress.... $350.00 – 450.00
    In formalwear. $400.00 – 1,100.00
Gibson Girl
    1962 – 1963... $550.00 – 650.00
Jacqueline
    1961 – 1962... $300.00 – 500.00
Margot
    1961 .... $525.00 – 625.00
Portrette
    1968 – 1973... $375.00 – 450.00
Queen
    1957 – 1958... $400.00 – 500.00
Sleeping Beauty, 1959, authorized Disney
    blue gown ...... $325.00 – 375.00
Tinker Bell, 1969...... $375.00 – 450.00
Cissy
1955–1959, 20", hard plastic, vinyl arms, jointed elbows and knees, high-heeled feet. Clothes are tagged "Cissy." MIB can bring double.

Madame Alexander

21" Cissy, ca. 1955, $2,200.00. *Photo courtesy of Morphy Auctions.*

Basic doll in undergarments
.... $400.00 – 450.00
In street dress. $500.00 – 1,000.00
In formalwear.$1,400.00 – 2,500.00
Model 2176, ca. 1957, aqua taffetta gown, MIB $5,600.00*
Miss Flora McFlimsey, 1953 only, Cissy, vinyl head, inset eyes
   15" .... $725.00 – 800.00
1996 on, 21", vinyl
   85th anniversary Cissy
   2008 .... $450.00 – 500.00
   Yardley
   2001 .... $350.00 – 450.00
Others, MIB can bring double.
Alice in Wonderland, 1949 – 1952, hard plastic, Margaret and/or Maggie
   14" .... $450.00 – 500.00
   15", 18", 23" ..... $400.00 – 600.00

24" Binnie Walker, $500.00. *Photo courtesy of Alderfer Auction & Appraisal.*

1996, vinyl
   14" .... $45.00 – 50.00
American Girl, 1962 – 1963, #388, seven-piece walker body, became McGuffey Ana in 1964 – 1965
   8" .... $130.00 – 160.00
Annabelle, 1951 – 1952, Maggie head
   14" .... $1,200.00 – 1,700.00
   20" – 23" ..... $800.00 – 1,000.00
Anne of Green Gables, 1993, in Concert dress
   8" .... $65.00 – 80.00
Babs Skater, 1948 – 1950, hard plastic, Margaret
   15" .... $800.00 – 1,000.00
   17" – 18".. $1,200.00 – 1,400.00
Bill/Billy, 1960, seven-piece walker body
   8" .... $325.00 – 375.00
Binnie Walker, 1954 – 1955, Cissy face, value varies depending on how elaborate the costume is
   15" .... $450.00 – 650.00
   18" .... $475.00 – 675.00
Model 1846, ca. 1955, bridesmaid
   MIB $5,000.00*
   25" .... $500.00 – 600.00
Brenda Starr, 1964 only, 12" hard plastic, vinyl arms, red wig
   In street dress.... $125.00 – 150.00
   In formalwear ... $175.00 – 210.00
Bunny, 1962 only
   18" .... $175.00 – 225.00
Caroline, 1961, #131, vinyl
   15" .... $140.00 – 180.00
Chatterbox, 1961, vinyl & plastic, talker
   24" .... $150.00 – 175.00
Cinderella
   1950 – 1951, Margaret face, 14", hard plastic
      Ballgown
      14" .... $425.00 – 500.00
      18" .... $500.00 – 600.00
      Poor Cinderella, gray dress, original broom
      14" .... $325.00 – 400.00

1967 – 1992, Mary Ann face, plastic and vinyl
14"..................... $35.00 – 45.00
Cowgirl & Cowboy, 1967 – 1970, hard plastic, jointed knees
8".................... $200.00 – 250.00
Cynthia, 1952 only, hard plastic
15"................. $450.00 – 500.00
18"................. $450.00 – 600.00
23"................. $700.00 – 800.00
Easter Doll, 1968, vinyl
14"................. $200.00 – 350.00
Edith, The Lonely Doll, 1958 – 1959, vinyl head, hard plastic body
8".................... $350.00 – 400.00
16"................. $150.00 – 200.00
22"................. $175.00 – 225.00
2003 – 2004, vinyl, with 3" Mr. Bear
8"....................... $75.00 – 80.00
Elise
1957 – 1964, 16½", hard plastic, vinyl arms, jointed ankles and knees
Street dress ...... $450.00 – 550.00
Ballerina.......... $200.00 – 300.00
Formalwear... $500.00 – 1,000.00
1963 only, 18", hard plastic, vinyl arms, jointed ankles and knees
Bouffant hairstyle.. $150.00 – 225.00
1966 – 1972, 17", hard plastic, one-piece vinyl arms, jointed ankles and knees
Street dress ...... $250.00 – 275.00

16½" Elise bride, ca. 1959, $550.00. *Photo courtesy of Morphy Auctions.*

1966 – 1991
Ballerina............ $75.00 – 100.00
1997, vinyl
16".................. $95.00 – 125.00
Fairy Queen, 1948 – 1950, Margaret face
14½".............. $350.00 – 400.00
Fashions of a Century, 1954 – 1955, 14" – 18", Margaret face, hard plastic
$1,200.00 – 1,600.00
First Ladies, 1976 – 1990
Set 1
1976 – 1978.... $90.00 – 110.00 ea.
Set 2
1979 – 1981....$70.00 – 90.00 ea.
Set 3
1982 – 1984....$70.00 – 80.00 ea.
Set 4
1985 – 1987..$60.00 – 80.00 ea.
Set 5, 1988 ....$40.00 – 45.00 ea.
Set 6
1989 – 1990..$40.00 – 65.00 ea.
Flower Girl, 1954, hard plastic, Margaret
15"................. $375.00 – 425.00
Glamour Girl Series, 1953 only, hard plastic, Margaret head, auburn wig, straight-leg walker
18"................. $750.00 – 900.00
Godey Bride, 1950 – 1951, Margaret, hard plastic
14"........... $1,000.00 – 1,200.00
18"........... $1,300.00 – 1,500.00
Godey Lady, 1950 – 1951, Margaret, hard plastic
14"........... $1,400.00 – 1,600.00
14", ca. 1949, MIB.... $9,750.00*
Godey Groom, 1950 – 1951, Margaret, hard plastic
14" .... $500.00 – 600.00
18"................ $600.00 – 700.00
Gold Rush, 1963 only, hard plastic, Cissette
10"................. $700.00 – 800.00
Grandma Jane, 1970 – 1972, #1420, Mary Ann, vinyl body
14"................. $200.00 – 225.00

Groom
 1949 – 1951, Margaret, hard plastic
 14" – 16"........ $750.00 – 850.00
 1953 – 1955, Wendy Ann, hard plastic
 7½"................ $525.00 – 575.00
Jacqueline, 1961 – 1962, 21", hard plastic, vinyl arms
 In street dress. $850.00 – 1,000.00
 In formalwear ... $900.00 – 950.00
 In riding habit ... $825.00 – 875.00
Janie, 1964 – 1966, #1156, toddler, vinyl head, hard plastic body, rooted hair
 12"................. $175.00 – 225.00
Jenny Lind and Listening Cat, 1970 – 1971,
 14"................. $230.00 – 260.00
John Robert Powers Model, 1952, with oval beauty box, hard plastic
 14".......... $1,700.00 – 2,000.00
Kelly
 1959 only, hard plastic, Lissy face
 12"................. $400.00 – 500.00
 1958 – 1959, hard plastic, Marybel face
 15" – 16"........ $225.00 – 300.00
 1958
 18" .... $350.00 – 375.00
 1958 – 1959
 22"................. $300.00 – 400.00
Leslie (black Polly), 1965 – 1971, 17", vinyl head, hard plastic body, vinyl limbs, rooted hair
 Ballerina .... $375.00 – 400.00
 In formalwear ... $300.00 – 350.00
Lissy, hard plastic, wigged
 1956 – 1958, 12", elbow and knee joints
 In undies.......... $250.00 – 300.00
 In street dress ... $500.00 – 600.00
 In formalwear... $600.00 – 900.00
 1957 Bridesmaid, MIB.$1,600.00*
 1959 – 1967, as above but no elbow and knee joints
 In street dress ... $150.00 – 225.00
 2006, vinyl
 12".................... $60.00 – 100.00

Little Shaver, 1963 – 1965, painted eyes, vinyl body
 12"................. $200.00 – 250.00
Little Women,
 1947 – 1956, Meg, Jo, Amy, Beth, plus Marme, Margaret and Maggie faces
 14" – 15".$300.00 – 400.00 each
 1955, Meg, Jo, Amy, Beth, plus Marme, Wendy Ann, straight-leg walker
 8"............$175.00 – 200.00 each
 1956 – 1959, Wendy Ann, bent-knee walker
 8"............$125.00 – 150.00 each
 1974 – 1992, straight-leg, #411 – #415
 8"................$45.00 – 55.00 each
 1957 – 1958, Lissy, jointed elbows and knees
 12"................. $300.00 – 400.00
 1959 – 1968, Lissy, one-piece arms and legs
 12".................... $75.00 – 120.00
 1983 – 1989, Nancy Drew face
 12"..............$40.00 – 50.00 each
Madeline, 1961, vinyl, multiple joints
 18"................. $450.00 – 600.00
Maggie, hard plastic
 1948 – 1954
 20" – 21"........ $350.00 – 400.00

12" Lissy, ca. 1956, $700.00. *Photo courtesy of Morphy Auctions.*

16

Madame Alexander

1949 – 1952
22" – 23"........ $400.00 – 450.00
1949 – 1953
17" – 18" .... $450.00 – 550.00
1949 – 1953, walker
15" – 18"........ $325.00 – 375.00
Maggie Mixup, 1960 – 1961, hard plastic,
freckles, price depends on outfit
8".................... $190.00 – 500.00
Maggie Teenager, 1951 – 1953, hard
plastic, price depends on outfit
15" – 18" .... $300.00 – 350.00
Margaret O'Brien, 1949 – 1951, hard plastic
14".............. $800.00 – 1,200.00
18" – 21"..... $600.00 – 1,100.00
Margot Ballerina, 1951 – 1953, Margaret
and Maggie, dressed in various colored outfits
15" – 18"........ $650.00 – 850.00
Marlo Thomas as "That Girl," 1967 only,
Polly face, vinyl
17".................. $300.00 – 400.00
Mary Ellen, 1954 only, rigid vinyl walker
31".................. $625.00 – 675.00
Mary Ellen Playmate, 1965 only, bendable
vinyl body
17".................. $300.00 – 350.00
Mary Martin, 1948 – 1952, South Pacific
character Nell, two-piece sailor outfit, hard plastic
14" – 17"..... $900.00 – 1,000.00
17" in sailor suit......... $1,600.00*
Marybel, "The Doll That Gets Well," 1959 –
1965, rigid vinyl, in case with accessories
16".................. $120.00 – 170.00
1998
75th anniversary
re-issue .... $90.00 – 100.00
McGuffey Ana
1948 – 1950, hard plastic, Margaret
14"........... $1,000.00 – 1,200.00
18".............. $950.00 – 1,050.00
21"........... $1,200.00 – 1,400.00
1956 only, hard plastic, #616, Wendy
Ann face

8" .... $675.00 – 750.00
1963 only, hard plastic, rare doll, Lissy
face
12" model 1258 MIB.. $4,400.00*
1977 – 1986, vinyl, Mary Ann face
14"..................... $35.00 – 45.00
Melanie, 1979 – 1980, dotted Swiss gown
pink trim
21"................. $130.00 – 150.00
Melinda, 1962 – 1963, plastic/vinyl, cotton dress
14" – 22"........ $250.00 – 275.00
Muffin, 1989 – 1990, Janie face, vinyl
12"..................... $25.00 – 35.00
Nancy Drew, 1967 only, vinyl body,
Literature Series
12"................. $250.00 – 300.00
Nina Ballerina, 1949 – 1951, Margaret
head, clover wrist tag
15"................. $300.00 – 400.00
19"................. $450.00 – 700.00
21" – 23"........ $700.00 – 900.00
Pamela, 1962 – 1963, Lissy face,
changeable wigs
12" in box with wardrobe
$900.00 – 1,100.00
Peggy Bride, 1950 – 1951, hard plastic,
Margaret face
14", MIB $1,600.00*
Peter Pan, 1953 – 1954, Margaret
15"................. $600.00 – 800.00
1969, 14" Wendy (Mary Ann head),
12" Peter, Michael (Jamie head), 10"
Tinker Bell (Cissette head)
Peter or Wendy. $200.00 – 225.00
Michael .... $225.00 – 250.00
Tinker Bell .... $300.00 – 350.00
Set of four $1,000.00
Pollyanna
1960 – 1961, vinyl, Marybel face
16"................. $400.00 – 450.00
1987 – 1988, Mary Ann face
14"..................... $45.00 – 55.00
2000 – 2001, Wendy face

8" Prince Charles, $400.00. *Photo courtesy of Withington Auction, Inc.*

8" .... $25.00 – 35.00
Polly Pigtails, 1949 – 1951 , hard plastic
   17" .... $450.00 – 500.00
Portraits, 1960 on, marked "1961," Jacqueline face, 21", early dolls have jointed elbows, later one piece. For models made over long periods the older dolls bring the higher end of the values listed, later dolls the lower end. MIB can bring double.
   Agatha, 1967 – 1980
   #2171 .... $160.00 – 325.00
   Cornelia, 1972
   #2191 .... $150.00 – 200.00
   Gainsborough, 1968 – 1978
   #2184 .... $150.00 – 325.00
   Godey, 1977, in ecru & red
   #2298 .... $125.00 – 150.00
   *Goya,*1968
   #2183 .... $250.00 – 300.00
   Jenny Lind, 1969 – 1970
   #2193 .... $700.00 – 750.00
   *Lady Hamilton,*1968
   #2182 .... $200.00 – 225.00
   Madame Alexander, 1988 – 1990
   $100.00 – 175.00
   Madame Pompadour, 1970
   #2197 .... $200.00 – 250.00
   Manet, 1982 – 1983
   #2225 .... $160.00 – 190.00

   Melanie, 1971
   #2162 .... $100.00 – 200.00
   Renoir, 1965
   #2154 .... $650.00 – 700.00
   *Scarlett,*1975 – 1977, green satin gown, white lace at cuffs.. $125.00 – 200.00
   Southern Belle, 1965
   #2155 .... $750.00 – 800.00
Prince Charles, 1957 only, #397, hard plastic, blue jacket, cap, and shorts
   8" .... $300.00 – 400.00
Prince Charming, 1948 – 1950, hard plastic, Margaret face, brocade jacket, white tights
   14" .... $700.00 – 775.00
   18" .... $825.00 – 875.00
Princess Margaret Rose
   1949 – 1953, hard plastic, Margaret face
   14" .... $750.00 – 800.00
   18" .... $875.00 – 925.00
   1953 only, #2020B, hard plastic, Beaux Arts Series, pink taffeta gown with red ribbon, tiara, Margaret face
   18" $2,400.00*
Queen, 1953, Margaret
   1953 only, #2020A, hard plastic, Beaux Arts Series, pink taffeta gown with red ribbon, tiara, Margaret face
   18" $2,500.00*
Quiz-Kin, 1953, hard plastic, back buttons, nods yes or no
   8" .... $450.00 – 500.00
Renoir Girl, 1972 – 1986, vinyl body, pink multi-tiered dress
   14" .... $25.00 – 35.00
Scarlett O'Hara
   1950 on, hard plastic, Margaret face
   14" – 16" .... $800.00 – 900.00
   1966 – 1972, jointed knees, Wendy Ann face
   8" .... $150.00 – 200.00
   1969 – 1986, vinyl, Mary Ann face, white gown
   14" .... $40.00 – 50.00

1970, #2180 green satin with white trimmed jacket

    21".................. $350.00 – 450.00

Shari Lewis, 1958 – 1959

    14".............. $600.00 – 1,000.00

    21"........... $1,000.00 – 1,200.00

Sleeping Beauty, 1959, Disneyland Special

    10"................. $300.00 – 350.00

    16"................. $600.00 – 650.00

    21"................. $850.00 – 900.00

Smarty, 1962 – 1963, vinyl body

    12"................. $125.00 – 175.00

Snow White

    1970 – 1985, Mary Ann face, Classic series, vinyl

    14"........................ 45.00 – 65.00

    1990 – 1992, Wendy face, vinyl

    8"........................ $45.00 – 55.00

    2002 – 2004, Cissette face, came with 5" dwarves

    10", complete set ..$100.00 – 125.00

Sonja Henie, 1951 only, Madeline face, vinyl head

    15"................. $300.00 – 400.00

Sound of Music, 1965 – 1970 (large), 1971 – 1973 (small), vinyl

    Brigitta

    10" .... $70.00 – 90.00

    14".................... $90.00 – 100.00

14" Shari Lewis and Lambchop, sold for $2,975.00. *Photo courtesy of Dollhappy.*

Friedrich

    8" .... $75.00 – 100.00

    10"................. $100.00 – 125.00

Gretl

    8" .... $75.00 – 100.00

    10"................. $100.00 – 125.00

Liesl

    10" .... $110.00 – 125.00

    14" .... $100.00 – 125.00

Louisa

    10" .... $110.00 – 125.00

    14" .... $100.00 – 125.00

Maria

    12" .... $100.00 – 125.00

    17" .... $125.00 – 140.00

Marta

    8" .... $100.00 – 125.00

    10" .... $100.00 – 125.00

Suzy, 1970 only, vinyl head, Janie face

    12".................... $80.00 – 100.00

Timmy Toddler, 1960 – 1961, vinyl head, hard plastic body

    23"................. $125.00 – 150.00

    1960 only

    30"................,,,, $200.00 – 250.00

Tommy Bangs, 1952 only, hard plastic, Little Men Series

    11"................. $825.00 – 875.00

Wendy, Wendy Ann, Wendy-kin: See Alexander-kins section.

Special Event dolls, limited edition

Collector's United

    Faith, 1992

    8"........................ $40.00 – 50.00

    Miss Tennessee Waltz, 1997

    8"........................ $30.00 – 40.00

Disney

    Morgan Le Fay, 1995, limit 500

    10"................. $125.00 – 150.00

    Mouseketeer, 1991, Disney theme parks only

    8"........................ $60.00 – 80.00

Madame Alexander Doll Club Convention

    Avalon Ball, 2008, limit 100

10".................... $75.00 – 100.00
Briar Rose, 1989, Cissette head, limit 804
8".................... $225.00 – 250.00
Southern Belle Cissy, 2003, limit 65
21"................. $450.00 – 500.00
U.F.D.C.
Annette, 2001, limit 350
10"................. $100.00 – 125.00
Susan, 2000, Limit 400, doll with wardrobe
8"...................... $25.00 – 50.00

6" French-style all-bisque with swivel neck and bare feet, $4,000.00. *Photo courtesy of Withington Auction, Inc.*

HENRI ALEXANDRE

1888 – 1891, Paris. Succeeded by Tourrel in 1892 and in 1895 merged with Jules Steiner.
Incised HA model, bisque socket head, paperweight eyes, closed mouth with space between lips, straight wrist body
17" – 20".. $5,500.00 – 6,900.00
Bébé Phénix, trademarked in 1895, bisque socket head, paperweight eyes, pierced ears, composition body
Child, closed mouth
10" – 14".. $2,200.00 – 3,600.00
16" – 18" . $5,000.00 – 5,500.00
20" – 24".. $6,000.00 – 7,000.00
Child, open mouth
16" – 18".. $2,100.00 – 2,400.00
20" – 24".. $2,400.00 – 2,800.00

ALL-BISQUE FRENCH

1880 on, made by various French and German doll companies. Sold as French products. Most are unmarked, some have numbers only. Allow more for original clothes and tags, less for chips or repairs.

Bare feet

5"............ $2,500.00 – 2,800.00
6"............. $3,200.00 – 4,000.00
Five-strap boots, glass eyes, swivel neck
5" – 6"...... $2,500.00 – 3,100.00
Glass eyes, swivel head, molded shoes or boots
2½" – 3½"... $800.00 – 1,200.00
4" – 5"...... $2,000.00 – 4,000.00
6" – 7"...... $4,500.00 – 5,500.00
10"........... $6,300.00 – 6,500.00
Later style, 1910 – 1920, glass eyes, molded shoes, swivel neck, long stockings
2½" .... $300.00 – 350.00
5" – 6"............ $575.00 – 625.00
7"................... $700.00 – 725.00
Painted eyes
2½" – 3½" ..... $500.00 – 600.00
4"................ $900.00 – 1,000.00

ALL-BISQUE GERMAN

1880s onward, made by various German doll companies including Alt, Beck & Gottschalck; Bähr & Pröschild; Hertel, Schwab & Co.; Kämmer & Reinhardt; Kestner; Kling; Limbach; Bruno Schmidt; and Simon & Halbig. Some incised "Germany" with or without numbers, others have paper labels glued onto their torsos. More for labels, less for chips and repairs.

All-Bisque, Black or Brown: See Black or Brown Dolls section.

Painted eyes, 1880 – 1910, stationary neck, molded painted footwear, dressed or undressed, all in good condition

2" – 3"	$100.00 – 150.00
4" – 5"	$150.00 – 250.00
6" – 8"	$300.00 – 350.00

Black or brown stockings, tan slippers

4" – 5"	$375.00 – 450.00
6"	$475.00 – 525.00

Early very round face

7"	$2,100.00 – 2,300.00

Molded hair

4½"	$225.00 – 300.00
6"	$325.00 – 350.00
6½", bare feet	$500.00 – 600.00

Ribbed hose or blue or yellow shoes

4" – 5"	$275.00 – 325.00
6"	$425.00 – 475.00
8"	$825.00 – 875.00

Molded clothing, 1890 – 1910, jointed at shoulders only or at shoulders and hips, painted eyes, molded hair, molded shoes or bare feet, excellent workmanship, no breaks, chips, or rubs

3½" – 4"	$115.00 – 145.00
5" – 6"	$125.00 – 180.00
7"	$200.00 – 275.00

Lesser quality

3"	$65.00 – 75.00
4"	$80.00 – 90.00
6"	$100.00 – 120.00

Molded on hat or bonnet

5" – 6½"	$365.00 – 395.00
8" – 9"	$500.00 – 550.00
5" pair, man and woman, exceptional quality	$5,200.00*

Stone bisque (porous)

4" – 5"	$90.00 – 115.00
6" – 7"	$125.00 – 145.00

10" German all-bisque by Kestner, mold 156 open/closed mouth, $1,400.00. *Photo courtesy of Dolls & Lace.*

Glass eyes, 1890 – 1910, stationary neck, molded painted footwear, excellent bisque, open or closed mouth, sleep or set eyes, good wig, nicely dressed, molded one-strap shoes. Includes doll with sticker reading "Prize Baby."

3" – 4"	$200.00 – 275.00
5"	$300.00 – 350.00
6" – 7"	$600.00 – 700.00
8" – 9"	$500.00 – 650.00

Elaborate footwear or stockings

3"	$325.00 – 350.00
4½"	$500.00 – 800.00
6" – 7"	$800.00 – 900.00
8" – 8½"	$1,200.00 – 1,300.00

Mold 100, 125, 150, 225 (preceded by 83/), rigid neck, fat tummy, jointed shoulders and hips, glass sleep eyes, open mouth, molded black one-strap shoes with tan soles, white molded stockings with blue band. Similarly molded dolls, imported in 1950s by Kimport, have synthetic hair, lesser quality bisque. Add more for original clothing. Mold number appears as a fraction with the following size numbers under 83; Mold "83/100," "83/125," "83/150," or "83/225." One marked "83/100" has a green label on torso reading, "Princess//Made in Germany."

5½" – 6½"	$300.00 – 400.00
7½" – 8½"	$500.00 – 600.00
10" – 12"	$1,200.00 – 1,400.00

All-Bisque German

Swivel neck and glass eyes, 1880 – 1910, molded painted footwear, pegged or wired joints, open or closed mouth. Allow more for unusual footwear such as yellow or multi-strap boots or flirty eyes.

3" – 4"	$450.00 – 500.00
5" – 6"	$600.00 – 700.00
7" – 8"	$800.00 – 900.00
9" – 10"	$1,000.00 – 1,500.00

Bare feet

5" – 6"	$2,000.00 – 2,800.00
8" – 10"	$3,200.00 – 3,500.00

Early round face

6"	$1,600.00 – 1,800.00
8"	$2,200.00 – 2,300.00

Jointed knees

6"	$3,500.00 – 4,000.00
8½"	$6,000.00 – 7,000.00
10"	$8,000.00 – 9,000.00

Mold 102, Wrestler (so called), fat thighs, arm bent at elbow, open mouth (can have two rows of teeth) or closed mouth, stocky body, glass eyes, socket head, individual fingers or molded fist

3½" – 5"	$1,500.00 – 1,600.00
8" – 9"	$3,000.00 – 4,000.00

Simon & Halbig or Kestner types, closed mouth, excellent quality. Molds 130, 150, 160, 184, 208, 602, 881, 886, 890, and others

4" – 5"	$1,000.00 – 2,000.00

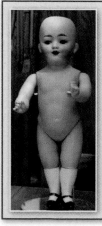

10" Kestner 150, stationary neck, glass eyes, $1,000.00. *Photo courtesy of Joan & Lynette Antique Dolls and Accessories.*

6" – 7"	$2,000.00 – 3,000.00
8"	$3,000.00 – 3,300.00
10"	$3,500.00 – 4,000.00

Slender dolls, 1900 on, stationary neck, slender arms and legs, glass eyes, molded footwear, usual wire or peg-jointed shoulders and hips. Allow much more for original clothes. May be in regional costumes. Add more for unusual color boots, such as gold, yellow, or orange, all in good condition.

3" – 4"	$200.00 – 250.00
5" – 6"	$275.00 – 325.00

Jointed knees and/or elbows with swivel waist

6"	$1,950.00 – 2,050.00
8"	$3,000.00 – 3,200.00

Swivel neck, closed mouth

4"	$275.00 – 300.00
5" – 6"	$450.00 – 500.00
8½"	$800.00 – 900.00
10"	$1,100.00 – 1,300.00

Swivel waist only

6"	$2,000.00 – 2,200.00

Baby, 1900 on, jointed at hips and shoulders, bent limbs, molded hair, painted features

2½" – 3½"	$80.00 – 90.00
5" – 6"	$175.00 – 225.00

Bye-Lo: See Bye-Lo section.

Character Baby, 1910 on, jointed at hips and shoulders, bent limbs, molded hair, painted features

Glass eyes, molds 391, 830, 833, and others

4" – 5"	$275.00 – 375.00
6" – 7"	$400.00 – 450.00
8"	$625.00 – 650.00
11"	$850.00 – 950.00

Painted eyes

3½"	$75.00 – 100.00
4" – 5"	$150.00 – 200.00
7"	$250.00 – 300.00
8"	$350.00 – 400.00

Swivel neck, glass eyes

5" – 6"	$850.00 – 1,000.00
8" – 10"	$1,300.00 – 1,500.00

Swivel neck, painted eyes

5" Bonnie Babe, $1,200.00. Photo courtesy of Withington Auction, Inc.

5" – 6"............ $325.00 – 350.00
7" – 8"............ $550.00 – 600.00
16"........................... $1,150.00*
Baby Bo Kaye, mold 1394, designed by Kallus, distributed by Borgfeldt
5"............. $1,500.00 – 1,900.00
7" – 8"...... $2,100.00 – 2,200.00
Baby Darling, mold 497, Kestner, 178, one-piece body, painted eyes
6".................... $850.00 – 950.00
8"............... $950.00 – 1,000.00
10".......... $1,100.00 – 1,200.00
Baby Peggy Montgomery, made by Louis Amberg, paper label, pink bisque with molded hair, painted brown eyes, closed mouth, jointed at shoulders and hips, molded and painted shoes/socks
3½"............... $325.00 – 375.00
5½"............... $525.00 – 575.00
Bonnie Babe, 1926 on, designed by Georgene Averill, glass eyes, swivel neck, wig, jointed arms and legs
5"............. $1,000.00 – 1,200.00
7"............. $1,400.00 – 1,500.00
8"............. $1,600.00 – 1,700.00
Mildred the Prize Baby, (* not to be confused with all bisque child dolls bearing the label Prize Baby), mold 880, 1914 on, made for Borgfeldt; molded, short painted hair; glass eyes; closed mouth; jointed at neck, shoulders, and hips; round paper label on chest; molded and painted footwear
5" – 7"...... $3,100.00 – 3,500.00
Mold 231 (A.M.), toddler, swivel neck, with glass eyes
9"............. $1,300.00 – 1,400.00
Mold 369, 372
7".................... $650.00 – 725.00
9"............. $1,000.00 – 1,100.00
11".......... $1,400.00 – 1,500.00
Mold 151, by Hertel, Schwab & Co.
10".................. $650.00 – 750.00
Our Darling, open mouth with teeth, glass eyes
5½"................. $160.00 – 200.00
Tynie Baby, made for E.I. Horsman, wigged or painted hair, glass eyes
8" – 10".... $1,600.00 – 2,200.00
Character doll with glass eyes, 1910
Heubach, Ernst, 1913 – 1920s, jointed at shoulders and hips, molded painted hair, some with ribbons etc., intaglio eyes, Our Golden Three, molds such as 9557, 9558, 10134, 10490, 10499, 10511, others
8" – 9"...... $1,800.00 – 2,000.00
9", swivel neck............. $2,400.00
Molds 155, 156
5" – 6"............ $400.00 – 500.00
7".................... $625.00 – 650.00

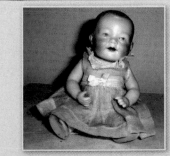

7" Mildred the Prize Baby. *Note: this character baby doll should not be confused with the all-bisque dolly-faced dolls bearing the sticker "Prize Baby." $3,500.00. Photo courtesy of Ann Lloyd Antique Dolls.

All-Bisque German

5" Vivi designed by Orsini, $2,500.00. *Photo courtesy of Withington Auction, Inc.*

4½" pair of Happifats in original box, $600.00. *Photo courtesy of Morphy Auctions.*

Orsini, 1919 on, designed by Jeanne Orsini for Borgfeldt, produced by Alt, Beck & Gottschalck, Chi Chi, Didi, Fifi, Mimi, Vivi
Glass eyes
    5"............. $2,200.00 – 2,700.00
    7"............. $3,500.00 – 4,000.00
Painted eyes
    5"................ $900.00 – 1,100.00
Our Fairy, mold 222, wigged, glass eyes
    4½" – 5"...... $800.00 – 1,000.00
    6" – 7"...... $1,500.00 – 1,800.00
    11"........... $2,000.00 – 2,200.00
Painted eyes, molded hair
    5".................... $450.00 – 550.00
    8".................... $750.00 – 850.00
    12".............. $950.00 – 1,500.00
Jointed animals, 1910 on, wire jointed shoulders and hips, crocheted clothing, makers such as Kestner, others, 2" – 3½"
Bear .... $500.00 – 600.00
Frog, Monkey, Pig....... $700.00 – 1,000.00
Rabbit...................... $425.00 – 500.00
Miniature dolls, painted eyes, crocheted clothing, various makers
    1" – 1¾"........... $80.00 – 100.00
Character Dolls, painted eyes, 1913 on
Campbell's Kid, molded clothes, Dutch bob
    5".................... $100.00 – 150.00
Chin-chin, Gebruder Heubach, 1919, jointed arms only, triangular label on chest

    4".................... $275.00 – 300.00
Happifats, designed by Kate Jordan for Borgfeldt, ca. 1913 – 1921
    4".................... $200.00 – 250.00
HEbee, SHEbee
    4" – 5"............ $350.00 – 400.00
    7".................... $400.00 – 500.00
Max, Moritz, Kestner, 1914, jointed at the neck, shoulders, and hips, many companies produced these characters from the Wilhelm Busch children's story
    4½" – 5". $1,600.00 – 2,000.00 each
Mibs, Amberg, 1921, molded blond hair, molded and painted socks and shoes, pink bisque, jointed at shoulders, legs molded to body, marked "C.//L.A.&S.192//GERMANY"
    3".................... $150.00 – 200.00
    5".................... $325.00 – 375.00
    8".................... $400.00 – 475.00

6½" Max & Moritz by Kestner, $4,000.00 pair. *Photo courtesy of Skinner, Inc.*

Peterkin, 1912, one-piece baby, side-glancing googly eyes, molded and painted hair, molded blue pajamas on chubby torso, arms molded to body with hands clasping stomach

5" – 6"............ $200.00 – 250.00

September Morn, jointed at shoulders and hips, Grace Drayton design, George Borgfeldt

4" – 5"......... $900.00 – 1,100.00

6"– 8"....... $1,300.00 – 1,700.00

Later issue with painted eyes, 1920 on, painted hair or wigged, molded painted single-strap shoes, white stockings, makers such as Limbach, Hertwig & Co., others

3½".................... $75.00 – 85.00

4" – 5"............ $110.00 – 125.00

6" – 7"............ $175.00 – 225.00

Molded "paper hat" and dagger in belt

4½" – 5½"...... $150.00 – 200.00

Infant,1920 on, so-called candy babies

3" – 4"................ $50.00 – 65.00

So-called Flapper, 1920, tinted bisque, molded bobbed hairstyle, painted features, molded single-strap shoes

Adult

5½"................ $325.00 – 375.00

Molded loop for bow

2⅛"................ $175.00 – 200.00

5".................... $300.00 – 350.00

6" – 7"............ $400.00 – 450.00

Molded hat

3½" – 4"......... $275.00 – 350.00

Aviatrix

5".................... $325.00 – 375.00

Swivel waist

4½"................ $375.00 – 400.00

Wigged

3½".................. $95.00 – 125.00

Child

2½" – 3½"...... $100.00 – 200.00

Nodders, 1920 on, immobile body, head attached with elastic, makers such as Hertwig & Co., others, when their heads are touched, they "nod," molded clothes

5" all-bisque with jointed shoulders, painted clothing, 1920s, $75.00. *Photo courtesy of Joan & Lynette Antique Dolls and Accessories.*

Animals, cat, dog, rabbit

3" – 5" ....$100.00 – 150.00 each

Child/adult

3" – 4".........$50.00 – 75.00 each

Comic characters

3" – 5"............ $120.00 – 135.00

Santa Claus or Indian

$200.00 – 225.00 each

Teddy bear .... $200.00 – 225.00

Immobiles, 1920, one-piece doll with molded clothing, top layer of paint not fired on and the color can be washed off, some have molded hats

Baby

3½".................... $40.00 – 50.00

5"....................... $50.00 – 60.00

Adults and children

3"................$50.00 – 60.00 each

5"................$65.00 – 70.00 each

Bathing Beauties, 1910 – 1930s, various German porcelain factories made these bisque figures, painted features

3".................... $100.00 – 300.00

6".................... $350.00 – 600.00

Mermaid tail

4".................... $300.00 – 325.00

Reclining woman, lying on stomach

2½"................ $135.00 – 165.00

4".................... $375.00 – 425.00

Two figures molded together

4½" – 5½" . $1,500.00 – 1,700.00

Wigged

4" painted bisque, 1920s – 1930s, $70.00. *Photo courtesy of The Museum Doll Shop.*

5"................... $700.00 – 750.00

Too few in database for a reliable range.

Painted bisque child, 1920 – 1930s, all in original clothing

    3" – 4"............... $45.00 – 70.00

ALL-BISQUE JAPANESE

1915 onward, made by a variety of Japanese companies. Quality varies widely, stationary dolls or jointed at shoulders and/or hips. Marked "Made in Japan" or "Nippon." Fired bisque, fired on color, some jointed at shoulders, some immobile

Characters such as Que San Baby, Cho Cho San, etc.

    4" – 4½"......... $175.00 – 250.00

Painted bisque, top layer of paint not fired on and the color can be washed off, usually one-piece figurines with molded hair, painted features, including clothes, shoes, and socks, some have molded hats

Baby

    3" – 5"............... $15.00 – 25.00

    5" – 7"............... $30.00 – 40.00

Black baby, with pigtails

    4" – 5"............... $35.00 – 60.00

Bye-Lo Baby-type, fine quality

    3½"................... $60.00 – 75.00

5"................... $100.00 – 120.00

Betty Boop, bobbed hairstyle, large eyes painted to side, head molded to torso

    4"...................... $18.00 – 25.00

    6"...................... $25.00 – 30.00

Bride & Groom, all-original costume

    4" .... $30.00 – 50.00

Child

    3" – 5"............... $15.00 – 30.00

Child with molded clothes

    4½"................... $30.00 – 45.00

    6"...................... $40.00 – 50.00

Child, 1920s – 1930s, pink or painted bisque with painted features, jointed at shoulders and hips, has molded hair or wig, excellent condition

    3"...................... $10.00 – 20.00

    4"...................... $15.00 – 35.00

Happifats

    3½"................ $100.00 – 125.00

HEbee, SHEbee

    4½"..................... $70.00 – 90.00

Immobile characters, Indian, Pirate, etc.

    5"...................... $15.00 – 25.00

Skippy

    6"................... $110.00 – 135.00

Snow White

    5"..................... $90.00 – 110.00

Boxed with Dwarfs.... $450.00 – 650.00

4" immobile, cold painted clothing, $20.00. *Photo courtesy of The Museum Doll Shop.*

Three Bears/Goldilocks
  Boxed set......... $325.00 – 400.00
Nippon mark
  4" – 6"................ $45.00 – 80.00
Occupied Japan mark
  2" – 3"................ $15.00 – 25.00
  4" – 6"................ $30.00 – 40.00
  7"...................... $40.00 – 50.00

ALT, BECK & GOTTSCHALCK

1854, Nauendorf, Thüringia, Germany. Produced bisque and china headed dolls for a variety of companies including Bergmann and Borgfeldt.

Shoulder Heads, china, 1880 on. Mold 639, 698, 784, 870, 890, 912, 974, 990, 1000, 1008, 1028, 1032, 1044, 1046, 1064, 1112, 1123, 1127, 1142, 1210, 1222, 1234, 1235, 1254, 1304, cloth or kid body, bisque lower limbs, molded hair or wig, no damage and nicely dressed. Allow more for molded hat or fancy hairdo.
  15" – 18"........ $300.00 – 350.00
  19" – 22"........ $400.00 – 500.00
  23" – 26"........ $550.00 – 625.00
  28"................ $775.00 – 850.00

Shoulder Heads, bisque, 1880. Cloth or kid body, bisque lower arms, closed mouth, molded hair or wig. Molds such as 784, 911, 912, 916, 990, 1000, 1008, 1028, 1044, 1046, 1064, 1127, 1142, 1210, 1234, 1254, 1304 and so-called Schoolboy style. More for molded hat or fancy hairdo.
Glass eyes, closed mouth
  9" – 11" .... $400.00 – 450.00
  15" –17"......... $500.00 – 600.00
  20" – 24"........ $650.00 – 800.00
Painted eyes, closed mouth
  14" – 18"........ $375.00 – 400.00
  21" – 23"........ $450.00 – 500.00

27" open mouth bisque turned shoulder head, $750.00. *Photo courtesy of Morphy Auctions.*

Turned bisque shoulder heads, 1885, solid dome head or plaster pate, kid body, bisque lower arms, glass eyes, wigged, all in good condition, nicely dressed. Dolls marked 639, 698, 870, 1032, 1123, 1235, "DEP" or "Germany" after 1888. Some have "Wagner & Zetzsche" marked on head, paper label inside top of body. Allow more for molded bonnet or elaborate hairdo.
Closed mouth, glass eyes
  16" – 18"........ $700.00 – 800.00
  20" – 22"........ $650.00 – 700.00
  26"................ $750.00 – 800.00
Open mouth
  16" – 18"........ $300.00 – 375.00
  20" – 22"........ $575.00 – 650.00

22" turned shoulder head, closed mouth, $700.00. *Photo courtesy of Withington Auction, Inc.*

19" Sweet Nell, $475.00. *Photo courtesy of Emmie's Antique Doll Castle.*

Character Baby, 1910s on, open mouth, sleep eyes, bent limb body. Allow more for flirty eyes or toddler body. Molds such as 1322, 1342, 1346, 1352, 1361.

    10" – 12"........ $375.00 – 425.00
    16" – 19"........ $450.00 – 575.00
    22" – 24"........ $675.00 – 750.00

Mold 1407, Baby Bo-Kaye

    8" – 9"...... $2,300.00 – 2,400.00
    15" – 19".. $1,600.00 – 2,000.00

Child, All-Bisque: See All-Bisque section.

Child, 1880 onward, bisque socket head, ball-jointed composition body, glass eyes, wig, closed mouth

Mold 630, glass eyes, closed mouth, ca. 1880

    20" – 22".. $1,800.00 – 2,000.00

Mold 911, 915, 916, swivel head, closed mouth, ca. 1890

    16" – 18".. $1,500.00 – 1,700.00
    20" – 22".. $1,900.00 – 2,100.00

Mold 1362, ca. 1912, Sweet Nell, more for flapper body

    14" – 16" .... $400.00 – 500.00
    18" – 20"........ $450.00 – 500.00
    22" – 24" .... $550.00 – 600.00
    26" – 28"........ $700.00 – 800.00
    29" – 32"..... $700.00 – 1,000.00

Character Child, ca. 1910 onward, bisque socket head, composition ball-jointed body

Mold 1322, 1342, 1352, 1361, glass eyes

    10" – 12"........ $325.00 – 400.00
    14" – 16"........ $425.00 – 500.00
    18" – 20"........ $550.00 – 650.00

Mold 1357, ca. 1912, solid dome or wigged, painted eyes, open mouth; mold 1358, ca. 1910, molded hair, ribbon, flowers, painted eyes, open mouth

    15" – 20"..... $975.00 – 1,700.00

Mold 1367, 1368, ca. 1914

    15"................. $450.00 – 475.00

LOUIS AMBERG & SONS

1878 – 1930, Cincinnati, Ohio, and New York City. Importer, wholesaler, and manufacturer. First company to manufacture all American-made composition dolls.

Newborn Babe, Bottle Babe, 1914 on, bisque head on cloth body, hands of celluloid, bisque, or rubber, sleep eyes, painted hair, closed or open mouth, molds such as 886, 371

Closed mouth

    8" – 10".......... $200.00 – 250.00
    12" – 14"........ $250.00 – 300.00
    16" – 18"........ $300.00 – 375.00

27" Vanta Baby, bisque head, $1,100.00. *Photo courtesy of Withington Auction, Inc.*

Louis Amberg & Sons

14" doll called Edwina, Sue, or It, $500.00.
Photo courtesy of Withington Auction, Inc.

Charlie Chaplin, 1915, composition head with molded mustache, cloth body, composition hands, cloth label on sleeve

    14" .... $625.00 – 650.00

AmKid, 1918, composition shoulder head, kidolene body, composition arms, sleep eyes, wig

    22" .... $100.00 – 150.00

Happinus, 1918, all-composition with head and torso molded in one piece, coquette-style, brown painted hair molded with hair ribbon

    10" .... $275.00 – 325.00

Baby Peggy, portrait of child-actress Peggy Montgomery

Composition, 1923, composition head, arms, and legs, cloth body, molded bobbed hair painted brown, painted eyes

    18" – 20" .... $600.00 – 800.00

Bisque, 1924, bisque socket head, composition or kid body, sleep eyes, brown mohair wig

Molds 972, 973, socket head

    18" – 22" .. $1,800.00 – 2,000.00

Molds 982, 983, shoulder head

    18" – 22".. $1,100.00 – 1,400.00

Baby Peggy, All-Bisque: See All-Bisque, German section.

Composition Toddler, 1928, composition head and body, molded hair, painted eyes

    13" – 15" .... $250.00 – 300.00

Little Phyllis May, 1921, composition shoulder head and lower arms, cloth body, molded hair

    14" .... $200.00 – 250.00

Mibs, 1921, composition turned shoulder head, designed by Hazel Drukker, cloth body with composition arms and legs, painted eyes, molded painted hair, molded painted shoes and socks or barefoot mama-style leg

    16" .... $1,000.00 – 1,200.00

Mibs, All-Bisque: See All-Bisque, German section.

Miss Victory, composition dolly-faced doll, ball-jointed composition body, wig, sleep eyes

    22" – 24" .... $200.00 – 275.00

Sunny Orange Maid, 1924, composition shoulder head, cloth body with composition arms and legs, head has molded "orange" bonnet

    14" .... $800.00 – 1,000.00

Vanta Baby, 1927 on, sold through Sears, advertising for Vanta baby clothes, bent-limb composition body, sleep eyes, open mouth with two teeth, painted hair

Bisque head

    14" – 18" .... $500.00 – 700.00

    22" – 27" ..... $850.00 – 1,100.00

Composition head

    10" – 14" .... $150.00 – 175.00

    18" – 23" .... $225.00 – 250.00

Edwina, Sue, or It, 1928, all-composition, painted features, molded side-part hair with swirl on forehead, body twist construction

    14" .... $475.00 – 500.00

Tiny Tots, Body Twists, 1929, all-composition, swivel waist attached to torso with a ball, molded hair, painted features, boy or girl

    7½" – 8½" ...... $100.00 – 150.00

13" Peter Pan, composition, $500.00.
Photo courtesy of McMasters Harris Auction Co.

Peter Pan, 1928, all-composition, round joint at waist, wearing original Peter Pan fashion dress

14".................. $400.00 – 500.00

AMERICAN CHARACTER DOLL COMPANY

1919 – 1963, New York City. Made composition dolls, in 1923 registered the trademark "Petite" for mama and character dolls, later made cloth, rubber, hard plastic, and vinyl dolls. In 1960 the company name was changed to American Character Doll & Toy Co.

Composition doll, marked "A.C." or "Petite," 1923, composition heads and limbs, cloth body

Baby

14".................. $125.00 – 175.00
18".................. $150.00 – 225.00

Mama doll, sleep eyes, human hair wig

16" – 18"........ $200.00 – 225.00
24" .... $300.00 – 350.00

Petite girls, 1930s, all-composition

16" – 18"........ $250.00 – 300.00
24"................. $325.00 – 350.00

Toddler

13"................. $200.00 – 225.00

Bottletot, 1926, composition head and bent limbs, cloth body, painted hair, open mouth, one arm molded to hold molded celluloid bottle

13".................. $200.00 – 225.00
18".................. $300.00 – 325.00

All-rubber, drink and wet, painted-eye doll in layette case, labeled "Bottletot, A Petite Baby," doll marked on back with Horsman horseshoe with "petite Dolls // Pt. Pending"

9½" .... $100.00 – 150.00

Puggy, 1928, all-composition, character face with frown and side-glancing painted eyes, molded painted hair, jointed at neck, shoulders, and hips, original outfits included baseball player, Boy Scout, cowboy, and newsboy. Mark: "A // Petite // Doll," clothes tagged "Puggy // A Petite Doll"

13".................. $400.00 – 475.00

Sally, 1930, Patsy-type, all-composition, molded hair or wig, marks: "Petite" or "American Char. Doll Co.," painted or sleep eyes

12".................. $150.00 – 200.00
14" – 16"........ $200.00 – 250.00
18" – 22"........ $250.00 – 300.00

Sally, Shirley-type wig

24".................. $350.00 – 375.00

Sally-Joy, composition head on cloth body

18".................. $325.00 – 350.00

13" Puggy, ca.1928, $450.00. *Photo courtesy of Joan & Lynette Antique Dolls and Accessories.*

21".................. $375.00 – 400.00
24" .... $400.00 – 425.00

Carol Ann Beery, 1935, portrait doll of child-actor, daughter of Wallace Beery, all-composition, mohair wig with two braids drawn up across top of head, marks: "Petite Sally" or "Petite"

13".................. $400.00 – 500.00
16".................. $600.00 – 700.00
20".................. $675.00 – 750.00

Little Love (also called Newborn Babe), 1942, composition flange neck head and hands, cloth body, molded hair, sleep eyes, a Bye-Lo type doll

16" – 20"........ $250.00 – 350.00

Vinyl, sleep eyes, molded hair

16".................. $125.00 – 150.00

Tiny Tears, 1950s, hard plastic head with tear ducts, drink and wet doll. Doll in excellent condition with layette can bring double values listed.

All-vinyl, 1963

11½"............... $150.00 – 200.00
13½"............... $225.00 – 250.00
16".................. $250.00 – 275.00
20" .... $300.00 – 325.00

Clothing and accessories

Bottle $35.00
Bubble pipe $25.00
Bracelet..................................... $30.00

18" Sweet Sue, $225.00. *Photo courtesy of Morphy Auctions.*

Plastic cradle............................ $200.00
Romper $35.00

Danbury Mint, 2000, re-issue, porcelain, with layette

10"...................... $50.00 – 75.00

Rubber body

11½"............... $250.00 – 350.00
13½"............... $350.00 – 450.00
16".................. $325.00 – 400.00
18".................. $450.00 – 500.00

Sweet Sue, 1953 – 1961, all-hard plastic or hard plastic and vinyl, saran wig, some on walker bodies others fully jointed including elbows, knees, and ankles, marks: "A.C." "Amer. Char. Doll" or "American Character" in a circle

15".................. $175.00 – 200.00
18" – 20"........ $225.00 – 300.00
22" – 25"........ $325.00 – 375.00
31" .... $400.00 – 425.00

Sweet Sue Sophisticate, vinyl head, earrings

20".................. $225.00 – 275.00

Annie Oakley, 1953, hard plastic walker

14".................. $400.00 – 450.00

Ricky Jr., 1954 –1956, personality doll based on character from *I Love Lucy* television show, baby

Hard plastic with rubber body, 1952

14" – 16" .... $350.00 – 500.00

16" Tiny Tears, hard plastic head and rubber body, $400.00. *Photo courtesy of Dollyology Vintage Dolls.*

22" Eloise, ca. 1955, $375.00. *Photo courtesy of Joan & Lynette Antique Dolls and Accessories.*

All-vinyl, 1953 – 1956
    13"................. $275.00 – 350.00
    21"................. $275.00 – 350.00
Toodles, 1956, hard rubber drink and wet doll
Teeny Toodles
    11"................. $225.00 – 250.00
    18" – 20"........ $250.00 – 300.00
    29"................. $325.00 – 350.00
Toodles Toddler, 1960, vinyl and hard plastic, "Peek-a-Boo" eyes
    24"................. $325.00 – 400.00
    30"................. $500.00 – 550.00
Eloise, 1955, cloth with molded mask face, yarn hair
    22"................. $325.00 – 425.00
Toni, 1958, vinyl head with rooted hair
    10½"............. $175.00 – 225.00
    14"................. $275.00 – 350.00
    20"................. $400.00 – 475.00
    25"................. $500.00 – 600.00
Little Miss Echo, 1964, vinyl, recorder mechanism in torso
    30" .... $180.00 – 225.00
Miss America, 1963 ..... $50.00 – 65.00
Tressy, 1963 – 1965, vinyl, grow hair doll, marks: "American Doll & Toy Corp. // 19C.63" in a circle. MIB dolls will bring double the values here.

    11"..................... $50.00 – 75.00
    MIB first year................ $300.00*
Black .... $150.00 – 200.00
Pre-teen Tressy, 1963
    15"................... $75.00 – 100.00
Tressy family and friends
Cricket
    9"....................... $40.00 – 45.00
Mary Make-Up, non-grow hair
    11½"................... $40.00 – 60.00
Chuckles, 1969, vinyl, rooted hair, painted eyes
    16"................. $100.00 – 125.00
    22"................. $250.00 – 300.00
Whimsies, 1960, all-vinyl characters
Dixie the Pixie, Hedda Get Bedda (three face), Miss Take, Tiller the Talker, Wheeler the Dealer, and others
    19" – 20"........ $200.00 – 350.00
Whimettes,1963 smaller doll modeled after the whimsies
    7½"................ $200.00 – 275.00
Cartwrights, Ben, Hoss, Little Joe, 1966, personality dolls based on characters from the *Bonanza* television show. MIB dolls will bring double the values here.
    9"....................... $65.00 – 70.00

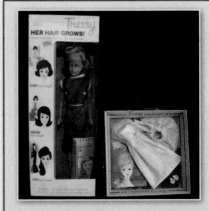

11" Tressy, grow-hair doll, MIB with extra packaged outfit, $200.00. *Photo courtesy of Emmie's Antique Doll Castle.*

ANNALEE MOBILITEE DOLL CO.

1934 to present, Meredith, New Hampshire. Dolls originally designed by Annalee Thorndike, cloth with wire armature "mobilitee" body, painted features.

Early dolls, 1934 – 1960

9" – 10½" .... $300.00 – 500.00

Later dolls, must be in excellent condition with tags

10" Folk Hero dolls

Robin Hood, 1983 – 1984 .$100.00 – 150.00

Johnny Appleseed

1983 – 1984... $100.00 – 150.00

Annie Oakley,

1985.................. $80.00 – 125.00

Mark Twain,

1986 .... $100.00 – 125.00

Ben Franklin,

1987 .... $100.00 – 120.00

Sherlock Holmes,

1988.......................$100.00 – 125.00

Abraham Lincoln,

1989 ....$100.00 – 125.00

Betsy Ross,

1990 .... $100.00 – 120.00

Christopher Columbus,

1991 .... $80.00 – 120.00

Uncle Sam,

Logo Kid, Goin' Fishin', 1995, $40.00. *Private collection.*

1992 .... $80.00 – 100.00

Pony Express,

1993 .... $75.00 – 125.00

"50's Style" Bean Nose Santa,

1994 .... $100.00 – 125.00

Pocahontas,

1995 .... $100.00 – 130.00

Logo Kid dolls

Milk & Cookies, 1985 . $75.00 – 140.00

Sweetheart, 1986......... $45.00 – 60.00

Naughty, 1987 .... $35.00 – 50.00

Raincoat, 1988............ $35.00 – 45.00

Christmas Morning,

1989 .... $35.00 – 45.00

Clown, 1990 .... $30.00 – 40.00

Reading, 1991 .... $25.00 – 35.00

Back to School, 1992.... $35.00 – 45.00

Ice Cream, 1993.......... $20.00 – 35.00

Dress-Up Santa, 1994 .. $20.00 – 35.00

Goin' Fishin', 1995 ...... $30.00 – 40.00

Little Mae Flowers,

1996 .... $22.00 – 28.00

Tea for Two?, 1997 ...... $25.00 – 30.00

15th Anniversary Kid,

1998 .... $15.00 – 20.00

Mending My Teddy,

1999 .... $25.00 – 30.00

Precious Cargo,

2000 .... $25.00 – 35.00

Mother's Little Helper,

2001 .... $30.00 – 40.00

Sand Castle Suzy,

2002 .... $30.00 – 40.00

Museum Collection Dolls

1997 Woman ...... $30.00 – 35.00

MAX OSCAR ARNOLD

1877 – 1930, Neustadt, Thüringia, Germany. Made dressed dolls and mechanical dolls including phonograph dolls.

Baby
Bisque socket head, composition body

12"	$125.00 – 175.00
16"	$245.00 – 265.00
19"	$430.00 – 480.00

Child
Bisque socket head, composition body, glass sleep eyes, wigged, molds such as 200, 201, 250, or MOA
High quality bisque

6½" on flapper body	$300.00 – 325.00
12"	$225.00 – 275.00
15" –18"	$300.00 – 350.00
21" – 24"	$425.00 – 500.00
32"	$800.00 – 850.00

Low quality bisque

15"	$125.00 – 145.00
18" – 20"	$225.00 – 275.00
24"	$300.00 – 375.00

Shoulder head, kid body, open mouth, glass sleep eyes, wigged

12" – 19"	$350.00 – 425.00

ARRANBEE DOLL CO.

1922 – 1958, New York City. Sold to the Vogue Doll Company who continued to use their molds until 1961. Some bisque heads used by Arranbee were made by Armand Marseille and Simon & Halbig. The company also produced composition, rubber, hard plastic, and vinyl dolls.
My Dream Baby, 1924
Bisque head, made by Armand Marseille: See Armand Marseille section for values.
Composition head, 1927, composition, lower arms and legs, cloth body, metal sleep eyes

8" – 10"	$100.00 – 200.00
17" – 19"	$150.00 – 250.00

Composition
Baby

8" composition My Dream Baby, $100.00. *Private collection.*

8"	$100.00 – 125.00
14"	$150.00 – 175.00
23"	$250.00 – 275.00

Bottletot, 1926, all-composition, molded bottle in hand

13"	$175.00 – 195.00
16"	$300.00 – 350.00

Child, 1930s and 1940s, all-composition, mohair wig, marks: "Arranbee" or "R & B"

9"	$100.00 – 125.00
15"	$150.00 – 200.00

Debu'teen, 1938 on, all-composition, elaborate costume brings higher end of price range

11"	$275.00 – 325.00
14"	$250.00 – 450.00
17"	$250.00 – 450.00
21"	$425.00 – 500.00

Skating costume

14"	$225.00 – 250.00
17"	$250.00 – 275.00
21"	$350.00 – 375.00

WAC

18"	$500.00 – 525.00

Kewty, 1934 – 1936, all-composition, mohair wig, marks: "Kewty"

14"	$225.00 – 300.00

Little Angel Baby, 1940s, composition head,

cloth body, molded painted hair

11"	$150.00 – 160.00
16"	$200.00 – 250.00
18"	$250.00 – 300.00

Hard plastic

18"	$150.00 – 225.00

Mama doll, 1920s on, composition and cloth

20" – 24"	$100.00 – 150.00

Nancy, 1930s, Patsy-type, all-composition, marks: "Arranbee" or "Nancy"

Molded hair, painted eyes

12"	$200.00 – 250.00
17" – 21"	$250.00 – 350.00

Nancy Lee, all-composition, mohair wig, sleep eyes

12" – 14"	$300.00 – 425.00
16" – 17"	$350.00 – 475.00

Storybook dolls, 1935, composition dolls dressed as storybook characters

8½" – 10"	$100.00 – 200.00

Hard plastic and vinyl

Cinderella, 1952, hard plastic

14"	$225.00 – 275.00
20"	$375.00 – 400.00

Coty Girl, 1958, vinyl, high-heeled fashion doll, allow more for rare outfits

10½"	$100.00 – 150.00

Lil' Imp, 1960, vinyl with red hair and freckles

14" Nanette Walker, 1957–1959, $150.00. *Photo courtesy of McMasters Harris Auction Co.*

10"	$75.00 – 100.00

Littlest Angel, 1956, hard plastic, bent-knee walker, mark: "R & B"

11"	$100.00 – 150.00

My Angel, 1961, hard plastic and vinyl

17"	$35.00 – 45.00
22"	$60.00 – 70.00
36"	$155.00 – 165.00

Walker, 1957 – 1959

30"	$130.00 – 150.00

Vinyl head on oilcloth body, 1959

22"	$50.00 – 60.00

Nancy, 1951 – 1952, vinyl head with hard plastic body, wigged

14"	$125.00 – 150.00

17" Nancy Lee, all original with box, $525.00. *Photo courtesy of Morphy Auctions.*

11" Littlest Angel, $100.00. *Photo courtesy of Emmie's Antique Doll Castle.*

18".................. $170.00 – 190.00
Nancy Lee, 1950 – 1959, hard plastic
    14" .... $325.00 – 375.00
    17"................. $375.00 – 425.00
    20"................. $450.00 – 550.00
Nancy Lee Baby, 1952, painted eyes, crying face
    15"................. $125.00 – 145.00
Nanette, 1949 – 1959, hard plastic, synthetic wig, sleep eyes, closed mouth
    14"................. $225.00 – 300.00
    17"................. $325.00 – 375.00
Nanette Walker, 1957 – 1959
    15"................. $100.00 – 150.00
    17"................. $200.00 – 275.00
    20"................. $325.00 – 375.00
Taffy, 1956, Cissy-type
    23"................. $125.00 – 145.00

ARTIST DOLLS

Original artist dolls may be one-of-a-kind pieces or limited edition pieces made by the designing artist. Production artist dolls are artist series produced in workshop or factory settings, worked on by people other than the designing artist, often limited editions. Values listed reflect secondary market prices, retail from the artist will differ.

Original Artist Dolls
Martha Armstrong-Hand, porcelain
Babies.............. $1,200.00 – 1,300.00
Children
    Brandon, Elizabeth
           $450.00 – 500.00
Mirren Barrie
Rob Roy, cloth
    12"................. $325.00 – 400.00
Bob and June Beckett, wood
Baby .... $100.00 – 150.00
Children.................. $300.00 – 350.00
Roberta Bell, wood
Historic figures .... $400.00 – 600.00

11" and 12" wooden artist dolls by Helen Bullard, ca. 1968, $400.00 each. *Photo courtesy of Withington Auction, Inc.*

Halle Blakeley, high-fire clay
Lady dolls................ $600.00 – 700.00
Carol Bowling, cloth over molded form
Baby
    11"................... $75.00 – 125.00
Frances Bringloe, wood
Pioneer children or parents
    6¼"................. $300.00 – 350.00
Muriel Bruyere, low-fire porcelain
Children
    8"................... $200.00 – 250.00
Helen Bullard, wood
Original artist dolls ... $350.00 – 500.00
Production artist dolls
    Holly, Barbry Allen
           $250.00 – 300.00
    Tennessee Mountain Kids
           $50.00 – 60.00
Emma Clear, porcelain
China or bisque ladies
    15" – 22"......... $300.00 – 600.00
George & Martha Washington
    Painted eyes ... $600.00 – 700.00 pair
    Glass eyes..$700.00 – 800.00 pair
Dewees Cochran, various media: latex composition
Grow Up Series

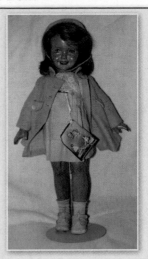

18" Dewees Cochran portrait doll, $1,800.00. *Doll courtesy of Jean Grout.*

18"........... $2,500.00 – 2,600.00
Look Alikes, portrait children
    15" – 16".. $1,400.00 – 1,700.00
    18" – 20".. $1,800.00 – 2,000.00
Production doll, Cindy
    15".............. $900.00 – 1,000.00
Judith Congdon, porcelain
Black children........... $250.00 – 400.00
Dianne Dengel, cloth
    3½"................ $100.00 – 125.00
    20" – 24"........ $200.00 – 250.00
Gertrude Florian, ceramic, composition

14½" Renauld Montauban, Medieval man, cloth, by Dorothy Heizer, $3,500.00. *Photo courtesy of Skinner, Inc.*

Ladies .... $250.00 – 375.00
Dorothy Heizer, cloth
20th Century Fashion Ladies
        $1,600.00 – 2,000.00
Historic figures, 10" – 11"
    Men and more simple costumes
        $2,600.00 – 3,200.00
    More elaborate costume (queens, etc.)
        $3,500.00 – 5,000.00
Maggie Head Kane, porcelain
        $400.00 – 450.00
Avis Lee, wood
Americanettes
    11".................. $500.00 – 800.00
Tykes, cloth body
    11".................. $400.00 – 500.00
Maryanne Oldenburg, porcelain
Children .... $200.00 – 250.00
Irma Park, wax
Wax over porcelain miniatures
    2" – 3"............ $250.00 – 375.00
Ann Parker, resin
Crepe paper
    8" – 11"............ $75.00 – 200.00
Frances & Bernard Ravca, various media
Crepe paper
    6" – 7".............. $90.00 – 120.00

17" poured wax peddler by Louis Sorenson, $1,000.00. *Doll courtesy of The Museum Doll Shop.*

Cloth, needle-sculpted
    Peasants
      10" – 14"........ $100.00 – 150.00
    Other figures
      10" – 14"........ $125.00 – 175.00
Composition, cloth and paper
    Historical figures
      10" – 14".......... $75.00 – 125.00
    21" & 23" Laurel & Hardy . $3,555.00*
Kathy Redmond, porcelain
Ladies
    13" – 14"........ $350.00 – 500.00
Regina Sandreuter, wood
            $550.00 – 650.00
Madeline Saucier, cloth
    15" – 19"........ $225.00 – 300.00
Sherman Smith, wood, 5" – 6"
Simple style.............. $250.00 – 325.00
More elaborate .... $375.00 – 500.00
Bisque head on wooden boy
            $300.00 – 400.00
Lewis Sorenson, wax
Kewpie type
    15"................. $100.00 – 150.00
Ladies
    14" – 25"........ $800.00 – 900.00
Peddler
    18" – 25".. $1,000.00 – 2,000.00

Tamara Steinheil
Victorian lady .... $400.00 – 500.00
Martha Thompson, porcelain
Early reproductions of antique dolls
    13" – 18" .... $300.00 – 400.00
Betsy .... $675.00 – 750.00
Prince Charles and Princess Anne
    10" – 11".$1,000.00 – 1,200.00 each
Fashion plate ladies
    8" – 14".... $1,200.00 – 4,000.00
Little Women .....$600.00 – 800.00 each
Ellery Thorpe, porcelain
Children .... $400.00 – 500.00
Vargas, wax
Ethnic figures
    10" – 11"........ $600.00 – 700.00
Clara Wade, porcelain, marked Clarmaid
Buster Brown, glass eyes
    18".................. $250.00 – 300.00
Faith Wick, porcelain
           $2,500.00 – 2,700.00
Fawn Zeller, porcelain
One-of-a-kind .... $1,000.00 – 2,000.00
US Historical Society
    Holly .... $200.00 – 300.00
    Polly II .... $175.00 – 225.00
Production Artist Dolls

15" Ellery Thorpe, ca. 1955, $500.00. *Photo courtesy of Withington Auction, Inc.*

28" Annette Himstedt Sidika, ca. 2005, $800.00. *Doll courtesy of The Museum Doll Shop.*

Sabine Esche, vinyl by Sigikid
    22".................. $250.00 – 300.00
Hildegard Gunzel, various media
Porcelain for Seymour Mann, limited 1,200
    26".................. $100.00 – 140.00
Vinyl
    Children
    24" – 30"........ $200.00 – 400.00
Sonja Hartmann, various media
Porcelain
    20".................. $275.00 – 300.00
Vinyl
    23".................. $150.00 – 200.00
Philip Heath, vinyl
World Children Collection
                 $375.00 – 450.00
Karin Heller, cloth
Children................... $200.00 – 250.00
Annette Himstedt, 1986 on. Distributed by Timeless Creations, a division of Mattel, Inc. Swivel rigid vinyl head with shoulder plate, cloth body, vinyl limbs, inset eyes, real lashes, molded eyelids, holes in nostrils, human hair wig, bare feet, original in box.
Barefoot Children, 1986, Bastian, Beckus, Ellen, Fatou, Kathe, Lisa, Paula
    26".................. $150.00 – 350.00
The World Children Collection, 1988, 31"
    Friederike......... $625.00 – 700.00

    Kasimir............ $625.00 – 700.00
    Makimura .... $625.00 – 700.00
    Malin .... $625.00 – 700.00
    Michiko .... $625.00 – 700.00
Reflections of Youth, 1989 – 1990, Adrienne, Ayoka, Kai, Mia Yin, Neblina, Tarea
    26" .... $300.00 – 350.00
World Children's Summit,
    35" .... $800.00 – 1,100.00
Maggie Iacono, cloth
Children
    11" – 16"........ $450.00 – 650.00
Helen Kish vinyl
Children
    7" .... $100.00 – 200.00
Lee Middleton, vinyl
Babies and toddlers....... $75.00 – 85.00
Bubba Chubbs
    22"................. $175.00 – 200.00
Harold Nabor resin
Children
    14" – 15".......... $75.00 – 125.00
Lynn & Michael Roche, porcelain and wood
Children
    17" – 22"........ $700.00 – 900.00
Robert Tonner, vinyl
Fashion Models
    19"................. $175.00 – 225.00
Robin Woods, 1980s on. Creative designer

12" R. John Wright's Abigail, souvenir for UFDC Region 14 conference, 2008, limited edition 300, $650.00. *Doll courtesy of The Museum Doll Shop.*

for various companies, including Le Petit Ami, Robin Woods Company, Madame Alexander (Alice Darling), Horsman, and Playtime Productions.

Cloth

    1985, clowns .... $40.00 – 50.00

Vinyl

    2000, Halle Angel, for Home Shopping Network

    14" .... $40.00 – 50.00

R. John Wright, cloth

Early adult peasant characters

                $1,000.00 – 1,200.00

Children .... $750.00 – 1,000.00

Max and His Pinocchio

    17" .... $1,400.00 – 2,000.00

Kewpies .... $300.00 – 400.00

Raggedy Ann .... $500.00 – 525.00

U.F.D.C. Souvenir dolls, various artists for special events

Muriel Kramer, 1982, Rose O'Neill

    16" .... $50.00 – 75.00

Kathy Redmond, Christopher Columbus, 1992, porcelain

    13" .... $100.00 – 200.00

R. John Wright, felt, 2003 Musette, candy container

                $200.00 – 300.00

Fawn Zeller, porcelain,1991, Janette

    13" .... $10.00 – 125.00

ASHTON-DRAKE

Located in Niles, Illinois, Ashton-Drake is a division of Bradford Industries. Manufactures dolls designed by a number of well-known artists. Sells its doll lines through distributors or via direct mail-order sales to the public. Dolls in perfect condition with original clothing and tags.

Yolanda Bello

Picture Perfect Babies

Jason, 1985 .... $100.00 – 140.00
Heather, 1986 .... $20.00 – 30.00
Jennifer, 1987 .... $20.00 – 30.00
Matthew, 1987 .... $20.00 – 30.00
Amanda, 1988............ $20.00 – 30.00
Sarah, 1989 .... $20.00 – 30.00
Jessica, 1989 .... $20.00 – 30.00
Michael, 1990............. $20.00 – 30.00
Lisa, 1990 .... $20.00 – 30.00
Emily, 1991................. $20.00 – 30.00
Danielle, 1991............. $20.00 – 30.00

Playtime Babies, 1994

Lindsey...........................$25.00 – 30.00
Shawna..........................$25.00 – 30.00
Todd ....$25.00 – 30.00
Lullaby Babies .... $20.00 – 25.00
Blythe, 2005, vinyl, reissue of Hasbro doll

    11½".......$125.00 – 175.00 each

Brigitte Duval

Fairy Tale Princesses series

    18" .... $40.00 – 50.00

Diana Effner

Heroines of Fairy Tales series, 16"

Cinderella.................... $25.00 – 40.00
Snow White................. $25.00 – 40.00
Goldilocks .... $25.00 – 40.00
Red Riding Hood .... $25.00 – 40.00

Ashton-Drake

Rapunzel .... $25.00 – 40.00
Mother Goose series, 14"
Mary Mary .... $60.00 – 75.00
Curl with a Curl .... $60.00 – 75.00
Curly Locks .... $60.00 – 75.00
Snips & Snails .... $60.00 – 75.00
Julie Good-Krueger
Amish Blessings series
Rebeccah .... $25.00 – 35.00
Rachel........................ $25.00 – 35.00
Adam .... $25.00 – 35.00
Joan Ibarolle
Little House on the Prairie series,
1992 – 1995
Laura .... $30.00 – 45.00
Mary .... $30.00 – 45.00
Carrie ....$30.00 – 45.00
Ma & Pa .... $30.00 – 45.00
Baby Grace .... $45.00 – 50.00
Nellie ....$25.00 – 35.00
Almanzo ....$25.00 – 35.00
Wendy Lawton
Little Women, set of five
16" .... $225.00 – 250.00
Mary Had a Little Lamb . $20.00 – 30.00

Little Bo Peep .... $20.00 – 30.00
Little Miss Muffet .... $20.00 – 30.00
Others
Glamour of the Gibson Girl, 1987, porcelain,
designed by Arlene Siegel
18" .... $25.00 – 30.00
Patti Playpal re-issues
35" – 37" .... $150.00 – 200.00
Princess Diana, porcelain
19" .... $50.00 – 100.00
Mel Odom
Gene
1995, designed by Mel Odom-marketed
through Ashton-Drake
Premier, 1st
1995 .... $350.00 – 450.00
Monaco, 2nd
1995 .... $50.00 – 65.00
Red Venus, 3rd
1995 .... $40.00 – 50.00
Other Genes
Bird of Paradise
1997 .... $40.00 – 50.00
Blue Goddess .... $60.00 – 75.00
Breathless

15" Gene doll designed by Mel Odom, manufactured by Ashton-Drake, $60.00. *Doll courtesy of The Museum Doll Shop.*

1999 .... $50.00 – 65.00
Iced Coffee........... $40.00 – 50.00
Midnight Romance
1997 .... $45.00 – 55.00
Song of Spain
1999 .... $50.00 – 75.00
White Hyacinth
1997 .... $30.00 – 40.00
Gene Specials
Champagne Flight MDCC, limited edition 250
2002 .... $150.00 – 200.00
Covent Garden, NALED
1998 .... $40.00 – 55.00
Diamond Evening
2001 .... $175.00 – 225.00
Dream Girl, Convention
1998 .... $225.00 – 250.00
Heart of Hollywood
2000 .... $55.00 – 75.00
Holiday Benefit Gala, limited editon 25
1998 .... $245.00 – 265.00
I'll Take Manhattan, Gene convention centerpiece, limited edition 50
2005 MIB.................. $1,264.00*
King's Daughter, NALED
1997 .... $40.00 – 65.00
Madra, Gene convention centerpiece, limited edition100
2005 .... $250.00 – 300.00
Moments to Remember, MDCC, limited edition 250
2000 .... $125.00 – 175.00
Night at Versailles, FAO Schwarz
1997 .... $50.00 – 90.00
On the Avenue, FAO Schwarz
1998 .... $100.00 – 130.00
Priceless, FAO Schwarz exclusive
1999 .... $75.00 – 90.00
Sparkling Seduction, NALED
1997 .... $50.00 – 80.00
Titus Tomescu
From This Day Forward bridal series

1994 .... $60.00 – 70.00
Barely Yours Series
Snug as a Bug in a Rug . $30.00 – 40.00
Clean as a Whistle ....$50.00 – 65.00
Cool as a Cucumber......$50.00 – 60.00
Cute as a Button,1993 .. $30.00 – 35.00
Pretty as a Picture, 1996 . $30.00 – 40.00
Special Delivery............ $50.00 – 65.00
I Am the Way, the Truth, and the Life
Collection .... $65.00 – 85.00

AUTOMATONS

Various manufacturers used many different mediums including bisque, wood, wax, cloth, and others to make dolls that performed some action. More complicated models performing more or complex actions bring higher prices. The unusual one-of-a-kind dolls in this category make it difficult to provide a good range. All these auction prices are for mechanicals in good working order.

Autoperipatetikos, 1860 – 1870s
Bisque, china, or papier-mâché by American Enoch Rice Morrison, key-wound mechanism
12".......... $1,000.00 – 1,200.00
With more elaborate,
head .... $2,500.00 – 3,000.00

9½" Autoperipatetikos, MIB, $4,000.00. *Photo courtesy of James D. Julia, Inc.*

Automatons

Ballerina
Bisque Simon & Halbig mold 1159, key rotates head and arms lower, leg extends, key-wound, Leopold Lambert, ca. 1900
    20".............................$4,000.00
Bébé with Fan and Flowers
Bisque Paris Bébé head, key-wound, moves hand, fans herself, sniffs flower, Leopold Lambert,
    19".............................$8,000.00
Clown Équilibriste
Roullet et Descamps, Jumeau head, clown raises his body to do a handstand on the back of the chair, turns head, lifts one arm
    18"........... $7,000.00 – 8,000.00
Edison Phonograph doll
Simon & Halbig or Jumeau bisque head doll with mechanism in torso of composition body
Jumeau head
    25" .... $8,000.00 – 10,000.00
Simon & Halbig head mold 719
    23" .... $4,900.00 – 5,400.00
Garden Tea Party
Three bisque children, painted eyes, move head and arms at tea table on 9" x 9" base
    12".............................$3,050.00
Girl with Doll in Arms

Bisque head by Jumeau, head turns, raises cage, and puppy pokes out its head, Leopold Lambert, ca. 1890
    18".......... $9,000.00 –12,000.00
Girl with Puppy
Bisque head by Simon & Halbig, rocks doll in arms, Roullet et Descamps
    16"........... $3,000.00 – 3,500.00
Laughing Girl with Kitten
Bisque laughing Jumeau socket head, carton torso, key-wound mechanism, turns head, smells flower, kitten pulls ribbon, Leopold Lambert, ca. 1890
    20"..........................$10,000.00
Magician
Jumeau black Portrait head, makes three heads under pots disappear, Roullet et Descamps
    28"..........................$80,580.00*
Marquis with Lorngette
French bisque Jumeau portrait head, key-wound, raises lorngette to eye as music plays, Leopold Lambert
    18"..........................$12,500.00*
Monkey Smoker
Papier-mâché head, smokes a cigarette, Roullet et Descamps
    30"....... $18,000.00 – 22,000.00

28" Roullet et Descamps Magician, sold at auction for $80,580.00. *Photo courtesy of Skinner, Inc.*

Négre Buveur
Roullet et Descamps, papier-mâché head, boy drinking brandy while holding a monkey on his lap

    30".......................... $28,200.00

Piano Player
Jumeau socket head, plays piano, Leopold Lambert,

    15"........................ $12,500.00*

Pushing a Carriage, key-wound toy with pressed fabric doll head

    Goodwin ... $1,900.00 – 2,400.00

Riding Toy, key-wound, fur covered horse with doll, metal with German bisque head, when wound the horse gallops across the floor, heads such as cowboys, Indians, and George Washington

    6".................... $450.00 – 500.00

Waltzing Couple, by Vichy, French poupee heads

    13"........... $5,000.00 – 7,000.00

Waltzing Lady, by Steiner

    16"........... $5,000.00 – 6,000.00

Walking doll
Roullet et Descamps, Simon & Halbig 1078 head

    23"........... $2,000.00 – 2,400.00

Steiner

    15"......... $8,000.00 – 10,000.00

15" Allie Kat, $15,000.00. *Photo courtesy of Skinner, Inc.*

also continued to manufacture their own dolls under the name Georgene Novelties.

Allie Kat, bisque head by Alt, Beck & Gottschalck, glass eyes, open mouth with wobble tongue and teeth, plush Puss in Boots-style body with composition boots

    15"....... $10,000.00 – 15,000.00

Allie Dog, bisque head by Alt, Beck & Gottschalck, glass eyes, open mouth with tongue and teeth, mold 1405

    12" – 15".. $7,000.00 – 7,500.00

Baby Dawn, 1950, vinyl with cloth body

    19"................. $300.00 – 325.00

Baby Georgene or Baby Hendron, composition

GEORGENE AVERILL

1913 – 1960s, New York City. Georgene and James Averill began their doll business dressing dolls. Georgene was the designer, James the businessman. They began as Averill Manufacturing Company. In 1915 they trademarked the name "Madame Hendron" for doll designs. In 1923 the Averills ended their association with Averill Manufacturing which continued to make dolls designed by other artists. The Averills

11" Bonnie Babe, $850.00. *Photo courtesy of Morphy Auctions.*

head, arms, and legs, cloth body, marked with name on head

13"................. $125.00 – 150.00
16"................. $175.00 – 225.00
20"................. $275.00 – 300.00
26"................. $475.00 – 525.00

Body Twists, 1927, composition with ball swivel joint in torso
Dimmie & Jimmie

14½"............. $425.00 – 475.00

Bonnie Babe, 1926 – 1930s, bisque heads made in Germany by Alt, Beck & Gottschalck, cloth bodies made in the USA by K&K toys.
Bisque head, open mouth with two lower teeth, composition or celluloid lower arms and legs, cloth body, molds 1368, 1402

12"................. $800.00 – 900.00
15"............. $900.00 – 1,000.00
18"........... $1,200.00 – 1,300.00
22"........... $1,300.00 – 1,400.00

Celluloid head

10"................. $450.00 – 500.00
16"................. $625.00 – 675.00

All-bisque Bonnie Babe: See All-bisque German section.

Brownies, Girl Scouts: See Girl Scout Dolls section.

Character animals, Uncle Wiggly, Nurse Jane, Krazy Kat, and others

19" Uncle Wiggly, cloth with mask face, $375.00.
Photo courtesy of Withington Auction, Inc.

18"................. $350.00 – 400.00

Character or ethnic doll, 1915 on, composition head, cloth or composition body, character faces, painted features
Indian, Sailor, Dutch Boy, etc.

12"................. $125.00 – 150.00
16"................. $225.00 – 275.00

Black

14"................. $375.00 – 400.00

Cloth, 1920s on, molded mask face, painted features, sometimes inset hair eyelashes, yarn hair, cloth body, many dressed in international costumes

12" – 15".......... $75.00 – 100.00
18"................. $120.00 – 150.00

Comic Characters, 1944 – 1965, cloth, molded mask face, cloth body, appropriate character clothing
Alvin, Nancy, Sluggo, Little Lulu, etc.

14"................. $300.00 – 400.00

Becassine, 1950s, French character doll

13"................. $650.00 – 700.00

Dolly Reckord, 1922 – 1928, composition head, arms, and legs, cloth body with record player inside, human hair wig, sleep eyes, open mouth with teeth

26"................. $750.00 – 900.00

Grace Drayton designs, 1923, flat faced cloth dolls with painted features, some with yarn hair
Chocolate Drop

10"................. $350.00 – 400.00
14"................. $500.00 – 550.00

Dolly Dingle

11"................. $375.00 – 400.00
15"................. $525.00 – 550.00

Maude Tousey Fangel designs, 1938, flat faced cloth dolls with painted features
Sweets, Snooks, etc.

12" – 14"........ $500.00 – 600.00
15" – 17"........ $625.00 – 675.00
21"................. $750.00 – 800.00

Kris Kringle, cloth mask face

14"................. $175.00 – 200.00

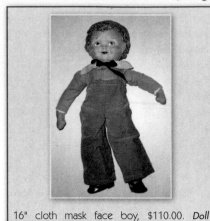

16" cloth mask face boy, $110.00. *Doll courtesy of Patty Asker.*

Little Cherub, designed by Harriet Flanders, composition with painted eyes

16".................. $300.00 – 375.00

Lullabye Baby, 1920 – 1925, composition head and hands, cloth body

15" – 19"........ $175.00 – 250.00

Mama doll, 1918 on, composition head, arms, and swing-style legs, cloth body, voice box in torso, molded hair or mohair wig, painted or sleep eyes

15" – 18"........ $200.00 – 300.00

20" – 22"........ $400.00 – 450.00

28".................. $500.00 – 550.00

Peaches,1928 on, Patsy-type, all-composition, jointed at hips and shoulders, molded hair or wigged, painted eyes or glass, open mouth or closed

14".................. $325.00 – 350.00

17".................. $400.00 – 425.00

Snookums, 1927, child actor at Universal Stern Brothers Studio, composition, laughing mouth with two rows of teeth

14".................. $300.00 – 500.00

Sunny Girl, 1927, celluloid head, cloth body, turtle mark

15".................. $375.00 – 425.00

Tear Drop Baby, designed by Dianne Dengel, cloth mask face, molded tear on cheek

16".................. $200.00 – 250.00

Whistling doll, 1925 – 1929, doll made a whistling noise when its head was pushed down

Whistling Dan, etc.

14" – 15"........ $350.00 – 450.00

BABYLAND RAG DOLL

Babyland Rag Dolls were a line of dolls sold by Horsman from 1893 to 1928. The actual manufacturer of these dolls is still unknown. The dolls were originally marked with paper tags which read "Genuine// Babyland//Trade//Mark." Dolls had flat cloth faces, cloth bodies, some with mohair wigs. Dolls listed are in good, clean condition with original clothing. Faded, stained, or worn examples can bring half the values listed.

Painted face

12" – 15"........ $850.00 – 950.00

18" – 22".. $1,000.00 – 1,200.00

30"........... $1,800.00 – 2,200.00

Black

15" – 17"..... $950.00 – 1,050.00

20" – 22".. $1,300.00 – 1,600.00

Topsy-Turvy

13" – 15"........ $800.00 – 900.00

30" Babyland Rag Doll, $1,800.00. *Photo courtesy of Joan & Lynette Antique Dolls and Accessories.*

Lithographed face, 1907 on

    12" – 15"........ $550.00 – 600.00

    24" – 30"..... $675.00 – 1,000.00

Topsy-Turvy

    14"................. $650.00 – 700.00

BADEKINDER

1860 – 1940. Most porcelain factories made china and bisque dolls in one-piece molds with molded or painted black or blond hair, and usually undressed. Sometimes called Bathing Dolls, they were dubbed "Frozen Charlotte" from a song about a girl who went dancing dressed lightly and froze in the snow. They range in size from under 1" to over 19". Some were reproduced in Germany in the 1970s to the present. Allow more for pink tint, extra decoration, or hairdo.

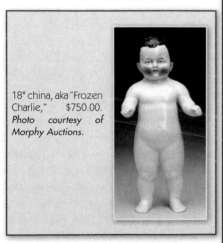

18" china, aka "Frozen Charlie," $750.00. *Photo courtesy of Morphy Auctions.*

All china

    2" – 3"............ $125.00 – 175.00

    4" – 5"............ $195.00 – 200.00

    6" – 7"............ $245.00 – 265.00

    9" – 10".......... $275.00 – 300.00

    14" – 15"........ $500.00 – 575.00

Black china

    5" – 6"............ $190.00 – 250.00

Blond hair, flesh tones head and neck

    9" – 12".......... $600.00 – 900.00

    14" – 15"..... $900.00 – 1,000.00

Molded boots

    4".................. $250.00 – 275.00

    8".................. $300.00 – 325.00

Molded clothes or hats

    1½" – 3"........ $250.00 – 375.00

    6".................. $300.00 – 350.00

    8".................. $425.00 – 475.00

Pink tint, hairdo

    3".................. $250.00 – 375.00

    5".................. $400.00 – 450.00

    13" – 14"........ $650.00 – 750.00

Pink tint, bonnet-head

    3".................. $450.00 – 475.00

    5".................. $550.00 – 575.00

Bisque

Good quality

    5".................. $200.00 – 275.00

Fancy hair, molded boots

    4" – 5"............ $275.00 – 300.00

Stone bisque, molded hair, one piece

    3"...................... $18.00 – 25.00

    6"...................... $30.00 – 40.00

Parian-type, 1860

    5".................. $200.00 – 225.00

    7".................. $250.00 – 275.00

BÄHR & PRÖSCHILD

1871 – 1930s, Orhdruf, Thüringia, Germany. Porcelain factory that made its own dolls as well as providing heads for companies such as Kley & Hahn, Bruno Schmidt, Heinrich Stier, and others.

Belton-type, 1880 on. Solid dome head with flat crown with small stringing holes in it, closed mouth, paperweight eyes, pierced ears, straight wrists, composition or kid body, molds in the 200 series

    12"........... $1,900.00 – 2,000.00

14" – 16".. $2,100.00 – 2,300.00
18" – 20".. $2,600.00 – 2,700.00
Child, 1888, bisque head, open or closed mouth, human hair or mohair wig, composition body in German or French style or kid body, molds 204, 224, 239, 246, 252, 273, 275, 277, 286, 289, 293, 297, 309, 325, 332, 340, 343, 379, 394

11" – 14"..... $700.00 – 1,000.00
16" – 18"..... $800.00 – 1,000.00
22" – 24".. $1,100.00 – 1,600.00

Kid body

13" – 16"........ $325.00 – 475.00
24"................ $675.00 – 725.00

Mold 224, with dimples

14" – 16"..... $900.00 – 1,000.00
22" – 24".. $1,400.00 – 1,800.00

Character child

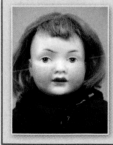

11" character child, mold 536, $2,000.00. *Photo courtesy of McMasters Harris Auction Co.*

Mold 247, open/closed mouth
26"........... $2,600.00 – 2,900.00
Mold 531
15" – 19"..... $800.00 – 1,200.00
Mold 536
18" – 20" ... $3,750.00 – 3,800.00
Mold 604
11" – 14"..... $900.00 – 1,000.00
18" – 22".. $1,100.00 – 1,300.00
Mold 624, open mouth
12" – 17"..... $900.00 – 2,000.00

Too few in database for a reliable range.

Character Baby, 1909 on, bisque socket head, solid dome or wigged, sleep eyes, open mouth, bent limb body, molds: 585,

586, 587, 602, 604, 619, 620, 624, 630, 641, 678

8" character baby, mold 604, $275.00. *Photo courtesy of Withington Auction, Inc.*

9" – 10".......... $300.00 – 400.00
12" – 14"........ $600.00 – 700.00
17" – 19"........ $750.00 – 900.00
22" – 24"..... $925.00 – 1,000.00

Toddler body

10" – 12"........ $800.00 – 900.00
18" – 20".. $1,200.00 – 1,300.00

BARBIE®

Barbie®, 1959 to present, Hawthorne, California, 11½" fashion doll manufactured by Mattel Inc. Values listed are for perfect condition dolls in original clothing and bearing all appropriate tags. Played with and undressed dolls should be valued at one-fourth to one-third the value of perfect. Mint-in-box examples will bring double the values listed here.

Lilli, 1955 – 1964, a German cartoon character, created by Reinhard Beuthien for the tabloid *Bild-Zeitung* in Hamburg, Germany, inspiration for Barbie design

7½".......... $1,100.00 – 1,700.00
12".......... $3,000.00 – 3,500.00

#1 Barbie®, 1959, heavy, solid vinyl torso, faded to pale white color, white irises, pointed arch eyebrows, soft texture ponytail hairstyle, black and white swimsuit, gold hoop earrings, metal lined holes in bottom of feet and shoes to accept doll stand

11½" #1 Barbie®, sold at auction for $7,000.00. *Photo courtesy of McMasters Harris Auction Co.*

Blond................ $6,500.00 – 7,000.00
Brunette............. $7,000.00 – 9,000.00
#2 Barbie®, 1959, doll same as previous doll, but with no holes in feet, some wore pearl earrings
Blond................ $3,400.00 – 3,800.00
Brunette............. $3,600.00 – 3,900.00
#3 Barbie®, 1960, same as #2 Barbie®, but now has blue irises and curved eyebrows
Blond................... $900.00 – 1,000.00
Brunette............. $1,400.00 – 1,600.00
#4 Barbie®, 1960, same as #3 Barbie®, but torso now has a flesh-tone color
Blond or brunette...... $300.00 – 350.00
#5 Barbie®, 1961, same as #4 Barbie®, but now has a hollow, hard plastic torso, and hair is now firmer texture saran
Blond, titian or brunette. $350.00 – 400.00
#6 Barbie®, 1962, same as #5 Barbie®, but now the doll is available in many more hair and lipstick colors and wears a red swimsuit
$225.00 – 275.00
Swirl Ponytail, 1964, smooth bangs swirled across forehead and to the side instead of the

Swirl Ponytail and Fashion Queen Barbie® dolls, $400.00 and $250.00. *Photo courtesy of Morphy Auctions.*

curly bangs of the previous ponytail dolls
$375.00 – 425.00
Bubble Cut Barbie®, 1961, same doll as others of this year but with new bubble cut hairstyle
Brown..................... $450.00 – 500.00
White Ginger........... $300.00 – 350.00

#5, ponytail, MIB, $700.00. *Photo courtesy of Morphy Auctions.*

Others ,........,\\........ $150.00 – 200.00
Side-part bubble cut .. $325.00 – 375.00
Barbie® Fashion Queen, 1963, doll has molded hair with a hair band and three interchangeable wigs, gold-and-white-striped swimsuit, and turban
$200.00 – 250.00
Miss Barbie®, 1964, doll has molded bendable legs, hair with a hair band and three interchangeable wigs, sleep eyes
$450.00 – 550.00
American Girl Barbie®, 1965, bobbed hairstyle with bangs, bendable legs
$400.00 – 600.00
Side-part American Girl
$600.00 – 700.00
Color Magic Barbie®, 1966, dolls hair can change color
Blond...................... $500.00 – 600.00
Midnight to ruby red . $575.00 – 750.00
Twist 'n Turn Barbie®, 1967, swivel jointed at waist .... $300.00 – 350.00
Talking Barbie®, 1968, doll now has pull-string talker .... $150.00 – 200.00
Living Barbie®, 1970, joints at neck, shoulder, elbow, wrist, hip, knee, and ankle
$130.00 – 150.00
Other Barbie® dolls. Dolls listed are in excellent condition, wearing original clothing, Mint-in-box can bring double the values listed.

Angel Face
1983 .... $15.00 – 20.00
Ballerina
1976 .... $25.00 – 35.00
Barbie Baby-sits
1974 .... $20.00 – 40.00
Beautiful Bride
1976 .... $95.00 – 120.00
Beauty Secrets
1980 .... $50.00 – 60.00
Bicyclin'
1994 .... $15.00 – 20.00
Busy Barbie
1972 .... $75.00 – 100.00
Dance Club
1989 .... $12.00 – 18.00
Day-to-Night
1985 .... $25.00 – 30.00
Doctor
1988 .... $12.00 – 15.00
Fashion Jeans, black
1982 .... $12.00 – 16.00
Fashion Photo
1978 .... $30.00 – 38.00
Free Moving
1975 .... $50.00 – 70.00
Gold Medal Skater
1975 .... $32.50 – 40.00
Golden Dream
1980 .... $50.00 – 75.00
Growin' Pretty Hair
1971 .... $75.00 – 100.00
Hair Fair
1967 .... $50.00 – 65.00
Hair Happenin's
1971 .... $375.00 – 550.00
Happy Birthday
1981 .... $15.00 – 20.00
Ice Capades, 50th
1990 .... $12.00 – 18.00
Kissing

Side-part American Girl, $700.00.
Photo courtesy of McMasters Harris Auction Co.

1979 .... $20.00 – 25.00
Live Action on Stage
1971 .... $120.00 – 150.00
Loving You
1983 .... $40.00 – 45.00
Magic Curl
1982 .... $12.00 – 18.00
Magic Moves
1986 .... $20.00 – 25.00
Malibu (Sunset)
1971 .... $25.00 – 32.00
Miss America Walk Lively
1972 .... $65.00 – 80.00
My First Barbie
1981 .... $12.00 – 18.00
My Size
1993 .... $40.00 – 60.00
Newport the Sport's Set
1973 .... $62.50 – 82.00
Peaches 'n Cream
1985 .... $40.00 – 50.00
Pink & Pretty
1982 .... $35.00 – 50.00
Rappin' Rockin'
1992 .... $12.00 – 15.00
Rocker
1986 .... $15.00 – 20.00
Roller Skating
1980 .... $20.00 – 25.00
Secret Hearts
1993 .... $10.00 – 12.00
Sensations
1988 .... $10.00 – 12.00
Silkstone Barbie, 2000
Fashion Editor ..... $50.00 – 60.00
Sun Lovin' Malibu
1979 .... $12.00 – 16.00
Sun Valley, The Sports Set
1973 .... $32.50 – 42.00
Super Fashion Fireworks
1976 .... $45.00 – 60.00
Super Size, 18"
1977 .... $35.00 – 60.00

Superstar Promotional
1978 .... $30.00 – 40.00
Talking Busy
1972 .... $40.00 – 55.00
Twinkle Lights
1993 .... $10.00 – 15.00
Walk Lively
1972 .... $50.00 –60.00
Western (three hairstyles)
1981 .... $25.00 – 30.00
Gift Sets
Mint-in-box prices; add more for NRFB (never removed from box), less for worn or faded.
Barbie Hostess
1966 .... $4,750.00
Beautiful Blues, Sears
1967 .... $3,300.00
Color Magic Gift Set, Sears
1965 .... $2,000.00
Fashion Queen Barbie & Friends
1963 .... $2,250.00
Fashion Queen & Ken Trousseau
1963 .... $2,600.00
Little Theatre Set
1964 .... $5,500.00
On Parade
1960 .... $2,350.00
Party Set
1960 .... $2,300.00
Pink Premier
1969 .... $1,600.00
Round the Clock
1964 .... $5,000.00
Sparkling Pink
1964 .... $2,500.00
Travel in Style, Sears
1964 .... $2,400.00
Trousseau Set
1960 .... $2,850.00
Wedding Party
1964 .... $3,000.00
Store Specials or Special Editions, mint-in-box
Avon Winter Velvet

1996 .... $20.00
Billy Boy Feelin' Groovy
1986 .... $80.00
Bloomingdale's
Savvy Shopper
1994 .... $35.00
Donna Karan
1995 .... $45.00
Ralph Lauren
1996 .... $40.00
Bob Mackie
Gold
1990 .... $200.00
Platinum
1991 .... $175.00
Starlight Splendor, black
1992 .... $200.00
Empress
1992 .... $400.00

Bob Mackie Goddess of Africa, $200.00.
Photo courtesy of The Museum Doll Shop.

Neptune Fantasy
1992 .... $300.00
Masquerade Ball
1993 .... $225.00
Queen of Hearts
1994 .... $120.00
Goddess of the Sun
1995 .... $80.00
Moon Goddess
1996 .... $80.00
Madame du Barbie®
1997 .... $200.00
Goddess of Africa
1999 .... $200.00
Goddess of the Americas
2000 .... $100.00
Goddess of the Arctic
2001 .... $130.00
Stling Silver Rose
2002 .... $25.00
Classique Series
Benefit Ball
1992 .... $30.00
City Style
1993 .... $35.00
Opening Night
1994 .... $30.00
Evening Extravaganza
1994 .... $25.00
Uptown Chic
1994 .... $30.00
Midnight Gala
1995 .... $40.00
Disney
Euro Disney
1992 .... $40.00
Disney Fun
1993 .... $15.00
Disney World, 25th anniversary
1996 .... $15.00
FAO Schwarz
Golden Greetings
1989 .... $40.00

Barbie®

Winter Fantasy
    1990 .... $90.00
Night Sensation
    1991 .... $40.00
Madison Avenue
    1991 .... $50.00
Rockette
    1993 .... $50.00
Silver Screen
    1994 .... $50.00
Jeweled Splendor
    1995 .... $45.00
La Papplion, Bob Mackie
    1999 .... $100.00

Great Eras
Gibson Girl
    1993 .... $25.00
Flapper
    1993 .... $30.00
Southern Belle
    1994 .... $25.00
French Lady
    1996 .... $20.00

Hallmark
Victorian Elegance
    1994 .... $20.00
Sentimental Valentine
    1996 .... $25.00
Holiday Voyage
    1997 .... $18.00

Hills
Party Lace
    1989 .... $18.00
Evening Sparkle
    1990 .... $15.00
Moonlight Rose
    1991 .... $15.00
Blue Elegance
    1991 .... $20.00

Holiday Barbie®
1988, red gown $550.00
1989, white gown $125.00
1990, fuchsia gown $75.00
1991, green gown $60.00
1992, silver gown $45.00
1993, red/gold gown $35.00
1994 .... $38.00
1995 .... $20.00
1996 .... $20.00
1997 .... $18.00
1998 .... $18.00
1999 .... $22.00
2000 .... $35.00
2001 .... $38.00
2002 .... $40.00
2003 .... $30.00
2004 .... $30.00
2005 .... $35.00
2006 .... $40.00
2007 .... $25.00
2008 .... $35.00
2009 .... $40.00

Hollywood Legends
Scarlett O'Hara, white gown
    1994 .... $25.00
Dorothy, Wizard of Oz
    1994 .... $30.00
Glinda, Good Witch
    1995 .... $30.00
Maria, Sound of Music
    1995 .... $25.00

Home Shopping Club
Evening Flame
    1991 .... $20.00

J.C. Penney
Evening Elegance
    1990 .... $35.00
Enchanted Evening
    1991 .... $25.00
Golden Winter
    1993 .... $30.00
Night Dazzle, blond
    1994 .... $35.00

K-Mart
Peach Pretty
    1989 .... $35.00

Barbie®

Pretty in Purple
1992 .... $15.00
Little Debbie
1993 .... $20.00
Mervyn's
Ballerina
1983 .... $75.00
Fabulous Fur
1986 .... $70.00
Montgomery Ward
#1 Replica, shipping box
1972 .... $710.00
#1 Replica, pink box
1972 .... $840.00
Nostalgia Series
35th Anniversary
1994 .... $30.00
Solo in the Spotlight
1994 .... $18.00
Busy Gal
1995 .... $20.00
Enchanted Evening
1996 .... $25.00
Poodle Parade
1996 .... $25.00
Fashion Luncheon
1997 .... $35.00
Prima Ballerina Music Box
Swan Lake, music box
1991 .... $30.00
Nutcracker, music box
1992 .... $30.00
Sears
Celebration, 100th Anniversary
1986 .... $20.00
Lilac & Lovely
1987 .... $25.00
Star Dream
1987 .... $20.00
Evening Enchantment
1989 .... $20.00
Blossom Beautiful
1992 .... $50.00

Ribbons & Roses
1995 .... $15.00
Service Merchandise
Blue Rhapsody
1991 .... $45.00
Satin Nights
1992 .... $20.00
Sparkling Splendor
1993 .... $20.00
Sea Princess
1996 .... $20.00
Spiegel
Sterling Wishes
1991 .... $30.00
Regal Reflections
1992 .... $30.00
Royal Invitation
1993 .... $25.00
Theatre Elegance
1994 .... $25.00
Shopping Chic
1995 .... $25.00
Winner's Circle
1996 .... $22.00
Target
Gold 'n Lace
1989 .... $30.00
Party Pretty
1990 .... $20.00
Golden Evening
1991 .... $35.00
35th Anniversary Barbie
1997 .... $20.00
Barbie & Kelly Easter Egg Hunt set
1997 .... $12.00
Stars & Stripes Collection
Air Force
1990 .... $20.00
Navy
1991 .... $25.00
Marine
1992 .... $30.00
Army Gift Set

1993 .... $40.00
Air Force Gift Set
1994 .... $40.00
Toys R Us
Dance Sensation
1985 .... $40.00
Pepsi Spirit
1989 .... $30.00
Vacation Sensation
1989 .... $25.00
Radiant in Red
1992 .... $16.00
Very Violet
1992 .... $25.00
Moonlight Magic
1993 .... $16.00
Harley-Davidson, #1
1997 .... $225.00
Firefighter
1995 .... $75.00
Walmart
Pink Jubilee, 25th Anniversary
1987 .... $25.00
Frills & Fantasy
1988 .... $25.00
Dream Fantasy
1990 .... $25.00
Wholesale Clubs
Party Sensation
1990 .... $15.00
Fantastica
1992 .... $15.00
Royal Romance
1992 .... $45.00
Season's Greetings
1994 .... $35.00
Winter Royale
1994 .... $25.00
After the Walk, Sam's Club
1997 .... $35.00
Country Rose, Sam's Club
1997 .... $20.00
Woolworth's

Special Expressions, white
1989 .... $30.00
Sweet Lavender
1992 .... $25.00
Family and other related dolls. Dolls listed are in excellent condition, wearing original clothing. Mint-in-box can bring double the values listed.
Allan, 1964 – 1967
Straight-leg .... $60.00 – 80.00
Bendable-leg .... $100.00 – 125.00
Buffy & Mrs. Beasley
$85.00 – 100.00
Cara, Quick Curl, 1974, African American
$85.00 – 100.00
Casey, Twist 'n Turn
1967 .... $95.00 – 120.00
Non-twist 'n turn . $80.00 – 100.00
Chris, brunette, bendable-leg
1967 .... $70.00 – 90.00
Francie
Bendable-leg
1966 .... $100.00 – 130.00
Straight-leg
1966 .... $100.00 – 150.00
Twist 'n Turn
1967 ....,,......... $175.00 – 225.00

Straight-leg Allan, MIB, $160.00. *Photo courtesy of McMasters Harris Auction Co.*

Francie, bendable legs, MIB, $250.00. *Photo courtesy of McMasters Harris Auction Co.*

Flocked hair Ken, $110.00. *Photo courtesy of McMasters Harris Auction Co.*

Black
    1967 .... $850.00 – 950.00
Malibu
    1971 .... $20.00 – 25.00
Growin' Pretty Hair
    1971 .... $100.00 – 120.00
Jamie, Walking
    1970 .... $100.00 – 120.00
Julia, Twist 'n Turn
    1969 .... $130.00 – 150.00
Talking
    1969 .... $100.00 – 110.00
Kelly
Quick Curl
    1973 .... $80.00 – 100.00
Yellowstone
    1974 .... $90.00 – 110.00
Ken, #1, straight-leg, blue eyes, hard plastic hollow body, flocked hair, 12", mark: "Ken® MCMLX//by//Mattel//Inc."
    1961 .... $90.00 – 110.00
Molded hair
    1962 .... $70.00 – 80.00
Bendable legs
    1965 .... $95.00 – 120.00
Talking
    1968 .... $60.00 – 70.00
Mod hair
    1968 .... $35.00 – 40.00

Busy Talking
    1971 .... $75.00 – 90.00
Walk Lively
    1971 .... $40.00 – 50.00
Living Fluff
    1971 – 1972....... $40.00 – 50.00
Midge
Straight-leg
    1963 .... $65.00 – 80.00
No freckles
    1963 .... $100.00 – 120.00
Bendable legs
    1965 .... $125.00 – 150.00

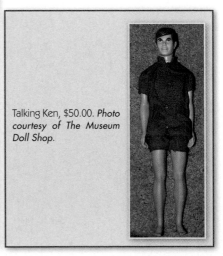

Talking Ken, $50.00. *Photo courtesy of The Museum Doll Shop.*

Living Fluff, $100.00. *Photo courtesy of Morphy Auctions.*

Skipper and Ricky, $200.00 and $150.00. *Photo courtesy of Morphy Auctions.*

P.J. Talking
1970 .... $150.00 – 200.00
Twist 'n Turn
1970 .... $65.00 – 85.00
Live Action/Stage
1971 .... $75.00 – 85.00
Ricky, straight legs
1965 .... $60.00 – 80.00
Skipper
Straight legs
1964 .... $75.00 – 90.00
Bendable legs
1965 .... $90.00 – 100.00

Twist 'n Turn
1968 .... $70.00 – 80.00
Living
1969 .... $65.00 – 80.00
Growing Up
1975 .... $45.00 – 60.00

Bendable-leg Midge, MIB, $300.00. *Photo courtesy of McMasters Harris Auction Co.*

Growing Up Skipper, $120.00. *Photo courtesy of McMasters Harris Auction Co.*

Barbie®

Skooter
Straight-leg
    1965 .... $65.00 – 75.00
Bendable-leg
    1966 .... $80.00 – 100.00
Stacey
Talking
    1968 .... $100.00 – 120.00
Twist 'n Turn
    1968 .... $120.00 – 150.00
Todd, bendable, posable
    1966 .... $40.00 – 60.00
Tutti, bendable, posable
    1967 .... $50.00 – 60.00
    Pairs in sets
    Tutti & Todd, Sundae Treat
        $150.00 –175.00
    Angie & Tangie.. $100.00 –125.00
    Lori & Rori........... $90.00 –110.00
Twiggy, Twist 'n Turn
    1967 .... $125.00 – 150.00
Barbie Accessories
Animals
All American (horse)
    1991 .... $35.00
Blinking Beauty (horse)
    1988 .... $25.00
Champion (horse)
    1991 .... $40.00
Dancer (horse)
    1971 .... $100.00
Midnight (horse)
    1980 .... $40.00
Fluff (kitten)
    1983 .... $20.00
Prancer (horse)
    1984 .... $35.00
Prince (poodle)
    1985 .... $35.00
Snowball (dog)
    1990 .... $35.00
Cases
Fashion Queen, black, zippered

    1964 .... $150.00
Barbie & Ken, black patent
    1965 .... $35.00
Miss Barbie, zippered
    1964 .... $160.00
Skooter, aqua
    1965 .... $50.00
Clothing
Name of outfit, stock number; price for mint
in package, much less for loose.
Aboard Ship
    1631 .... $550.00
All That Jazz
    1848 .... $350.00
Arabian Knights
    874 .... $495.00
Ballerina
    989 .... $325.00
Barbie in Japan
    821 .... $500.00
Beautiful Bride
    1698 .... $2,100.00
Benefit Performance
    1667 .... $1,400.00
Black Magic Ensemble
    1609 .... $420.00
Bride's Dream
    947 .... $350.00
Busy Gal
    981 .... $450.00
Campus Sweetheart
    1616 .... $1,750.00
Career Girl
    954 .... $225.00
Cinderella
    872 .... $550.00
Commuter Set
    916 .... $1,400.00
Country Club Dance
    1627 .... $490.00
Dancing Doll
    1626 .... $525.00
Debutante Ball

Barbie®

1666 .... $1,300.00
Dog 'n Duds
1613 .... $350.00
Drum Majorette
875 .... $225.00
Easter Parade
971 .... $4,500.00
Evening Enchantment
1695 .... $595.00
Fabulous Fashion
1676 .... $595.00
Formal Occasion
1697 .... $550.00
Fashion Editor
1635 .... $850.00
Formal Luncheon
1656 .... $1,400.00
Garden Wedding
1658 .... $575.00
Gay Parisienne
964 .... $4,300.00
Glimmer Glamour
1547 .... $5,000.00
Gold 'n Glamour
1647 .... $1,750.00
Golden Glory
1645 .... $495.00
Here Comes the Bride
1665 .... $1,200.00
Holiday Dance
1639 .... $625.00
International Fair
1653 .... $500.00
Intrigue
1470 .... $425.00
Invitation to Tea
1632 .... $600.00
Junior Prom
1614 .... $695.00
Knitting Pretty, pink
957 .... $450.00
Let's Have a Ball
1879 .... $325.00

Magnificence
1646 .... $625.00
Make Mine Midi
1861 .... $350.00
Masquerade
944 .... $250.00
Maxi 'n Midi
1799 .... $375.00
Midnight Blue
1617 .... $850.00
Miss Astronaut
1641 .... $700.00
On the Avenue
1644 .... $575.00
Open Road
985 .... $385.00
Orange Blossom
987 .... $600.00
Pajama Pow
1806 .... $300.00
Pan American Stewardess
1678 .... $5,000.00
Patio Party
1692 .... $375.00
Plantation Belle
966 .... $600.00
Poodle Parade
1643 .... $985.00
Rainbow Wraps
1798 .... $350.00
Reception Line
1654 .... $600.00
Red Fantastic, Sears
1817 .... $850.00
Riding in the Park
1668 .... $625.00
Roman Holiday
968 .... $5,000.00
Romantic Ruffles
1871 .... $250.00
Satin 'n Rose
1611 .... $395.00
Saturday Matinee

1615 .... $950.00
Sears Pink Formal
1681 .... $2,450.00
Shimmering Magic
1664 .... $1,550.00
Smasheroo
1860 .... $275.00
Solo in the Spotlight
982 .... $200.00
Sorority Meeting
937 .... $300.00
Suburban Shopper
969 .... $350.00
Sunday Visit
1675 .... $595.00
Swirley-Cue
1822 .... $300.00
Trailblazers
1846 .... $250.00
Travel Togethers
1688 .... $300.00
Tunic 'n Tights
1859 .... $300.00
Under Fashions
1655 .... $695.00
Velveteens, Sears
1818 .... $850.00
Weekenders, Sears
1815 .... $950.00
Wedding Wonder
1849 .... $375.00
Wild 'n Wonderful
1856 .... $300.00
Furniture, Suzy Goose
Canopy Bed, display box
1960s $250.00
Chifferobe, cardboard box
1960s $250.00
Queen Size Bed, pink
1960s $600.00
Vanity, pink $75.00
Vehicles
Austin Healy, orange & aqua

1964 .... $300.00
Beach Bus
1974 .... $45.00
Mercedes, blue-green
1968 .... $450.00
Speedboat, blue-green
1964 .... $1,100.00
Sport Plane, blue
1964 .... $3,000.00
Sun 'n Fun Buggy
1971 .... $150.00
United Airlines
1973 .... $75.00

E. BARROIS

1846 – 1877, Paris, France. Assembled, sold, and distributed lady-type dolls with bisque heads, closed mouths, on kid and cloth bodies. It is still largely unknown which French and German porcelain factories made heads for Barrois, although it is known that the heads Barrois supplied to Steiner and Blampoix were made by Frayon.

Mark: EB

Poupée (Fashion-type)

14", painted eyes, $2,000.00. *Photo courtesy of Joan & Lynette Antique Dolls and Accessories.*

Painted eyes

    14" – 16".. $1,800.00 – 2,200.00

    19" – 21".. $2,600.00 – 3,000.00

Glass eyes

    14" – 16".. $3,500.00 – 4,000.00

    19" – 21".. $4,500.00 – 4,800.00

    23" – 24".. $4,800.00 – 5,000.00

BELTON-TYPE

1875 on, made by various German manufacturers including Bähr & Pröschild, Kestner, Simon & Halbig, and others. Solid dome bisque socket head doll with small holes in crown for stringing and/or wig application. Paperweight eyes, straight-wristed wood and composition body, closed mouth, pierced ears. Belton-type is a name applied to this type of doll by modern doll collectors and is not a reference to a specific maker. Mark: none or mold numbers only.

Bru-look face

    12" – 14".. $2,000.00 – 2,600.00

French-Trade, dolls with a French look that were manufactured for the French market, mold 137 or 138

    9" – 15"....... $800.00 – 2,000.00

    18" – 20".. $1,000.00 – 2,000.00

    22" – 24".. $2,500.00 – 3,000.00

12" French-Trade, made in Germany, $1,400.00. *Photo courtesy of Joan & Lynette Antique Dolls and Accessories.*

German look dolls

    8"............. $1,000.00 – 1,600.00

    12" – 15".. $1,700.00 – 1,950.00

    18" – 20".. $2,000.00 – 2,200.00

Mold 200: See Bähr & Pröschild section.

C.M. BERGMANN

1888 – 1931, Walterhausen, Thuringia, Germany. Doll factory that distributed in the United States through L. Wolfe & Co. Bergmann had bisque doll heads made for them by Alt, Beck & Gottschalck, Armand Marseille, Simon & Halbig, and others. Registered trademarks: Cinderella 1897, Columbia 1904, My Gold Star 1926. Dolls listed are in good condition, appropriately dressed.

30" Dolly-faced doll, $600.00. *Photo courtesy of Morphy Auctions.*

Character Babies, bisque socket head on bent-limb composition body

Open mouth

    12" – 14"........ $325.00 – 400.00

    15" – 18"........ $450.00 – 600.00

Mold 612, open/closed mouth

    15"........... $2,000.00 – 2,200.00

Mold 134, character toddler

    12".............. $950.00 – 1,000.00

Child, bisque socket head, open mouth, wigged, sleep or set eyes, ball-jointed composition body, mold 1916 or others, some marked with Simon & Halbig/Bergmann mark

10"	$275.00 – 350.00
14" – 18"	$375.00 – 400.00
20" – 24"	$500.00 – 750.00
26" – 28"	$500.00 – 600.00
30" – 32"	$600.00 – 625.00
42"	$1,100.00 – 1,300.00

Flapper-type body

12"	$625.00 – 650.00
16"	$1,100.00 – 1,200.00

Eleonore

18"	$550.00 – 600.00
25"	$700.00 – 800.00

BETSY McCALL

Dolls based on *McCall's* magazines paper doll Betsy McCall. Dolls listed are in excellent condition wearing original clothing; mint-in-box can bring double the values listed.

Ideal Toy Corp., 1952 – 1953
Doll with vinyl head, on a hard plastic Toni body, saran wig

14"	$200.00 – 275.00

1958, vinyl, four hair colors, rooted hair, flat feet, slim body, round sleep eyes, may have swivel waist or one-piece torso, mark: "McCall 19©58 Corp." in circle

14"	$100.00 – 200.00

1959, vinyl, rooted hair, slender limbs, some with flirty eyes, one-piece torso, mark: "McCall 19©58 Corp." in a circle

19" – 20"	$225.00 – 275.00

1961, vinyl, five colors of rooted hair, jointed wrists, ankles, waist, blue or brown sleep eyes, four to six outfits available, mark: "McCall 19©61 Corp." in a circle

22"	$125.00 – 175.00
29"	$200.00 – 225.00

American Character Doll Co., 1957 to 1963, 8" hard plastic doll with jointed knees, sleep eyes, molded eyelashes, metal barrettes in hair. First year these dolls had mesh cap saran wigs and plastic pin joints in knees. Second year they had vinyl skull-caps on their wigs and metal knee pins.

In undies	$225.00 – 275.00
In street dress	$300.00 – 400.00
In formalwear	$400.00 – 475.00

Designer studio gift set B-498, MIB

$1,879.00*

8" doll clothing

Dresses	$35.00 – 65.00
Shoes and socks	$28.00 – 30.00
Complete outfit	$50.00 – 75.00
Boxed outfit	$100.00 – 125.00

Vinyl doll, 1958 on, jointed at shoulder, neck, and hip, sleep eyes

14"	$250.00 – 375.00
20"	$350.00 – 400.00
30"	$500.00 – 550.00
36"	$600.00 – 700.00

Additional joints at wrists, waist, knees, and ankles

22"	$350.00 – 400.00
29"	$375.00 – 425.00

Companion-size Betsy McCall, 1959, vinyl, rooted hair, mark: "McCall Corp//1959" on head

8" American Character Betsy McCall, $300.00. *Photo courtesy of Fourty Fifty Sixty.*

34".................. $400.00 – 450.00

Linda McCall (Betsy's cousin), 1959, vinyl, Betsy face, rooted hair, mark: "McCall Corp//1959" on head

34".................. $350.00 – 450.00

Sandy McCall (Betsy's brother), 1959, vinyl, molded hair, sleep eyes, red blazer, navy shorts, mark: "McCall 1959 Corp."; tag reads "I am Your Life Size Sandy McCall"

35".................. $350.00 – 450.00

Uneeda

1964, vinyl, rooted hair, rigid vinyl body, brown or blue sleep eyes, slim pre-teen body, wore mod outfits, some mini-skirts, competitor of Ideal's Tammy, mark: none

11½".............. $160.00 – 250.00

Horsman

1974, vinyl with rigid plastic body, sleep eyes, came in Betsy McCall Beauty Box with extra hairpiece, brush, bobby pins on card, eye pencil, blush, lipstick, two sponges, mirror, and other accessories, mark: "Horsman Doll Inc.//19©67" on head; "Horsman Dolls Inc." on torso

12½".................. $35.00 – 45.00

1974, vinyl with rigid plastic teen type body, jointed wrists, sleep eyes, lashes, rooted hair with side part (some blond with ponytails), closed mouth, original clothing marked "BMc" in two-tone blue box marked "©1974//Betsy McCall – she WALKS with you," marks: "Horsman Dolls 1974"

29".................. $175.00 – 200.00

Tomy

1984, porcelain head, arms, legs, cloth bodies, stationary eyes, wigged

16"..................... $15.00 – 20.00

Rothchild

1986, 35th anniversary Betsy, hard plastic, sleep eyes, painted lashes below eyes, single stroke eyebrows, tied ribbon emblem on back, marks: hang tag reads "35th Anniversary//BetsyMcCall//by   Rothschild

(number) 'Betsy Goes to a Tea Party,' or 'Betsy Goes to the Fair,' box marked "Rothchild Doll Company//Southboro, MA 01722"

8"....................... $25.00 – 35.00

Robert Tonner

1996 to present, vinyl (some porcelain), rooted hair, rigid vinyl body, glass eyes, closed smiling mouth, mark: "Betsy McCall// by//Robert Tonner//©Gruner & Jahr USA PUB." Values below are secondary market prices, dolls still available at retail as well.

8"

In undies.............. $20.00 – 30.00

Dressed .... $35.00 – 50.00

14"..................... $40.00 – 70.00

29"..................... $70.00 – 85.00

BING ART DOLLS

Germany, 1921 – 1932. Gebrüder Bing was founded in 1882. In 1921 it became a part of a conglomerate called the Bing Werke Corporation, this is when they began making their cloth "art dolls." Molded cloth face, sometimes with a heavy coating of gesso giving a composition appearance, cloth head and body, oil-painted features, wigged or painted hair, pin-jointed at neck, shoulders, and hips, seams down front of legs, mitt hands.

10" girl, $500.00. *Doll courtesy of Jean Grout.*

Painted hair or wigged, cloth or felt, unmarked or "Bing" on bottom of foot

8" – 10".......... $475.00 – 500.00
13"................ $550.00 – 600.00
15"................ $750.00 – 950.00

BISQUE, UNKNOWN OR LITTLE KNOWN MAKERS

Various manufacturers of bisque-headed child dolls working from 1870 on. No separate listing for these makers. No damage, appropriately dressed.

French

Unknown maker

Early desirable very French-style face, marks such as "J.D.," "J.M. Paris," and "H. G." (possibly Henri & Granfe-Guimonneau)

12".......... $9,000.00 – 11,000.00
17"....... $17,000.00 – 18,000.00
21"....... $19,000.00 – 21,000.00
27"....... $25,000.00 – 27,000.00

Jumeau or Bru-style face, may be marked "W. D." (Wilhalm Dehler, German doll for French trade) or "R. R."

13" – 14".. $4,000.00 – 4,200.00
19".......... $4,500.00 – 4,600.00
24".......... $4,600.00 – 4,900.00
27".......... $5,000.00 – 5,250.00

Closed mouth, marks: "J," "137," "136," or others

Excellent quality, unusual face
10" – 12".. $3,600.00 – 3,900.00
15" – 17".. $4,200.00 – 5,200.00
23" – 25".. $6,200.00 – 8,000.00

Standard quality, excellent bisque
13".......... $2,200.00 – 2,450.00
18".......... $3,200.00 – 3,450.00
23".......... $4,300.00 – 4,500.00

Lesser quality, may have poor painting and/or blotches on cheeks

15".......... $1,100.00 – 1,200.00
21".......... $1,600.00 – 1,800.00
26".......... $2,100.00 – 2,300.00

Open mouth

Excellent quality, ca. 1890 on, French body
15".......... $1,300.00 – 1,500.00
18".......... $2,100.00 – 2,300.00
21".......... $2,300.00 – 2,400.00
24".......... $3,000.00 – 3,100.00

High cheek color, ca. 1920s, may have five-piece papier-mâché body

15"................ $575.00 – 625.00
19"................ $750.00 – 800.00
23"................ $900.00 – 950.00

Known makers

Danel & Cie, 1889 – 1895, Paris, France. Bisque socket head on composition body, paperweight eyes, wigged, pierced ears

Paris Bébé
15".......... $4,000.00 – 4,500.00
18".......... $4,000.00 – 5,000.00
22" .... $6,000.00 – 6,500.00
24".......... $7,000.00 – 8,000.00
28"......... $9,000.00 – 11,000.00

Bébé Francaise
14".......... $3,500.00 – 3,600.00
20".......... $4,300.00 – 4,400.00

Delcroix, Henri, 1887, Paris and Montreuil sous Bois. Pressed bisque socket head, closed mouth, paperweight eyes, marked Pan Bébé

12"....... $10,000.00 – 14,000.00
18" ...... $15,000.00 – 19,000.00

Falck & Roussel, 1880s, socket head, closed mouth, paperweight eyes, wood and composition body, marked: F.R.

15" – 16".. $13,000.00 – 15,000.00
18"....... $16,000.00 – 17,000.00

Halopeau, A., 1881 – 1889, Paris, pressed bisque socket head, closed mouth, paperweight eyes, cork pate, French wood and composition body, marked: H

Bisque, Unknown or Little Known Makers

18"   Joanny, $18,000.00. *Photo courtesy of Skinner, Inc.*

13" $36,000.00
16" – 18"..$58,000.00 – 65,000.00
21" – 24".....$76,000.00 – 95,000.00
Lefebvre et Cie., Alexander, 1975, pressed bisque socket head, closed mouth, paperweight eyes, French wood and composition body, marked: A.L.
22" $35,000.00
Too few in database for a reliable range.
Joanny, Joseph Louis, 1888, pressed bisque socket head, closed mouth, paperweight eyes, French wood and composition body, marked: J.
12" – 15".. $9,000.00 – 12,00.00
17" – 18" .$16,000.00 – 18,000.00
22" – 23" .$11,000.00 – 18,000.00
J.M. Bébé 0, 1880s, pressed bisque socket head, closed mouth, paperweight eyes, French wood and composition body, marked: J.M.
19" – 26" $9,000.00 – 14,000.00
Too few in database for a reliable range.
M. Bebe, 1890s, pressed bisque socket head, closed mouth, paperweight eyes, pierced ears, French wood and composition body, marked: M with size number
12" – 14".. $3,000.00 – 4,000.00
19" – 23".. $2,900.00 – 3,900.00
Marque, Albert, 1914, fewer than 100 dolls

are believed to have been made
21" – 22"..............$263,000.00*
May Frères Cie, 1890 – 1897, later Steiner (1898 on), closed mouth paperweight eyes, pierced ears, composition body, marked: Bébé Mascotte
19" – 20".. $4,000.00 – 5,500.00
Mothereau, Alexandre, 1880 – 1895, pressed bisque socket head, closed mouth, paperweight eyes, French wood and composition body, marked: B.M.
12" – 15"..$16,000.00 – 18,000.00
22" – 24"..$20,000.00 – 22,000.00
28" – 29"..$23,000.00 – 25,000.00
Pannier, 1875, pressed bisque socket head, closed mouth, paperweight eyes, French wood and composition body, marked: C.P.
20"..........................$59,000.00
Too few in database for a reliable range.
Petite et Dumontier, 1878 – 1890, Paris. Pressed bisque socket head, closed mouth, paperweight eyes, French wood and composition body, some with metal hands, marked: P. D. with size number
16"....... $10,000.00 – 11,000.00
18" – 19"..$12,000.00 – 14,000.00
23"....... $15,000.00 – 16,000.00
Pintel et Godchaux, 1880 – 1889, Montreuil, France, pressed bisque socket head, closed

21" closed-mouth Bébé by Pintel et Godchaux, $4,800.00. *Photo courtesy of Gloria's Antique Dolls.*

65

18" Verlingue doll, marked Petite Française, $900.00. *Photo courtesy of Morphy Auctions.*

mouth, paperweight eyes, French wood and composition body, trademark: Bébé Charmant

10".......... $1,600.00 – 1,800.00
20" – 22".. $4,000.00 – 5,000.00
Open mouth
18" – 20".. $1,800.00 – 2,000.00

Verlingue, 1915 – 1921, Montreuil & Boulogne, France, bisque socket head, open mouth, glass eyes, composition body, trademark: J V with anchor

14"................. $700.00 – 800.00
18" – 22"..... $900.00 – 1,000.00

German

Various German manufacturers of bisque-headed dolls working from 1870 on. No separate listing for these makers. Marks: May be unmarked or only a mold or size number or Germany.

Baby

Character Baby, 1910 on, solid dome or wigged, open mouth, glass eyes, bent-limb composition body, marks: G.B., P.M. (Porzellanfabrik Mengersgereuth), F.B., or unmarked

9" – 12".......... $275.00 – 375.00
14" – 16"........ $450.00 – 500.00
19" – 21"........ $650.00 – 700.00
My Sweet Baby
23" toddler .... $900.00 – 1,000.00

Newborn Baby, 1924, bisque head on cloth body, bisque or celluloid hands, marks: Baby Weygh, IV, others.

10" – 12"........ $200.00 – 250.00
14" – 17"........ $350.00 – 400.00
Gerling Baby
17"................. $575.00 – 625.00

Dolly face child, 1880 on, bisque socket-head, wigged, glass eyes, open mouth, ball-jointed composition body or kid body with bisque lower arms, mark: G.B., K inside H, L.H.K., P.Sch, D.& K., and/or unmarked

8" – 10" .... $275.00 – 375.00
12" – 15"........ $325.00 – 425.00
18" – 20"........ $375.00 – 475.00
23" – 25"........ $375.00 – 475.00

13" socket-head dolly-faced doll, $400.00. *Photo courtesy of The Museum Doll Shop.*

21" character baby, mold 914, by Porzellanfabrik Mengersgereuth, $700.00. *Photo courtesy of McMasters Harris Auction Co.*

Bisque, Unknown or Little Known Makers

10½" German bisque Schoolboy-type, $350.00. *Photo courtesy of Skinner, Inc.*

30" .... $500.00 – 600.00
Mold 50, 51, square teeth
14" – 16".. $1,000.00 – 1,100.00
Mold 422, 444, 457, 478
17"................. $600.00 – 650.00
23"................. $800.00 – 825.00
My Girlie, My Dearie, Pansy, Princess, Special, Sweetheart, Viola, G.&S., MOA, A.W.
13".,.............. $350.00 – 375.00
18" – 20"........ $300.00 – 375.00
22" – 24" .... $425.00 – 475.00
26" – 28" .... $450.00 – 525.00
32".,.............. $550.00 – 600.00
Shoulder head, wigged, 1880 – 1890, glass eyes, open mouth, kid or cloth body, special

and other molds or no mold mark
10" – 12"........ $125.00 – 200.00
15" – 17"........ $250.00 – 325.00
20" – 23"........ $300.00 – 400.00
Closed mouth
Mold 50, shoulder head
14" – 16"........ $450.00 – 650.00
22" – 24".. $1,200.00 – 1,275.00
Mold 120, 126, 132, Bru-look
13"........... $2,500.00 – 2,600.00
19" – 21".. $3,800.00 – 4,000.00
Mold 51, swivel neck shoulder head
17".............. $950.00 – 1,100.00
German-look doll, composition body
11" – 13".. $1,200.00 – 1,300.00
16" – 18".. $1,600.00 – 1,800.00
Mold 136, French-look
12" – 14".. $1,900.00 – 2,000.00
19" – 20".. $1,600.00 – 1,700.00
E.G., maker Ernst Grossman
16"........... $2,500.00 – 2,600.00
Shoulder head with molded hair, 1880 on
American Schoolboy-type
12" – 14"........ $400.00 – 475.00
18" – 20"........ $500.00 – 600.00
Small child, 1890 to mid-1910s, bisque socket head, open mouth, set or sleep eyes, five-piece composition body
High quality bisque, flapper style body

20" shoulder head dolly faced doll, $300.00. *Photo courtesy of Alderfer Auction & Appraisal.*

5" – 6"............ $375.00 – 425.00

8" – 10".......... $400.00 – 500.00

Crude five-piece body

7" – 8"............ $175.00 – 200.00

Fully jointed body

7" – 8"............ $575.00 – 600.00

  Closed mouth

4" – 5"............ $475.00 – 500.00

8"................... $750.00 – 800.00

Character, 1910 on, glass eyes, open or open/closed mouth, solid dome or wigged, composition body

Mold 125, smiling

13"........... $6,000.00 – 6,500.00

Mold 159

23"........... $1,100.00 – 1,200.00

Mold 213, 214, maker Bawo & Dotter

13" – 14".. $4,900.00 – 5,200.00

Mold 221, toddler

16"........... $2,500.00 – 2,600.00

Mold 411, shoulder head lady

14"............................. $3,500.00

Too few in database for a reliable range.

Mold 838, P.M. Coquette

11"................. $550.00 – 575.00

K&K Mama doll, 1924, German bisque shoulder head, American-made cloth Mama-style body with composition limbs, glass eyes, made for George Borgfeldt

15" – 23"........ $300.00 – 400.00

Wolfe, Louis & Co., 1870 – 1930 on, Sonneberg, Germany, Boston, and New York City. Made and distributed dolls, also distributed dolls made for them by other companies such as Hertel, Schwab & Co. and Armand Marseille. They made composition as well as bisque dolls and specialized in babies and Red Cross nurses before World War I. May be marked "L.W. & C."

Baby, open or closed mouth, sleep eyes

12"................. $400.00 – 475.00

28" toddler body

$1,200.00 – 1,500.00

26"................. $675.00 – 725.00

Sunshine Baby, solid dome, cloth body, glass eyes, closed mouth

15"........... $1,000.00 – 1,300.00

Too few in database fro a reliable range.

Japanese

1915 on, Japan. Bisque head dolls often in imitation of the German bisque dolls. Distributed in the United States by companies such as Morimura Brothers, Yamato Importing Co., and others, marks: 1915 to 1921 marked Nippon, after 1921 marked Japan.

Character baby, bisque socket head, solid dome or wigged, open mouth with teeth, bent limb composition body

11" – 12"........ $150.00 – 200.00

13" – 15"........ $200.00 – 240.00

19" – 21"........ $250.00 – 275.00

Hilda look-alike

13"................. $500.00 – 550.00

19"................. $700.00 – 900.00

Heubach pouty look-alike, 300 series

17" .... $800.00 – 900.00

Child, bisque head, mohair wig, glass sleep eyes, open mouth, composition or kid body

9" – 11".......... $175.00 – 225.00

13" – 15"........ $200.00 – 225.00

19" – 21"........ $250.00 – 400.00

24" Japanese bisque character baby by Morimura Brothers, $275.00. *Photo courtesy of Morphy Auctions.*

Shoulder head dolly
12" – 15"........... $80.00 – 125.00

BLACK OR BROWN DOLLS

Dolls both homemade and made by various European and American manufacturers. Shades range from black to tan. Sometimes Caucasian mold in dark color, other times ethnic sculpted mold was used. Dolls listed are in good condition, appropriately dressed.

All-bisque
Glass eyes, wigged
    4" – 5"............. $375.00 – 525.00
Hertwig, character
    2½"................... $85.00 – 100.00
Kestner, swivel neck
    5" – 6"...... $1,800.00 – 1,900.00
Gebruder Kuhnlenz
    3½" – 4" .... $550.00 – 650.00
    5" – 6"...... $1,100.00 – 1,200.00
Simon & Halbig, 886
    5" – 7"...... $1,200.00 – 1,700.00
Bisque, 1880 on, French and German makers. Bisque socket head, painted black or black color in slip, brown composition or kid body
French
Poupée (fashion-type), kid body
    Unmarked
    14" – 15".. $3,000.00 – 3,400.00
    FG
    14"........... $3,400.00 – 3,600.00
    Bru
    14"........................ $19,000.00*
    17"......... $9,500.00 – 10,000.00
    Jumeau
    15"........... $8,500.00 – 9,000.00
Bébé
    Bru

Circle Dot
    13"....... $28,000.00 – 30,000.00
    17" – 19" .$32,000.00 – 42,000.00
Bru Jne
    23"....... $33,000.00 – 35,000.00
E.D., open mouth
    16"........... $2,300.00 – 2,400.00
    22"........... $2,600.00 – 2,700.00
Eden Bébé, open mouth
    15"........... $2,300.00 – 2,500.00
Gaultier, Francois, closed mouth
    12"........... $5,000.00 – 6,000.00
Jumeau
E.J., closed mouth
    10"........... $6,500.00 – 7,500.00
    15" – 17".. $8,200.00 – 9,300.00
Tété, open mouth
    10"........... $1,800.00 – 2,100.00
    15"........... $2,500.00 – 2,700.00
    20".......... $3,200.00 – 3,300.00
Tété, closed mouth
    15"........... $4,500.00 – 4,700.00
    18"........... $4,900.00 – 5,100.00
    22" – 24".. $5,200.00 – 6,500.00
DEP, open mouth
    16"........... $2,400.00 – 2,600.00
Lanternier
    18" – 20".. $1,000.00 – 1,300.00
Mothereau
    15" – 16"..$16,500.00 – 18,000.00
Paris Bébé, closed mouth
    13"........... $3,900.00 – 4,300.00
    16"........... $4,500.00 – 4,600.00
    19"........... $5,300.00 – 5,500.00
S.F.B.J.
Molds 226, 235
    15" – 17".. $2,600.00 – 3,000.00
Molds 301, 60 (Unis France mark also), jointed composition body, open mouth
    8" – 10".......... $175.00 – 225.00
    14" – 17"........ $350.00 – 525.00
Steiner
Figure A series, closed mouth

Black or Brown Dolls

10" – 11".. $4,500.00 – 5,000.00
14"........... $5,000.00 – 6,000.00
18" – 22".. $6,500.00 – 7,000.00
Open mouth
13"........... $4,200.00 – 4,400.00
16"........... $4,600.00 – 4,900.00
Series C
18"........... $6,000.00 – 6,200.00
21"........... $6,400.00 – 6,600.00

German

Unmarked
    Closed mouth
    10" – 11"........ $350.00 – 400.00
    14"................. $450.00 – 500.00
    17"................. $600.00 – 675.00
    21"................. $825.00 – 875.00
    Open mouth
    9" – 10"......... $500.00 – 600.00
    13"................. $700.00 – 750.00
    15"................. $900.00 – 950.00
    Painted bisque
    Closed mouth
    16"................. $400.00 – 450.00
    19"................. $550.00 – 600.00
    23".............. $900.00 – 1,000.00
    Open mouth
    12"................. $180.00 – 200.00
    14"................. $300.00 – 350.00
    18"................. $500.00 – 550.00

Ethnic features
    15"........... $3,000.00 – 3,200.00
    18"........... $3,800.00 – 4,000.00
    Indian, open mouth, often scowling expression, glass eyes, wigged
    10" – 15"........ $225.00 – 300.00
Bähr & Pröschild, open mouth, mold 277, ca. 1891
    10"................. $850.00 – 900.00
    12"........... $1,100.00 – 1,300.00
    Mold 244, Indian or native
    14" – 16".. $2,100.00 – 2,300.00
Bye-Lo Baby
    9"............... $900.00 – 1,100.00
    16"........... $2,700.00 – 3,000.00
Handwerck, Heinrich, mold 79, 119
    Open mouth
    12" – 16"..... $900.00 – 1,300.00
    18" – 21".. $1,600.00 – 1,900.00
    29"........... $2,500.00 – 2,600.00
Heubach, Ernst (Koppelsdorf)
    Mold 145, dolly faced, socket head, glass eyes, open mouth, five-piece composition body
    10"................. $275.00 – 325.00
    Mold 271, 1914, shoulder head, painted eyes, closed mouth
    10"................. $425.00 – 475.00
    Mold 320, 339, 350

11" Ernst Heubach, mold 399, bisque (center) and two SNF celluloid babies, 10" each. $400.00 for center baby and $300.00 each for other two. *Photo courtesy of Morphy Auctions.*

10"................ $375.00 – 425.00
13"................ $500.00 – 525.00
18"................ $650.00 – 700.00
Mold 399, allow more for toddler
10" – 14"........ $375.00 – 425.00
17"................ $550.00 – 600.00
Mold 414
9".................. $340.00 – 450.00
17"................ $715.00 – 950.00
Mold 418 (grin)
9".................. $675.00 – 725.00
14"................ $850.00 – 900.00
Mold 444, 451
9".................. $250.00 – 300.00
14"................ $550.00 – 600.00
Mold 452, brown
7½"................ $425.00 – 475.00
10"................ $525.00 – 600.00
15"................ $675.00 – 700.00
Mold 458
10"................ $465.00 – 495.00
15"................ $700.00 – 775.00
Mold 463
12"................ $650.00 – 750.00
16".............. $950.00 – 1,050.00
Mold 473
13"................ $425.00 – 475.00
Mold 1900
14"................ $500.00 – 600.00
17"................ $675.00 – 775.00
Heubach, Gebruder, Sunburst mark
Boy, eyes to side, open-closed mouth
12" – 14".. $2,300.00 – 2,500.00
Mold 7657, 7658, 7668, 7671
9" – 10".... $1,800.00 – 2,100.00
12" – 13".. $1,700.00 – 2,000.00
Mold 7620, 7661, 7686
10"........... $1,800.00 – 2,100.00
14"........... $3,500.00 – 4,000.00
17"........... $4,100.00 – 4,200.00
Mold 8457, 9467, Indians
14"........... $2,400.00 – 2,500.00
Kämmer & Reinhardt (K * R)

Child, no mold number
14" –16"...... $900.00 – 1,100.00
17" – 19".. $1,200.00 – 1,500.00
Mold 100
10" – 11"........ $850.00 – 950.00
17" – 20".. $1,600.00 – 1,900.00
Mold 101, painted eyes
15" – 18".. $3,300.00 – 3,500.00
Mold 101, glass eyes
15" – 17".. $4,300.00 – 4,800.00
Mold 114
13"........... $5,000.00 – 5,500.00
Mold 116, 116a
15"........... $4,000.00 – 4,500.00
19"........... $5,900.00 – 6,200.00
Mold 122, 126, baby body
12"................ $700.00 – 750.00
18"........... $1,000.00 – 1,125.00
Mold 126, toddler
18"........... $1,400.00 – 1,600.00
Mold 192, open mouth child
12".............. $900.00 – 1,100.00
Kestner, J. D.
Baby, no mold number, open mouth, teeth
10"............................ $1,500.00
Too few in database for a reliable range.
Hilda, mold 245
12" – 14".. $2,800.00 – 3,100.00
18"........... $4,000.00 – 4,500.00
Child, no mold number
Closed mouth
14".............. $900.00 – 1,100.00
17"........... $1,500.00 – 1,700.00
Open mouth
12"................ $550.00 – 625.00
16" – 18"..... $750.00 – 1,100.00
Five-piece body
9".................. $285.00 – 300.00
12"................ $350.00 – 400.00
Long face with letter mark, open mouth
18" – 19".. $2,000.00 – 2,500.00
Knoch, Gebruder, mold 185 dolly face child,

Black or Brown Dolls

five-piece composition body

    8" – 10".......... $150.00 – 250.00

Konig & Wernicke (KW/G)

    10" – 14"........ $600.00 – 900.00

    18" – 20"..... $900.00 – 1,200.00

    Ethnic features

    17"........... $1,000.00 – 1,100.00

Too few in database for a reliable range.

Kuhnlenz, Gebruder

    Closed mouth

    15"................. $675.00 – 900.00

    18"........... $1,350.00 – 1,800.00

    Open mouth, mold 34.14, 34.16, 34.24, etc.

    7" – 9"......... $700.00 – 1,100.00

    12"........... $1,300.00 – 1,400.00

    Ethnic features

    16"........... $3,800.00 – 4,000.00

Marseille, Armand

    No mold number, ebony

    11"................................$850.00

Too few in database for a reliable range.

    Mold 341, 351, 352, 362

    8" – 10".......... $450.00 – 550.00

    14" – 16"........ $650.00 – 700.00

    20"................. $800.00 – 900.00

    Mold 390, 390n

    16"................. $550.00 – 600.00

    19"................. $775.00 – 825.00

    23"................. $895.00 – 920.00

    28"........... $1,100.00 – 1,200.00

    Mold 966, 970, 971, 992, 995 (some in composition)

    9".................... $265.00 – 290.00

    14"................. $550.00 – 600.00

    18"................. $875.00 – 900.00

    Mold 1894, 1897, 1902, 1912, 1914

    12"................. $500.00 – 550.00

    14"................. $700.00 – 750.00

    18"................. $800.00 – 850.00

Recknagel, marked "R.A.," mold 126, 138

    9" – 10".......... $375.00 – 425.00

    16"................. $800.00 – 950.00

19" Recknagel, sold for $3,081.00. *Photo courtesy of Skinner, Inc.*

    19"........................... $3,081.00*

    22"........... $1,275.00 – 1,430.00

Schmidt, Franz

    Mold 1255, baby

    21"............. $900.00 – 1,000.00

    Closed mouth child, glass eyes, wig

    15"........... $2,300.00 – 3,000.00

Schoenau & Hoffmeister (S PB H)

    Hanna

    7" – 8"............. $475.00 – 550.00

    10" – 12"........ $600.00 – 650.00

    15"................. $750.00 – 800.00

    18"................. $900.00 – 950.00

    Painted bisque Hanna, glass eyes, wig

    9".................... $350.00 – 400.00

    Mold 1909

    16"................. $575.00 – 625.00

    19"................. $750.00 – 850.00

Simon & Halbig

    Mold 126

    8" toddler body.....$875.00 – 925.00

    Mold 639

    14"........... $6,400.00 – 6,800.00

    18"......... $9,000.00 – 10,000.00

    Mold 739, open mouth

    10"........... $1,000.00 – 1,200.00

    16"........... $1,500.00 – 1,800.00

    22"........... $2,800.00 – 3,000.00

    Closed mouth

Black or Brown Dolls

20" Simon & Halbig, mold 1358, $15,000.00. *Photo courtesy of Skinner, Inc.*

13"............................. $1,500.00
Too few in database for a reliable range.
    17"........... $2,400.00 – 2,600.00
    Mold 939
    Closed mouth
    18"........... $3,000.00 – 3,300.00
    21"........... $4,300.00 – 4,500.00
    Open mouth
    13"......... $2,300.00 original outfit
Too few in database for a reliable range.
    Mold 949
    Closed mouth
    18"........... $3,200.00 – 3,400.00
    21"........... $3,750.00 – 3,950.00
    Open mouth
    15"........... $2,600.00 – 2,800.00
    Mold 1009, 1039, 1078, 1079, 1248,
open mouth
    11" – 12".. $1,000.00 – 1,200.00
    15" – 16".. $1,400.00 – 1,500.00
    18" – 19".. $1,900.00 – 2,100.00
    34"........... $1,900.00 – 2,000.00
    Pull-string sleep eyes
    19"........... $2,200.00 – 2,300.00
    Mold 1248, open mouth
    15"........... $1,400.00 – 1,500.00
    18"........... $1,600.00 – 1,800.00
    Mold 1272
    20"........... $1,800.00 – 2,000.00

    Mold 1302, closed mouth, glass eyes, character face
    18"......... $9,000.00 – 10,000.00
    Indian, sad expression, brown face
    18"........... $7,000.00 – 7,400.00
    Mold 1303, Indian, thin face, man or woman
    15" – 16".. $6,000.00 – 6,500.00
    21"........... $7,800.00 – 8,000.00
    Mold 1339, 1368
    16"........... $5,700.00 – 5,900.00
    Mold 1348
    15"........... $5,000.00 – 6,000.00
    Mold 1358
    13" – 15" .$10,000.00 – 12,500.00
    19" – 24"..$13,000.00 – 17,000.00
Papier-mâché, shoulder head on cloth or leather body
    10" – 13"........ $425.00 – 525.00
    Squeeze toy, molded head, glass eyes
    10" – 13"........ $200.00 – 300.00
China
Frozen Charlie/Charlotte
    3".................... $100.00 – 135.00
    6".................... $225.00 – 250.00
    8" – 9"............ $300.00 – 350.00
Shoulder head doll
    9" – 11"....... $400.00 – 1,000.00
Celluloid
All-celluloid, German or American
    10"................. $150.00 – 200.00
    15"................. $275.00 – 350.00
    18"................. $500.00 – 600.00
Celluloid shoulder head, kid body, add more for glass eyes
    17"................. $275.00 – 350.00
    21"................. $375.00 – 450.00
French-type, marked "SNF"
    14"................. $350.00 – 400.00
    16" – 18"........ $500.00 – 600.00
Kämmer & Reinhardt, mold 775, 778
    11"................. $175.00 – 200.00
    18"................. $425.00 – 475.00

Black or Brown Dolls

Cloth

Alabama Baby: See Alabama Baby section.

Babyland Rag Doll: See Babyland Rag Doll section.

Brazilian, embroidered features, shell fingernails

    17" – 19"........ $500.00 – 600.00

Bruckner: See Albert Bruckner section.

Homemade, painted, embroidered, or appliquéd features, values vary according to the skill of the maker and the charm of the doll

Mid-nineteenth to early twentieth century

    8" – 12"....... $400.00 – 1,600.00

    15" – 20"..... $600.00 – 2,200.00

1900 – 1920

    15" – 18"........ $250.00 – 600.00

1920 – 1940

    15" – 18"........ $175.00 – 250.00

1930s Mammy-type

    14"................. $400.00 – 500.00

    18"................. $500.00 – 600.00

Chase: See Chase Doll Company section.

Golliwog, 1895 to present. Character from 1895 book *The Adventures of Two Dutch Dolls and a Golliwogg,* all-cloth, various English makers. See also Deans Rag Book Co.

1895 – 1920

    13"................. $750.00 – 800.00

1930 – 1950

    11"................. $400.00 – 500.00

    15"................. $500.00 – 675.00

    18"................. $600.00 – 700.00

1950 – 1970s

    13" – 18"........ $250.00 – 325.00

Steiff, 1996

    Molly Golli & Peg $450.00

Mask face, 1920 – 1930s, American

    13" – 18".......... $65.00 – 100.00

Stockinette Baby (often mis-called Black Beecher), embroidered features, glass eyes

    20" – 22".. $2,500.00 – 3,500.00

Composition, doll in good condition with

7" cloth doll, $900.00.
Photo courtesy of Skinner, Inc.

original clothing

Unknown maker

Baby with three pigtails, painted eyes

    8" – 10"............ $75.00 – 100.00

Averill

Madame Hendron, designed by Grace Drayton

    13"................. $400.00 – 500.00

Cameo

Scootles, 1925 on, Rose O'Neill design, all-composition, no marks, painted side-glancing eyes, paper wrist tag

    12" .... $400.00 – 500.00

Effanbee

Baby Grumpy

    12" – 16"........ $525.00 – 700.00

Bubbles

    17" – 22"........ $650.00 – 750.00

Candy Kid, original shorts, robe, and gloves

    12"................. $300.00 – 350.00

Patsy baby

    10"................. $575.00 – 625.00

Skippy, with original outfit

    14"............................... $900.00

Too few in database for a reliable range.

Horsman

Baby Bumps

    12"................. $200.00 – 225.00

Ideal

Marama, Shirley Temple body, from the movie *Hurricane*

    13".............. $900.00 – 1,000.00

Konig & Wernicke, mold 134

    14"................. $450.00 – 500.00

Leo Moss-type .... $2,500.00 – 8,000.00

Patsy-type

    13" – 14"........ $200.00 – 300.00

Skookum Apple character head, googly look

    14"................................. $300.00

Too few in database for a reliable range.

Tony Sarg Mammy with baby

    18".............. $900.00 – 1,100.00

Topsy-type, cotton pigtails

    10" – 12"........ $175.00 – 225.00

Rubber

Amosandra, from *Amos & Andy* radio show

    10"................. $150.00 – 175.00

Sun Rubber So-Wee

    10"..................... $55.00 – 65.00

Hard plastic

Terri Lee

Benji, painted plastic, brown, 1946 – 1962, black lamb's wool wig

    16"........... $1,800.00 – 2,000.00

Bonnie Lou, black

    16"........... $1,200.00 – 1,800.00

Patty Jo, 1947 – 1949

    16"........... $1,200.00 – 1,500.00

Vogue

Strung Ginny, 1950 – 1953, hard plastic, sleep eyes, strung joints, marked "Vogue" on head, "Vogue Doll" on body, painted eyes, molded hair with mohair wig, clothing tagged "Vogue Dolls" or "Vogue Dolls, Inc. Medford Mass.," inkspot tag on white with blue letters

    8"............................. $1,249.00*

Vinyl

Dee & Cee, 1960 – 1970s, Canada, vinyl head and body, rooted hair. See also Vinyl section.

    12" – 15".......... $75.00 – 100.00

Drowsy, Mattel, 1965 – 1974, vinyl head,

15" Vinyl by Dee & Cee, $75.00. *Doll courtesy of Pat Buckley.*

stuffed body, sleepers, pull-string talker

    15½"................ $75.00 – 100.00

Effanbee Fluffy, 1957 on

    8"....................... $30.00 – 40.00

FloJo, Florence Griffith Joyner, made by LJN

    11½"................... $15.00 – 20.00

Götz

World of Children Series

    23"................. $150.00 – 180.00

Mindy, 1957, Earl Pullan Co. Canada, vinyl head with molded braids, stuffed vinyl body

    15"................. $200.00 – 250.00

Miss Peep, Cameo

    18"................. $100.00 – 150.00

Sara Lee, Ideal, 1950, vinyl head and limbs, cloth body, sleep eyes

    17"................. $350.00 – 400.00

BLEUETTE

1905 – 1960, France. This premium doll was first made in bisque and later in composition for a weekly children's periodical, *La Semanine de Suzette* (The Week of Suzette), that also produced patterns for Bleuette. Premiere Bleuette was a bisque socket head, Tété Jumeau, marked only with a "1" superimposed on a "2," and 10⅝" tall. She had set blue or brown glass eyes, open mouth with four teeth, wig, and pierced ears. The composition jointed body was marked "2" on back and "1" on the sole of each foot. This mold was made only in 1905. S.F.B.J., a bisque socket head, began production in 1905, using a Fleischmann and Bloedel mold marked "6/0," blue or brown glass eyes, wig, open mouth, and teeth. S.F.B.J. mold marked "SFBJ 60" or "SFBJ 301 1" was a bisque socket head, open mouth with teeth, wig, and blue or brown glass eyes. All Bleuettes were 10⅝" tall prior to 1933, after that all Bleuettes were 11⅜".

Bisque
Premiere, 1905, Jumeau head
    10⅝"......... $4,800.00 – 6,000.00
SFJB 6/0, 1905 – 1915, head made in Germany by Fleischman
    10⅝"......... $2,800.00 – 3,100.00
SFBJ 60 8/0, 1916 – 1933
    10⅝"........ $2,200.00 – 3,000.00
SFBJ 301 1
    10⅝"......... $2,800.00 – 3,300.00
71 Unis France 149 60 8/0
    10⅝"......... $1,900.00 – 2,500.00
71 Unis France 149, 1933 on
    11⅜"......... $1,400.00 – 1,600.00
Composition, 1930 – 1933

SFBJ 301 or 71 Unis France 149 251, 1930 – 1933
    10⅝"......... $1,500.00 – 1,700.00
SFBJ or 71 Unis France 149 251, 1933 on
    11⅜"............... $600.00 – 900.00

BONNET HEAD
1860s – 1940s on, dolls made of a variety of materials by numerous manufacturers, all with molded bonnets or hats. More elaborate hat brings higher end of range.
All-bisque, German immobiles, painted eyes
    5"................... $125.00 – 175.00
    7" – 8"............ $275.00 – 325.00
    10"................. $350.00 – 375.00
Stone bisque immobile
    3½" – 5".............. $25.00 – 35.00
Bisque, socket or shoulder head, five-piece composition body, kid body or cloth body
Painted eyes
    5" – 8"............., $150.00 – 235.00
    11" – 14"........ $300.00 – 500.00
    18" – 20"........ $400.00 – 500.00
Glass eyes
    7" – 9"............ $250.00 – 350.00
    12" – 15"........ $500.00 – 750.00

10⅝" Bleuette, marked SFBJ 60 8/0 with trunk and clothes, $4,000.00. *Photo courtesy of Withington Auction, Inc.*

Bonnet Head

10½" bisque shoulder head with molded bonnet, 1890s, sold for $1,422.00 at auction. *Photo courtesy of Skinner, Inc.*

Alt, Beck & Gottschalck
Painted eye
    16".......... $1,500.00 – 2,000.00
Glass eye
    18"............................$1,530.00
Too few in database for a reliable range.
Handwerck, Max, WWI military figure, painted eyes, mark: Elite
Bisque socket head, glass eyes, molded helmet
    10" – 14".. $1,900.00 – 2,200.00
Heubach, Gebruder
Mold 7975, "Baby Stuart," ca. 1912, glass eyes, removable molded bisque bonnet
    9" – 13".... $1,600.00 – 3,000.00
Molds 7877, 7977, "Baby Stuart," ca. 1912, molded bonnet, closed mouth, painted eyes
    8" – 9"......... $975.00 – 1,025.00
    11" – 13".. $1,400.00 – 1,600.00
    15".......... $1,600.00 – 1,700.00
Hertwig, molded bonnet, jointed shoulders
    8" – 10"......... $175.00 – 225.00
    14" – 16"........ $250.00 – 350.00
Japan
    8" – 9"................ $85.00 – 95.00
    12"................. $125.00 – 145.00
Molded shirt or top

    15"................. $750.00 – 850.00
    21"........... $1,200.00 – 1,305.00
Recknagel, Bonnet head baby, painted eyes, open-closed mouth, teeth, molds 22, 28, 44, molded white boy's cap, bent-leg baby body
    8" – 9"............ $450.00 – 550.00
    11" – 12"........ $600.00 – 700.00
Stone bisque
    8" – 9"............ $125.00 – 175.00
    12" – 15"........ $200.00 – 300.00
Papier-mâché, leather body, wood lower limbs
Painted eyes
    12" – 18".. $1,500.00 – 1,800.00
Man, molded military hat, 1840s – 1850s
    16"........... $4,500.00 – 5,500.00
Glass eyes
    13"........... $5,000.00 – 6,000.00
Parian-type, cloth body with composition or wood lower limbs
Painted eyes
    4" – 6"......... $400.00 – 1,000.00
    10" – 17"..... $600.00 – 1,700.00
Glass eyes
    10" – 14".. $2,500.00 – 5,000.00
China, blond or black hair, painted eyes
Common style and quality
    10" – 13"......... $125.00 – 200.00
High quality

15" papier-mâché man, ca. 1850, $5,000.00. *Photo courtesy of Skinner, Inc.*

8" – 10½". $5,000.00 – 7,000.00
12" – 14".. $6,000.00 – 8,000.00
Wax-over composition, cloth body with composition or wood lower limbs, glass eyes
7" – 13".......... $250.00 – 500.00
15"................. $575.00 – 800.00
19" – 23"..... $600.00 – 1,500.00
29"........... $2,000.00 – 2,200.00

BOUDOIR DOLLS

1915 – 1940s, made in France, Italy, and United States usually. Long-limbed dolls of a variety of materials, used primarily as decorative items, fancy costumes, usually 28" – 30".
Cloth mask face, 1920s

32", with cloth face, $400.00. *Photo courtesy of Joan Gourgas.*

High quality with silk floss hair
$550.00 – 700.00
Average quality........ $300.00 – 400.00
Composition head, 1920 – 1940s
Smoker .... $500.00 – 900.00
High quality............. $400.00 – 700.00
Average quality........ $165.00 – 350.00
Hard plastic, 1940s
$100.00 – 175.00

BRU

1866 – 1899, Bru Jne. & Cie, Paris and Montreuil-sous-Bois, France. Bru eventually became one of the members of the S.F.B.J. syndicate (1899 – 1953). Bébés Bru with kid bodies are some of the most collectible dolls, highly sought after because of the fine quality of bisque, delicate coloring, and fine workmanship. Brus are made of pressed bisque and have a metal spring stringing mechanism in the neck. Add more for original clothes and rare body styles.
Poupée (Fashion-type lady), 1866 –1877, pressed bisque socket head attached to bisque shoulder plate with metal spring stringing, painted or glass eyes, pierced ears, cork pate, mohair wig, kid body, mark: numbers only, some marked "B. Jne et Cie" on shoulder plate
12" – 13".. $3,900.00 – 4,200.00
15" – 17".. $3,200.00 – 3,500.00
20" – 21".. $4,200.00 – 4,800.00
Wooden lower arms
16" – 17".. $5,700.00 – 6,000.00
Wooden body
15" – 16".. $8,900.00 – 9,500.00
Smiler, 1873 on, closed smiling mouth, mark: size letters A through O
Kid body with kid or bisque lower arms

16" Smiler poupée, $5,500.00. *Photo courtesy of Sweetbriar Auctions.*

16" Bru Breveté, $28,000.00. *Photo courtesy of James D. Julia, Inc.*

19" circle dot bébé, $29,000.00. *Photo courtesy of Withington Auction, Inc.*

11"........... $3,800.00 – 4,000.00
13" – 15".. $4,500.00 – 5,500.00
20" – 21".. $7,500.00 – 8,500.00
Wooden lower arms
16" – 19".. $5,500.00 – 7,500.00
Wooden body
15" – 16".. $8,500.00 – 9,500.00
18" – 21"..$10,000.00 – 15,000.00
Surprise Doll, poupée with two faces
13"....... $12,000.00 – 15,000.00
Bru Breveté, 1879 – 1880, pressed bisque socket head on bisque shoulder plate, paperweight eyes, multi-stroked eyebrows, closed mouth with space between the lips, full cheeks, pierced ears, cork pate, skin wig, kid or wood articulated body, size number only on head
10" – 12" . $23,000.00 – 28,000.00
14" – 16".. $26,000.00 – 28,000.00
19" – 22"..$27,000.00 – 30,000.00
Circle dot or crescent mark Bru, 1879 – 1884, pressed bisque socket head on bisque shoulder plate, paperweight eyes, multi-stroked eyebrows, open-closed mouth with molded, painted teeth, full cheeks, pierced ears, cork pate, mohair or human hair wig, gusseted kid body with bisque lower arms
12" size 1....................$28,000.00*
13" – 14".. $22,000.00 – 23,000.00

18" – 19"..$23,000.00 – 29,000.00
22" – 24"..$28,000.00 – 31,000.00
31"....... $32,000.00 – 35,000.00
Bru Jne, 1880 – 1891, pressed bisque socket head on bisque shoulder plate with deeply molded shoulders, paperweight eyes, multi-stroked eyebrows, open-closed mouth with molded, painted teeth, pierced ears, cork pate, mohair or human hair wig, gusseted kid body with wood upper arms, bisque lower arms and kid or wooden lower legs
10" ...... $34,000.00 – 36,000.00
12" – 14".. $32,000.00 – 38,000.00
15" – 17",. $33,000.00 – 40,000.00
20" – 24".. $36,000.00 – 42,000.00

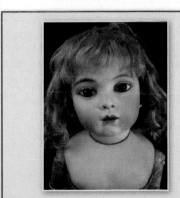

21" Bru Jne, $38,000.00. *Photo courtesy of Withington Auction, Inc.*

30" – 35". $30,000.00 – 40,000.00

37" Size 14..................$57,500.00*

Bru Jne R, 1891 – 1899, pressed bisque socket head on bisque shoulder plate with deeply molded shoulders, paperweight eyes, multi-stroked eyebrows, open-closed mouth with four to six teeth, pierced ears, cork pate, mohair or human hair wig, articulated wood and composition body

Open mouth

12"........... $1,900.00 – 2,100.00

18" – 21".. $3,200.00 – 3,400.00

Closed mouth

10½"........ $4,500.00 – 5,000.00

12" – 13".. $5,500.00 – 7,000.00

15" – 16"..$9,500.00 – 10,000.00

19" – 21".. $7,500.00 – 8,500.00

27" – 29".. $8,500.00 – 9,500.00

Mechanical specialty dolls

Bébé Baiser (kiss throwing), 1892 on, pull-string mechanism raises doll's arm and simulates throwing a kiss

11"........... $4,100.00 – 4,200.00

15"........... $4,300.00 – 4,400.00

22"........... $5,500.00 – 6,000.00

Bébé Gourmand (eating), 1880 on, open mouth with tongue, bisque lower legs, when fed food pellets went in through mouth and out through holes on the bottom of the feet, special shoes with a flap opening on the bottom allowed for food removal

16" – 18".. $40,000.00 – 50,000.00

Bébé Modele, 1880 on, Breveté face, carved wood body

16" – 19".. $34,000.00 – 40,000.00

Bébé Respirant (breathing), 1892 on, key or lever in torso activates mechanism to simulate chest movement

20" – 24"..$12,000.00 – 15,000.00

Bébé Teteur (nursing), 1879 –1898, open mouth for insertion of bottle, screw key at back of head allowed doll to drink

13" .... $7,500.00 – 8,500.00

15" – 17".. $8,000.00 – 9,000.00

19" – 24"..$9,000.00 – 10,000.00

Bru shoes

$600.00 – 1,100.00

ALBERT BRUCKNER

1901 – 1930 on, Jersey City, New Jersey. Made some dolls for the Horsman Babyland line. These dolls had molded cloth mask faces, cloth bodies, and printed features. Later made flat faced cloth dolls.

Molded cloth, mask faces

12" – 14"........ $200.00 – 275.00

17" Bébé Teteur, nursing baby, $9,000.00. *Photo courtesy of Withington Auction, Inc.*

12" Bruckner, $200.00. *Photo courtesy of Susan Holeman.*

Black .... $350.00 – 450.00
Topsy-Turvy .... $450.00 – 550.00
Flat faced, printed, 1925 on, such as Dollypop, Pancake Baby, others
    12" – 13" .... $200.00 – 250.00

BUCHERER

1921 – 1930s, Armisil, Switzerland. Metal bodies with metal ball joints, composition head, hands and feet, mark: "MADE IN SWITZERLAND PATENTS APPLIED FOR"
    6½" – 7" .... $250.00 – 400.00

8" Metal Becassine, $500.00. *Doll courtesy of Alfred Edward.*

Regional and characters such as baseball player, fireman, military, Pinocchio, others
    $300.00 – 500.00
Comic characters such as Charlie Chaplin, Happy Hooligan, Katzenjammers, Maggie & Jiggs, Mutt & Jeff, others
    $400.00 – 550.00
Becassine .... $600.00 – 800.00

BUDDY LEE

1920 – 1962, United States. Made by the H.D. Lee Co., Inc. as an advertising doll to spotlight their overalls and work gear. Doll with molded hair, painted side-glancing eyes, jointed shoulders, legs molded apart, all original clothing, mark: embossed Buddy Lee.

13" composition Buddy Lee, $425.00. *Photo courtesy of Marie Novocin.*

Composition, 1920 –1948, 13"
Engineer, Cowboy, Phillips 66
    $350.00 – 500.00
Football uniform, Gulf Oil, Minneapolis Moline uniform
    $1,500.00 – 2,000.00
Too few in database for a reliable range.
Hard plastic, 1949 – 1962
    13" .... $300.00 – 350.00
Black Magic, made for Gandy Dancer's
    $1,290.00*
Vinyl reissue, 1997
    13" .... $100.00 – 125.00

BURGARELLA

1925 to WWII, Rome, Italy. Made by Gaspare Burgarella, designed by Ferdinando Stracuzzi. Mark: cloth label sewn into outfit BURGARELLA Made in Italy.
Child, high quality composition, expressively painted eyes with heavy shading, high quality

human hair or mohair wig, jointed at neck, shoulders, hips, and knees.

16" – 18".. $1,200.00 – 1,400.00
22".......... $1,600.00 – 1,800.00

BYE-LO BABY

1922 – 1952. Baby doll designed by Grace Storey Putnam to represent a three-day old infant. Distributed by George Borgfeldt & Co. Bisque heads made by German makers such as Hertel, Schwab & Co., Kestner, Kling, others. Cloth bodies made by K & K in the United States. Composition bodies made by Konig & Wernicke in Germany. Composition head made by Cameo Doll Co.

All-bisque, 1925 on, made by Kestner, some with pink or blue booties, mark: G. S. Putnam on back, paper sticker on chest reads Bye-Lo Baby
Painted eyes
4" – 5" .... $350.00 – 400.00
4" immobile, feet kicking in air
$350.00 – 400.00
6".................... $500.00 – 550.00
8".................... $700.00 – 800.00

5" all-bisque, bare feet, $800.00. *Photo courtesy of Withington Auction, Inc.*

18" bisque, $500.00. *Photo courtesy of Morphy Auctions.*

Glass eyes, wigged
5" – 6"......... $800.00 – 1,000.00
8"............. $1,400.00 – 1,500.00
Swivel neck, glass eyes
5".................... $850.00 – 950.00
8"............. $1,250.00 – 1,350.00
Bisque head, flange neck head on cloth body with "frog" style legs or straight legs, closed mouth, molded, painted hair, blue sleep eyes, celluloid or composition hands, mark: head incised, some bodies stamped Bye-Lo Baby
8" – 9"............ $350.00 – 450.00
9" black .... $900.00 – 950.00
10" – 12"........ $350.00 – 450.00
14" – 16"....... $450.00 – 500.00
18" – 22"........ $500.00 – 600.00
Socket head on composition body
13" – 15".. $1,000.00 – 1,500.00
Composition head, 1924 on, molded painted hair, sleep or painted eyes, closed mouth, cloth body
12" – 13"........ $250.00 – 325.00
16".................. $450.00 – 500.00
Celluloid, made by Karl Standfuss, Saxony, Germany
All-celluloid
4".................... $150.00 – 200.00
6".................... $225.00 – 275.00

Celluloid head on cloth body
    10" .... $300.00 – 350.00
    12" .... $425.00 – 450.00
Wax, 1925, sold in New York boutiques
    18" – 20".. $1,500.00 – 2,000.00
Wood, 1925, made by Schoenhut
              $1,700.00 – 2,000.00
Vinyl, Horsman, 1972, mark: Grace Storey Putnam on head
    14" – 16" .... $40.00 – 50.00
Other Putnam dolls
Fly-Lo, 1926 –1930, bisque, ceramic, or composition head, glass or metal sleep eyes, molded painted hair, flange neck on cloth body, celluloid hands, satin wings in pink, green, or gold, mark: "Corp. by //Grace S. Putnam" on head
Bisque, less for ceramic
    10" – 11".. $3,000.00 – 4,000.00
Composition
    12" – 14" .... $700.00 – 900.00

CABBAGE PATCH KIDS

1978 to present, initially designed by Xavier Roberts as an all-cloth, needle-sculpted doll. The dolls were made in varying skin tone and hair and eye color combinations giving them each a unique look and "personality." Kids were 22", Newborns 17", and Preemies 15". Later licensing agreement led to vinyl headed dolls made by Coleco. In 1988 rights for the vinyl headed dolls went to Hasbro and in 1994 to Mattel. In 2004 rights for vinyl production were sold to Play Along Toys and 4Kids Entertainment. Dolls listed are in perfect condition with original clothing and tags or paperwork.
1978 on, Babyland General Hospital, Cleveland, Georgia, cloth, needle-sculpted, signature color changes year to year.

"A" blue edition
    1978 .... $1,300.00 – 1,400.00
"B" red edition
    1978 .... $1,000.00 – 1,100.00
"C" burgundy edition
    1979 .... $800.00 – 900.00
"D" purple edition
    1979 .... $700.00 – 800.00
    black $1,000.00
"E" bronze edition
    1980 .... $300.00 – 400.00
Preemie edition
    1980 .... $300.00 – 400.00
New Ears edition
    1981 .... $300.00 – 400.00
Ears edition
    1982 .... $300.00 – 400.00
Green edition
    1983 .... $300.00 – 400.00
"KP" dark green edition
    1983 .... $300.00 – 400.00
"KPR" red edition
    1983 .... $300.00 – 400.00
"KPB" burgundy edition
    1983 .... $300.00 – 400.00
"KPZ" edition
    1983 – 1984 ..... $85.00 – 150.00
Champagne edition
    1983 – 1984 ..... $80.00 – 200.00
"KPP" purple edition
    1984 .... $80.00 – 200.00
"KPF," "KPG," "KPH," "KPI," "KPJ" editions
    1984 – 1985 ... $100.00 – 150.00
Emerald edition
    1985 .... $80.00 – 150.00
Aquamarine edition
    1988 .... $80.00 – 200.00
1989 through 1990s
Kid, Newborn, or Preemie
              $125.00 – 175.00
2004 on
    Kid .... $200.00 – 400.00
Tray Mountain, limited edition, 2005

1988 .... $125.00 – 150.00
Coleco Cabbage Patch Kids, 1983 on, vinyl head, cloth body, black signature stamp
Kid, Newborn, or Preemie
                    $12.00 – 40.00
Red Hair Boys, fuzzy hair
                    $50.00 – 75.00
Popcorn hairdos, rare
                    $85.00 – 200.00
Cornsilk Kid................. $30.00 – 50.00
Porcelain, 1985, made by Shaders
  Kid.................... $60.00 – 100.00

CAMEO DOLL CO.

1922 – 1930 on, New York City, Port Allegheny, Pennsylvania. Joseph L. Kallus's company made composition dolls, some with wood segmented bodies and cloth bodies. All dolls listed are in good condition with original clothing, allow less for crazed or undressed dolls.

Bisque
Baby Bo Kaye
Bisque head, made in Germany, molded hair, open mouth, glass eyes, cloth body, composition limbs, good condition, mark: "J.L. Kallus: Corp. Germany//1394/30"
  7" – 9" ..... $1,200.00 – 2,000.00
  17" – 20".. $1,600.00 – 2,100.00
All-bisque, molded hair, glass sleep eyes, open mouth, two teeth, swivel neck, jointed arms and legs, molded pink or blue shoes, socks, unmarked, some may retain original round sticker on body
  5".............. $1,100.00 – 1,200.00
  7" – 8"...... $1,500.00 – 1,600.00

Celluloid
Baby Bo Kaye
Celluloid head, made in Germany, molded hair, open mouth, glass eyes, cloth body
  12" – 16"........ $750.00 – 950.00

Composition
Annie Rooney, 1926, Jack Collins, designer,

all-composition, yarn wig, legs painted black, molded shoes
  13"................ $475.00 – 500.00
  17"................ $650.00 – 700.00
Baby Blossom, 1927, "DES, J.L.Kallus," composition upper torso, cloth lower body and legs, molded hair, open mouth
  19" – 20"........ $550.00 – 650.00
Baby Bo Kaye
Composition head, molded hair, open mouth, glass eyes, light crazing
  14"................ $650.00 – 675.00
Bandy, 1929, composition head, wood segmented body, marked on hat "General Electric Radio," designed by J. Kallus
  18½".............. $800.00 – 900.00
Betty Boop, 1932, composition head character, wood segmented body, molded hair, painted features, label on torso
  11"................ $600.00 – 700.00
  20".......... $1,000.00 – 1,100.00
Champ, 1942, composition with freckles
  16"................ $575.00 – 600.00
Eugene the Jeep, composition and wood segmented doll from Popeye comics
  6"............................ $1,600.00*
  14".......... $1,000.00 – 1,200.00
Felix the Cat, composition and wood segmented doll

7" Pinkie, $425.00. *Photo courtesy of Sharing My Dolls 'N Stuff.*

Cameo Doll Co.

13".................. $200.00 – 275.00

Giggles, 1946, "Giggles Doll, A Cameo Doll," composition with molded loop for ribbon

12" – 14"........ $300.00 – 350.00

Ho-Ho, 1940, painted plaster, laughing mouth

5½".................. $175.00 – 200.00

Joy, 1932, composition head character, wood segmented body, molded hair, painted features, label on torso

10"................. $275.00 – 325.00

15"................. $375.00 – 425.00

Margie, 1929, composition head character, wood segmented body, molded hair, painted features, label on torso

10"................. $190.00 – 215.00

15"................. $350.00 – 400.00

17"................. $450.00 – 500.00

Pete the Pup, 1930 – 1935, composition head character, wood segmented body, molded hair, painted features, label on torso

9" – 12"........... $250.00 – 400.00

Pinkie, 1930 – 1935, composition head character, wood segmented body, molded hair, painted features, label on torso

7" – 10"........... $425.00 – 475.00

Popeye, 1935, composition head character, wood segmented body, molded hair, painted features, label on torso

14"................. $200.00 – 300.00

Pretty Bettsie, composition head, molded hair, painted side-glancing eyes, open-closed mouth, composition one-piece body and limbs, wooden neck joint, molded and painted dress with ruffles, shoes, and socks, triangular red tag on chest marked "Pretty Bettsie//Copyright J. Kallus"

18"................. $450.00 – 500.00

Scootles, 1925 on, Rose O'Neill design, all-composition, no marks, painted side-glancing eyes, paper wrist tag

7" – 8"............ $375.00 – 425.00

14" Popeye, composition head, wood segmented body, $300.00. *Photo courtesy of Morphy Auctions.*

12"................. $350.00 – 400.00

15"................. $550.00 – 600.00

22".............. $900.00 – 1,000.00

26"........... $1,550.00 – 1,650.00

Composition, sleep eyes

15"................. $650.00 – 700.00

Black composition

12"................. $650.00 – 750.00

Hard plastic and vinyl, dolls listed here are in good condition wearing original clothing, allow double for mint-in-box.

Baby Mine, 1962 – 1964, vinyl and cloth,

15" Scootles, $450.00. *Doll from private collection.*

sleep eyes

    16"................. $100.00 – 125.00

    19"................. $150.00 – 200.00

Ho Ho, "Rose O'Neill," laughing mouth, squeaker, tag

Black

    7"................... $225.00 – 275.00

White

    7"................... $150.00 – 200.00

Miss Peep, 1957 – 1970s, pin jointed shoulders and hips, vinyl

    15"..................... $60.00 – 70.00

    18"..................... $70.00 – 80.00

Black

    18"................. $100.00 – 125.00

1984, Jesco re-issue, all vinyl

    16"..................... $25.00 – 30.00

Miss Peep, Newborn, 1962, vinyl head and rigid plastic body

    14" – 18"............ $30.00 – 40.00

Pinkie, 1950s

    10" – 11"........ $125.00 – 150.00

Scootles, 1964, vinyl

    14"................. $125.00 – 175.00

    20"................. $225.00 – 275.00

1980s, Jesco

    12"..................... $25.00 – 30.00

    16"..................... $40.00 – 50.00

    19"..................... $60.00 – 80.00

CATTERFELDER PUPPENFABRIK

1906 on, Catterfeld, Thuringia, Germany. Had heads made by Kestner. Trademark: My Sunshine

C.P. child, 1902 on, dolly face, bisque socket head, glass sleep eyes, wigged, open mouth with teeth, ball-jointed composition body

Mold 264 and others

    9"................... $250.00 – 300.00

    14" – 16"........ $300.00 – 350.00

    25" – 28"........ $400.00 – 500.00

C.P. character child, 1910 on, bisque socket head, painted eyes, wigged, open mouth with teeth, ball-jointed composition body

Mold 207, 210, 215, 219, 217, others

    15" –16"... $8,500.00 – 9,000.00

Mold 220, glass eyes

    14"........... $8,300.00 – 8,500.00

Mold 524, painted eyes, closed mouth, wigged

    18"........................... $5,750.00*

Character baby, 1910 on, bisque socket head, molded hair or wig, painted or glass sleep eyes, composition baby body

Mold 200, 201, 207, 208, others

    8" – 10".......... $550.00 – 650.00

    14" – 16"........ $750.00 – 800.00

    19" – 21"........ $875.00 – 925.00

201, toddler

    8" – 10"....... $900.00 – 1,200.00

Mold 262, 263

    15" – 17"........ $400.00 – 450.00

    20" – 22"........ $550.00 – 600.00

262 toddler, five-piece composition body

    18"................. $675.00 – 725.00

34", mold 264, $550.00. *Photo courtesy of McMasters Harris Auction Co.*

CELLULOID

Early form of plastic made from nitrocellulose and a plasticizer such as camphor. Came into use in 1869 and an improved version became popular about 1905.

Made in numerous countries:

England – Wilson Doll Co., Cascelliod Ltd. (Palitoy)

France – Petitcollin (profile of eagle head), Widow Chalory, Convert Cie, Parisienn Cellulosine, Neuman & Marx (dragon), Société Industrielle de Celluloid (SIC), Société Nobel Francaise (SNF in diamond), Sicoine, others.

Germany – Bähr & Pröschild, Buschow & Beck (helmet Minerva), Catterfelder Puppenfabrik Co., Cuno & Otto Dressel, E. Maar & Sohn (3M), Emasco, Kämmer & Reinhardt, Kestner, Konig & Wernicke, A. Hagendorn & Co., Hermsdorfer Celluloidwarenfabrik (ladybug), Dr. Paul Hunaeus, Kohn & Wengenroth, Rheinsche Gummi und Celluloid Fabrik Co. later known as Schildkröte (turtle mark), Max Rudolph, Bruno Schmidt, Franz Schmidt & Co., Schoberl & Becker (mermaid) who used Cellba as a trade name, Karl Standfuss, Albert Wacker, others.

USA – Averill, Bo-Peep (H.J. Brown), DuPont Viscaloid Co., Horsman, Irwin, Marks Bros., Parsons-Jackson (stork mark), Celluloid Novelty Co., others.

All-celluloid

Baby, 1910 on, painted eyes

4" – 8"	$65.00 – 90.00
12" – 15"	$150.00 – 165.00
19" – 21"	$200.00 – 225.00

Marked France

5" – 9"	$120.00 – 250.00
16" – 18"	$350.00 – 450.00

Marked German character baby

12"	$325.00 – 400.00

Marked Japan

4" – 5"	$18.00 – 22.00
8" – 10"	$65.00 – 75.00
13" – 15"	$145.00 – 165.00

Occupied Japan

24"	$150.00 – 175.00

Child, painted eyes, jointed at shoulder and hips

5" – 7"	$75.00 – 100.00
11" – 14"	$150.00 – 200.00
18" – 20"	$250.00 – 275.00

Glass eyes

12" – 13"	$200.00 – 250.00
15" – 16"	$300.00 – 400.00

Marked France

7" – 9"	$150.00 – 175.00
14" – 18"	$300.00 – 325.00
22" – 24"	$375.00 – 425.00

Marked Japan

With molded clothing

3" – 4"	$50.00 – 60.00
8" – 9"	$125.00 – 150.00

Jointed shoulders only

3" – 4"	$18.00 – 22.00
8" – 10"	$30.00 – 40.00

12" pair of celluloid dolls by Gura, $200.00. *Photo courtesy of The Museum Doll Shop.*

10" Kämmer & Reinhardt, mold 728, $225.00.
Doll courtesy of The Museum Doll Shop.

Occupied Japan

6" – 8"............... $90.00 – 100.00

In regional costume, tagged LeMinor, Poupée Carnival-type, may have feathers glued on head or body

8" – 12"............... $25.00 – 35.00

Magali, others

8"....................... $40.00 – 55.00

12" – 15"........ $120.00 – 135.00

19"................. $150.00 – 175.00

Kewpie: See Kewpie section.

Shoulder head child, 1900 on, German, molded hair or wig, open or open-closed mouth, kid or cloth body, sometimes arms of other materials

Glass eyes

16" – 18"........ $225.00 – 300.00

22" – 24"........ $300.00 – 400.00

Painted eyes

11" – 14".......... $75.00 – 100.00

16" – 18"........ $150.00 – 175.00

Bye-Lo Baby: See Bye-Lo Baby section.

Socket head child, 1910 on, open mouth, glass sleep eyes, wig, composition body

French, such as Petitcolin, others, glass eyes, wigged

18" – 19"........ $350.00 – 400.00

Jumeau

13"................. $450.00 – 500.00

16"................. $575.00 – 600.00

German, various makers

Molded hair, painted eyes

11" – 13"....... $200.00 – 300.00

16" – 19"........ $225.00 – 325.00

Glass eyes

14" – 17"........ $200.00 – 400.00

Heubach Köppelsdorf, mold 399

11"................... $75.00 – 100.00

Kämmer & Reinhardt

Baby, mold 721, 728

10" – 15"........ $225.00 – 275.00

17" – 21"........ $350.00 – 450.00

Child, socket head, mold 701, 717

12" – 14"........ $650.00 – 750.00

18" – 25"........ $800.00 – 850.00

Toddler, flirty eyes

17"................. $500.00 – 600.00

Kestner, mold 203 character baby

12"................. $425.00 – 450.00

Konig & Wernicke (K & W)

Toddler

15" – 19"........ $375.00 – 500.00

Max & Moritz

7"............$300.00 – 350.00 each

American

Parsons-Jackson (stork mark)

Baby

10" – 12"........ $150.00 – 200.00

14"................. $200.00 – 250.00

Toddler

12" – 15"........ $150.00 – 200.00

CENTURY DOLL CO.

1909 – 1930, New York City. Founded by Max Scheuer and Sons, used bisque heads on many later dolls. In about 1929,

Century merged with Domec to become the Doll Corporation of America. Some heads were made by Kestner, Herm Steiner, and other firms for Century. Dolls listed here are in good condition, with original clothes or appropriately dressed. More for boxed, tagged, or labeled exceptional doll.

Bisque

Baby, 1926, by Kestner, bisque head, molded and painted hair, sleep eyes, open-closed mouth, cloth body

13".................. $325.00 – 400.00
16" – 18"........ $475.00 – 600.00

Mold 275, solid dome, glass eyes, closed mouth, cloth body, composition limbs

14".................. $900.00 – 950.00

Child

Molds 285, 287, by Kestner, bisque socket head, glass eyes, wig, ball-jointed body

14".................. $625.00 – 675.00
19" – 24"........ $600.00 – 650.00

Molds 279, by Kestner, bisque socket head, molded bobbed hair, glass eyes, wig, ball-jointed body, looks like Patsy

15".................. $475.00 – 525.00

Composition

Century Baby, 1920s, composition flange head and hands, cloth baby body

13" – 15"........ $125.00 – 175.00

Child, composition shoulder head, cloth body, composition arms and legs, molded hair, painted eyes

13" – 17"........ $100.00 – 175.00

Chuckles, 1927 – 1929, composition shoulder head, arms, and legs, cloth body with crier, open mouth, molded short hair, painted or sleep eyes, two upper teeth, dimples in cheeks, came as a bent-leg baby or toddler

14" – 16"........ $125.00 – 200.00
18" – 22"........ $200.00 – 300.00

Mama dolls, 1922 on, composition head, tin sleep eyes, cloth body, with crier, swing legs and composition arms

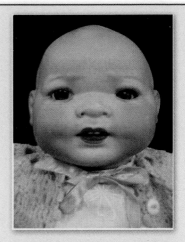

16" Century baby, $475.00. *Photo courtesy of McMasters Harris Auction Co.*

16".................. $175.00 – 200.00
23".................. $300.00 – 325.00

Bisque shoulder head, mold 281

21".................. $650.00 – 750.00

CHAD VALLEY

1917 – 1930s, Harbonne, England. Founded by Johnson Bros. in 1897, in 1917 began making all types of cloth dolls, early ones had stockinette faces, later felt, with velvet body, jointed neck, shoulders, hips, glass or painted eyes, mohair wig, used designers such as Mabel Lucie Atwell and Norah Wellings.

Animals

Bonzo, cloth dog with painted eyes, almost closed and smile

4".................... $210.00 – 230.00
12".................. $750.00 – 800.00

Bonzo, eyes open

5½".................. $275.00 – 300.00
14".................. $575.00 – 600.00

Cat

12".................. $215.00 – 230.00

Dog, plush

8½" felt dwarf, $225.00. *Photo courtesy of Cybermogul Dolls.*

12".................. $260.00 – 280.00
Characters
Captain Blye, Fisherman, Long John Silver, Pirate, Policeman, Train Conductor, etc.
Glass eyes
    10" – 12"........ $225.00 – 250.00
    18" – 20"..... $900.00 – 1,100.00
Painted eyes
    13" – 15"........ $375.00 – 400.00
    18" – 20"........ $675.00 – 775.00
Ghandi/India
    13".................. $625.00 – 675.00
Rahmah-Jah
    26".................. $850.00 – 900.00
Child
Glass eyes
    12" – 16"........ $250.00 – 400.00
    18" – 21"........ $425.00 – 525.00
Painted eyes
    9" – 10".......... $175.00 – 250.00
    12" – 15"........ $250.00 – 300.00
    18".................. $350.00 – 425.00
Mabel Lucie Atwell design, wide impish face, glass eyes
    14".................. $600.00 – 700.00

    18".............. $900.00 – 1,000.00
Royal Family, all with glass eyes, 16" – 18"
Princess Alexandra
        $1,400.00 – 1,500.00
Prince Edward, Duke of Windsor
        $900.00 – 1,100.00
Princess Elizabeth
        $1,500.00 – 2,000.00
Princess Margaret Rose
        $1,500.00 – 2,000.00
Story Book Dolls
Golliwog
    14" – 16"........ $150.00 – 300.00
Red Riding Hood
    14" – 19"........ $350.00 – 500.00
Snow White & Dwarfs
Dwarf, 6½"............. $250.00 – 275.00
Set 10" dwarves, 16" Snow White
        $2,200.00 – 2,800.00

CHASE DOLL COMPANY

1889 to 1981, Pawtucket, Rhode Island. Founded by Martha Chase, earlier dolls had heads of molded stockinette with heavily painted features including thick lashes, closed mouth, painted textured hair, jointed shoulder, elbows, knees, and hips, later dolls jointed only at shoulders and hips, later dolls had latex heads on vinyl coated bodies, all in good condition with original or appropriate clothing.
Baby or child, short hair with curls around face
    12" – 16"..... $850.00 – 1,000.00
    17" – 20".. $1,000.00 – 1,200.00
    22" – 24" ..$1,200.00 – 1,400.00
    26" – 30".. $1,600.00 – 2,000.00
    37" with trunk and wardrobe
        $5,000.00*
Hospital-type, weighted doll with pierced

Rare Alice in Wonderland set, Frog Footman, Duchess, Mad Hatter, and Alice, sold at auction for $40,290.00. *Photo courtesy of Skinner, Inc.*

nostrils and ear canals

    20".................. $500.00 – 550.00

    29".................. $450.00 – 550.00

Child

Molded bobbed hair

    12" – 15".. $1,400.00 – 1,600.00

    20" – 22".. $1,900.00 – 2,500.00

Side-part painted hair

    15" – 16".. $4,600.00 – 5,200.00

Characters, 1905 to 1920s, produced characters based on Alice in Wonderland, Dickens, Joel Chandler Harris books, and George Washington

Alice in Wonderland Characters

    12" set of four, Alice, Duchess, Frog Footman, Mad Hatter $40,290.00*

Dickens Characters, needle-sculpted hairstyles including buns, curls, etc.,15"

Lady or man ...... $1,800.00 – 2,000.00

Mrs. Gamp $4,740.00*

Mrs. Micawber ....,,........ $4,740.00*

Little Nell, braids .. $2,000.00 – 2,500.00

George Washington

    15" .... $3,900.00 – 4,200.00

Mammy

    26"....... $10,000.00 – 12,000.00

Later dolls, latex heads

Baby

    12".................. $150.00 – 200.00

Black

    12".................. $200.00 – 250.00

Child

    15".................. $225.00 – 275.00

Black

    15" .... $250.00 – 300.00

Hospital Baby

    14" – 15"........ $200.00 – 250.00

    19".................. $250.00 – 300.00

CHINA OR GLAZED PORCELAIN HEAD

1840 on. Most china shoulder head dolls were made in Germany by various firms. Prior to 1880, most china heads were pressed into the mold; later ones poured. Pre-1880, most china heads were sold separately with purchaser buying commercial body or making one at home. Original commercial costumes are rare; most clothing was homemade. Early unusual features are glass eyes or eyes painted brown. After 1870, pierced ears and blond hair were found and, after 1880, more child chinas with shorter hair and shorter necks were popular. Most common in this period were flat tops and low brows and the latter were made until the mid-1900s. Later innovations were china arms and legs with molded boots. Most heads are unmarked or with size or mold number only, usually on the back shoulder plate. Identification tips: hairstyles, color, complexion tint, and body help date the doll. Dolls listed are in good condition with original or appropriate clothes. More for exceptional quality.

1840 styles

China shoulder head with long neck, painted features, black or brown molded hair, may have exposed ears and pink complexion, with red-orange facial detail, may have bust modeling, cloth, leather, or wood body, nicely dressed, good condition.

Early marked china (Nuremberg, Rudolstadt)
    12" – 14".. $1,800.00 – 3,000.00
    17" – 24".. $4,000.00 – 6,000.00

Pink complexion, bun or coronet
    13" – 15".. $7,000.00 – 9,000.00
    18" – 21" .$11,000.00 – 12,000.00

Wooden body, with china lower arms, 1840s on
    5" – 8"..... $4,000.00 – 6,000.00

Covered wagon
Center part, combed back to form sausage curls, pink tint complexion
    7" – 10"......... $500.00 – 600.00
    14" – 17"........ $750.00 – 900.00
    20" – 25".. $1,000.00 – 1,200.00
    31"........... $1,400.00 – 1,500.00

Kinderkopf (child-head)
Pink tint child-head doll, brushstrokes around face
    12" – 16".. $1,900.00 – 3,200.00
    21"........... $3,500.00 – 4,000.00

KPM (Königliche Porzellan Manufaktur, Berlin) 1840s – 1850s on, marked KPM inside shoulder plate

Lady, brown hair in bun
    14" – 18"..$7,000.00 – 13,000.00
    20" – 24"..$12,000.00 – 15,000.00

Man, brown hair
    16" – 18"..$8,000.00 – 11,000.00
    22" – 23" .$12,000.00 – 14,000.00

8½" china on wooden body with china lower arms, ca. 1850, $5,000.00. *Photo courtesy of Skinner, Inc.*

China or Glazed Porcelain Head

25" brown-eyed Greiner-style china doll, $2,200.00. *Photo courtesy of Morphy Auctions.*

1850 styles

China shoulder head, painted features, bald with black spot or molded black hair, may have pink complexion, cloth, leather, or wood body, china arms and legs, nicely dressed, good condition.

Various unnamed styles, variations of buns and side waves

  12" – 16".. $6,000.00 – 8,000.00

Alice in Wonderland, snood, headband

  12" – 14"........ $750.00 – 850.00
  16" – 18"..... $975.00 – 1,025.00
  20" – 22".. $1,150.00 – 1,300.00
  On Taufling-style body
  14"......... $9,000.00 – 12,000.00

Bald head (so-called Biedermeier style), glazed china with black spot, human hair or mohair wig

  12"................ $650.00 – 750.00
  14" – 16"..... $900.00 – 1,200.00
  20" – 24".. $2,000.00 – 3,000.00

Badekinder (Frozen Charlies or Charlottes): See Badekinder section.

French, 1850s on, some heads may have been made in Germany for the French makers.

Jacob Petit, pink tint to skin, black painted pate

  17" – 22".. $5,000.00 – 6,000.00

Morning Glory, brown hair with molded morning glories

  21" – 24" . $9,000.00 – 10,250.00

Poupée-type, glass or painted eyes, open crown, cork pate, wig, kid body, china arms

  12" – 14".. $4,500.00 – 5,000.00
  17" – 21".. $8,500.00 – 9,000.00

Greiner–type, painted black eyelashes

Glass eyes

  13" – 15".. $3,700.00 – 4,200.00
  18" – 22".. $4,400.00 – 5,200.00

Painted eyes

  14" – 15".. $1,200.00 – 1,800.00
  18" – 22".. $1,500.00 – 1,900.00

Sophia Smith, straight sausage curls ending in a ridge around head, rather than curved to head shape

  17" – 24".. $4,000.00 – 6,000.00

24" Sophia Smith style, $6,000.00. *Photo courtesy of Skinner, Inc.*

25" Kister china with braids looped around her ears and a bun in back, often referred to by modern collectors as a young Victoria style, $7,000.00. *Photo courtesy of Skinner, Inc.*

Young Queen Victoria, molded braids looped around ears, bun in back

   16" – 18".. $3,000.00 – 4,000.00
   22" – 23".. $4,500.00 – 5,000.00

1860 styles

China shoulder head, center part, smooth black curls, painted features, seldom brush marks or pink tones, all-cloth bodies or cloth with china arms and legs, may have leather arms. Decorated chinas with fancy hairstyles embellished with flowers, ornaments, snoods, bands, ribbons, may have earrings.

Flat-top Civil War

Black hair, center part, with flat top, curls on sides and back

   5" – 7"............. $200.00 – 250.00
   10" – 14"........ $250.00 – 325.00
   18" – 22"........ $450.00 – 550.00
   24" – 26"........ $550.00 – 650.00
   34"................. $625.00 – 675.00

Swivel neck

   15"........... $1,300.00 – 1,500.00

8½" high brow style, rare all-original presentation, $1,000.00. *Photo courtesy of Joy's Antique Dolls.*

Molded necklace

   21" – 24"........ $700.00 – 800.00

High brow, curls, high forehead, round face

   9".................... $450.00 – 500.00
   12" – 13"........ $350.00 – 450.00
   15" – 18"........ $500.00 – 700.00
   19" – 22"........ $600.00 – 800.00
   25" – 32"........ $800.00 – 950.00

Conta & Boehme, pierced ears

   9" – 10".......... $400.00 – 700.00
   14" – 16"..... $900.00 – 1,100.00

14" Conta & Boehme china doll, $900.00. *Photo courtesy of James D. Julia, Inc.*

China or Glazed Porcelain Head

18" Curly Top, $1,000.00. *Photo courtesy of Sweetbriar Auctions.*

18" – 20".. $1,100.00 – 2,000.00
Curly Top
    12"................. $700.00 – 800.00
    19"........... $1,200.00 – 1,500.00
Currier & Ives, long hair lying on shoulders
    15" – 17"........ $700.00 – 800.00
Dagmar, curls on forehead, curls gathered at nape with barrette
    13" – 18".. $1,100.00 – 1,300.00
    22" – 25".. $1,400.00 – 1,600.00
Dolley Madison, with molded bow
    9"................... $300.00 – 350.00
    14" – 16"..,,.... $600.00 – 700.00
    20" – 24"........ $800.00 – 950.00

16" Grape Lady, $2,000.00. *Photo courtesy of Withington Auction, Inc.*

Man or boy with curls
    17" – 19".. $1,300.00 – 1,800.00
Grape Lady, with cluster of grape leaves and blue grapes
    15" – 18".. $1,800.00 – 2,200.00
Mary Todd Lincoln, black hair, gold snood, gold luster bows at ears
    14" – 15"........ $700.00 – 800.00
    18" – 21"..... $900.00 – 1,200.00
Blond, with snood
    15" – 16"........ $800.00 – 900.00
    18" – 21".. $1,000.00 – 1,300.00
Spill Curls, with or without headband, a lot of single curls across forehead, around back to ringlets in back
    13" – 15"........ $800.00 – 900.00
    18" – 20".. $1,000.00 – 1,100.00
    24" – 26".. $1,200.00 – 1,400.00
1870 styles
China shoulder head, poured, finely painted, well molded, black or blond hair, all-cloth or cloth and leather bodies, now with pink facial details instead of earlier red-orange.
    14" – 16"........ $350.00 – 400.00
    18" – 24"........ $425.00 – 475.00
Adelina Patti, hair pulled up and away, center part, brushstroke temples, partly exposed ears, ringlets across back of head
    13" – 15"........ $600.00 – 700.00
    18" – 22"........ $800.00 – 900.00
    26"........... $1,000.00 – 1,100.00
Bangs, full cut across forehead, sometimes called Highland Mary
    14" – 16"........ $300.00 – 425.00
    19" – 21"........ $475.00 – 525.00
Jenny Lind, black hair pulled back into a bun or coronet
    12" – 15"..... $900.00 – 1,400.00
    20" – 24".. $1,600.00 – 2,000.00
1880 styles
Now may also have many blond as well as black hair examples, more curls, and overall curls, narrower shoulders, fatter cheeks, irises

China or Glazed Porcelain Head

24" Kloster Veilsdorf, $7,000.00. *Photo courtesy of Skinner, Inc.*

outlined with black paint, may have bangs, china legs have fat calves and molded boots *Child,* short black or blond curly hairdo with exposed ears, makers such as Alt, Beck & Gottschalck, Kling, and others.

 14" – 18"........ $300.00 – 400.00
 20" – 24"........ $550.00 – 650.00
 27" – 30"........ $750.00 – 850.00

Bawo & Dotter, patented 1880

 13" – 14"........ $250.00 – 325.00
 18" – 20"........ $275.00 – 350.00

1890 styles

Shorter, fatter arms and legs, may have printed body with alphabet, emblems, flags
Common or low brow, black or blond center-part wavy hairdo that comes down low on forehead

 4" – 8".............. $75.00 – 125.00
 10" – 14"........ $150.00 – 250.00
 16"................. $200.00 – 250.00
 19" – 23"........ $250.00 – 300.00
 27" – 28"........ $350.00 – 400.00

With jeweled necklace

 8".................... $160.00 – 190.00

 20" – 22"........ $425.00 – 475.00

Pet names, 1899 – 1930 on
Agnes, Bertha, Daisy, Dorothy, Edith, Esther, Ethel, Florence, Helen, Mabel, Marion, Pauline, and Ruth, made for Butler Brothers by various German firms, china head and limbs on cloth body, molded blouse marked in front with name in gold lettering, molded blond or black allover curls

 9".................... $125.00 – 150.00
 12" – 14"........ $200.00 – 275.00
 17" – 21"........ $325.00 – 400.00

Japanese, 1910 – 1920, marked or unmarked, black or blond hair

 10"................. $100.00 – 125.00
 15"................. $160.00 – 190.00

CLOTH

Various American and European manufacturers of cloth headed dolls working from 1850 on. No separate listing for these makers. Many are unmarked or carried paper hang tags.

Becassine, French comic character, originally drawn by Emile Joseph Porphyre Pinchon for *La Semaine de Suzette.* Made in doll form by various makers, needle-sculpted nose, painted features.

Reine Dégrais, 1947 – 1972

 8" – 14"......... $200.00 – 450.00

Minerve, 1972 on

 12" – 16"........ $250.00 – 350.00

See Georgene Averill section for additional listing.

Homemade, nineteenth and early twentieth centuries. Makers unknown, many one-of-a-kind type dolls. Embroidered or painted features. Dolls vary greatly according to the skill of the maker. Values may differ substantially for individual examples.

Mid-nineteenth century – 1900

 8" – 12"....... $400.00 – 1,000.00
 15" – 20"..... $900.00 – 2,000.00

Cloth

25" homemade cloth doll, $1,500.00. *Photo courtesy of Withington Auction, Inc.*

13½" Maggie Bessie doll, ca. 1918, sold for $15,795.00 at auction. *Photo courtesy of Morphy Auctions.*

1900 – 1930

15" – 18"........ $250.00 – 600.00
16" – 24"..... $700.00 – 1,200.00
Known makers
Baps, 1946 on, Burgkunstadt, Germany. Made by Edith von Arps. Felt doll with felt over wire armature body, yarn hair, metal feet, painted features. Many represent storybook characters. Allow more for sets.
2½" – 6", single figures
$50.00 – 150.00
Blossom, 1920s on, New York, New York. Made cloth, mask-faced dolls depicting children as well as long-limbed lady dolls (Also see Boudoir Dolls section)
11"................... $75.00 – 125.00
Hol-Le Toy, 1950s, New York, New York
Eloise, cloth mask face based on the fictional character created by Kay Thompson
21"................. $175.00 – 225.00
Maggie Bessie dolls, 1890s on, Salem, North Carolina, Sisters Margaret and Elizabeth Pfohl made cloth dolls with oil painted faces in three sizes, 13/14", 17/18", and 20/22"
13" – 18"..$15,000.00 – 17,000.00
Molded cloth shoulder head dolls, mid-nineteenth century on. Makers such as George H. Hawkins, Carl Weigand, and others both

known and unknown. Dolls resemble the china and papier-mâché dolls of the era.
19" – 24"........ $600.00 – 750.00
Nelke, 1917 to 1930, Philadelphia, Pennsylvania. Harry Nelke founded the Elke Knitting Mills Co. in 1901 and began making stockinette crib dolls in 1917. The dolls were made of a silky stockinette fabric with painted features. Clothing integral to body, added band of stockinette around neck, and/or added collars, hats, etc. Doll in clean, unfaded condition.
8" – 10"..............,,... $60.00 – 75.00
13" – 15"........ $100.00 – 125.00
Tebbetts Sisters, 1922 on, Pittsburgh,

7" Tebbetts Petiekin clown, $400.00. *Photo courtesy of The Museum Doll Shop.*

14" Worsted doll by Emil Wittzack, $100.00.
Photo courtesy of Withington Auction, Inc.

Pennsylvania, Mary, Elizabeth, Marion, and Ruth Tebbetts patented and made cloth dolls. Petiekins, cloth mask face, crepe or flannel body

6½".............. $375.00 – 425.00

Baby Sister, needle-sculpted stockinette doll with painted features, wigged

18"........... $1,500.00 – 2,000.00

Tiny Town, 1949 into the 1950s, San Francisco, California. Alma LeBlanc took out a patent under the business name of Lenna Lee's Tiny Town Dolls for these dolls. The dolls have felt faces with painted features, mohair wigs, and wrapped wire armature bodies with metal feet

4" – 7"................ $75.00 – 90.00
(double for MIB)

Worsted dolls, 1878 – 1900s, Emil Wittzack of Gotha, Thuringia, Germany. Woolen crib dolls with needle-sculpted features, bead eyes, chenille embroidered designs on bodies, some had bells sewn on them

7" – 10".............. $50.00 – 75.00
15" – 18"........ $125.00 – 150.00

CLOTH, PRINTED

1876 on. Made by various American, British, and German firms including Arnold Print Works, North Adams, Massachusetts, Cocheco Manufacturing Co., Art Fabric Mills, and other lesser or unknown firms who printed fabric for making cutout dolls to be sewn together and stuffed. Dolls listed are in good, clean condition, uncut sheets bring double the values listed here.

Improved Life Size Doll, with printed underwear

16" – 18"........ $200.00 – 250.00
20" – 24"........ $225.00 – 275.00
30"................. $300.00 – 325.00

Punch and Judy, pair

27"................. $550.00 – 650.00

Brownies, 1892 – 1907, produced by Aronld Print Works. Printed cloth dolls based on copyrighted figures of Palmer Cox; 12 different figures, including Canadian, Chinaman, Dude, German, Highlander, Indian, Irishman, John Bull, Policeman, Sailor, Soldier, and Uncle Sam

Single doll

7½"................ $125.00 – 175.00

Printed underwear, Dolly Dear, Flaked Rice,

15" printed cloth Columbian Sailor by Arnold Print Works, $175.00. *Photo courtesy of Withington Auction, Inc.*

Merry Marie, etc.

    7" – 9"............. $95.00 – 115.00

    16" – 18"........ $200.00 – 225.00

    20" – 24"........ $250.00 – 300.00

Child with printed clothing, 1903

    12" – 14"........ $175.00 – 225.00

    17" – 19"........ $250.00 – 300.00

Columbian Sailor, Arnold Print Works, 1892

    16"................. $250.00 – 300.00

Foxy Grandpa

    18"................. $200.00 – 225.00

Gutsell, Ida, 1893 on, made by Cocheco Manufacturing. Designed and patented by Ida Gutsell of Ithaca, New York. Printed boy doll with a center-seam face, removable clothing with printed detail

    16"................. $400.00 – 500.00

Mother's Congress, 1900 on, Philadelphia, Pennsylvania. Designed and patented by Madge L. Meade. The uniquely styled pattern piece used for the head included a round section to produce the crown and several darts in the neck area. Unbleached muslin doll with lithographed facial features, blond hair with a blue bow and black Mary Jane-style shoes, marked with a stamp: "Mother's Congress Doll//Baby Stuart//Children's Favorite//

Philadelphia, Pa.//Pat. Nov. 6, 1900"

    17" – 24"........ $500.00 – 800.00

Our Soldier Boys ...... $125.00 – 150.00

Red Riding Hood ...... $150.00 – 175.00

Peck, 1886 Santa Claus/St. Nicholas

    15"................. $250.00 – 300.00

COLUMBIAN

1891 on, Oswego, New York. Emma E. Adams designed and made rag dolls, sold directly or through stores such as Marshall Field & Co. Won awards at the 1893 Chicago World's Fair. Succeeded by her sister, Marietta Adams Ruttan. Cloth dolls had hand–painted features, stitched fingers and toes. Values are for dolls in good condition wearing appropriate clothing, exceptional condition examples will sell for more.

    14" – 15".. $5,000.00 – 5,600.00

    19" – 23".. $5,800.00 – 6,200.00

    28".......... $7,000.00 – 9,000.00

23" Columbian, $4,500.00. *Photo courtesy of Joan & Lynette Antique Dolls and Accessories.*

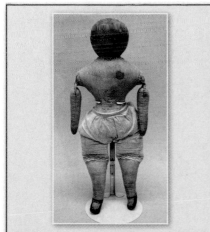

10" Mother's Congress, Baby Stuart, $300.00. *Photo courtesy of Alderfer Auction & Appraisal.*

COMPOSITION

Dolls listed are in good condition with original or appropriate dress. Allow more for exceptional dolls with elaborate costume or accessories.

Composition

American
Animal head doll, 1930s, all-composition on Patsy-type five-piece body, could be wolf, rabbit, cat, or monkey

    10"................. $300.00 – 350.00

Baby, 1910 on, wigged or molded hair, painted or sleep eyes, composition or cloth body with bent legs

    12" – 14"........ $175.00 – 225.00

    18" – 20"........ $250.00 – 300.00

Bester Doll Company, 1918 – 1921, Bloomfield and Newark, New Jersey. Composition doll in the style of German dolly-faced dolls, ball-jointed body, sleep eyes, wigged

    18" – 22"........ $400.00 – 425.00

Character baby

    18"................. $250.00 – 300.00

Child, costumed in ethnic or theme outfit, all-composition, sleep or painted eyes, mohair wig, closed mouth, original costume

Lesser quality

    9" – 11".............. $65.00 – 75.00

Better quality

    9" – 11".......... $100.00 – 125.00

    16"................. $200.00 – 250.00

Coleman walker

    24" – 28"........ $200.00 – 225.00

Denny Dimwitt, Toycraft Inc, 1948, all-composition, nodder, painted clothing

    11½".............. $200.00 – 225.00

Early child, 1910 – 1920, all-composition, unmarked, painted features, may have molded hair

    12"................. $145.00 – 165.00

    18" – 19"........ $200.00 – 250.00

Character face, 1910 – 1920, unmarked, cork-stuffed cloth body, painted features, may have molded hair

    12" – 15"........ $150.00 – 200.00

    18" – 20"........ $250.00 – 300.00

    24"................. $375.00 – 400.00

Jackie Robinson, complete in box

    13".............. $900.00 – 1,000.00

Kewty, 1930, made by Domec of Canada, all-composition Patsy-type, molded bobbed hair, closed mouth, sleep eyes, bent left arm

    14"................. $300.00 – 350.00

Lone Ranger, "TLR Co, Inc.//Doll Craft Novelty Co. NYC," cloth body, hat marked

    20"................. $400.00 – 450.00

Louis Vuitton, 1955, ceramic, composition, with labeled case and wardrobe

    19"............................ $2,200.00

Too few in database for a reliable range.

Maiden America, "1915, Kate Silverman," all-composition, patriotic ribbon

    8½"................. $165.00 – 185.00

Mama doll, 1922 on, wigged or painted hair, sleep or painted eyes, cloth body, with crier and swing legs, lower composition legs and arms

    16" – 18"........ $225.00 – 275.00

    20" – 22"........ $325.00 – 375.00

    24" – 26"........ $425.00 – 500.00

Miss Curity, composition, eye shadow, nurse's uniform

    18"................. $450.00 – 500.00

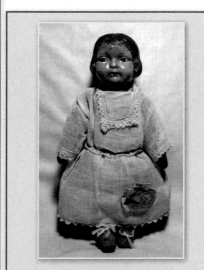

10", maker unknown, early twentieth century, $150.00. *Photo courtesy of Joan & Lynette Antique Dolls and Accessories.*

Composition

Patsy-type girl, 1928 on, molded and painted bobbed hair, sleep or painted eyes, closed pouty mouth, composition or hard stuffed cloth body

    9" – 10"......... $125.00 – 150.00
    14" – 16"....... $225.00 – 275.00
    19" – 20"....... $275.00 – 300.00

With molded hair loop

    12" – 15"....... $125.00 – 150.00

Pinocchio, composition and wood character

    16½" .... $400.00 – 425.00

Puzzy, 1948, "H of P"

    15"................ $400.00 – 450.00

Quintuplets, 1934 on, all-composition, jointed five-piece baby or toddler body, molded hair or wig, with painted or sleep eyes, closed or open mouth

    7" – 8"........... $140.00 – 160.00
    13"................ $225.00 – 250.00

Santa Claus, composition molded head, composition body, original suit, sack

    19"................ $450.00 – 500.00

Shimmy Doll, 1920s, key-wound shimmy dancer

    12" – 18"....... $150.00 – 300.00

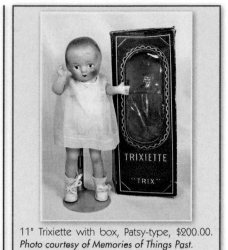

11" Trixiette with box, Patsy-type, $200.00.
Photo courtesy of Memories of Things Past.

Shirley Temple-type girl, 1934 on, all-composition, five-piece jointed body, blond curly wig, sleep eyes, open mouth, teeth, dimples

    16" – 19"....... $250.00 – 300.00

Sizzy, 1948, "H of P"

    14"................ $350.00 – 400.00

Thumbs-Up, to raise money for ambulances during WWII, see photo first edition

    8".................. $140.00 – 155.00

Uncle Sam, various makers

All original, cloth body

    13"............................... $900.00

Too few in database for a reliable range.

Whistler, composition head, cotton body, composition arms, open mouth

    14½"............. $200.00 – 225.00

Canadian, Pullan

Little Lulu

    14"................ $350.00 – 450.00

German, composition head, composition or cloth body, wig or molded and painted hair, closed or open mouth with teeth, dressed, may be Amusco, Sonneberger Porzellanfabrik, Winkler, or others

Character baby

Cloth body

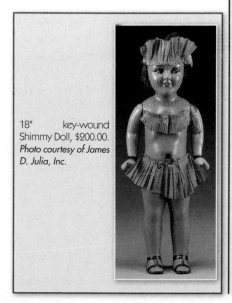

18" key-wound Shimmy Doll, $200.00.
Photo courtesy of James D. Julia, Inc.

20", Sayco, $300.00. *Photo courtesy of Quality Vintage Doll Patterns.*

18"................ $275.00 – 325.00
Composition baby body, bent limbs
16"................ $275.00 – 325.00
Child
Composition shoulder head, cloth body, composition arms
20"................ $275.00 – 300.00
Socket head, all-composition body
12" – 14"........ $200.00 – 300.00
19" – 21"........ $425.00 – 450.00
Japanese
Quintuplets
7" – 9"............ $175.00 – 250.00

11", unmarked, Asian costume, $65.00. *Photo courtesy of The Museum Doll Shop.*

COSMOPOLITAN DOLL & TOY CORP.

1950s on, Jackson Heights, New York. Dolls listed are in perfect condition with original clothing. Mint-in-box can be double the values listed here, naked dolls bring one-third the values listed here.

8", Ginger, straight-leg walker, $65.00. *Photo courtesy of Alderfer Auction & Appraisal.*

Ginger, 1955 on, 7½", hard plastic
Painted lash straight-leg walker
$60.00 – 75.00
Molded lash straight-leg walker
$50.00 – 65.00
Bent-knee walker .... $40.00 – 60.00
Vinyl head................... $35.00 – 45.00
Boxed outfit .... $50.00 – 60.00
Cardboard house and furniture
$130.00 – 150.00
Miss Ginger, 1957 on, vinyl, rooted hair, sleep eyes, teen doll, tagged clothes
10½"................ $65.00 – 100.00
Boxed outfit .... $80.00 – 90.00
Little Miss Ginger, 1958 on, vinyl, rooted hair, sleep eyes, teen doll, tagged clothes
8"..................... $80.00 – 125.00

CRÈCHE

Figures of various materials made

especially for religious scenes such as the Christmas manger scene. Usually not jointed, some with elaborate costumes. Some early created figures were gesso over wood head and limbs, fabric covered bodies with wire frames, later figures made of terra cotta or other materials, some with inset eyes.

9½" wooden crèche figure, $650.00. *Photo courtesy of Withington Auction, Inc.*

Wood, carved
Angel
    10" – 16".. $2,000.00 – 2,800.00
Man or woman, shoulder head, glass eyes, wire body
    8"................... $400.00 – 500.00
    10" – 14"..... $700.00 – 1,000.00
    17" – 19" $1,4000.00 – 2,000.00
Too few in database for a reliable range.
Terra cotta, mid nineteenth century, shoulder head, wire frame
Man or woman
    12" –15"... $1,400.00 – 2,000.00
    17" – 22"... $2000.00 – 2,500.00

DE FUISSEAUX

1909 – 1912, Baudour, Belgium.

19" De Fuisseaux portrait-style lady, $1,800.00. *Photo courtesy of The Museum Doll Shop.*

Porcelain heads, often highly colored. Marked with D.F.B, or F1 (and other #s), D1 (and other numbers).
Open mouth dolly face, sleep eyes, wig, cardboard and composition ball-jointed body
    18" – 22"........ $300.00 – 350.00
Character doll
Painted eyes, resembles Kämmer & Reinhardt 101, various body types
    8"................... $400.00 – 450.00
Glass eyes, resembles Heubach, ball-jointed composition body
    12" – 18".. $1,100.00 – 1,700.00
Portrait-style girl or lady, cloth body
    19" – 23".. $1,800.00 – 2,200.00

DEAN'S RAG BOOK CO.

1905 on, London. Subsidiary of Dean & Son, Ltd., a printing and publishing firm, used

16" doll, $500.00. *Doll courtesy of Cathy Ellis O'Brien.*

"A1" to signify quality, made Knockabout Toys, Tru-to-Life, Evripoze, and others. An early designer was Hilda Cowham.

Child, painted eyes
    10"................ $275.00 – 300.00
    16" – 17"........ $500.00 – 600.00
    24"................ $600.00 – 700.00
Printed cloth, cut-and-sew-type
    9" – 10".............. $85.00 – 95.00
    15" – 16"........ $175.00 – 225.00
Mask face, velvet, with cloth body and limbs
    12" – 15"........ $125.00 – 175.00
    18" – 24"........ $275.00 – 350.00
    30" – 34"........ $475.00 – 550.00
    40"................ $625.00 – 675.00
Dancing Dolls, cloth dolls sewn together at hands to look like a dancing couple, on a string.
    12" – 14"........ $110.00 – 125.00
Lupino Lane
    12"................ $200.00 – 250.00
Mickey Mouse
    12" – 13"........ $400.00 – 500.00
Golliwogs (English black character doll)

    11"................ $400.00 – 500.00
    15"................ $500.00 – 675.00
    18"................ $600.00 – 700.00
Ronnie, 1950s, molded rubber head, plush body
    15"................ $150.00 – 175.00

DELUXE READING

1955 – 1972, Elizabeth, New Jersey. Also used the names Deluxe Toy Creations, Deluxe Premium Corp., Deluxe Topper, Topper Toys, and Topper Corp. Dolls listed are complete, all-original, in good condition, wearing original clothes, hard plastic or vinyl, allow double for mint-in-box.

Baby
Baby Boo, 1965, battery-operated
    21"................ $100.00 – 125.00
Baby Catch a Ball, 1969 (Topper Toys), battery-operated
    18"..................... $70.00 – 80.00
Baby Magic, 1966, blue sleep eyes, rooted saran hair, magic wand has magnet that opens/closes eyes
    18".................. $60.00 – 100.00
Baby Party, 1968, blows horns, balloons, etc.
    18".................. $20.00 – 25.00
Baby Peek 'n Play, 1969, battery-operated
    18"..................... $20.00 – 25.00
Baby Tickle Tears
    14"..................... $20.00 – 30.00
Nancy Nurse, 1963
    21"..................... $25.00 – 30.00
Suzy Cute, move arm and face changes expressions
    7"......................... $25.00 – 35.00
Child or adult
Betty Bride, 1957, also called Sweet Rosemary, Sweet Judy, Sweet Amy, one-piece vinyl body and limbs, more if many accessories
    30"..................... $40.00 – 50.00
Candy Fashion, 1958, made by Deluxe

6" Dawn Series, $25.00. *Photo courtesy of The Museum Doll Shop.*

21" Suzy Homemaker, ca. 1964, $40.00. *Photo courtesy of The Museum Doll Shop.*

Premium, a division of Deluxe Reading, sold in grocery stores, came with three dress forms, extra outfits

21".................. $100.00 –125.00

Dawn Series, circa 1969 – 1970s, all-vinyl doll with additional friends, Angie, Daphne, Denise, Glori, Jessica, Kip, Long Locks, Majorette, Maureen, black versions of Van and Dale, accessories available, included Apartment, Fashion Show, outfits

Dawn and friends

6"...................... $20.00 – 25.00

Dawn & other outfits

Loose, but complete.......... $10.00+

NRFP................... $35.00 – 45.00

Go Gos, 1965, soft vinyl bendable body. Cool Cat, Private Ida, Tom Boy

6"...................... $30.00 – 35.00

Little Miss Fussy, battery-operated

18"..................... $15.00 – 20.00

Little Red Riding Hood, 1955, vinyl, synthetic hair, rubber body, book, basket

23"..................... $50.00 – 75.00

Penny Brite, 1963 on, all-vinyl, rooted blond hair, painted eyes, bendable and straight legs, extra outfits, case, furniture available, marks: "A – 9/B150 (or B65) DELUXE READING CORP.//c. 1963"

8"...................... $15.00 – 20.00

Outfit, NRFP .... $30.00 – 40.00

Kitchen set................... $50.00 – 60.00

Suzy Homemaker, 1964, hard plastic and vinyl, jointed knees, mark: "Deluxe Reading Co."

21"..................... $40.00 – 50.00

Suzy Smart, ca. 1962, vinyl, sleep eyes, closed mouth, rooted blond ponytail, hard plastic body, The Talking School Doll, desk, chair, easel

25"............... $100.00 – 150.00

Sweet Rosemary, vinyl head, soft vinyl body, high-heel foot

28".................... $50.00 – 80.00

DEP

The "DEP" mark on the back of bisque heads stands for the French "Depose" or the German "Deponirt," which means registered claim. Some dolls made by Simon & Halbig have the "S&H" mark hidden above the "DEP" under the wig. Bisque head, swivel neck, appropriate wig, paperweight eyes, open or closed mouth, good condition, nicely dressed on French style wood and composition body.

20" DEP open mouth on Jumeau body, $1,200.00. *Photo courtesy of Morphy Auctions.*

Dolls listed are in good condition with original or appropriate clothing.

Closed mouth

15".......... $2,100.00 – 2,250.00
18" – 20".. $2,600.00 – 3,000.00
23" – 25".. $3,150.00 – 3,800.00

Open mouth, including those marked Jumeau

13" – 15"........ $925.00 – 975.00
18" – 20".. $1,100.00 – 1,200.00
23" – 25".. $1,200.00 – 1,300.00
28" – 30".. $1,000.00 – 1,200.00

DOLLHOUSE DOLLS

Small German dolls generally under 8" usually dressed as member of a family or in household-related occupations, often sold as a group. Made of any material, but usually bisque head by 1880. Dolls listed are in good condition with original clothes.

Bisque

Adult, man or woman,

Painted eyes, molded hair, wig

7½", bisque, in soldier's uniform, $900.00. *Photo courtesy of Skinner, Inc.*

4" – 5"............ $100.00 – 300.00
6" – 7"............ $250.00 – 400.00

Glass eyes

Molded hair

6"................... $350.00 – 450.00

Wigged

6"................... $500.00 – 550.00

Black man or woman, molded hair, original clothes

6"................... $400.00 – 650.00

Chauffeur, molded cap

6"................... $245.00 – 285.00

Grandparents, with molded-on hats

6"................... $235.00 – 265.00

Military man, mustache, original clothes

6"................... $475.00 – 575.00

With molded-on helmet

6"................... $600.00 – 900.00

Children, all-bisque

4"................... $100.00 – 150.00

China

With early hairdo

4"................... $300.00 – 600.00

With low brow or common hairdo, 1900 on
    4".....................$75.00 – 125.00
Composition, papier-mâché, plaster, etc.
    5"....................$150.00 – 200.00

DOOR OF HOPE

1901 – 1950, Shanghai, China. Cornelia Bonnell started the Door of Hope Mission in Shanghai to help poor girls sold by their families. As a means to learn sewing skills, the girls dressed carved pear wood heads from Ning-Po. The heads and hands were natural finish, stuffed cloth bodies were then dressed in correct representation for 26 different Chinese classes. Carved wooden head with cloth or wooden arms, original handmade costumes, in very good condition. Dolls listed are in good condition with clean, bright clothing. Exceptional dolls could be higher. Values are lower for dolls in faded costumes.

Adult, man or woman
    11" – 13".. $1,400.00 – 2,800.00
Amah with Baby
    11" – 13".. $3,000.00 – 4,000.00
Boy or girl in silk
    6" – 9"....... $2,000.00 –4,000.00
Boy with western hairstyle
    8" – 9"............ $800.00 – 950.00
Bride and groom
    12"....$3,000.00 – 4,000.00 each
Farmer in bamboo raincoat
    12"........... $2,200.00 – 2,400.00
Kindergarten child
    6".............. $4,025.00 – 4,200.00
Male Mourner
    12"........... $1,600.00 – 3,000.00
Manchu Woman
    11"........... $7,500.00 – 8,500.00
Policeman
    11½"........ $5,000.00 – 7,000.00
Priest
    11½"........ $3,000.00 – 4,000.00

CUNO & OTTO DRESSEL

1857 – 1943, Sonneberg, Thüringia, Germany. The Dressel family began its business in the early 1700s and was dealing in toys from a very early date. Cunno & Otto became involved in the 1880s. The Dressels made wood, wax, wax-over-composition, papier-mâché, composition, china, and bisque heads for their dolls which they produced, distributed, and exported. Their bisque heads were made by Simon & Halbig, Armand Marseille, Ernst Heubach, Schoenau & Hoffmeister, and others. Dolls listed are in good condition with appropriate clothing.

Bisque
Baby, 1910 on, character face, marked "C.O.D.," more for toddler body
    12" – 14"........ $325.00 – 375.00
    15" – 17"........ $375.00 – 425.00
    19" – 23"........ $550.00 – 600.00
Child, mold 1912, others, open mouth, jointed composition body
    14" – 16"........ $350.00 – 400.00
    18" – 24"........ $400.00 – 500.00

20" dolly-faced doll, marked "COD," $450.00.
Photo courtesy of Alderfer Auction & Appraisal.

18" Santa Claus, $4,500.00. *Photo courtesy of Skinner, Inc.*

On flapper body, flirty eyes

    22"................. $800.00 – 900.00

Shoulder head child

Molds 93, 1896, or no mold #, bisque, wigged, open mouth, kid or cloth body, glass eyes

    13" – 15"........ $150.00 – 200.00

    18" – 24"........ $200.00 – 275.00

Bisque, closed mouth, molded hair, kid or cloth body, glass eyes

    14"................. $300.00 – 325.00

Child, character face, closed mouth, jointed child or toddler body

Painted eyes

    14" – 16".. $1,200.00 – 1,300.00

    18" – 20" ... $1,500.00 – 1,700.00

    19" girl resembles Kammer Reinhardt

    101........................... $5,800.00*

Glass eyes

    12" – 15".. $2,400.00 – 2,700.00

    18" – 20".. $3,000.00 – 3,200.00

Flapper, mold 1469, lady doll, closed mouth, five-piece composition body with thin legs and high-heeled feet, painted-on hose up entire leg, mold 1469

    12" – 15".. $3,500.00 – 4,000.00

Composition

Holz-Masse, 1875 on, shoulder head, wigged or molded hair, painted or glass eyes, cloth body, composition limbs, molded-on boots

    13" – 15"........ $350.00 – 400.00

    18" – 20"........ $450.00 – 525.00

    24" – 29"........ $575.00 – 650.00

Glass eyes

    12"................. $400.00 – 500.00

    16" – 18"........ $550.00 – 650.00

Wigged

    18"................. $650.00 – 750.00

Jutta

Baby open mouth, bent-leg body

    16" – 18"........ $425.00 – 475.00

    20" – 24"........ $500.00 – 650.00

Child, 1906 – 1921, open mouth, marked with "Jutta" or "S&H" mold 1914, 1348, 1349, etc.

    14" – 16"........ $450.00 – 525.00

    17" – 19"........ $550.00 – 625.00

    21" – 24"........ $700.00 – 750.00

    25" – 29"........ $800.00 – 900.00

Toddler

    8".................... $525.00 – 550.00

    14" – 16"........ $575.00 – 625.00

    17" – 19"........ $700.00 – 750.00

Portrait dolls, 1896 on, bisque head, glass eyes, composition body

Admiral Dewey, Admiral Byrd, other military

    8"............. $1,600.00 – 2,000.00

    12" – 14".. $5,500.00 – 6,000.00

Buffalo Bill

    8" – 10".... $2,500.00 – 3,500.00

Farmer, Old Rip, Witch

    8"............. $1,200.00 – 1,500.00

    12"........... $2,600.00 – 3,000.00

Father Christmas

    18"........... $4,000.00 – 4,500.00

Uncle Sam

    10" – 13". $1,300.00 – 1,600.00

E.D.

1857 – 1899, Paris. E.D. Bébés

marked with "E.D." and a size number and the word "Depose" were made by Etienne Denamur. It is important to note that other dolls marked E.D. with no Depose mark were made when Emile Douillet was director of Jumeau and should be priced as Jumeau Tété face dolls. Denamur had no relationship with the Jumeau firm and his dolls do not have the spiral spring made to attach heads used by Jumeau. Denamur bébés have straighter eyebrows, the eyes slightly more recessed, large lips, and lesser quality bisque. Smaller sizes of Denamur E.D. bébés may not have the Depose mark. Dolls listed are in good condition, appropriately dressed. Allow more for exceptional clothing.

Closed mouth

    11" – 15".. $4,000.00 – 5,000.00
    18" – 22".. $5,000.00 – 6,500.00
    25" – 28".. $7,000.00 – 8,000.00

Open mouth

    14" – 16".. $2,000.00 – 2,300.00
    18" – 21".. $3,000.00 – 3,100.00
    25" – 27".. $3,500.00 – 3,800.00

14" French bisque closed mouth bébé, marked "ED," $4,500.00. *Photo courtesy of Withington Auction, Inc.*

EDEN BÉBÉ

1890 – 1899, made by Fleischmann & Bloedel; 1899 – 1953, made by Société Francaise de Fabrication de Bébés & Jouet (S.F.B.J.). Dolls had bisque heads, jointed composition bodies. Dolls listed are in good condition, appropriately dressed.

14", open mouth, $1,700.00. *Photo courtesy of Withington Auction, Inc.*

Closed mouth, pale bisque

    14" – 16".. $2,200.00 – 2,900.00
    18" – 24".. $3,600.00 – 5,000.00

Open mouth

    15" – 18".. $2,000.00 – 2,500.00
    20" – 26".. $2,600.00 – 2,800.00

High color, five-piece body

    13"............... $600.00 – 1000.00
    19"........... $1,300.00 – 1,500.00
    22"........... $1,900.00 – 2,100.00

EEGEE

1917 on, Brooklyn, NY. Owned by E. G. Golderberger, assembled and made dolls, some of their dolls had bisque heads imported from Armand Marseille. Eegee also

Eegee

made their own heads and complete dolls of composition, hard plastic, and vinyl. Dolls listed are in all-original, good condition. Add more for exceptional doll, tagged, extra outfits, or accessories.

Composition

Baby, cloth body, bent limbs

16".................. $100.00 – 125.00

Child, open mouth, sleep eyes

14".................. $145.00 – 160.00

18".................. $200.00 – 220.00

MaMa Doll, 1920s – 1930s, composition head, sleep or painted eyes, wigged or molded hair, cloth body with crier, swing legs, composition lower arms and legs

16".................. $225.00 – 250.00

20".................. $325.00 – 350.00

Miss Charming or Little Miss Movie, 1936, all-composition, Shirley Temple look-alike

19" – 22"........ $350.00 – 400.00

Pin-back button $50.00

Hard Plastic and Vinyl

Andy, 1963, vinyl, teen-type, molded and painted hair, painted eyes, closed mouth

12"..................... $25.00 – 35.00

Annette, 1961 on, PlayPal type

19"..................... $40.00 – 50.00

32" – 35"........ $100.00 – 140.00

Walker, all-vinyl rooted long blond hair or short curly wig, blue sleep eyes, closed mouth

25"..................... $35.00 – 40.00

28"..................... $45.00 – 55.00

36"..................... $65.00 – 75.00

Annette or Babette, 1963, vinyl, teen-type fashion, rooted hair, painted eyes

11½".................. $45.00 – 55.00

Babette, 1970, vinyl head, stuffed limbs, cloth body, painted or sleep eyes, rooted hair

15"..................... $30.00 – 40.00

25"..................... $55.00 – 65.00

Baby Care, 1969, vinyl, molded or rooted hair, sleep or set glassine eyes, drink and wet doll, with complete nursery set

18"..................... $35.00 – 45.00

Baby Carrie, 1970, rooted or molded hair, sleep or set glassine eyes with plastic carriage or carry seat

24"..................... $50.00 – 60.00

Baby Luv, 1973, vinyl head, rooted hair, painted eyes, open/closed mouth, marked "B.T. Eegee," cloth body, pants are part of body

14"..................... $30.00 – 40.00

Baby Susan, 1958, marked "Baby Susan" on head

8"........................ $20.00 – 30.00

Baby Tandy Talks, 1963, pull-string activates talking mechanism, vinyl head, rooted hair, sleep eyes, cotton and foam-stuffed body and limbs

14"..................... $25.00 – 35.00

20"..................... $55.00 – 65.00

Ballerina

1964, vinyl head and hard plastic body

31"..................... $75.00 – 100.00

1967, vinyl head, foam-filled body

18"..................... $30.00 – 40.00

Barbara Cartland, painted features, adult

15"..................... $45.00 – 52.00

Beverly Hillbillies, Clampett family from 1960s TV sitcom

Car $350.00

Granny Clampett, gray rooted hair

14"..................... $55.00 – 65.00

Bundle of Joy, 1964, vinyl head, arms, legs, cloth body, rooted hair, sleep eyes

19"..................... $30.00 – 40.00

Fields, W. C., 1980, vinyl ventriloquist doll by Juro, division of Goldberger

30".................. $150.00 – 200.00

Flowerkins, 1963, marked "F–2" on head; seven dolls in series

Boxed

16"..................... $50.00 – 60.00

Gemmette, 1963, rooted hair, sleep eyes,

jointed vinyl, dressed in gem colored dress, includes child's jeweled ring
Misses Amethyst, Diamond, Emerald, Ruby, Sapphire, and Topaz
15½".............................$50.00
Georgie, Georgette, 1971, vinyl head, cloth bodies, redheaded twins
22"...................... $40.00 – 50.00
Gigi Perreau, 1951, early vinyl head, hard plastic body, open/closed smiling mouth
17"................. $550.00 – 700.00
Honey, 1949, hard plastic
12"................. $125.00 – 150.00
Karena Ballerina, 1958, vinyl head, rooted hair, sleep eyes, closed mouth, hard plastic body, jointed knees, ankles, neck, shoulders, and hips, head turns when walks
21"...................... $45.00 – 55.00
Little Debutantes, 1957, vinyl head, rooted hair, sleep eyes, closed mouth, hard plastic body, swivel waist, high-heeled feet
15"................... $80.00 – 100.00
17"................. $120.00 – 140.00
Debutante, 1958
28"................. $130.00 – 150.00
Little Miss Debutante, 1958
10½"...................,..... $60.00 – 90.00
My Fair Lady, 1958, all-vinyl, fashion type, swivel waist, fully jointed
20"...................... $65.00 – 75.00
Parton, Dolly, 1978
11½"................... $20.00 – 25.00
18"...................... $40.00 – 45.00
Posi Playmate, 1969, vinyl head, foam-filled vinyl body, bendable arms and legs, painted or rooted hair, sleep or painted eyes
12"...................... $15.00 – 20.00
Puppetrina, 1963 on, vinyl head, cloth body, rooted hair, sleep eyes, pocket in back for child to insert hand to manipulate doll's head and arms
22"...................... $70.00 – 80.00
Shelly, 1964, Tammy-type, grow hair

12"..................... $12.00 – 18.00
Sniffles, 1963, vinyl head, rooted hair, sleep eyes, open/closed mouth, marked "13/14 AA–EEGEE"
12"..................... $15.00 – 20.00
Susan Stroller, 1955, vinyl head, hard plastic walker body, rooted hair, closed mouth
20"...................... $60.00 –90.00
23"................. $125.00 – 150.00
26"................. $140.00 – 160.00
Tandy Talks, 1961, vinyl head, hard plastic body, freckles, pull-string talker
20"...................... $75.00 – 85.00
Ventriloquist dolls, 1960s, Bozo, Charlie McCarthy, Howdy Doody, Suzie Sez, vinyl and cloth
14" – 31"................. $70.00 – 150.00
Winky the Wurlitzer walking doll, vinyl
36"................. $100.00 – 125.00

EFFANBEE

1910 to present, New York City. Founded by Bernard Fleischaker and Hugo Baum. This company began selling composition headed dolls. These heads were made for them by Otto Ernst Denivelle (marked "Deco"). Effanbee eventually did their own manufacturing. By the late 1920s they were one of the leading manufacturers of American composition dolls. They went on to make dolls of hard plastic and vinyl. In 2002 the company was purchased by Robert Tonner. The new management of the company is currently re-issuing many of the designs from the past as well as new pieces. Values shown are for early dolls in good condition with original clothing, dolls from 1950 on in perfect condition with appropriate tags. More for exceptional dolls with wardrobe or accessories.
Bisque/Composition
Mary Jane, 1920, dolly-faced doll to compete

Effanbee

with German bisque. Some with bisque heads, others composition; bisque head, manufactured by Lenox Potteries, New Jersey, for Effanbee, sleep eyes, composition body, wooden arms and legs, kid body with wood and composition limbs. Composition shoulder head marked with Effanbee sticker on kid body, wooden ball-jointed arms and legs, composition hands, wigged, sleep eyes

24" .... $450.00 – 500.00

Early composition

Babies

Baby Bud, 1918 on, all-composition, painted features, molded hair, open-closed mouth, jointed arms, legs molded to body, one finger goes into mouth

6" .... $175.00 – 195.00

Black .... $200.00 – 225.00

Baby Dainty, 1912 on, name given to a variety of dolls, with composition heads, cloth bodies, some toddler types, some mama-types with criers

12" – 14" .... $170.00 – 190.00

15" .... $200.00 – 250.00

11" Baby Grumpy, $400.00. *Photo courtesy of Cybermogul Dolls.*

Vinyl

10" .... $30.00 – 40.00

Baby Effanbee, 1925, composition head, cloth body

12" – 13" .... $165.00 – 185.00

Baby Evelyn, 1925, composition head, cloth body 17" .... $250.00 – 275.00

Baby Grumpy, 1915 on, also later variations, composition character, heavily molded and painted hair, frowning eyebrows, painted intaglio eyes, pin-jointed limbs, cork-stuffed cloth body, gauntlet arms, pouty mouth

Mold #172, 174, 176

12" – 16" .... $425.00 – 500.00

Black .... $550.00 – 600.00

Baby Grumpy Variations

Baby Grumpy Gladys, 1923, composition shoulder head, cloth body, marked in oval, "Effanbee//Baby Grumpy// corp. 1923"

15" .... $300.00 – 350.00

Grumpy Aunt Dinah, black, cloth body, striped stocking legs

14½" .... $400.00 – 425.00

Grumpykins, 1927, composition head, cloth body, composition arms, some with cloth legs, others with composition legs

12" .... $200.00 – 250.00

Black .... $325.00 – 375.00

Grumpykins, Pennsylvania Dutch Dolls, 1936, dressed by Marie Polack in Mennonite, River Brethren, and Amish costumes

12" .... $225.00 – 250.00

Bubbles, 1924 on, composition shoulder head, open-closed mouth, painted teeth, molded and painted hair, sleep eyes, cloth body, bent-cloth legs, some with composition toddler legs, composition arms, finger of left hand fits into mouth, wore heart necklace, various marks including "Effanbee//Bubbles//Copr. 1924//Made in U.S.A."

16" – 18" .... $325.00 – 400.00

20" – 22" .... $450.00 – 500.00

24" – 29" .... $600.00 – 900.00

30" Lovums, $900.00. *Photo courtesy of Alderfer Auction & Appraisal.*

Lamkin, 1930 on, composition molded head, sleep eyes, open mouth, cloth body, crier, chubby composition legs, with feet turned in, fingers curled, molded gold ring on middle finger

16" .... $375.00 – 425.00

Lovums, 1928 on, child doll, composition swivel head, shoulder plate and limbs, cloth body, sleep eyes, molded and painted hair or wigged, can have bent baby legs or toddler legs

16" – 18" .... $375.00 – 425.00

20" – 22" .... $400.00 – 450.00

24" – 28" .... $500.00 – 700.00

Pat-o-Pat, 1925 on, composition head, painted eyes, cloth body with mechanism which, when pressed, causes hands to clap

13" .... $200.00 – 250.00

15" .... $250.00 – 275.00

Cloth mask-faced

15" .... $575.00 – 600.00

Sugar Baby, 1936 on, composition molded head, sleep eyes, cloth body, composition legs and hands

22" – 25" .... $250.00 – 350.00

Character Children, 1912 on, composition, heavily molded hair, painted eyes, pin-jointed cloth body, composition arms, cloth or composition legs, some marked "Deco"

Cliquot Eskimo, 1920, painted eyes, molded hair, felt hands, mohair suit

18" .... $450.00 – 525.00

Coquette, Naughty Marietta, 1915, composition girl, molded bow in hair, side-glancing eyes, cloth body

12" – 14" .... $375.00 – 600.00

Harmonica Joe, 1923, cloth body, with rubber ball, when squeezed provides air to open mouth with harmonica

15" .... $425.00 – 450.00

Irish Mail Kid, 1915, or Dixie Flyer, composition head, cloth body, arms sewn to steering handle of wooden wagon

10" .... $300.00 – 325.00

Johnny Tu-face, 1912, composition head with face on front and back, painted features, open-closed crying mouth, closed smiling mouth, molded and painted hair, cloth body, red striped legs, cloth feet, dressed in knitted romper and hat

16" .... $375.00 – 425.00

Pouting Bess, 1915, composition head with heavily molded curls, painted eyes, closed mouth, cloth cork-stuffed body, pin jointed, mark; "162" or "166" on back of head

15" .... $300.00 – 325.00

Whistling Jim, 1916, composition head, with heavily molded hair, painted intaglio eyes, perforated mouth, cloth cork-stuffed body, black sewn-on cloth shoes, wears red striped shirt, blue overalls, mark, label: "Effanbee// Whistling Jim//Trade Mark"

15" .... $300.00 – 325.00

MaMa Dolls, 1921 on, including Rosemary and Marilee, composition shoulder head, painted or sleep eyes, molded hair or wigged, cloth body, swing legs, crier, with composition arms and lower legs

14" .... $275.00 – 300.00

17" – 19" .... $300.00 – 375.00

24" – 27" .... $350.00 – 400.00

Late composition

Effanbee

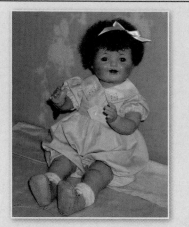

18" Touselhead Lovums, $425.00. *Photo courtesy of Dollyology Vintage Dolls*

American Children, 1936 – 1939 on, all-composition, designed by Dewees Cochran, open mouth, separated fingers can wear gloves, marks: heads may be unmarked, "Effanbee//Anne Shirley" on body

> *Barbara Joan, Barbara Ann*
> 14" – 17"........ $600.00 – 750.00
> *Barbara Lou*
> 21".............. $900.00 – 925.00

Closed mouth, separated fingers, sleep or painted eyes, marks: "Effanbee// American//Children" on head; "Effanbee// Anne Shirley" on body

Painted eye such as Peggy Lou and others

> 14" – 17"..... $900.00 – 1,200.00
> 19" – 21".. $1,800.00 – 1,900.00
> *Sleep eye* such as Gloria Ann and others
> 17" – 21".. $1,400.00 – 1,900.00

Anne Shirley, 1936 – 1940, never advertised as such, same mold used for Little Lady, all-composition, more grown-up body style, mark: "EFFANBEE//ANNE SHIRLEY"

> 10".............. $300.00 – 350.00
> 14" – 15"........ $350.00 – 400.00
> 17" – 18"........ $400.00 – 475.00
> 21".............. $400.00 – 475.00
> 27".............. $450.00 – 500.00

Movie Anne Shirley, 1935 – 1940. 1934 RKO movie character, Anne Shirley from *Anne of Green Gables* movie, all-composition, marked "Patsy" or other Effanbee doll, red braids, wearing Anne Shirley movie costume and gold paper hang tag stating "I am Anne Shirley." The Anne Shirley costume changes the identity of these dolls.

Mary Lee/Anne Shirley, open mouth, head marked "©Mary Lee," on marked "Patsy Joan" body

> 16".............. $300.00 – 400.00

Patsyette/Anne Shirley, body marked "Effanbee// Patsyette// Doll"

> 9½".............. $325.00 – 375.00

Patricia/Anne Shirley, body marked "Patricia"

> 15".............. $500.00 – 550.00

Patricia-kin/Anne Shirley, head marked "Patricia-kin," body marked "Effanbee// Patsy Jr.," hang tag reads "Anne Shirley"

17" American Child, designed by Dewees Cochran, $750.00. *Photo courtesy of McMasters Harris Auction Co.*

Effanbee

11½".............. $325.00 – 375.00
Babyette, 1943, eyes molded closed, composition head, hands, legs, cloth body

13"................. $300.00 – 400.00
Bright Eyes, 1940, composition head, hands, legs, cloth body, molded hair

14" – 16"........ $250.00 – 350.00
Brother or Sister, 1943, composition head, hands, cloth body, legs, yarn hair, painted eyes

12" – 16" .... $275.00 – 325.00
Butin-nose: See Patsy Family and Vinyl categories in this section.

Candy Kid, 1946 on, all-composition, sleep eyes, toddler body, molded and painted hair, closed mouth

13" .... $450.00 – 600.00
Charlie McCarthy, 1937, composition head, hands, feet, painted features, mouth opens, cloth body, legs, marked: "Edgar Bergen's Charlie McCarthy//An Effanbee Product"

17" – 19"........ $400.00 – 600.00
Happy Birthday Doll, 1940, music box in body, heart bracelet

17"................. $450.00 – 550.00

19" Charlie McCarthy, $600.00. *Photo courtesy of Morphy Auctions.*

Historical Dolls, 1939 on, all-composition, jointed body, human hair wigs, painted eyes, made only three sets of 30 dolls depicting history of apparel, 1492 – 1939, very fancy original costumes, metal heart bracelet, head marked "Effanbee//American//Children," on body, "Effanbee//Anne Shirley"

21"........... $2,250.00 – 2,500.00
Historical Replicas, 1939 on, all-composition, jointed body, copies of Historical Dolls, but smaller, human hair wigs, painted eyes, original costumes

14"................. $450.00 – 600.00
Honey, 1947 – 1948, all-composition jointed body, human hair wig, sleep eyes, closed mouth

18" – 21"........ $200.00 – 325.00
All hard plastic, ca. 1949 – 1955, see Hard Plastic and Vinyl later in this category.

Ice Queen, 1937 on, composition, open mouth, skater outfit

17"................. $625.00 – 750.00
Little Lady, 1939 on, used Anne Shirley mold, all-composition, wigged, sleep eyes, more grown-up body, separated fingers, gold paper hang tag, many in formals, as brides, or fancy gowns with matching parasol, during war years yarn hair was used, may have gold hang tag with name, like Gaye or Carole

12" Candy Kid (on left, doll on right is Averill's Little Cherub), $550.00 and $350.00. *Photo courtesy of Sweetbriar Auctions.*

15".................. $275.00 – 375.00
18".................. $325.00 – 400.00
21".................. $375.00 – 450.00
27".................. $475.00 – 550.00

Mae Starr, 1928, talking doll, composition shoulder head, cloth body, open mouth, four teeth, with cylinder records, marked: "Mae// Starr// Doll"

29".................. $600.00 – 800.00

Marionettes, 1937 on, puppets designed by Virginia Austin, composition, painted eyes
Clippo, clown

15".................. $125.00 – 175.00

Emily Ann

14".................. $175.00 – 225.00

Kilroy Cop

15".................. $100.00 – 150.00

Portrait Dolls, 1940 on, all-composition, Bo-Peep, Ballerina, Bride, Groom, Gibson Girl, Colonial Maid, etc.

12".................. $275.00 – 350.00

Suzanne, 1940, all-composition, jointed body, sleep eyes, wigged, closed mouth, may have magnets in hands to hold accessories, more for additional accessories or wardrobe

14".................. $250.00 – 300.00

14" Historical Replica doll, $550.00. *Photo courtesy of Withington Auction, Inc.*

23" Sweetie Pie, $400.00. *Photo courtesy of Joan & Lynette Antique Dolls and Accessories.*

Suzette, 1939, all-composition, fully jointed, painted side-glancing eyes, closed mouth, wigged

12".................. $250.00 – 275.00

Sweetie Pie, 1939 on, also called Baby Bright Eyes, Tommy Tucker, Mickey, composition bent limbs, sleep eyes, caracul wig, cloth body, crier, issued again in 1952+ in hard plastic, cloth body, and vinyl limbs, painted hair or synthetic wigs, wore same pink rayon taffeta dress with black and white trim as Noma doll

16" – 18"........ $275.00 – 300.00
20" – 24"........ $350.00 – 425.00

W. C. Fields, 1929 on, composition shoulder head, painted features, hinged mouth, painted teeth
1980, vinyl, Legend Series, marked: "W.C. Fields//An Effanbee Product"

17½".............. $900.00 – 950.00

Patsy Family, 1928 on, composition through 1947, later issued in vinyl and porcelain, many had gold paper hang tag and metal bracelet that read "Effanbee Durable Dolls," more for black, special editions, costumes, or with added accessories

Effanbee

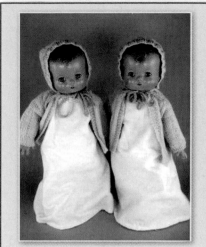

13" pair of Patsy babies, $300.00 each. *Photo courtesy of McMasters Harris Auction Co.*

Babies

Patsy Baby, 1931, painted or sleep eyes, wigged or molded hair, composition baby body, advertised as Babykin, came also with cloth body, in pair, layettes, trunks, marks: on head, "Effanbee//Patsy Baby"; on body, "Effanbee //Patsy// Baby"

    10" – 13"........ $250.00 – 300.00

Patsy Babyette, 1932, sleep eyes, marked on head "Effanbee," on body "Effanbee//Patsy //Babyette"

    9".................... $300.00 – 375.00

Patsy Baby Tinyette, 1934, painted eyes, bent-leg composition body, marked on head "Effanbee," on body "Effanbee//Baby// Tinyette"

    7".................... $250.00 – 300.00

Quints, 1935, set of five Patsy Baby Tinyettes in original box, from FAO Schwarz, organdy christening gowns and milk glass bottles, excellent condition

Set of five

    7"............. $1,700.00 – 2,100.00

Children

Patsy

1924, cloth body, composition legs, open mouth, upper teeth, sleep eyes, painted or human hair wig, with composition legs to hips, marked in half oval on back shoulder plate: "Effanbee//Patsy"

    15"................. $300.00 – 350.00

1928, all-composition jointed body, painted or sleep eyes, molded headband on red molded bobbed hair, or wigged, bent right arm, with gold paper hang tag, metal heart bracelet, marked on body: "Effanbee//Patsy// Pat. Pend.//Doll"

    14"................. $550.00 – 600.00

Oriental with black painted hair, painted eyes, in fancy silk pajamas and matching shoes

    14"................. $750.00 – 800.00

1946, all-composition jointed body, bright facial coloring, painted or sleep eyes, wears pink or blue checked pinafore

    14"................. $400.00 – 450.00

Patsy Ann, 1929, all-composition, closed mouth, sleep eyes, molded hair, or wigged, marked on body:"Effanbee//'Patsy-Ann'//©//Pat. #1283558"

    19"................. $400.00 – 450.00

1959, limited edition, vinyl, sleep eyes, white organdy dress, with pink hair ribbon, marked "Effanbee//Patsy Ann//©1959" on head, "Effanbee" on body

    15"................. $245.00 – 285.00

Patsyette, 1931, composition

    9".................... $325.00 – 375.00

Black, Dutch, George & Martha Washington

    9" ....$350.00 – 400.00 each

Patsy Fluff, 1932, all-cloth, with painted features, pink checked rompers and bonnet

    16"............................ $1,000.00

Effanbee

Too few examples in database for a reliable range.

Patsy Joan, 1931, composition

16"................. $450.00 – 475.00

1946, marked "Effandbee" on body, with "d" in "Effanbee"

17"................. $325.00 – 425.00

Patsy Jr., 1931, all-composition, advertised as Patsykins, marks: "Effanbee//Patsy Jr.//Doll"

11½"............. $350.00 – 400.00

Patsy Lou, 1930, all-composition, molded red hair or wigged, marks: "Effanbee//Patsy Lou" on body

22"................. $350.00 – 425.00

Patsy Mae, 1934, shoulder head, sleep eyes, cloth body, crier, swing legs, marks: "Effanbee//Patsy Mae" on head, "Effanbee//Lovums//c//Pat. No. 1283558" on shoulder plate

29"........... $1,500.00 – 1,600.00

Patsy Ruth, 1934, shoulder head, sleep eyes, cloth body, crier, swing legs, marks: "Effanbee//Patsy Ruth" on head, "Effanbee//Lovums//©//Pat. No. 1283558" on shoulder plate

26"........... $1,400.00 – 1,700.00

Patsy Tinyette Toddler, 1935, painted eyes, marks: "Effanbee" on head, "Effanbee//Baby//Tinyette" on body

7¾"................. $325.00 – 375.00

Tinyette Toddlers, tagged "Kit & Kat"

In Dutch costumes. $800.00 pair

Wee Patsy, 1935, head molded to body, molded and painted shoes and socks, jointed arms and hips, advertised only as "Fairy Princess," pin-back button, marks on body: "Effanbee//Wee Patsy"

5¾"................. $400.00 – 500.00

Related items

Metal heart bracelet, reads "Effanbee Durable Dolls".................... $25.00

Metal personalized name bracelet for Patsy family....................... $65.00

Patsy Ann, Her Happy Times, ca. 1935, book by Mona Reed King.....$75.00

Patsy For Keeps, c 1932, book by Ester Marian Ames.................. $125.00

Patricia Series, 1935, all sizes advertised in *Patsytown News,* all-composition slimmer bodies, sleep eyes, wigged, later WWII-era Patricia dolls had yarn hair and cloth bodies

Patricia, wig, sleep eyes, marked, "Effanbee Patricia" body

15"................. $475.00 – 600.00

Patricia Ann, wig, marks unknown

19"................. $600.00 – 650.00

Patricia Joan, wig, marks unknown, slimmer legs

16"................. $500.00 – 550.00

Patricia-Kin, wig, mark: "Patricia-Kin" head; "Effanbee//Patsy Jr." body

11½"............. $350.00 – 400.00

Patricia Lou, wig, marks unknown

22"................. $475.00 – 525.00

Patricia Ruth, head marked: "Effanbee//Patsy Ruth," no marks on slimmer composition body

27"........... $1,200.00 – 1,350.00

Patsy, related dolls and variations

Betty Bee, 1932, all-composition, short

14" Skippy Aviator, $1,300.00. *Photo courtesy of Morphy Auctions.*

tousle wig, sleep eyes, marked on body: "Effanbee//Patsy Lou"

22".............. $375.00 – 400.00

Betty Bounce, tousle head, 1932 on, all-composition, sleep eyes, used Lovums head on body, marked: "Effanbee//'Patsy Ann'//©//Pat. #1283558"

19".............. $350.00 – 400.00

Betty Brite, 1932, all-composition, short tousle wig, sleep eyes, some marked: "Effanbee//Betty Brite" on body and others marked on head "© Mary-Lee," on body "Effanbee Patsy Joan," gold hang tag reads "This is Betty Brite, The lovable Imp with tiltable head and movable limbs, an Effanbee doll."

16".............. $300.00 – 350.00

Butin-nose, 1936 on, all-composition, molded and painted hair, features, distinct feature is small nose, usually has regional or special costume

8".............. $200.00 – 300.00

Oriental, with layette

8".............. $525.00

Mary Ann, 1932 on, composition, sleep eyes, wigged, open mouth, marked: "Mary Ann" on head, "Effanbee//'Patsy Ann'//©//Pat. #1283558" on body

19".............. $350.00 – 375.00

Mary Lee, 1932, composition, sleep eyes, wigged, open mouth, marked: "©//Mary Lee" on head, "Effanbee//Patsy Joan" on body

16½".............. $325.00 – 350.00

Patsy/Patricia, 1940, used a marked Patsy head on a marked Patricia body, all-composition, painted eyes, molded hair, may have magnets in hands to hold accessories, marked on body: "Effanbee//'Patricia'"

15".............. $400.00 – 450.00

Skippy, 1929, advertised as Patsy's boyfriend, composition head, painted eyes, molded and painted blond hair, composition or cloth body, with composition molded shoes and legs, marked on head: "Effanbee//Skippy//©//P. L. Crosby," on body "Effanbee//Patsy//Pat. Pend// Doll"

14"

Military outfit .... $600.00 – 700.00
Baseball player.................. $1,600.00*
Boy's outfit .... $500.00 – 550.00
Boy Scout $3,250.00*

Rubber

Dy-Dee, 1934 on, hard rubber head, sleep eyes, jointed rubber bent-leg body, drink/

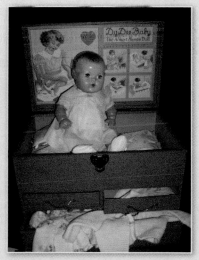

14" Dy-Dee, hard rubber head with layette, $450.00. *Photo courtesy of Withington Auction, Inc.*

Effanbee

wet mechanism, molded and painted hair. Early dolls had molded ears, after 1940 had applied rubber ears, nostrils, and tear ducts, later made in hard plastic and vinyl, marked: "Effanbee//Dy-Dee Baby" with four patent numbers

Dy-Dee Wee

    9".................. $275.00 – 300.00
    11"................. $200.00 – 225.00
    13"................. $250.00 – 280.00
    15"................. $375.00 – 400.00
    20"................. $425.00 – 450.00

Dy-Dee in Layette Trunk, with accessories

    11" – 13"........ $700.00 – 850.00

Vinyl reissue, 1984 molded hair or curly rooted hair

    14"..................... $60.00 – 75.00

Hard plastic and vinyl, dolls listed are all in good condition wearing original clothing, allow more for MIB

Alyssa, 1960 – 1961, vinyl head, hard plastic jointed body, walker, including elbows, rooted saran hair, sleep eyes

    23"................. $200.00 – 225.00

Baby Lisa, 1980, vinyl, designed by Astri Campbell, represents a three-month-old baby, in wicker basket with accessories

    11"..................... $25.00 – 30.00

Baby Lisa Grows Up, 1983, vinyl, toddler body, in trunk with wardrobe

                     $40.00 – 50.00

Brenda Starr, 2002 – 2007, designed and produced under Robert Tonner

    16"..................... $40.00 – 75.00

Butterball, 1969, all vinyl, molded hair or rooted, sleep eyes

    12"..................... $40.00 – 50.00

1989 version, molded hair

    12"..................... $18.00 – 22.00

Button Nose, 1968 – 1971, vinyl head, cloth body

    18"..................... $25.00 – 35.00

2004 version, produced under Robert Tonner

    18"..................... $45.00 – 60.00

Champagne Lady, 1959, vinyl head and arms, rooted hair, blue sleep eyes, lashes, hard plastic body, from Lawrence Welk's TV show, Miss Revlon-type

    21"................. $225.00 – 275.00
    23"................. $250.00 – 300.00

Currier & Ives, vinyl and hard plastic

    12"..................... $15.00 – 20.00

Disney dolls, 1977 – 1978, Snow White, Cinderella, Alice in Wonderland, and Sleeping Beauty

    14"................. $100.00 – 125.00
    16½".............. $150.00 – 225.00

Fluffy, 1954+, all-vinyl

Molded hair

    8"........................ $20.00 – 28.00

Rooted hair

    8"........................ $18.00 – 22.00
    11"..................... $35.00 – 45.00

Grand Dames, 1970 on, vinyl, sleep eyes, rooted hair elaborate costumes

    11"..................... $12.00 – 18.00
    15"..................... $20.00 – 25.00
    18"..................... $18.00 – 22.00

Gumdrop, 1962 on, vinyl, jointed toddler, sleep eyes, rooted hair

    16"..................... $20.00 – 25.00

Hagara, Jan, designer, all-vinyl, jointed, rooted hair, painted eyes, Christina 1984, Larry 1985, Laurel 1984, Lesley 1985

    15"..................... $12.00 – 18.00

Half-Pint, 1966 – 1983, all-vinyl, rooted hair, sleep eyes, lashes

    11"..................... $35.00 – 40.00

Happy Boy, 1960, vinyl, molded hair, tooth, freckles, painted eyes

    11"..................... $45.00 – 50.00

Hibel, Edna, designer, 1984 only, all-vinyl

Contessa .... $30.00 – 45.00

Flower Girl .... $25.00 – 35.00

Honey, 1949 – 1958, hard plastic (see

Effanbee

14" Honey, hard plastic, $400.00. *Photo courtesy of Morphy Auctions.*

also composition), saran wig, sleep eyes, closed mouth, marked on head and back, "Effanbee," had gold paper hang tag that read: "I am//Honey//An//Effanbee// Sweet/ /Child"
Honey, 1949 – 1955, all hard plastic, closed mouth, sleep eyes

14"..................	$350.00 – 400.00
18"..................	$400.00 – 500.00
24"..................	$500.00 – 525.00

Honey Walker, 1952 on, all hard plastic with walking mechanism, Honey Walker Junior Miss, 1956 – 1957, hard plastic, extra joints at knees and ankles permit her to wear flat or high-heeled shoes, add $50.00 for jointed knees, ankles

14"..................	$225.00 – 275.00
19"..................	$275.00 – 325.00

Humpty Dumpty, 1985 .. $55.00 – 75.00
Katie, 1957, molded hair

8½"..................... $40.00 – 50.00
Legend Series, vinyl, 15½", allow double for MIB
1980, W.C. Fields .... $35.00 – 40.00
1981, John Wayne, cowboy
                    $30.00 – 35.00

1982, John Wayne, cavalry
                    $30.00 – 35.00
1982, Mae West.......... $20.00 – 25.00
1983, Groucho Marx ... $20.00 – 25.00
1984, Judy Garland, Dorothy
                    $40.00 – 45.00
1985, Lucille Ball.......... $35.00 – 40.00
1986, Liberace .... $25.00 – 30.00
1987, James Cagney.... $20.00 – 25.00
Lil Sweetie, 1967, nurser with no lashes or brow
    16"...................... $40.00 – 45.00
Limited Edition Club, vinyl
1975, Precious Baby.. $150.00 – 175.00
1976, Patsy Ann ...... $160.00 – 180.00
1977, Dewees Cochran . $65.00 – 75.00
1978, Crowning Glory .. $40.00 – 50.00
1979, Skippy........... $125.00 – 150.00
1980, Susan B. Anthony . $40.00 – 50.00
1981, Girl with Watering Can
                    $60.00 – 70.00
1982, Princess Diana . $100.00 – 125.00
1983, Sherlock Holmes. $35.00 – 45.00
1984, Bubbles .... $45.00 – 50.00
1985, Red Boy .... $25.00 – 30.00
1986, China head .... $25.00 – 30.00
1987 – 1988,
Porcelain Grumpy (2,500)
                    $100.00 – 125.00
    Vinyl Grumpy .... $40.00 – 50.00
Martha and George Washington, 1976 – 1977, all-vinyl, fully jointed, rooted hair, blue eyes, molded lashes
    11" ....$50.00 – 75.00 pair
Mickey, 1956 – 1972, all-vinyl, fully jointed, some with molded hat, painted eyes
    10"...................... $40.00 – 50.00
Miss Chips, 1966 – 1981, all-vinyl, fully jointed, side-glancing sleep eyes, rooted hair
    17"...................... $45.00 – 50.00
Black
    17"...................... $50.00 – 55.00
Most Happy Family, 1958, vinyl, 21" mother,

10" brother and sister, 8" baby

    Set .... $125.00 – 175.00

Noma, The Electronic Doll, 1950, hard plastic, cloth body, vinyl limbs, battery-operated talking doll, wore pink rayon taffeta dress with black and white check trim

    27" .... $450.00 – 475.00

Polka Dottie, 1954, vinyl head, with molded pigtails on fabric body, or with hard plastic body

    21" .... $145.00 – 165.00

Latex body

    11" .... $100.00 – 120.00

Personality Series

1984, Sir Winston Churchill

                $50.00 – 60.00

1984, Louis Armstrong .. $65.00 – 75.00

1984, Mark Twain .... $50.00 – 60.00

1985, Eleanor Roosevelt . $45.00 – 50.00

Presidents, 1983 on

Abraham Lincoln, 1983

    18" .... $35.00 – 40.00

George Washington, 1983

    16" .... $35.00 – 40.00

Teddy Roosevelt, 1984

    17" .... $50.00 – 55.00

Franklin D. Roosevelt

    1985 .... $40.00 – 45.00

Andrew Jackson

    1989 .... $40.00 – 45.00

Princess Diana, 1982, vinyl

    18" .... $20.00 – 25.00

Pun'kin, 1966 – 1983, all-vinyl, fully jointed toddler, sleep eyes, rooted hair

    11" .... $15.00 – 20.00

Regal Heirloom Collection, 1965, vinyl, rooted hair, sleep eyes

    18" .... $30.00 – 35.00

Rootie Kazootie, 1954, vinyl head, cloth or hard plastic body, smaller size has latex body

    11" .... $100.00 – 120.00

    21" .... $145.00 – 165.00

Santa Claus, 1982 on, designed by Faith Wick, "Old Fashioned Nast Santa," No. 7201, vinyl head, hands, stuffed cloth body, molded and painted features, marked "Effanbee//7201 c//Faith Wick"

    18" .... $65.00 – 75.00

Storybook Series, 1976, Heidi, Red Riding Hood, Alice in Wonderland, others

    11" .... $12.00 – 18.00

Sugar Pie, 1960, vinyl nurser, rooted or molded hair, sleep eyes

    14" – 16" .... $30.00 – 40.00

Suzie Sunshine, 1961 – 1979, designed by Eugenia Dukas, all-vinyl, fully jointed, rooted hair, sleep eyes, lashes, freckles on nose, add $25.00 more for black

    18" .... $30.00 – 35.00

Sweetie Pie, 1952, hard plastic

    27" .... $300.00 – 325.00

Tintair, 1951, hard plastic, hair color set, to compete with Ideal's Toni

    14" – 16" .... $150.00 – 200.00

    20" .... $200.00 – 300.00

Wicket Witch, 1981 – 1982, designed by Faith Wick. No. 7110, vinyl head, blond rooted hair, painted features, cloth stuffed body, dressed in black, with apple and basket, head marked: "Effanbee//Faith Wick//7110 19cc81"

    18" .... $30.00 – 40.00

FARNELL-ALPHA TOYS

1915 – 1930s, Acton, London. Cloth dolls with molded felt or velvet heads, cloth bodies, painted features, mohair wigs.

Baby

    15" .... $300.00 – 350.00

    18" .... $400.00 – 500.00

Child

15" King George VI, $500.00. *Photo courtesy of McMasters Harris Auction Co.*

10" .... $350.00 – 400.00
14" – 15" .... $400.00 – 450.00
20" .... $450.00 – 500.00
Black
    13" – 15"........ $500.00 – 600.00
Too few in database for a reliable range.
Characters such as islanders, pirates etc.
    15" .... $100.00 – 225.00
Long-limbed lady doll
    26" .... $800.00 – 850.00
Too few in database for a reliable range.
King George VI, "H.M. The King"
    13" .... $450.00 – 550.00
Palace Guard, "Beefeater"
    15" .... $175.00 – 250.00

FISHER-PRICE

Fisher-Price, 1931 on, New York. Began to make infants' and children's toys. Eventually, the product line was expanded to include dolls. Values are for secondary market dolls in perfect condition wearing original clothing. Many are still available retail.
My Friend Mandy, 1977 on, vinyl head and limbs, cloth body, rooted hair, painted eyes

    16" .... $20.00 – 30.00
My Baby Beth, 1978, vinyl head and limbs, cloth body, rooted hair, painted eyes
    18" .... $50.00 – 60.00

FRANKLIN MINT

The Franklin Mint, 1964 on, began to make legal tender coins for foreign countries, as well as commemorative medallions, casino tokens, and precious metal ingots. Eventually, the product line was expanded to include sculptures, deluxe games, precision die-cast models, and collector dolls. Since 2003 the doll lines have been reduced in production, some phased out completely. Values are for secondary market dolls in perfect condition wearing original clothing. Many are still available retail.
Vinyl

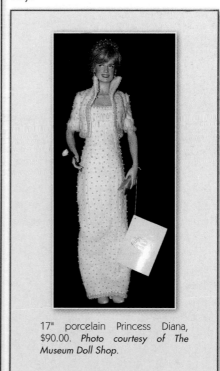

17" porcelain Princess Diana, $90.00. *Photo courtesy of The Museum Doll Shop.*

Cinderella
  15½".................. $75.00 – 85.00
Jackie Kennedy
  14½".................. $40.00 – 55.00
Marilyn Monroe
  16"..................... $50.00 – 80.00
Princess Diana
  15½"................ $90.00 – 100.00
Porcelain
Arwen Evenstar
  22"................. $100.00 – 110.00
Country Store advertising logo dolls, 1986 on
  13"..................... $20.00 – 40.00
Gibson Girl
  21"..................... $55.00 – 75.00
Jackie Kennedy
  15"................... $60.00 – 100.00
With trunk and wardrobe
                    $200.00 – 300.00
Marilyn Monroe
  19",,................ $100.00 – 175.00
Scarlett O'Hara, in wedding gown
  19"................. $100.00 – 125.00
Princess Diana
  18½"................ $70.00 – 130.00

FRENCH POUPÉE

1869 on. Glass eyes, doll modeled as an adult lady, with bisque shoulder head, stationary or swivel neck, closed mouth, earrings, kid or kid and cloth body, nicely dressed, good condition. Add more for original clothing, special body such as Gesland, Kintzbach, Terrenne, black, or exceptional doll.

Poupée Peau (kid body), unmarked or with size number only
Glass eyes
  12" – 14" ... $2,800.00 – 4,500.00
  16" – 18" ... $6,000.00 – 9,000.00
  21"......... $9,000.00 – 11,000.00

12" Poupée Peau, $2,800.00. *Photo courtesy of Morphy Auctions.*

  27"....... $10,000.00 – 12,000.00
Painted eyes, kid body
  14" – 16".. $1,600.00 – 1,900.00
Poupée Bois (wood body), unmarked or with size number only, articulated body, glass eyes
  13"........... $6,500.00 – 9,000.00
  15",.......... $7,000.00 – 8,500.00
  18"........... $7,500.00 – 8,000.00
Kid-over wood body
  15" – 18" ... $6,000.00 – 8,000.00
Blown kid body
  14" .... $9,000.00 – 11,000.00
Too few in database for a reliable range.
Barrois: See E. Barrios section.
B.S., Blampoix
  12" – 14" ... $2,600.00 – 3,000.00
  16" – 17" ... $4,000.00 – 8,000.00
A. Dehors, 1860, swivel neck, bisque lower arms
Generic face, wooden body
  14"........... $3,400.00 – 3,900.00
  17" – 20" ... $5,000.00 – 9,000.00
Portrait face
  17" – 18"..$17,000.00 – 20,000.00
L.D., Louis Doleac, kid body
  17" – 20" ... $3,000.00 – 5,300.00
Too few in database for a reliable range.

Simonne
Kid body
 16" – 17".. $6,000.00 – 7,000.00
Wood body
 14"........... $7,500.00 – 8,500.00
 18"....... $10,500.00 – 12,000.00
Fortune Teller Dolls, fashion-type head with swivel neck, glass or painted eyes, kid body, skirt made to hold many paper "fortunes," exceptional doll may be more
Closed mouth
 15" – 18".. $4,100.00 – 7,000.00
Open mouth
 18"...........................$3,100.00+
China, glazed finish, 1870 – 1880 hairstyle
 14" – 15" ... $5,000.00 – 5,500.00
 18"........... $8,500.00 – 9,000.00
Accessories
Dress .... $600.00+
Shoes, marked by maker .... $500.00+
Unmarked $250.00
Trunk .... $250.00+
Wig .... $250.00+

RALPH A. FREUNDLICH

1924 – 1945, New York City, later Clinton, Massachusetts. Ralph Freundlich worked for Jeanette Doll Co. then opened Silver Doll & Toy Manufacturing Co. in 1923. In 1924 became Ralph Freundlich Inc. and made composition dolls. Dolls listed are in good condition wearing original clothing.
Baby Sandy, 1939 – 1942, all-composition, jointed toddler body, molded hair, painted or sleep eyes, smiling mouth
 8".................... $200.00 – 250.00
 12"................. $250.00 – 300.00
 15"................. $300.00 – 400.00
 20"................. $575.00 – 650.00
Dummy Dan, ventriloquist doll, Charlie

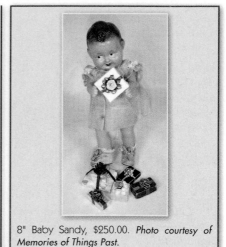

8" Baby Sandy, $250.00. *Photo courtesy of Memories of Things Past.*

McCarthy look-alike
 15"..................... $50.00 – 75.00
 21"................... $75.00 – 100.00
General Douglas MacArthur, 1942, all-composition, jointed body, bent arm salutes, painted features, molded hat, jointed, in khaki uniform, with paper tag
 18"................. $300.00 – 400.00
Military dolls, 1942+, all-composition, molded hats, painted features, original clothes, with paper tag Soldier, Sailor, WAAC, or WAVE
 15"................. $225.00 – 300.00
Orphan Annie and her dog, Sandy
 12"................. $500.00 – 600.00
Pig Baby, 1930s, composition pig head, with painted features on unmarked five-piece body, Freundlich presumed maker of similar composition cat, rabbit, and monkey dolls
 9".................... $350.00 – 400.00
Pinocchio, composition and cloth, with molded hair, painted features, brightly colored cheeks,large eyes, open/closed mouth, tagged: "Original as portrayed by C. Collodi"
 16"................. $400.00 – 425.00
Red Riding Hood, Wolf, Grandma, 1934,

composition, in schoolhouse box, original clothes, set of three

9".................. $775.00 – 875.00

Trixbe (Patsy-type), all-composition girl, painted features, molded painted hair with bow pinned on head

11"................. $100.00 – 125.00

FULPER POTTERY CO.

1918 – 1921, Flemington, New Jersey. Made dolls with bisque heads and all-bisque dolls. Sold dolls to Amberg, Colonial Toy Mfg. Co., and Horsman. "M.S." monogram stood for Martin Stangl, in charge of production. Dolls listed are in good condition with original or appropriate clothes.

Baby, bisque socket head, glass eyes, open mouth, teeth, mohair wig, bent-leg body

14" – 16"........ $400.00 – 500.00

17" – 22"........ $475.00 – 575.00

Toddler

16" – 18"........ $575.00 – 625.00

Child, socket head, glass eyes, open mouth

Kid body

18" – 22"........ $300.00 – 375.00

27"................. $450.00 – 500.00

Composition body

16" – 18"........ $300.00 – 450.00

22" – 24"........ $550.00 – 650.00

GABRIEL

The Lone Ranger Series, 1970s, vinyl action figures with horses, separate accessory sets available. Dolls in very good condition with original clothing and accessories. Mint-in-box can bring double values listed.

Dan Reed on Banjo, blond hair, figure on palomino horse

14" Fulper baby doll, bisque socket head, $400.00. *Photo courtesy of The Museum Doll Shop.*

9"..................... $75.00 – 110.00

Butch Cavendish on Smoke, black hair, mustache, on black horse

9"..................... $90.00 – 130.00

Hopi Medicine Man

9".................,,. $110.00 – 120.00

Lone Ranger on Silver, masked figure on white horse

9"..................... $75.00 – 100.00

Lone Ranger, no horse

9"....................... $50.00 – 60.00

Mysterious Prospector set, Mule and mining items

$50.00 – 60.00

Tonto on Scout, Indian on brown and white horse

9"................... $110.00 – 120.00

Tonto, no horse

9"....................... $60.00 – 70.00

GANS & SEYFARTH PUPPENFABRIK

1908 – 1922, Waltershausen, Thüringia. Made bisque dolls; had a patent for flirty and

22" dolly-faced, doll, $500.00. *Photo courtesy of Morphy Auctions.*

googly eyes. Partners separated in 1922, Otto Gans opened his own factory.

Baby, bent-leg, original clothes or appropriately dressed

16"	$400.00 – 475.00
20"	$525.00 – 600.00
25"	$750.00 – 825.00

Child, open mouth, composition body, original clothes or appropriately dressed, no mold number or molds 120, 6589

13" – 15"	$325.00 – 425.00
21" – 24"	$425.00 – 550.00
28"	$600.00 – 700.00

FRANCOIS GAULTIER

1860 – 1899. After 1899, became part of S.F.B.J., located near Paris. They made bisque doll heads and parts for lady dolls and for bébés and sold to many French makers of dolls including Gesland, Jullien, Petite et Dumontier, Rabery et Delphieu, and Thuillier. Also made all-bisque dolls marked "F.G." Dolls listed are in good condition, appropriately dressed.

Poupée (fashion-type), 1860 on, F.G., marked swivel head on bisque shoulder plate, kid body, may have bisque lower arms

Glass eyes

10" – 11"	$1,900.00 – 2,500.00
12" – 13"	$3,000.00 – 4,000.00
15" – 17"	$3,750.00 – 4,000.00
18" – 20"	$5,000.00 – 6,000.00
23" – 24"	$6,000.00 – 6,200.00
30" – 32"	$4,000.00 – 5,000.00

Painted eyes

16" – 17"	$1,800.00 – 2,000.00

Wood body

16" – 18"	$10,000.00 – 10,200.00

Later one-piece shoulder head, kid body, often in regional dress

Glass eyes

18"	$900.00 – 1,000.00

Painted eyes

12" – 15"	$700.00 – 900.00

Bébé (child), "F.G." in block letters, 1879 – 1887, closed mouth, excellent quality bisque socket head, glass eyes, pierced ears, cork pate

Composition and wood body with straight wrists

10" – 11"	$8,000.00 – 11,000.00

20" bébé, block letter mark "FG," $7,500.00. *Photo courtesy of Joan & Lynette Antique Dolls and Accessories.*

13" – 16" ... $7,000.00 – 9,000.00
18" – 22" ... $7,000.00 – 8,000.00
27" – 29" . $8,000.00 – 10,000.00
Kid body, may have bisque forearms
10" – 12" ... $4,900.00 – 6,000.00
13" – 15" ... $7,000.00 – 9,000.00
17" – 19" . $10,000.00 – 11,000.00
Bébé (child), "F.G." inside scroll, 1887 – 1900,
Composition body, closed mouth
9½", size 0 .... $3,948.00*
12" – 13".. $2,000.00 – 3,000.00
15" – 17" ... $3,000.00 – 3,800.00
22" – 24" ... $4,000.00 – 4,200.00
28" .... $5,000.00 – 5,200.00
Composition body, open mouth
14" – 16" ... $1,500.00 – 1,700.00
20" – 24" ... $1,900.00 – 2,400.00

GESLAND

1860 – 1928, Paris. Made, repaired, exported, and distributed dolls, patented a doll body, used heads from Francois Gaultier with "F.G." block or scroll mark. In 1926 became part of the Société Industrielle de France. Gesland's dolls' bodies had metal articulated armatures covered with padding and stockinette, with bisque or wood/composition hands and legs. Dolls listed are in good condition, appropriately dressed. Allow more for exceptional original clothing.
Poupée (fashion-type) Gesland, stockinette covered metal articulated fashion-type body, bisque lower arms and legs
14" – 15".. $5,500.00 – 6,000.00
16" – 17" ... $6,000.00 – 8,000.00
23" – 24".$10,000.00 – 11,000.00
Bébé (child), on marked Gesland body, closed mouth
12" – 15" ... $5,600.00 – 8,000.00
17" – 20" ... $5,500.00 – 6,000.00
22" – 24" ... $6,100.00 – 6,500.00
28" – 30" ... $5,000.00 – 7,000.00

23" Poupée with FG head on a Gesland body, $10,000.00. *Photo courtesy of Morphy Auctions.*

RUTH GIBBS

1946 on, Flemington, New Jersey. Made dolls with china heads and limbs on cloth bodies. The dolls were designed by Herbert Johnson. Dolls listed are in good condition wearing original clothing, in original box. Can bring double the values listed.
Godey's Lady Book Dolls, pink tinted or white shoulder head, cloth body
7" .... $70.00 – 90.00
12" .... $95.00 – 110.00

7" Godey Lady Book Doll, $80.00. *Doll courtesy of Elaine Holda.*

Blond special for G Fox 100th anniversary CT,
    12".......... $150.00 – 180.00 MIB
With molded necklace
    12"................ $100.00 – 135.00
Black
    12"................ $145.00 – 155.00
Caracul wig, original outfit
    10"................ $150.00 – 225.00

GILBERT TOYS

1909 – 1966, New Haven, Connecticut. Company founded on the invention of the Erector Set, went on to make dolls based on popular television characters. Dolls listed are in very good condition with all-original clothing and accessories, mint-in-box can bring double the values listed.
Honey West, 1965, vinyl head and arms, hard plastic torso and legs, rooted blond hair, painted eyes, painted beauty spot near mouth, head marked "K73" with leopard
    11½".............. $100.00 – 125.00
Accessories, MOC....... $80.00 – 90.00
The Man from U.N.C.L.E. characters from 1960s TV show
Ilya Kuryakin (David McCallum)
    12¼".............. $200.00 – 250.00
Napoleon Solo (Robert Vaughn)
    12¼".............. $100.00 – 125.00
James Bond, Secret Agent 007, character from James Bond movies
    12¼".............. $100.00 – 125.00

GIRL SCOUT DOLLS

1917 on, listed chronologically. Dolls made for the Girl Scouts of America, various manufacturers. Dolls listed are in good condition with original clothing, MIB can bring double the values listed.
1917, all-composition doll, painted features, mohair wig

    6½"............... $225.00 – 250.00
1920s Girl Scout doll in camp uniform, pictured in Girls Scout 1920 handbook, all-cloth, mask face, painted features, wigged, gray-green uniform
    13"............................ $600.00+
Grace Corry, Scout 1929, composition shoulder head, designed by Grace Corry, cloth body with crier, molded hair, painted features, original uniform, mark on shoulder plate: "by Grace Corry," body stamped "Madame Hendren Doll//Made in USA"
    13"................ $550.00 – 675.00
Averill Mfg. Co, 1936, all-cloth, printed and painted features
    16"................ $350.00 – 400.00
Georgene Novelties
1940 – 1946, all-cloth, flat-faced painted features, yellow yarn curls, wears original silver green uniform with red triangle tie, hang tag reads: "Genuine Georgene Doll//A product of Georgene Novelties, Inc., NY// Made in U.S.A."
    15"................ $250.00 – 300.00
1946 – 1955, all-cloth, mask face, painted

8" Tiny Terri Lee Girl Scout (doll Ginger by Cosmopolitan), $100.00. *Photo courtesy of Memories of Things Past.*

features and string hair

13½".............. $125.00 – 150.00

1955 – 1957, same as previous listing, but now has a stuffed vinyl head

13"................. $200.00 – 250.00

Terri Lee, 1949 – 1958, hard plastic, felt hats, oilcloth saddle shoes

16"................. $450.00 – 550.00

Outfit only..................... $160.00*

Tiny Terri Lee, 1955 – 1958, hard plastic, walker, sleep eyes, wig, plastic shoes

10"................. $125.00 – 175.00

Ginger, 1956 – 1958, made by Cosmopolitan for Terri Lee, hard plastic, straight-leg walker, synthetic wig

7½" – 8"........... $75.00 – 100.00

Effanbee Honey, 1949 – 1957, hard plastic, mohair wig

14"................. $125.00 – 150.00

18"................. $250.00 – 300.00

Vogue, Painted Lash Walker Ginny, 1954, hard plastic

8"................... $225.00 – 275.00

Nancy Ann Storybook, 1957, Muffie, hard plastic

8"................... $125.00 – 150.00

Effanbee, Patsy Ann, 1959 on, all-vinyl jointed body, saran hair, with sleep eyes, freckles on nose, Brownie or Girl Scout

15"................. $225.00 – 275.00

Effanbee Suzette, ca. 1960, jointed vinyl body, sleep eyes, saran hair, thin body, long legs

15"................. $300.00 – 350.00

Uneeda, 1961 – 1963, Ginny look-alike, vinyl head, hard plastic body, straight-leg walker, Dynel wig, marked "U" on head

8"..................... $75.00 – 100.00

Effanbee Fluffy, 1964 – 1972, vinyl dolls, sleep eyes, curly rooted hair, Brownie had blond wig, Junior was brunette, box had clear acetate lid, printed with Girl Scout trademark and catalog number

8"....................... $55.00 – 65.00

Related, Fluffy Camp Fire Girl

8"..................... $75.00 – 100.00

Effanbee Fluffy Cadette, 1965, vinyl, rooted hair, sleep eyes

11"................. $200.00 – 250.00

Effanbee Pun'kin Jr., 1974 – 1979, all-vinyl, sleep eyes, long, straight rooted hair, Brownie and Junior uniforms

11½"................. $40.00 – 50.00

Related, Fluffy Camp Fire Girl

11½"................. $55.00 – 65.00

Hallmark, 1979, all-cloth, Juliette Low, from 1916 handbook, wearing printed 1923 uniform

6½"..................... $25.00 – 30.00

Jesco, 1985, Katie, all-vinyl, sleep eyes, long straight rooted hair, look-alike Girl Scout, dressed as Brownie and Junior

9"....................... $45.00 – 55.00

Dakin, Ginny, 1986 – 1995, all vinyl

8"....................... $60.00 – 90.00

Madame Alexander, 1992, vinyl, unofficial Girl Scout, sleep eyes

8"....................... $60.00 – 80.00

Avon, 1995, Tender Memories series, porcelain, carries box of cookies

14"..................... $25.00 – 40.00

GLADDIE

1928 – 1930 on. Trade name of doll designed by Helen Webster Jensen, made in Germany, body made by K&K, for Borgfeldt. Flange heads made of bisque or biscaloid (a ceramic imitation of bisque), with molded hair, glass or painted eyes, open-closed mouth with two upper teeth and laughing expression, composition arms, lower legs, cloth torso, some with crier and upper legs, mark "copyriht" (misspelled). Dolls listed are in good condition, appropriately dressed. Biscaloid ceramic head

18" – 20" ... $1,100.00 – 1,400.00

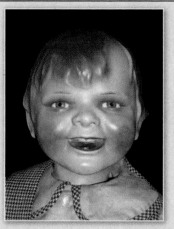

22" Gladdie with biscaloid head, $1,100.00.
Photo courtesy of Withington Auction, Inc.

27" Goebel, $700.00. *Photo courtesy of Glenda Antique Dolls & Collectables.*

23" – 24" ... $1,200.00 – 1,500.00
29" .... $1,500.00 – 1,900.00
Bisque head
14" .... $2,600.00 – 2,800.00
18" – 20" ... $3,800.00 – 4,800.00

WM. AND F. & W. GOEBEL

1867 – 1930 on, Oeslau, Thüringia. Made porcelain and glazed china dolls, as well as bathing dolls, Kewpie-types, and others. Earlier mark was triangle with half moon. Supplied heads to other doll makers including Max Handwerck. Dolls listed are in good condition, appropriately dressed. Exceptional dolls may be more.
Child, 1895
Shoulder head, open mouth, kid or cloth body, glass eyes
24" .... $195.00 – 210.00
Socket head, open mouth, composition body, sleep or set eyes, no mold number or mold 120
7" – 10" .... $150.00 – 200.00
12" – 16" .... $275.00 – 350.00

17" – 23" .... $400.00 – 500.00
25" – 27" .... $600.00 – 700.00
Baby body
13" .... $200.00 – 275.00
Character Child, after 1909
Molded hair, may have flowers or ribbons, painted features, with five-piece papier-mâché body
5½" – 7" .... $300.00 – 500.00
Molded-on bonnet or hat, closed mouth, five-piece papier-mâché body, painted features
9" .... $525.00 – 550.00
Character Baby, after 1909, open mouth, sleep eyes, five-piece bent-leg baby body
13" – 15" .... $425.00 – 600.00
18" – 21" .... $650.00 – 700.00
Toddler body
14" .... $425.00 – 500.00

GOOGLY

Popular 1900 – 1925, various manufacturers. Doll with exaggerated side-glancing eyes. Round eyes were painted, glass, tin, or celluloid, when they move to side they are called flirty eyes. Most doll

Googly

manufacturers of this period made dolls with googly eyes. With painted eyes, they could be painted looking to side or straight ahead; with inserted eyes, the same head can be found with and without flirty eyes. May have closed smiling mouth, composition or papier-mâché body, molded hair or wigged. Dolls listed are in good condition, appropriately dressed. Exceptional dolls can be more. Warning: Many bisque googly dolls are now being reproduced and sold as antique.

All-bisque, jointed shoulders, hips, molded shoes, socks

Painted intaglio eyes, no maker's mark

 3".................... $350.00 – 400.00

 5" – 6"............ $500.00 – 600.00

Rigid neck, glass eyes, no maker's mark

 3".................... $325.00 – 375.00

 4" – 5"............ $500.00 – 600.00

 6" – 7"............ $625.00 – 725.00

Swivel neck, glass eyes, no maker's mark

 5".................... $575.00 – 650.00

 7".................... $875.00 – 950.00

No mold number, jointed knees

 7"............. $2,500.00 – 2,800.00

Marked by maker, Molds 217, 330, 501

 4" – 5"............ $725.00 – 775.00

 6" – 7"............ $900.00 – 950.00

Hertel & Schwab, mold 189

 5" – 6½"....... $800.00 – 1,300.00

5" Kestner, mold 292, all-bisque, $1,100.00. *Photo courtesy of Gloria's Antique Dolls.*

 8"............. $1,500.00 – 1,600.00

Hertwig, molded clothing, wire jointed at shoulders and hips, painted eyes

 4" – 7"............ $100.00 – 125.00

Kestner, mold 111, jointed knees and elbows

 4½" – 6".... $1,000.00 – 1,200.00

Molds 192, 292, .glass eyes, watermelon smile

 4" – 5"....... $1,000.00 –1,200.00

Mold 211, with jointed elbows, knees, neck

 5"............. $2,800.00 – 3,000.00

Too few in database for a reliable range.

 7"............. $3,750.00 – 4,200.00

Too few in database for a reliable range.

6" all-bisque googly with sleep eyes, $700.00. *Photo courtesy of Morphy Auctions.*

11" Our Fairy, $2,100.00. *Photo courtesy of Dolls and Lace.*

Limbach, painted eyes, stiff neck baby, resemble Campbell's kids

    5½" – 7".......... $200.00 – 275.00

Our Fairy, mold 222, ca. 1914, wigged, glass eyes

    4½" – 5"....... $800.00 – 1,000.00

    6" – 7"...... $1,500.00 – 1,800.00

    11"........... $2,000.00 – 2,200.00

Painted eyes, molded hair

    5"................... $450.00 – 550.00

    8"................... $750.00 – 850.00

    12".............. $950.00 – 1,500.00

Peek-a-boo kids, designed by Chloe Preston, 1914 on, bisque immobile with painted features including wide lashes

    1¾" – 2½" .... $35.00 – 50.00

    4" – 5"............ $135.00 – 250.00

Bisque head, painted or glass eyes, composition body

Bähr & Pröschild, marked "B.P.," mold 686, ca. 1914, glass eyes

    10"........... $4,000.00 – 4,200.00

Demacol, made for Dennis Malley & Co., London, bisque socket head, glass eyes, closed watermelon mouth, mohair wig, five-piece composition toddler body

    8" – 13"....... $750.00 – 1,200.00

Goebel, mold 268, others

Painted eyes

    6" – 7"............ $600.00 – 650.00

    9" – 10".......... $800.00 – 850.00

    12".............. $900.00 – 1,000.00

Glass eyes

    7" – 8"......... $900.00 – 1,200.00

    10" – 11".. $1,500.00 – 1,600.00

    13"........... $2,200.00 – 2,500.00

Round open-closed mouth, molded painted hair, toddler body, resembles Recknagel mold 50

    Glass eyes

    9½" .... $3,400.00 – 3,600.00

    Painted eyes

    7"................ $900.00 – 1,050.00

Handwerck, Max

Marked "Elite," molded military helmet, bisque socket head, glass eyes, closed mouth

    10" – 14".. $1,900.00 – 2,100.00

Marked "Elite," molded military helmet, painted eyes, open mouth

    10"........................... $2,600.00*

Marked "Elite," bellhop-style molded hat

    11" – 12".. $2,700.00 – 3,000.00

Hertel, Schwab & Co., 1914 on

Mold 163, solid dome, glass eyes, molded hair, closed smiling mouth, toddler body

    12"........... $4,000.00 – 4,500.00

10" bisque-head googly by Demacol, $1,000.00. *Photo courtesy of Morphy Auctions.*

16"........... $6,700.00 – 7,200.00
21½"....................... $13,000.00
Jubilee, socket head, glass eyes, closed smiling mouth
  Mold 165, toddler
  11" – 12".. $4,000.00 – 7,500.00
  15" – 16" .$6,500.00 – 10,000.00
  Mold 172, baby, solid dome
  11" – 12".. $3,500.00 – 4,000.00
  16"........... $5,000.00 – 6,000.00
Mold 173, solid dome, glass eyes, closed smiling mouth
  Baby
  10" – 11".. $3,500.00 – 3,800.00
  16"........... $5,800.00 – 6,200.00
  Toddler
  10" – 12".. $4,000.00 – 5,000.00
  16"........... $7,000.00 – 7,400.00
Heubach, Ernst
  Molds 262, 264, ca. 1914, "EH" painted eyes, closed mouth
  6" – 8"............ $450.00 – 550.00
  10" – 12"........ $650.00 – 900.00
Mold 291, ca. 1915, "EH" glass eyes, closed mouth
  7" – 9"...... $1,200.00 – 1,400.00
Mold 318, ca. 1920, "EH" character, closed mouth
  11"........... $1,100.00 – 1,285.00
  14"........... $1,900.00 – 2,050.00
Mold 319, ca. 1920, "EH" character, painted eyes, tearful features
  12"........................ $24,000.00*
Mold 417, character, small eye cuts, glass eyes, closed mouth with pursed lips, wigged
  11".................. $750.00 – 900.00
Heubach, Gebrüder
No mold number, painted eyes
  6" – 7"............ $575.00 – 650.00
  9" – 11"....... $800.00 – 1,000.00
  13"........... $1,500.00 – 1,700.00
Mold 8590, painted eyes, molded touseled hair with pronounced curl on top

16"......................... $4,750.00*
Mold 8676, painted eyes
  9"................... $800.00 – 850.00
  11".............. $950.00 – 1,050.00
Mold 8678, glass eyes
  6" – 7"......... $900.00 – 1,000.00
  9" – 11".... $1,400.00 – 1,600.00
Mold 8723, 8995, glass eyes
  13"........... $2,600.00 – 2,900.00
Mold 8764, Einco, shoulder head, glass eyes, closed mouth, for Eisenmann & Co.
  11"........... $4,500.00 – 5,000.00
  18" – 20".. $11,500.00 – 13,500.00
Mold 9056, ca. 1914, square, painted eyes closed mouth
  8"................... $650.00 – 700.00
Mold 9141, winker, one eye painted closed
  7" – 10"....... $900.00 – 1,100.00
Mold 9573, glass eyes
  6" – 8"...... $1,000.00 – 1,100.00
  9" – 11".... $1,500.00 – 2,000.00
Mold 10342, glass eyes, wigged, rosebud mouth
  8" .... $1,300.00 – 1,600.00

7" Gebrüder Heubach, mold 9573, $1,500.00.
Photo courtesy of Gloria's Antique Dolls.

Googly

Kämmer & Reinhardt
Mold 131, ca. 1914, "S&H//K*R," glass eyes, closed mouth

    7" – 8½"...... $4,500.00 – 5,500.00
    13"........... $6,000.00 – 7,000.00
    15" – 16".. $10,000.00 – 12,000.00

Kestner
Mold, 221, ca. 1913, "JDK ges. gesch," character, glass eyes, smiling closed mouth

    7"............. $6,500.00 – 6,700.00
    11" – 13" . $6,000.00 – 10,000.00
    14" – 16".. $12,000.00 – 14,000.00

Kley & Hahn, mold 180, ca. 1915, "K&H" by Hertel Schwab & Co. for Kley & Hahn, character, glass eyes, laughing open-closed mouth

    15"........... $2,700.00 – 3,000.00
    17"........... $3,400.00 – 3,500.00

Lenci: See Lenci section.

Limbach, marked with crown and cloverleaf, socket head, large round glass eyes, pug nose, closed smiling mouth

    7" – 8"...... $1,800.00 – 2,100.00

Armand Marseille
Mold 200, ca. 1911, glass eyes, closed mouth

    8" – 9"...... $1,250.00 – 1,400.00
    11" – 14".. $2,000.00 – 2,500.00

Mold 210, ca. 1911, painted intaglio eyes, character, solid-dome head, painted eyes, closed mouth

    6" – 8"........... $300.00 – 500.00
    11" – 12"........ $800.00 – 900.00

Mold 232, ca. 1913, character, closed mouth

    7"............... $900.00 – 1,200.00
    11"........... $1,200.00 – 1,300.00

Mold 241, ca. 1914, wigged, glass eyes, closed mouth

    9" – 10".... $3,000.00 – 3,600.00

Mold 252, "AM 248," ca. 1912, solid dome, painted intaglio eyes, molded tuft, painted eyes, closed mouth

    9"............. $1,000.00 – 1,200.00

9" Armand Marseille, mold 252, $1,000.00. *Photo courtesy of Skinner, Inc.*

    12" – 15".. $1,800.00 – 1,900.00

Mold 253, "AM Nobbikid Reg. U.S. Pat. 066 Germany," ca. 1925

    6" – 7"...... $1,300.00 – 1,700.00
    9" – 11".... $1,400.00 – 1,800.00

Mold 254, ca. 1912, "AM" dome, painted eyes, closed mouth

    6" .... $575.00 – 650.00
    9".................... $675.00 – 750.00

Mold 320, "AM 255," ca. 1913, dome, painted eyes

    9"................ $900.00 – 1,000.00
    12",.......... $1,200.00 – 1,300.00

Mold 322, "AM," ca. 1914, dome, painted eyes

7" Armand Marseille, 253, $1,700.00. *Photo courtesy of Withington Auction, Inc.*

7" Armand Marseille, 323, $1,100.00. *Photo courtesy of Morphy Auctions.*

6½" Recknagel, mold 46, $375.00. *Photo courtesy of Joan & Lynette Antique Dolls and Accessories.*

8".................. $600.00 – 650.00
11"................. $800.00 – 850.00
Mold 323, 1914 – 1925, glass eyes, also composition
    7" – 9"...... $1,100.00 – 1,200.00
    11" – 12".. $1,100.00 – 1,800.00
Mold 325, ca. 1915, character, closed mouth
    9".................... $675.00 – 725.00
    14".............. $900.00 – 1,000.00
Nippon, baby, painted eyes, five-piece body
    6½" – 7½"...... $100.00 – 150.00
    15" glass eyes with molded tuft of
    hair $567.00*
P.M. Porzellanfabrik Mengersgereuth, ca. 1926, "PM" character, closed mouth, previously thought to be made by Otto Reinecke, mold 950
    6½" – 7"......... $800.00 – 900.00
Recknagel, no mold number, glass eyes
    7" – 8"......... $900.00 – 1,100.00
    10" – 11".. $1,500.00 – 1,600.00
    13"........... $2,200.00 – 2,500.00
Mold 43, intaglio eyes, molded hat and hair tufts, closed mouth
    7" – 8"............. $700.00 – 900.00
Mold 45, 46, 49, 54, 55, intaglio eyes, molded hair, closed mouth

7" – 9"............ $375.00 – 600.00
Mold 50, round open/closed mouth, intaglio eyes, molded hair
    7" – 8"............ $600.00 – 850.00
S.F.B.J.
Mold 245, glass eyes
    7" – 8"...... $4,000.00 – 6,000.00
Fully jointed body
    10"........... $5,800.00 – 6,500.00
Steiner, Hermann, mold 133, ca. 1920, "HS," closed mouth, papier-mâché body
    7" – 8"...... $1,300.00 – 1,500.00
Walthur & Sohn, mold 208, ca. 1920, "W&S" closed mouth, five-piece papier-mâché body, painted socks/shoes
    7" – 9" .... $400.00 – 700.00
Composition face, 1911 – 1914, all-composition head or composition mask face, cloth body, includes Hug Me Kids, Little Bright Eyes, and others.
    9" – 12".... $1,100.00 – 1,500.00

LUDWIG GREINER

1840 – 1874. Succeeded by sons, 1890 – 1900, Philadelphia, Pennsylvania. Papier-mâché shoulder head dolls, with molded hair, painted/glass eyes, usually made up to be large dolls. Dolls listed are in good condition, appropriately dressed.

Some wear is acceptable for these dolls but highly worn condition examples will bring half the value of good condition examples.

21", with 1858 patent label, $1,000.00. *Photo courtesy of Withington Auction, Inc.*

With "1858" label

12" – 13".. $1,100.00 – 1,200.00
15" – 17"........ $800.00 – 950.00
20" – 23".. $1,000.00 – 1,300.00
28" – 30".. $1,400.00 – 1,800.00

Glass eyes

21"........... $2,100.00 – 2,200.00
26"........... $2,500.00 – 2,800.00

With "1872" label

15"................. $300.00 – 400.00
18" – 24"........ $600.00 – 775.00
26" – 30".......... $750.00 – 800.00
32" – 33"........ $700.00 – 750.00

GUND

1898 on, Connecticut and New York. Adolph Gund founded the company, making stuffed toys.

Character

Cloth mask face, painted features, cloth body

19"– 24"......... $175.00 – 225.00

Little Lulu

16"..................... $40.00 – 50.00

Flat-faced cloth

6½"..................... $20.00 – 25.00

Plastic mask face, 1940s – 1950s, cloth body, Perki and others

14" – 16"............ $25.00 – 30.00
21"..................... $35.00 – 40.00

Vinyl mask face, 1950s – 1960s, on plush body, included characters such as Popeye, Disney's Pinocchio, Seven Dwarfs, and others

9" – 12".............. $35.00 – 40.00

Christopher Robin, cloth body

18".................... $75.00 – 100.00

The Now Kids, 1970s, cloth dolls, yarn hair, hippies named Desmond and Rhoda

Pair..................... $50.00 – 60.00

HALF DOLLS

1900 – 1930s, Germany, Japan. Half dolls can be made of bisque, china, composition, or papier-mâché, and were used not only for pincushions but on top of jewelry or cosmetic boxes, brushes, lamps, and numerous other items of decor. The hardest to find have arms molded away from the body as they were easier to break with the limbs in this position and thus fewer survived. Dolls listed are in good condition, add more for extra attributes. Rare examples may bring more. Dolls listed are German except where otherwise noted.

5¼" half doll by Kister, both arms away, exceptional quality, $650.00. *Photo courtesy of Joan & Lynette Antique Dolls and Accessories.*

2½", both arms away and back, $60.00. *Photo courtesy of The Museum Doll Shop.*

Arms Away

Lady, good quality, molded hair, marked by maker or mold number

    3" – 4"............ $100.00 – 140.00
    5" – 6"............ $225.00 – 500.00
    5" Deco style, arms raised above head, hands joined $750.00*
    8".................... $375.00 – 600.00
    12"................. $850.00 – 900.00

Bald head with wig

    4".................... $100.00 – 140.00
    6".................... $150.00 – 210.00

Child, molded hair

    2½".................... $50.00 – 90.00

Elaborate hat or special headwear, or applied decoration in hair

    3½" – 4½"...... $500.00 – 600.00
    5" – 6"............ $500.00 – 600.00
    5" medieval lady by Dressel & Kister
            $2,000.00 – 2,200.00

Galluba and Hoffman, unglazed area at base which flares out, wigged

    4" – 5"............ $450.00 – 600.00
    7½"............. $800.00 – 1,600.00

Holding items in hand, such as letter, flower, book, etc.

    3½" – 4"......... $400.00 – 700.00
    4½" – 5"...... $700.00 – 1,500.00

Flapper

    3½" – 4"......... $150.00 – 300.00
    4½" – 5"......... $200.00 – 400.00

One arm away and back to body, common German type

    2" – 3½"........... $80.00 – 130.00
    4½" – 6½"...... $250.00 – 500.00

Flapper

    2½" – 3".............. $80.00 – 300.00
    4" – 5"............ $400.00 – 600.00

Both arms away and back to body

    2½" – 3½"......... $45.00 – 90.00
    5"..................... $55.00 – 125.00
    7"..................... $60.00 – 130.00

Flapper

    2½" – 4"......... $200.00 – 400.00

Arms in, close to figure

4½" Japanese, arms in, $30.00. *Photo courtesy of Cybermogul Dolls.*

    3" – 4".............. $40.00 – 100.00
    5" – 6".............. $75.00 – 125.00

Bald head, wigged

    3" – 4"................ $50.00 – 60.00
    6"..................... $80.00 – 100.00

Decorated bodice, necklace, fancy hair or holding article

    3" – 5"............ $200.00 – 250.00

Double faced

    2½" – 3½"...... $325.00 – 375.00

Man .... $375.00 – 400.00
Papier-mâché or composition
    2" – 3½".............. $15.00 – 25.00
    5" – 6"................. $35.00 – 45.00
China lady
Marked Japan
    3"....................... $15.00 – 25.00
    6"....................... $40.00 – 50.00
    Occupied Japan
    3"....................... $55.00 – 60.00
Jointed shoulders
China or bisque, molded hair
    3" – 4"................ $50.00 – 80.00
    5" – 7"............ $120.00 – 200.00

20", mold 109, $600.00. *Photo courtesy of Morphy Auctions.*

HEINRICH HANDWERCK

1855 – 1932, Waltershausen, Thüringia, Germany. Made composition doll bodies, sent Handwerck molds to Simon & Halbig to make bisque heads. Trademarks included an eight-point star with French or German wording, a shield, and "Bébé Cosmopolite," "Bébé de Reclame," or "Bébé Superior." Sold dolls through Gimbels, Macy's, Montgomery Ward, and others. Bodies marked "Handwerck" in red on lower back torso. Patented a straight-wrist body. Dolls listed are in good condition, appropriately dressed. Exceptional dolls may be more.

Socket head child, 1885 on. Open mouth, sleep or set eyes, ball-jointed body, bisque socket head, pierced ears, appropriate wig, nicely dressed

Molds 69, 79, 89, 99, 109, 119, or No Number
    10" – 12"........ $600.00 – 650.00
    14" – 16"........ $600.00 – 650.00
    18" – 24"........ $550.00 – 650.00
    26" – 28"........ $700.00 – 800.00
    30" – 33". $1,100.00 – 1,200.00

Mold 79, 89, closed mouth
    15"........... $1,700.00 – 1,800.00
    18" – 20".. $2,200.00 – 2,300.00
    24"........... $2,700.00 – 2,900.00
    41", mold 79............. $4,313.00*
Mold 189, open mouth
    15"................. $800.00 – 850.00
    18" – 22"..... $950.00 – 1,100.00
Bébé Cosmopolite
    19" – 20".. $1,100.00 – 1,300.00
    24" – 28" . $1,200.00 – 1,500.00
Shoulder head child, 1885 on, open mouth,

23", with flirty eyes, no mold number, $700.00. *Photo courtesy of Morphy Auctions.*

glass eyes, kid or cloth body
Molds 139 or no numbers

12"	$125.00 – 150.00
15" – 16"	$175.00 – 225.00
18" – 22"	$250.00 – 300.00
24" – 25"	$325.00 – 350.00

MAX HANDWERCK

1899 – 1928, Waltershausen, Thüringia, Germany. Made dolls and doll bodies, registered trademark, "Bébé Elite."
Used heads made by Goebel.

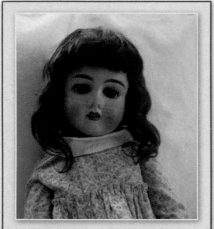

24" Dolly by Max Handwerck, $500.00. *Doll courtesy of Lucy DiTerilzzi.*

Child

Bisque socket head, open mouth, sleep or set eyes, jointed composition body. Size numbers only or molds 283, 285, 286, 291, 297, 307, and others

16" – 18"	$300.00 – 325.00
22" – 26"	$400.00 – 600.00
28" – 32"	$500.00 – 700.00

Bébé Elite, 1900 on, bisque socket head, mohair wig, glass sleep eyes, mohair lashes, open mouth, pierced ears, jointed composition/wood body, marks: "Max Handwerck Bébé Elite 286 12 Germany" on back of head

13" – 15"	$300.00 – 375.00
19" – 21"	$425.00 – 500.00
27" – 29"	$575.00 – 625.00

Googly: See Googly section.

HARD PLASTIC

Hard plastic was developed during WWII and became a staple of the doll industry after the war ended. Numerous companies made hard plastic dolls from 1948 through the 1950s; dolls have all-hard plastic jointed bodies, sleep eyes, lashes, synthetic wig, open or closed mouths. Marks: none, letters, little known, or other unidentified companies.
Hard plastic child, 1950s, maker unknown, some marked U.S.A., original clothing and wig

14" – 16"	$175.00 – 200.00
18" – 20"	$250.00 – 300.00

Advance Doll & Toy Company, 1954 on. Made heavy walking hard plastic dolls, metal rollers on molded shoes, named Winnie and Wanda, later models had vinyl heads

18" – 24"	$100.00 – 125.00

Artisan Novelty Company, 1950s, hard plastic, wide crotch
Raving Beauty

20"	$100.00 – 125.00
Black	$225.00 – 275.00

Duchess Doll Corporation, 1948 – 1950s, made small hard plastic adult dolls, mohair wigs, painted or sleep eyes, jointed arms, stiff or jointed neck, molded and painted shoes, about 7" – 7½" tall, costumes stapled onto body, elaborate costumes, exceptional dolls may be more

7"	$15.00 – 20.00

Eugenia Doll Co., 1950s, New York City

18" – 20".......... $90.00 – 150.00

Fortune Doll Company, a subsidiary of the Beehler Arts Company

Pam (Ginny-type), hard plastic, sleep eyes, synthetic wig, closed mouth

8"....................... $35.00 – 55.00

Furga, Italy

Simonna outfit, MIB

1967 .... $300.00 – 330.00

Imperial Crown Toy Co. (Impco), 1950s, made hard plastic or vinyl dolls, rooted hair, synthetic wigs

Hard plastic walker

14".................... $45.00 – 55.00

20"................... $85.00 – 100.00

Vinyl

16"..................... $55.00 – 65.00

Kendall Company

Miss Curity, 1953, hard plastic, jointed only at shoulders, blond wig, blue sleep eyes, molded-on shoes, painted stockings, uniform sheet vinyl, "Miss Curity" marked in blue on hat

7½"..................... $30.00 – 40.00

Nun doll, all hard plastic, sleep eyes, unmarked

12"..................... $45.00 – 65.00

17"................. $100.00 – 125.00

Pedigree Dolls & Toys, England, 1950s on, made hard plastic and vinyl dolls

Posey Walker, walker, sleep eyes, wig

20" – 22"....... $100.00 – 120.00

Roberta Doll Co.

Walker

17"..................... $75.00 – 85.00

Roddy of England, 1950 – 1960s, made by D.G. Todd & Co. Ltd., Southport, England, hard plastic walker, sleep or set eyes

11" – 12½"..... $100.00 – 160.00

22"................. $175.00 – 225.00

Rosebud of England, 1950s – 1960s, started in Raunds, Northamptonshire, England, by T. Eric Smith shortly after WWII

Miss Rosebud, hard plastic, various shades of blue sleep eyes, glued-on mohair wig, jointed at the neck and hips, marked "Miss Rosebud" in script on her back and head and "MADE IN ENGLAND" on her upper back, more for rare examples or mint-in-box dolls

7½"................. $95.00 – 115.00

Ross Products

Tina Cassini, designed by Oleg Cassini, hard plastic, marked on back torso, "TINA CASSINI," clothes tagged "Made in British Crown Colony of Hong Kong"

12"................. $175.00 – 200.00

Costume, MIB .... $100.00 – 125.00

Royal Doll Co.

Hard plastic girl, 1950s, similar to Sweet Sue by American Character

Wearing formal

20"................. $200.00 – 225.00

Virga, a subsidiary of the Beehler Arts Company, marketed Ginny-type dolls under various lines such as Playmates, Lolly Pop, Play-Pals, Lucy, and Schiaparelli Go-Go

Lolly Pop dolls, hair colors such as pink, blue,

22" Posey Walker by Pedigree, $120.00. *Photo courtesy of Alderfer Auction & Appraisal.*

bright yellow
8".................... $60.00 – 120.00

HARTLAND PLASTICS

1954 – 1963, Hartland, Wisconsin. Made action figures and horses, many figures from Warner Brothers television productions. Purchased by Revlon Cosmetics in 1963 and stopped making toys. Others have bought the molds and make these products today. Dolls discussed here are the 1954 to 1963 dolls. Values listed are for good condition with approriate accessories, MIB can bring double. Television or movie characters, 8"

Annie Oakley, 1953 – 1956, played by Gail Davis in *Annie Oakley*
8" ... $160.00 – 200.00 with horse

Bret Maverick, ca. 1958, played by James Garner in *Maverick*
8".................... $200.00 – 250.00

Clint Bonner, 1957 – 1959, played by John Payne in *The Restless Gun*
8".................... $100.00 – 120.00

Colonel Ronald MacKenzie, ca. 1950s, played by Richard Carlson in *Mackenzie's Raiders*
8".... $325.00 – 350.00 with horse

Dale Evans, ca. 1958, #802, with horse, Buttermilk, from *The Roy Rogers Show*
8".................... $75.00 – 125.00

Davy Crockett, 1956, played by Fess Parker
8".... $150.00 – 200.00 with horse

Jim Hardie, 1958, played by Dale Robertson in *Tales of Wells Fargo*
8".................... $125.00 – 150.00

Josh Randall, ca. 1950s, played by Steve McQueen in *Wanted Dead or Alive*
8".... $300.00 – 400.00 with horse

Major Seth Adams, 1957 – 1961, #824, played by Ward Bond in *Wagon Train*
8".................... $100.00 with horse

Paladin, 1957 – 1963, played by Richard Boone in *Have Gun, Will Travel*
8".... $160.00 – 180.00 with horse

Roy Rogers, ca. 1955, and Trigger, from *The Roy Rogers Show*
8".................... $125.00 – 175.00
With Trigger.................... $485.00

The Rifleman, Chuck Connors
8".................... $125.00 – 140.00

Sgt. Lance O'Rourke RCMP
8"...... $90.00 – 140.00 with horse

Sgt. William Preston, ca. 1958, #804, played by Richard Simmons in *Sgt. Preston of the Yukon*
8".... $250.00 – 265.00 with horse

Tom Jeffords, ca. 1958 – 1961 played by John Lupton
8".... $225.00 – 255.00 with horse

Other figures
Brave Eagle, #812, and horse, White Cloud
Buffalo Bill, #819, Pony Express Rider
Chief Thunderbird and horse, Northwind
Cochise, #815, with pinto horse from *Broken Arrow*
General George Custer, #814, and horse, Bugler
General George Washington, #815, and horse, Ajax
General Robert E. Lee, #808, and horse, Traveler
Jim Bowie, #817, with horse, Blaze
Lone Ranger, #801, and horse, Silver
Tonto, #805, and horse, Scout
8".................... $200.00 – 225.00

All others
8"............$125.00 – 225.00 each

CARL HARTMANN

1889 – 1930s, Neustadt, Germany. Made and exported bisque and celluloid dolls, especially small dolls in regional costumes, called Globe Babies.

Child, bisque socket head, open mouth, jointed composition and wood body

    22" – 24"........ $450.00 – 625.00

Globe Baby, bisque socket head, glass sleep eyes, open mouth, four teeth, mohair or human hair wig, five-piece papier-mâché or composition body with painted shoes and stockings

    8"................... $325.00 – 375.00

    12"................. $400.00 – 425.00

KARL HARTMANN

1911 – 1926, Stockheim, Germany. Doll factory, made and exported dolls. Advertised ball-jointed dolls, characters, and papier-mâché dolls. Marked "KH."

Child, bisque socket head, open mouth, glass eyes, composition body

No mold number

    18" – 22"........ $275.00 – 300.00

    24" – 26"........ $400.00 – 475.00

    27" – 32"........ $575.00 – 625.00

Mold 283, 287

25" Karl Hartmann, $450.00. *Photo courtesy of Morphy Auctions.*

22 – 24"........ $350.00 – 400.00

HASBRO

1923, Pawtucket, Rhode Island. Founded by the Hassenfeld Brothers. Began making toys in 1943. One of their most popular toys was the G.I. Joe series which came out in 1964. Dolls listed are in good condition with original clothing and accessories, mint-in-package usually bring double the values listed. Dolls in played-with condition bring one-third to one-half the value of complete examples.

Aimee, 1972, rooted hair, amber sleep eyes, jointed vinyl body, long dress, sandals, earrings

    18"..................... $30.00 – 40.00

Baby Alive, 1992, eats, drinks, wets, vinyl

    14"..................... $30.00 – 35.00

Bridal Sewing Set, 1950s, hard plastic dolls (6"), boxed with fabric and sewing supplies

    Complete set.... $135.00 – 165.00

Charlie's Angels, 1977, vinyl, Jill, Sabrina, Kelly, Kris

    8½"..................... $18.00 – 20.00

    Set of three .... $70.00 – 80.00

Dolly Darlings, 1965

    4½" ....$35.00 – 40.00 each

4½" Dolly Darlings, Fancy Pants, by Hasbro, MOC, $75.00. *Photo courtesy of The Museum Doll Shop.*

11" Kristen, from Maxie line, $22.00. *Photo courtesy of The Museum Doll Shop.*

9" Love, from the World of Love series, c. 1971, $40.00. *Photo courtesy of The Museum Doll Shop.*

John and His pets .... $45.00 – 50.00
Flying Nun
    4⅞",.................... $45.00 – 55.00
    12"................. $125.00 – 135.00
Jem: See Jem listings in this section.
Leggie, 1972
    10"..................... $30.00 – 40.00
Black, 11".................... $50.00 – 60.00
Little Miss No Name, 1965
    15"................. $125.00 – 150.00
Maxie, 1987, and her friends Rob, Ashley, Kimberly and others, vinyl fashion doll
    11½".................. $18.00 – 25.00
My Buddy, 1985, vinyl and cloth boy
    24"................. $100.00 – 125.00
My Buddy's Kid Sister
    20"...................... $40.00 – 50.00
Peteena Poodle, 1966, vinyl fashion doll poodle
    9½"................ $225.00 – 275.00
Pippi Longstocking, 1973, vinyl
    12"...................... $20.00 – 30.00
Real Baby, 1984, designed by J. Turner
    18"...................... $40.00 – 60.00
Show Biz Babies, 1967, 4"

Mama Cass Elliott..... $150.00 – 180.00
Bobby Gentry .... $125.00 – 150.00
Monkees
Individual ,.................... $75.00 – 80.00
Set of four .... $325.00 – 350.00
Storykins, 1967, 3", includes Cinderella, Goldilocks, Prince Charming, Rumpelstiltskin, Sleeping Beauty....$35.00 – 45.00 each
Snow White and Dwarfs
    Set...................... $60.00 – 75.00
Sweet Cookie, 1972, vinyl, with cooking accessories
    18"................. $100.00 – 125.00
World of Love Dolls, 1971
Love, Peace, or Flower
    9"...................... $28.00 – 35.00
Soul (black).................. $60.00 – 65.00
Adam......................... $30.00 – 40.00
G.I. Joe action figures, 1964, hard plastic head with facial scar, painted hair and no beard. Dolls listed are in good condition with original clothing and accessories, MIB can bring double the values listed.
G.I. Joe Action Soldier, flocked hair, Army

fatigues, brown jump boots, green plastic cap, training manual, metal dog tag, two sheets of stickers

11½".............. $200.00 – 275.00

Painted hair .... $200.00 – 250.00

Black................ $250.00 – 300.00

Green Beret, teal green fatigue jacket, four pockets, pants, Green Beret cap with red unit flashing, M-16 rifle, 45 automatic pistol with holster, tall brown boots, four grenades, camouflage scarf, and field communication set

11".................. $150.00 – 200.00

G.I. Joe Action Marine, camouflage shirt, pants, brown boots, green plastic cap, metal dog tag, insignia stickers, and training manual

11".................. $150.00 – 225.00

G.I. Joe Action Sailor, blue chambray work shirt, blue denim work pants, black boots, white plastic sailor cap, dog tag, rank insignia stickers

11".................. $200.00 – 250.00

G.I. Joe Action Pilot, orange flight suit, black boots, dog tag, stickers, blue cap, training manual

11".................. $200.00 – 300.00

Dolls only, nude .... $100.00 – 125.00

G.I. Joe Action Soldier of the World, 1966, figures in this set may have any hair and eye color combination, no scar on face, hard plastic heads

Australian Jungle Fighter

$395.00 – 450.00

British Commando, boxed

$525.00 – 600.00

French Resistance Fighter

$425.00 – 500.00

German Storm Trooper

$500.00 – 600.00

Japanese Imperial Soldier

$500.00 – 600.00

Russian Infantryman.. $475.00 – 500.00

Talking G.I. Joe, 1967 – 1969, talking mechanism added, semi-hard vinyl head, marks: "G.I. Joe®//Copyright 1964//By Hasbro®//Pat. No. 3,277,602//Made in U.S.A."

Talking G.I. Joe Action Marine, camouflage fatigues, metal dog tag, Marine training manual, insignia sheets, brown boots, green plastic cap, comic, and insert

$385.00 – 400.00

Talking G.I. Joe Action Pilot, blue flight suit, black boots, dog tag, Air Force insignia, blue cap, training manual, comic book, insert

$460.00 – 500.00

Talking G.I. Joe Action Sailor, denim pants, chambray sailor shirt, dog tag, black boots, white sailor cap, insignia stickers, Navy training manual, illustrated talking comic book, insert examples of figure's speech

$475.00 – 500.00

Talking G.I. Joe Action Soldier, green fatigues, dog tag, brown boots, insignia, stripes, green plastic fatigue cap, comic book, insert with examples of figure's speech

$330.00 – 360.00

G.I. Joe Action Nurse, 1967, vinyl head, blond rooted hair, jointed hard plastic body, nurse's uniform, cap, red cross armband, white shoes, medical bag, stethoscope, plasma bottle, two crutches, bandages, splints, marks: "Patent Pending//©1967 Hasbro®//Made in Hong Kong"

$900.00 – 1,000.00

G.I. Joe, Man of Action, 1970 – 1975, flocked hair, scar on face, dressed in fatigues with Adventure Team emblem on shirt, plastic cap, marks: "G.I. Joe®//Copyright 1964// By Hasbro®//Pat. No. 3, 277, 602//Made in U.S. A."

Kung Fu Grip .... $250.00 – 300.00

Talking .... $300.00 – 400.00

G.I. Joe, Adventure Team, marks: "©1975 Hasbro ®//Pat. Pend. Pawt. R.I.," flocked hair and beard, six team members:

Hasbro

11" G.I. Joe Adventurer, ca. 1970, $400.00.
Photo courtesy of McMasters Harris Auction Co.

Air Adventurer, orange flight suit
$265.00 – 285.00
Astronaut, talking, white flight suit, molded scar, dog tag, pull-string
$150.00 – 200.00
Land Adventurer, black, tan fatigues, beard, flocked hair, scar ..... $275.00 – 300.00
Land Adventurer, talking, camouflage fatigues .... $200.00 – 225.00
Sea Adventurer, light blue shirt, navy pants
$250.00 – 300.00
Talking Adventure Team Commander, flocked hair, beard, green jacket, and pants
$400.00 – 450.00
G.I. Joe Land Adventurer, flocked hair, beard, camouflage shirt, green pants
$100.00 – 150.00
G. I. Joe Negro Adventurer, flocked hair
$250.00 – 300.00
G. I. Joe, "Mike Powers, Atomic Man"
$45.00 – 55.00
G.I. Joe Eagle Eye Man of Action
$100.00 – 125.00
G.I. Joe Secret Agent, unusual face, mustache
$400.00 – 450.00
Sea Adventurer w/Kung Fu Grip
$125.00 – 145.00

Bulletman, muscle body, silver arms, hands, helmet, red boots ..... $100.00 – 125.00
Others
G.I. Joe Air Force Academy, Annapolis, or West Point Cadet ..... $350.00 – 400.00
G.I. Joe Secret Service Agent, limited edition of 200 .... $225.00 – 275.00
Accessory sets, mint, no doll included
Adventures of G.I. Joe
Adventure of the Perilous Rescue
$250.00
Adventure Caprure of the Pygmy Gorilla
$130.00
Eight Ropes of Danger Adventure
$200.00
Fantastic Free Fall Adventure
$275.00
Hidden Missile Discovery Adventure
$150.00
Mouth of Doom Adventure.. $150.00
Accessory packs or boxed uniforms and accessories
Air Force, Annapolis, West Point Cadet
$200.00
Action Sailor $350.00
Astronaut $250.00
Crash Crew Fire Fighter $275.00

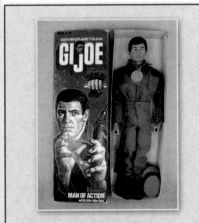

G.I. Joe with Kung Fu grip, ca. 1974, $500.00.
Photo courtesy of McMasters Harris Auction Co.

Deep Freeze with Sled $250.00
Deep Sea Diver $250.00
Frogman Demolition Set........... $375.00
Green Beret $450.00
Landing Signal Officer.............. $250.00
Marine Jungle Fighter............... $850.00
Marine Mine Detector............... $275.00
Military Police $325.00
Pilot Scramble Set ......:............ $275.00
Rescue Diver $350.00
Secret Agent $150.00
Shore Patrol........................... $300.00
Ski Patrol............................... $350.00

G.I. Joe vehicles and other accessories, mint in package

Adventure Team Helicopter, yellow . $70.00
Amphibious Duck, green plastic, Irwin
$600.00
Armored Car, green plastic, one figure
$150.00
Crash Crew Fire Truck, blue.... $1,400.00
Desert Patrol Attack Jeep, tan, one figure
$1,400.00
Footlocker, with accessories .... $400.00+
Iron Knight Tank, green plastic
$1,400.00
Jeep Combat Set $200.00
Jet Aeroplane, dark blue plastic .. $550.00
Jet Helicopter, green, yellow blades
$350.00
Motorcycle and Side Car, Irwin
$225.00
Personnel Carrier and Mine Sweeper
$700.00
Sea Sled and Frogman $325.00
Space Capsule and Suit, gray plastic
$425.00
Staff Car, four figures, green plastic, Irwin
$900.00

Jem, 1986 – 1987
Jem dolls were patterned after characters in the animated *Jem* television series, ca. 1985 – 1988, and include a line of 27 dolls. All-vinyl fashion-type with realistically proportioned body, jointed elbows, wrists, and knees, swivel waist, rooted hair, painted eyes, open or closed mouth, and hole in bottom of each foot. All boxes say "Jem" and "Truly Outrageous!" Most came with cassette tape of music from *Jem* cartoon, plastic doll stand, poster, and hair pick. All 12½" tall, except Starlight Girls, 11". Dolls listed are in excellent condition, wearing complete original outfits. MIB can bring double.

Jem and Rio
Jem/Jerrica, 1st issue
4000 .... $25.00 – 35.00
Jem/Jerrica, star earrings
$50.00 – 60.00
Glitter 'n Gold Jem
4001 .... $25.00 – 45.00
Rock 'n Curl Jem
4002 .... $25.00 – 30.00
Flash 'n Sizzle Jem
4003 .... $48.00 – 56.00
Rio, 1st issue
4015 .... $25.00 – 40.00
Glitter 'n Gold Rio
4016 .... $25.00 – 30.00
Glitter 'n Gold Rio, pale vinyl
4016 .... $125.00 – 150.00

Holograms
Synergy
4200 .... $40.00 – 50.00
Aja, 1st issue
4201/4005 .... $32.00 – 40.00
Aja, 2nd issue
4201/4005 .... $100.00 – 125.00
Kimber, 1st issue
4202/4005 .... $32.00 – 40.00
Kimber, 2nd issue
4202/4005 .... $60.00 – 70.00
Shana, 1st issue
4203/4005 .... $32.00 – 40.00
Shana, 2nd issue
4203/4005 .... $200.00 – 250.00

Danse

4208 .... $50.00 – 55.00

Video

4209 .... $25.00 – 30.00

Raya

4210 .... $125.00 – 150.00

Starlight Girls, 11", no wrist or elbow joints Ashley (4211/4025), Krissie (4212/4025), or Banee (4213/4025).$30.00 – 35.00 each

Misfits

Pizzazz, 1st issue

4204/4010 .... $50.00 – 60.00

Pizzazz, 2nd issue

4204/4010 .... $45.00 – 55.00

Stormer, 1st issue

4205/4010 .... $50.00 – 60.00

Stormer, 2nd issue

4205/4010 .... $60.00 – 80.00

Roxy, 1st issue

4206/4010 .... $55.00 – 60.00

Roxy, 2nd issue

4206/4010 .... $40.00 – 50.00

Clash

4207/4010 .... $20.00 – 30.00

Jetta

4214 .... $50.00 – 65.00

Accessories

Concert Clash game, by Milton Bradley,

1986.................................. $25.00

Glitter 'n Gold

Roadster .... $100.00 – 150.00

Rock 'n Roadster........... $35.00 – 40.00

Jem Guitar.....................$30.00 – 40.00

Backstager................... $30.00 – 35.00

Star Stage .... $40.00 – 45.00

MTV jacket (promo) .. $100.00 – 125.00

Jem fashions

Prices reflect NRFB (never removed from box or card), with excellent packaging. Damaged boxes or mint and complete, no packaging prices are approximately 25 percent less.

$32.00 – 60.00

HERTEL, SCHWAB & CO.

1910 – 1930s, Stutzhaus, Germany. Porcelain factory founded by August Hertel and Heinrich Schwab, both designed doll heads used by Borgfeldt, Kley and Hahn, Koenig & Wernicke, Louis Wolf, and others. Made china and bisque heads as well as all-porcelain, most with character faces. Molded hair or wigs, painted blue or glass eyes (often blue-gray), open mouth with tongue or closed mouth, socket or shoulder heads. Usually marked with mold number and "Made in Germany" or mark of company that owned the mold.

Baby, 1910 on, bisque head, molded hair or wig, open or open-closed mouth, teeth, sleep or painted eyes, bent-leg baby composition body

Mold 130, 142, 150, 151, 152, 159

9" – 12".......... $275.00 – 325.00

15" – 16"........ $350.00 – 400.00

19" – 21"........ $450.00 – 600.00

22" – 24"........ $600.00 – 650.00

10", mold 142, $300.00. *Photo courtesy of Cybermogul Dolls.*

11½" character mold 134, $3,000.00. *Photo courtesy of Gloria's Antique Dolls.*

Toddler body
14".................. $450.00 – 500.00
20".................. $750.00 – 850.00
Mold 125 (so-called Patsy Baby)
12".................. $800.00 – 900.00
Mold 126 (so-called Skippy Baby)
9".................... $825.00 – 875.00
Child
Mold 111, character face, closed mouth, glass sleep eyes, wigged
11"........... $7,200.00 – 7,400.00
17" – 18" .$16,000.00 – 17,000.00
Mold 127, ca. 1915, character face, solid dome with molded hair, sleep eyes, open mouth, Patsy-type
15"........... $1,350.00 – 1,450.00
17"........... $2,000.00 – 2,400.00
Mold 131, ca. 1912, character face, solid dome, painted closed mouth
18"............................. $1,300.00
Too few in database for a reliable range.
Mold 134, ca. 1915, character face, sleep eyes, closed mouth
15"........... $3,500.00 – 4,000.00
Mold 136, ca. 1912, "Made in Germany," character face, open mouth

7".................... $325.00 – 375.00
18" – 20"........ $400.00 – 450.00
24" – 25" .... $500.00 – 600.00
Mold 140, ca. 1912, character, glass eyes, open-closed laughing mouth
12" – 15".. $3,400.00 – 4,200.00
Mold 141, ca. 1912, character, painted eyes, open-closed mouth
12" – 14".. $2,800.00 – 3,300.00
17" – 18".. $7,400.00 – 9,000.00
Mold 178, character, open-closed mouth, wigged, ball-jointed body
6" – 7"............ $375.00 – 435.00
Mold 182, dolly-faced doll, open mouth, wigged, ball-jointed body
18" – 23"........ $600.00 – 700.00
Googly: See Googly section.

HERTWIG & CO.

1864 – 1940s, Kutzhütte, Thüringia, Germany. Porcelain factory producing china and bisque dolls. Some distributed by Butler Brothers. Half-bisque dolls, 1911 on, bisque head and torso, molded clothing, lower body cloth, lower arms and legs bisque
Child
4½"................ $175.00 – 200.00

10 – 10½" bonnet head dolls, $200.00 – 225.00 each. For values on Hertwig Bonnet Head dolls, see Bonnet Head section. *Photo courtesy of McMasters Harris Auction Co.*

7" all-bisque pair, $450.00. *Photo courtesy of McMasters Harris Auction Co.*

Adult

   6½"................ $300.00 – 325.00

All bisque: including animals in crochet outfits, see all-bisque German section.

China Name Dolls: See China or Glazed Porcelain Head section.

Bisque Bonnet Head: See Bonnet Head section.

ERNST HEUBACH

   1887 – 1930s, Köppelsdorf, Germany. In 1919, the son of Armand Marseille married the daughter of Ernst Heubach and merged the two factories. Mold numbers range from 250 to 452. They made porcelain heads for Dressel (Jutta), Revalo, and others. Dolls listed are in good condition, appropriately dressed.

Child, 1888 on

Mold 1900, 225, 275, or Horseshoe mark, shoulder head, open mouth, glass eyes, kid or cloth body

   10" – 12".......... $95.00 – 110.00

   18" – 22"........ $180.00 – 220.00

   26"................. $275.00 – 300.00

Molds 250, 251, 302, and others, socket head, composition body, open mouth, glass eyes

   8" – 10".......... $200.00 – 275.00

8" – 9" on flapper body

                     $325.00 – 375.00

   13" – 15"........ $225.00 – 250.00

   16" – 19"........ $300.00 – 350.00

   23" – 25"........ $350.00 – 475.00

   27" – 32"........ $400.00 – 495.00

   36"................. $550.00 – 650.00

Painted bisque

   8" – 12"............ $90.00 – 100.00

   16"................. $125.00 – 150.00

Baby, 1910 on, open mouth, glass eyes, socket head, wig, five-piece bent-leg composition body, add more for toddler body, flirty eyes

Molds 300, 320, 321, 342, and others

   5" – 6½"......... $250.00 – 275.00

   8" – 11".......... $200.00 – 225.00

   14" – 17"........ $300.00 – 375.00

   19" – 21"........ $400.00 – 475.00

   25" – 27"........ $525.00 – 650.00

Painted bisque, flirty eyes

   16" – 24"........ $375.00 – 500.00

Character child, 1910 on, painted eyes

Molds 261, 262, 271, and others, bisque shoulder head, cloth body

   12"................. $300.00 – 400.00

Mold 312 (for Seyfarth & Reinhard)

   14"................. $275.00 – 300.00

   18"................. $350.00 – 375.00

24", mold 250, $425.00. *Photo courtesy of McMasters Harris Auction Co.*

32" Mold 267, $600.00. *Photo courtesy of McMasters Harris Auction Co.*

28"................. $500.00 – 550.00
Mold 417, glass eyes, resembles Armand Marseille's Just Me
    11" – 12".. $1,200.00 – 1,400.00
Baby, Newborn, 1925 on solid dome, molded and painted hair, glass eyes, closed mouth, cloth body, composition or celluloid hands
Molds 338, 339, 340, 348, 349
    10" – 12"........ $375.00 – 425.00
    14" – 16"........ $475.00 – 575.00
    17"................. $600.00 – 650.00
Black, mold 444
    12"................,..... $375.00 – 425.00

GEBRÜDER HEUBACH

1910 – 1938, Lichte, Thüringia, Germany. Porcelain factory founded in 1804 but did not make dolls until 1910. Made bisque heads and all-bisque dolls, characters, either socket or shoulder head, molded hair or wigs, sleeping or intaglio eyes, in heights from 4" to 26". Provided heads to other companies including Bauersachs, Cuno & Oto Dressel, Eisemann & Co., and Gebruder Ohlhaver. Mold numbers from 556 to 10633. Sunburst or square marks, more dolls

12½" lady, $2,400.00. *Photo courtesy of The Museum Doll Shop.*

with square marks. Dolls listed are in good condition, appropriately dressed.
Marked "Heubach," no mold number
Closed mouth, intaglio eyes, wigged
    8".................... $400.00 – 700.00
Closed-mouth pouty, intaglio eyes
    6½" .... $150.00 – 200.00
    14" .... $500.00 – 600.00
Smile, painted eyes
    15"........... $3,400.00 – 3,500.00
Lady doll, open or closed mouth, glass eyes, mold 76325, 7635, 7925, 7926, others
    10" – 11".. $2,000.00 – 2,400.00
    14" – 16".. $3,800.00 – 4,400.00
Animal head, bears, cats, etc. on five-piece composition child doll bodies
    6" – 8"...... $1,600.00 – 1,800.00
Marked "Heubach Googly": See Googly section.
Character Child
Shoulder head
Mold 5777, Dolly Dimple, shoulder head version

151

Gebrüder Heubach

7" shoulder head dolls, mold 6692, $750.00 pair. *Photo courtesy of Morphy Auctions.*

17" – 19".. $1,600.00 – 1,700.00
Mold 6692, ca. 1912, shoulder head version, sunburst, intaglio eyes, closed-mouth pouty
    14" – 16"........ $700.00 – 750.00
    20"................. $875.00 – 900.00
Mold 6736, ca. 1912, square mark, painted eyes, laughing mouth
    12" – 13"........ $500.00 – 700.00
    16"........... $1,100.00 – 1,200.00
Mold 7072, ca. 1912, closed mouth, molded hair, painted eyes

13", mold 6692 with flocked hair, $700.00. *Photo courtesy of Morphy Auctions.*

    22"................. $750.00 – 850.00
Mold 7644, ca. 1910, "Our Pet," sunburst or square mark, painted eyes, open-closed laughing mouth
    9" – 10".......... $350.00 – 400.00
    14"................. $750.00 – 850.00
    17"........... $1,000.00 – 1,100.00
    20"........... $1,450.00 – 1,550.00
Mold 7844, ca. 1912, open-closed laughing mouth, molded hair, intaglio eyes
    12" – 13"........ $275.00 – 300.00
Mold 7850, ca. 1912, "Coquette," open-closed mouth
    10" – 12"........ $550.00 – 650.00
    15"................. $625.00 – 675.00
Mold 7851, ca. 1912, open-closed mouth, molded hair with molded bow, upward side-glancing intaglio eyes
    16"............................ $1,800.00
Too few in database for a reliable range.
Mold 7853, ca. 1912, downcast eyes
    14"........... $1,600.00 – 1,800.00
Mold 8191, baby, solid dome with molded hair, open-closed mouth, intaglio eyes
    8" – 12".......... $700.00 – 875.00
Mold 8221, square mark, dome, intaglio eyes, open-closed mouth
    14"................. $650.00 – 700.00
Mold 8457, Princess Angeline, Native American woman, wrinkled face, downcast eyes, wigged, believed to be a portrait of the daughter of Chief Seattle
    13"......... $7,500.00 – 10,000.00
Mold 8724, closed mouth, intaglio eyes, hair molded with tufts
    12"............................... $650.00
Too few in database for a reliable range.
Mold 8792, closed mouth, intaglio eyes, hair molded
    16"................. $750.00 – 800.00
Too few in database for a reliable range.
Mold 9355, ca. 1914, square mark, glass eyes, open mouth

Gebrüder Heubach

13".................. $800.00 – 850.00

19"........... $1,100.00 – 1,250.00

Socket head

Mold 5636, ca. 1912, glass eyes, open-closed laughing mouth, teeth

    12" – 13".. $1,700.00 – 1,800.00

    15" – 18".. $2,300.00 – 2,600.00

Mold 5689, ca. 1912, sunburst mark, smiling open mouth

    14"........... $1,600.00 – 1,700.00

    17"........... $2,000.00 – 2,100.00

    22"........... $2,700.00 – 2,800.00

Mold 5730, "Santa," ca. 1912, sunburst mark, made for Hamburger & Co.

    16"........... $1,600.00 – 1,700.00

    19" – 22".. $1,900.00 – 2,100.00

    24" – 26".. $2,400.00 – 2,600.00

Mold 5777, "Dolly Dimple," ca. 1913, open mouth, for Hamburger & Co.

    12" – 14".. $2,400.00 – 2,500.00

    16" – 19".. $2,800.00 – 3,000.00

    22" – 24".. $3,200.00 – 3,400.00

Mold 6682, intaglio eyes, closed mouth

    14".................. $350.00 – 400.00

Mold 6894, intaglio eyes, closed mouth

    9" – 12".......... $400.00 – 450.00

Mold 6969, ca. 1912, socket head, square mark, glass eyes, closed mouth

    7" – 9"...... $1,050.00 – 1,250.00

    12" – 13".. $2,100.00 – 2,200.00

    16" – 18".. $2,600.00 – 2,800.00

    20" – 24".. $3,100.00 – 3,700.00

Mold 6970, ca. 1912, sunburst, glass eyes, closed mouth

    7" – 9"............ $850.00 – 950.00

    12" – 13".. $2,800.00 – 3,000.00

    16" – 18".. $3,000.00 – 3,300.00

    20" – 24".. $3,500.00 – 3,900.00

Mold 7246, 7247, 7248, ca. 1912, sunburst or square mark, closed mouth, glass eyes

    7" – 10".......... $800.00 – 900.00

    12" – 13".. $1,900.00 – 2,200.00

    16" – 18".. $3,000.00 – 3,400.00

11", mold 7763, Coquette socket head character, $900.00. *Photo courtesy of Withington Auction, Inc.*

    20" – 24".. $3,900.00 – 4,100.00

    26" – 28".. $4,300.00 – 4,900.00

Mold 7407, character, glass eyes, open-closed mouth

    7" – 9"............ $850.00 – 950.00

    12" – 13".. $2,100.00 – 2,400.00

    16" – 18".. $3,100.00 – 3,500.00

    20" – 24".. $4,100.00 – 4,900.00

Mold 7602, 7603, ca. 1912, molded hair tufts, intaglio eyes

    10" – 12"........ $600.00 – 700.00

    15" – 18"........ $750.00 – 950.00

Mold 7604, ca. 1912, open-closed mouth, intaglio eyes

    12" – 14"........ $650.00 – 700.00

    20"........... $1,100.00 – 1,200.00

Mold 7608, pouty

    9".................... $400.00 – 500.00

Mold 7622, 7623, ca. 1912, intaglio eyes, closed or open-closed mouth

    16" – 18".. $1,100.00 – 1,300.00

Mold 7633, ca. 1912, laughing child, glass eyes

    12" – 13".. $1,700.00 – 1,800.00

    15" – 18".. $2,300.00 – 2,600.00

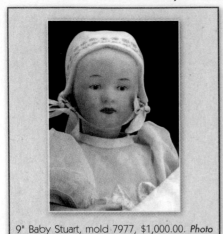

9" Baby Stuart, mold 7977, $1,000.00. *Photo courtesy of Morphy Auctions.*

Mold 7711, ca. 1912, glass eyes, open mouth, flapper body

    9" – 10".... $1,000.00 – 1,200.00
    18"........... $6,000.00 – 7,000.00

Mold 7759, ca. 1912, dome, painted eyes, closed mouth

    12"................. $800.00 – 900.00

Molds 7763, 7788, 7850 (Coquette), ca. 1912, molded hair with bow

    11"................. $900.00 – 950.00
    14" – 15".. $1,100.00 – 1,300.00
    20"........... $1,500.00 – 1,600.00

Mold 7911, ca. 1912, intaglio eyes, laughing open-closed mouth

    9" – 11".......... $775.00 – 850.00
    15" – 16".. $1,100.00 – 1,200.00

Mold 8145, small side-glancing intaglio eyes, molded hair

    20"......................... $11,258.00*

Mold 8178, intaglio eyes, open-closed mouth, wigged

    7½"............... $275.00 – 325.00

Mold 8191, "Crooked Smile," ca. 1912, square mark, intaglio eyes, laughing mouth

    11½"........ $1,200.00 – 1,300.00
    14"........... $1,500.00 – 1,600.00
    16"........... $2,800.00 – 3,000.00

Mold 8192, ca. 1914, sunburst or square mark, sleep eyes, open mouth

    11" – 13"..... $900.00 – 1,000.00
    16" – 20".. $1,500.00 – 2,100.00

Mold 8317, wig, open-closed smiling mouth, eight teeth, glass eyes

    16"........... $3,200.00 – 3,400.00
    19"........... $4,600.00 – 4,800.00

Mold 8381, "Princess Juliana," molded hair, ribbon, painted eyes, closed mouth

    14" – 16".. $10,000.00 – 13,000.00

Mold 8413, ca. 1914, wig, sleep eyes, open-closed mouth with teeth

    16" .... $2,800.00 – 3,437.00

Mold 8429, square mark, closed mouth

    15"............................ $2,500.00

Too few in database for a reliable range.

Mold 8774, "Whistling Jim," ca. 1914, smoker or whistler, square mark, flange neck, intaglio eyes, molded hair, cloth body, bellows

    9"............. $1,000.00 – 1,100.00
    13" – 14".. $1,100.00 – 1,200.00

Mold 8950, laughing girl, blue hair bow

    18"........... $6,900.00 – 7,200.00

Mold 8970, closed mouth, intaglio eyes, wigged

    9"............. $1,200.00 – 1,300.00

Mold 9457, ca. 1914, square mark, dome, intaglio eyes, closed mouth, Eskimo

    15"........... $2,300.00 – 2,500.00
    18"........... $3,800.00 – 4,000.00

Mold 9590, closed mouth, intaglio eyes, molded page boy hairstyle with molded bow

    7" .... $650.00 – 800.00

Mold 10532, ca. 1920, square mark, open mouth, five-piece toddler body

    8½".......... $1,000.00 – 1,100.00
    13½"........ $1,450.00 – 1,550.00
    20" – 22".. $1,900.00 – 2,100.00
    25"........... $2,400.00 – 2,500.00

Mold 11173, "Tiss Me," socket head, wig

    8"............. $1,900.00 – 2,000.00

Too few in database for a reliable range.

20" socket head character doll, mold 8245, sold for $9,500.00 at auction. *Photo courtesy of Skinner, Inc.*

Character Baby, socket head, 1911 on, bisque head, bent-limb body
Mold 6894, 6897, 7759, 7602, 7604, all ca. 1912, sunburst or square mark, intaglio eyes, closed mouth, molded hair

6" – 7"	$475.00 – 525.00
9" – 12"	$575.00 – 675.00
15"	$700.00 – 800.00
20"	$900.00 – 1,000.00

Toddler

14"	$850.00 – 950.00

Molds 7877, 7977, "Baby Stuart," ca. 1912, molded bonnet, closed mouth, painted eyes

8" – 9"	$1,000.00 – 1,100.00
11" – 13"	$1,400.00 – 1,600.00
15"	$1,700.00 – 2,000.00

Mold 7975, "Baby Stuart," ca. 1912, glass eyes, removable molded bisque bonnet

9" – 13"	$2,200.00 – 2,400.00

Mold 8420, ca. 1914, square mark, glass eyes, closed mouth

10"	$650.00 – 750.00
15"	$1,200.00 – 1,400.00

Mold 9377, sleep eyes, open mouth, dimples, prominent ears, wigged

27"	$2,000.00 – 2,400.00

Too few in database for a reliable range.
All-Bisque: See All-Bisque German section.

E.I. HORSMAN

1878 – 1980s, New York City. Founded by Edward Imeson Horsman as company importing, assembling, wholesaling, and distributing various dolls and doll lines. From 1909 to 1919 they distributed Aetna Doll & Toy company's dolls, in 1919 the two companies merged. Eventually Horsman made their own dolls as well as distributed other lines. They took out their first patent for a complete doll in 1909 for a Billiken doll. They made dolls of composition, rubber, hard plastic, and vinyl.
Early composition on cloth body, composition head, sometimes lower arms, cloth body. Dolls listed are in good condition with original clothing, add more for exceptional doll.
Baby Bumps, 1910 – 1917, composition head, cloth cork-stuffed body, blue and white cloth label on romper, copy of K*R #100 Baby mold

11"	$250.00
Black	$300.00 – 350.00

Baby Butterfly, 1914 on, composition head, hands, cloth body, painted hair and features

13"	$250.00 – 300.00
15"	$350.00 – 400.00

Billiken, 1909, composition head, molded hair, slanted eyes, smiling closed mouth, on stuffed mohair or velvet body, cloth label on body, "Billiken" on right foot

12"	$200.00 – 400.00

Campbell's Kids, 1910 on, designed by Helen Trowbridge, based on Grace Drayton's drawings, composition head, painted and molded hair, side-glancing painted eyes, closed smiling mouth, composition arms,

E.I. Horsman

12" Campbell's kid doll, $350.00. *Photo courtesy of Skinner, Inc.*

cloth body and feet, mark: "EIH © 1910"; cloth label on sleeve, "The Campbell Kids// Trademark by //Joseph Campbell// Mfg. by E.I. Horsman Co."

10" – 11"	$325.00 – 350.00
15" – 16"	$375.00 – 400.00

Can't Break 'Em Characters, 1911 on

Child, boy or girl

11" – 13" .... $200.00 – 275.00

Cotton Joe, black

13" .... $350.00 – 400.00

Little Mary Mix-up

15" .... $350.00 – 375.00

Master & Miss Sam, in patriotic outfits

15" .... $350.00 – 375.00

Polly Pru

13" .... $325.00 – 350.00

Fairy, 1911, composition head and hands, molded hair, painted side-glancing eyes, cloth body, designed by Helen Trowbridge, based on Little Fairy Soap advertising by N.K. Fairbanks Co., mark "EIH © 1911"

13" .... $325.00 – 400.00

Gene Carr Kids, 1915 – 1916, composition head, molded and painted hair, painted eyes, open-closed smiling mouth with teeth, big ears, cloth body, composition hands, original outfit, cloth tag reads: "MADE GENE CARR KIDS U.S.A.//FROM NEW YORK WORLD'S//LADY BOUNTIFUL COMIC SERIES//By E.I. HORSMAN CO. NY"

Blink, Lizzie, Mike, Skinney

14" .... $250.00 – 300.00

Snowball, black .... $450.00 – 500.00

Gold Medal Baby, 1911 on, line of baby dolls with composition head and limbs, upper and lower teeth, included Baby Suck-a-Thumb, Baby Blossom, Baby Premier, and others

10" .... $200.00 – 225.00

12" .... $225.00 – 275.00

19" .... $300.00 – 340.00

Early all-composition dolls

Peek-a-Boo, 1913, designed by Grace Drayton

8" .... $100.00 – 125.00

Peterkin, 1914 – 1930

11" .... $250.00 – 300.00

Puppy & Pussy Pippin, 1911, designed by Grace Drayton, composition head, plush body .... $450.00 – 550.00

Composition dolls on cloth body, 1920 on

15" Bright Star, hard plastic, $500.00. *Photo courtesy of Joy Macielle, Quality Vintage Doll Patterns.*

E.I. Horsman

Brother & Sister, 1937, marked: "Brother//1937//Horsman//©" & "Sister//1937//Horsman//©" Brother 21" and Sister 23"
.... $300.00 – 400.00 each

Ella Cinders, 1928 – 1929, based on a cartoon character, composition head, black painted hair or wig, round painted eyes, freckles under eyes, open/closed mouth, also came as all-cloth, mark: "1925//MNS"

14"................. $400.00 – 450.00
18"................. $650.00 – 700.00

Jackie Coogan, "The Kid," 1921 – 1922, composition head, hands, molded hair, painted eyes, turtleneck sweater, long gray pants, checked cap, button reads: "HORSMAN DOLL// JACKIE// COOGAN// KID// PATENTED"

13½"............. $450.00 – 475.00
15½"............. $500.00 – 550.00

Jeanie Horsman, 1937, composition head and limbs, painted molded brown hair, sleep eyes, mark: "Jeanie© Horsman"

14"................. $225.00 – 250.00

All-Composition Dolls, 1930 on

Body Twist, 1930, with jointed waist

11"................. $175.00 – 200.00

Bright Star, 1937 – 1946,

14".............. $150.00 – 200.00
20"................. $300.00 – 350.00

Campbell's Kids, 1930 – 1940s, all-composition

13"................. $200.00 – 250.00

Child, including Gold Medal child

13" – 14"........ $175.00 – 200.00
16" – 18"........ $200.00 – 225.00
21"................. $225.00 – 250.00

HEbee-SHEbees, 1925 – 1927, based on drawings by Charles Twelvetrees, painted features, molded undershirt and booties or various costumes

10½"............. $425.00 – 375.00

All-bisque HEbee & SHEbee: See All-Bisque German section.

16" Roberta, $400.00. *Photo courtesy of Withington Auction, Inc.*

Jo Jo, 1937, blue sleep eyes, wigged, over molded hair, toddler body, mark: "HORSMAN JO JO//©1937"

13"................. $275.00 – 325.00

Naughty Sue, 1937, jointed body

16"................. $400.00 – 450.00

Patsy-type, names such as Sue, Babs, and Joan were given to the various sizes

12"................. $250.00 – 275.00
14"................. $275.00 – 300.00

Roberta, 1937, all-composition

16"................. $375.00 – 450.00

Sweetheart, 1938, composition, hard rubber arms

24" – 28"........ $325.00 – 400.00

21" Sweetheart, composition, $325.00. *Photo courtesy of Withington Auction, Inc.*

E.I. Horsman

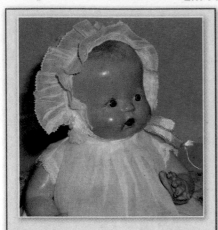

12" Baby Buttercup, ca. 1931, $585.00. *Photo courtesy of Dollyology Vintage Dolls.*

Composition Baby, 1920s – 1940s

Buttercup, 1931, composition flange neck head, arms, legs, cloth body, closed mouth, sleep, marked

    12" – 19" .... $250.00 – 650.00

Dimples, 1927 – 1937 on, composition head, arms, cloth body, bent-leg body or bent-limb baby body, molded dimples, open mouth, sleep or painted eyes, marked "E.I.H."

    13" – 14"........ $180.00 – 225.00
    16" – 18"........ $275.00 – 375.00
    20" – 22"........ $300.00 – 400.00

Toddler

    20"................. $300.00 – 350.00
    24"................. $425.00 – 475.00

Tynie Baby, ca. 1924 – 1929, bisque or composition head, sleep or painted eyes, cloth body, some all-bisque, marks: "©1924//E.I. HORSMAN//CO. INC." or "E.I.H. Co. 1924" on composition or "©1924 by//E I Horsman Co. Inc//Germany//37" incised on bisque head

All-bisque, with wardrobe, cradle

    9".............................. $2,500.00

Bisque, head circumference

    9" $600.00

    12" $200.00
    15"................................ $300.00

Composition heads and arms, cloth body

    14"................. $100.00 – 125.00
    18"................. $150.00 – 175.00
    21"................. $200.00 – 225.00

Vinyl, 1950s, boxed

    15".................... $90.00 – 110.00

Mama Dolls, 1920 on, composition head, arms, and lower legs, cloth body with crier and stitched hip joints so lower legs will swing, painted or sleep eyes, mohair or molded hair, models include Peggy Ann, Rosebud, and others

    14" – 15"........ $180.00 – 225.00
    19" – 21"........ $275.00 – 310.00
    23" – 24"........ $300.00 – 375.00

Hard plastic and vinyl, dolls listed are in excellent condition with original clothing and tags, allow more for mint-in-box dolls, add more for accessories or wardrobe

Angelove, 1974, plastic/vinyl made for Hallmark

    12"..................... $20.00 – 25.00

Answer Doll, 1966, button in back moves head

    10"..................... $10.00 – 15.00

Baby Dimples, vinyl reissue

    19" – 21"............. $45.00 – 55.00

Baby First Tooth, 1966, vinyl head, limbs, cloth body, open-closed mouth with tongue and one tooth, molded tears on cheeks, rooted blond hair, painted blue eyes, mark: "©Horsman Dolls Inc. //10141"

    16"..................... $30.00 – 40.00

Baby Grow Up, 1966, vinyl, one body with interchangeable child arms and legs, girl's head, baby arms and legs, baby head

    16"..................... $15.00 – 20.00

Baby Sofskin, 1972 on, vinyl

    12" – 15" .... $40.00 – 60.00

Baby Tweaks, 1967, vinyl head, cloth body, inset eyes, rooted saran hair, mark: "54//

158

E.I. Horsman

HORSMAN DOLLS INC.//Copyright 1967/67191" on head

20".................... $20.00 – 30.00

Ballerina, 1957, vinyl, one-piece body and legs, jointed elbows

18".................... $60.00 – 75.00

Betty, 1951, all-vinyl, one-piece body and limbs

14".................... $50.00 – 60.00

Vinyl head, hard plastic body

16".................... $20.00 – 25.00

Betty Ann, vinyl head, hard plastic body

19".................... $50.00 – 60.00

Betty Jane, vinyl head, hard plastic body

25".................... $65.00 – 75.00

Betty Jo, vinyl head, hard plastic body

16".................... $20.00 – 30.00

Bright Star, ca. 1952 on, all-hard plastic

15".................... $375.00 – 500.00

Bye-Lo Baby, 1972, reissue, molded vinyl head, limbs, cloth body, white nylon organdy bonnet dress, mark: "3 (in square)// HORSMAN DOLLS INC.//©1972"

14".................... $25.00 – 30.00

1980 – 1990s

14".................... $15.00 – 20.00

Celeste, portrait doll, in frame, eyes painted to side

12".................... $30.00 – 35.00

Cinderella, 1965, vinyl head, hard plastic body, painted eyes to side

11½".................... $25.00 – 30.00

Cindy, 1950s, all-hard plastic child, "170"

15".................... $125.00 – 175.00

17".................... $175.00 – 200.00

19".................... $200.00 – 225.00

Cindy fashion-type doll, vinyl head, soft vinyl stuffed high-heel body

15".................... $65.00 – 90.00

18".................... $100.00 – 150.00

Vinyl head, solid vinyl body jointed at shoulders and hips, high-heel foot

10".................... $25.00 – 30.00

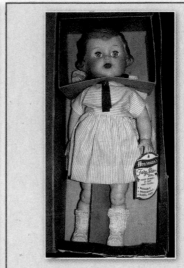

15" Gold Medal Doll, vinyl, $150.00. *Photo courtesy of Joy Macielle, Quality Vintage Doll Patterns.*

Cindy Kay, 1950s+, all-vinyl child with long legs

15".................... $70.00 – 80.00

20".................... $110.00 – 125.00

27".................... $200.00 – 225.00

Crawling Baby, 1967, vinyl, rooted hair

14".................... $20.00 – 25.00

Disney Exclusives, 1981, Cinderella, Snow White, Mary Poppins, Alice in Wonderland

8".................... $35.00 – 40.00

Elizabeth Taylor, 1976

11½".................... $45.00 – 50.00

Floppy, 1958, vinyl head, foam body and legs

18".................... $20.00 – 25.00

Flying Nun, 1965, TV character portrayed by Sally Field

12".................... $100.00 – 125.00

Gold Medal Doll, 1953, vinyl head, soft vinyl foam stuffed body, molded hair

17" – 26".................... $80.00 – 125.00

1954, vinyl, boy

12".................... $35.00 – 40.00

15".................... $65.00 – 75.00

159

E.I. Horsman

18" Ruthie, $75.00. *Photo courtesy of Emmie's Antique Doll Castle.*

Hansel & Gretel, 1963, vinyl head, hard plastic body, rooted synthetic hair, closed mouth, sleep eyes, marks: "MADE IN USA" on body, on tag, "HORSMAN, Michael Meyerberg, Inc.," "Reproduction of the famous Kinemins in Michael Myerberg's marvelous Technicolor production of Hansel and Gretel"

    15".................. $200.00 – 225.00

HEbee-SHEbees, 1987, vinyl reissues

                       $12.00 – 18.00

Jackie, 1961, vinyl doll, rooted hair, blue sleep eyes, long lashes, closed mouth, high-heeled feet, small waist, nicely dressed, designed by Irene Szor who says this doll named Jackie was not meant to portray Jackie Kennedy, mark: "HORSMAN//19©61//BC"

    18" – 25"....... $120.00 – 155.00

Joey Stivic, Archie Bunker's grandson, 1976, vinyl, rooted hair

    14".................... $15.00 – 20.00

Li'l David & Li'l Ruth, 1970s, all vinyl, anatomically correct babies

    12".................... $20.00 – 25.00

Lullabye Baby, 1967 – 1968, vinyl bent-leg body, rooted hair, inset blue eyes, drink and wet feature, musical mechanism, Sears 1968 catalog, came on suedette pillow, in terrycloth p.j.'s, mark: "2580//B144 8 // HORSMAN DOLLS INC//19©67"

    12".................... $10.00 – 15.00

Mary Poppins, 1965, all in good condition with original clothing, mint-in-box can bring double the values listed

    12".................... $50.00 – 65.00
    16".................... $60.00 – 80.00
    26", 1966........ $75.00 – 100.00
    36"................ $150.00 – 200.00

Mary Poppins with Michael and Jane, 1966

    12" and 8"...... $150.00 – 160.00

1970s version Mary Poppins

    12" .... $10.00 – 20.00

Patty Duke, ca. 1965, vinyl, rooted hair, painted eyes

    12"................ $100.00 – 125.00

Peggy Pen Pal, ca. 1970, vinyl, rooted hair, came with writing desk and pen

    18".................... $60.00 – 70.00
    Black.................. $70.00 – 80.00

Pippi Longstocking, ca. 1972, vinyl, rooted hair, painted eyes

    11".................... $60.00 – 70.00

Police Woman, ca. 1976, vinyl, fully articulated plastic body, rooted hair

    9"...................... $35.00 – 40.00

Poor Pitiful Pearl, 1963, from cartoon by William Steig, marked on neck: "Horsman 1963"

    11"................ $100.00 – 120.00
    17"................ $160.00 – 200.00

Ruthie, 1962

    15".................... $35.00 – 40.00
    19".................... $45.00 – 50.00

Softee, 1959, vinyl baby

    15".................... $20.00 – 25.00

Thirsty Walker, 1962

    26".................... $25.00 – 35.00

28" Walk-a-Bye, ca. 1960, $250.00. *Photo courtesy of Joy Macielle, Quality Vintage Doll Patterns.*

Ventriloquist dolls, 1973 on, Tessi Talk, Willie Talk, Simon Sez

    16".....................$50.00 – 70.00

MARY HOYER DOLL MFG. CO.

1937 – 1968, 1990 – present, Reading, Pennsylvania. Designed by Bernard Lipfert, all-composition, later hard plastic, then vinyl, swivel neck, jointed body, mohair or human hair wig, sleep eyes, closed mouth, original clothes, or knitted from Mary Hoyer patterns, company re-opened by Hoyer's granddaughter in 1990. Dolls listed are in good condition with appropriate clothing.

Composition, less for painted eyes

    14".................$325.00 – 400.00

Hard plastic

In knit outfit

    14".................$500.00 – 525.00

In tagged Hoyer outfit

    14".................$700.00 – 900.00

14" hard plastic Mary Hoyer, $800.00. *Photo courtesy of Morphy Auctions.*

Boy in original wig

    14"................$525.00 – 575.00

Modern, values are for secondary market dolls, dolls are still available at retail

    14".............$80.00 – 100.00 MIB

Gigi, circa 1950, with round Mary Hoyer mark found on 14" dolls, only 2,000 made by the Frisch Doll Company

    18"..,,..........$700.00 – 1,300.00

13" Modern Mary Hoyer doll. $100.00. *Photo courtesy of Alderfer Auction & Appraisal.*

Vinyl, circa 1957 on

Vicky, all-vinyl, high-heeled doll, body bends at waist, rooted saran hair, two larger sizes 12" and 14" were discontinued

10½".............. $90.00 – 100.00

Margie, circa 1958, toddler, rooted hair, made by Unique Doll Co.

10"................... $90.00 – 125.00

Cathy, circa 1961, infant, made by Unique Doll Co.

10"..................... $20.00 – 25.00

Janie, circa 1962, baby

8"...................... $20.00 – 25.00

ADOLPH HÜLSS

1915 – 1930+, Waltershausen, Germany. Made dolls with bisque heads, jointed composition bodies. Trademark: "Nesthakchen," "h" in mold mark often resembles a "b." Heads made by Simon & Halbig.

Baby, bisque socket head, sleep eyes, open mouth, teeth, wig, bent-leg baby, composition body, add more for flirty eyes

Mold 156

9"................... $275.00 – 300.00

10", mold 156, $300.00. *Photo courtesy of Cybermogul Dolls.*

14" – 15"........ $400.00 – 475.00
17" – 19"........ $625.00 – 675.00
23"................. $800.00 – 825.00

Toddler

9" – 10".......... $850.00 – 900.00
16"................. $775.00 – 800.00
20"................. $900.00 – 925.00

Painted bisque

22"................. $200.00 – 225.00

Child, bisque socket head, wig, sleep eyes, open mouth, teeth, tongue, jointed composition body

Mold 176

15"................. $650.00 – 675.00
18"................. $650.00 – 750.00
22"................. $950.00 – 975.00

MAISON HURET

1812 – 1930 on, France. May have pressed, molded bisque, or china heads, painted or glass eyes, closed mouths, bodies of cloth, composition, gutta-percha, kid, or wood, sometimes metal hands. Used fur or mohair for wigs, had fashion-type body with defined waist. Look for dolls with beautiful painting on eyes and face; painted eyes are more common than glass, but the beauty of the painted features and/or wooden bodies increases the price.

Poupée

Bisque shoulder head, kid body with bisque lower arms, glass eyes

15"....... $13,000.00 – 14,000.00
17" – 18".. $16,000.00 – 20,000.00

Gutta-percha body

17"....... $14,000.00 – 20,000.00

Round face, painted blue eyes, cloth body

16" – 18".. $11,000.00 – 14,000.00

Wood body

17" ...... $20,000.00 – 24,000.00

China shoulder head, kid body, china lower arms

17"....... $15,000.00 – 20,000.00

18" Prevost Era Lady, $6,500.00. *Photo courtesy of Withington Auction, Inc.*

Wood body
   17"....... $30,000.00 – 33,000.00
Gutta-percha body
   17"....... $20,000.00 – 25,000.00
Huret Bébé,1878, bisque head, glass eyes, closed mouth
Composition body
   13"......... $7,000.00 – 11,000.00
   20"....... $19,000.00 – 21,000.00
Gutta-percha body
   18"....... $70,000.00 – 80,000.00
Wooden body
   18"....... $34,000.00 – 36,000.00
Prevost Era Lady or Gentleman, 1914 – 1918, elongated face on composition body
   17" – 18"...... $6,000.00 – 7,000.00

IDEAL NOVELTY AND TOY CO.

1906 – 1980s, Brooklyn, New York. Produced their own composition dolls in early years. Later made dolls of rubber, hard plastic, vinyl, and cloth. Up to 1950 dolls listed are in good condition with appropriate clothing, after 1950 dolls listed are in excellent condition with original clothing and tags for values listed.

Cloth
Dennis the Menace, 1976, all-cloth, printed doll, comic strip character by Hank Ketcham, blond hair, freckles, wearing overalls, striped shirt
   7"...................... $10.00 – 15.00
   14"..................... $18.00 – 25.00
Internationals, 1920s on, cloth mask faces, cloth bodies............... $75.00 – 100.00
Peanuts Gang, 1976 – 1978, all-cloth, stuffed printed dolls from *Peanuts* comic strip by Charles Schulz; Charlie Brown, Lucy, Linus, Peppermint Patty, and Snoopy
   7"...................... $15.00 – 20.00
   14"..................... $20.00 – 30.00
Snow White and the Seven Dwarfs, 1939 on, cloth mask face dolls, cloth body
Snow White, black mohair wig, dress with dwarfs printed on skirt
   16"................. $375.00 – 475.00
Dwarfs
   10"..........$200.00 – 225.00 each
Strawman, 1939, all-cloth, scarecrow character played by Ray Bolger in *Wizard of Oz* movie, yarn hair, all-original, wearing dark jacket and hat, tan pants, round paper hang tag
   17".............. $900.00 – 1,200.00
   21"........... $1,400.00 – 1,500.00
Composition
Early composition character children, composition heads, lower arms and sometimes shoes on cloth body, excelsior stuffed
Cracker Jack Boy, 1917, sailor suit, carries package of Cracker Jack
   14"................. $350.00 – 375.00
Happy Hooligan, 1910
   21"................. $475.00 – 525.00

15" Uneeda Kid, composition, $450.00. *Photo courtesy of Alderfer Auction & Appraisal.*

Liberty Boy, 1917, molded uniform
  12"................. $190.00 – 225.00
Naughty Marietta (Coquette-type), 1912
  14"................................. $150.00
Snookums, 1910, plush body
  14"................. $500.00 – 600.00
Uneeda Kid, 1914 – 1919, original clothing including rain slicker and biscuit box
  15"................. $425.00 – 475.00
Zu Zu Kid, 1916 – 1917
  14"................. $225.00 – 275.00
Child or toddler, 1913 on, composition head, molded hair, or wigged, painted or sleep eyes, cloth or composition body, may have Ideal diamond mark or hang tag, original clothes
  13"................. $155.00 – 225.00
  15" – 16"........ $230.00 – 255.00
  18"................. $295.00 – 325.00
Baby doll, 1913 on, composition head, molded hair or wigged, painted or sleep eyes, cloth or composition body, models such as Baby Mine, Our Pet, Prize Baby, and others
  15" – 16"........ $180.00 – 250.00

Mama Doll, 1921 on, composition head and arms, molded hair or wigged, painted or sleep eyes, cloth body with crier and stitched swing leg, lower part composition
  16"................. $225.00 – 250.00
  20"................. $275.00 – 300.00
  24"................. $325.00 – 350.00
Babies, mid 1920s – 1940s, composition head, arms and legs, cloth body
Flossie Flirt, 1924 – 1931, composition head, limbs, cloth body, crier, tin flirty eyes, open mouth, upper teeth, original outfit, dress, bonnet, socks, and shoes, mark: "IDEAL" in diamond with "U.S. of A"
  14"................. $225.00 – 250.00
  18"................. $275.00 – 300.00
  20"................. $325.00 – 350.00
  22"................. $350.00 – 375.00
  24"................. $375.00 – 400.00
  28"................. $400.00 – 525.00
Tickletoes, 1928 – 1939, composition head, rubber arms, legs, cloth body, squeaker in each leg, flirty sleep eyes, open mouth, two painted teeth, original organdy dress, bonnet, paper hang tag, marks: "IDEAL" in diamond with "U.S. of A." on head
  14"................. $225.00 – 275.00

18" Baby Beautiful, composition, $350.00. *Photo courtesy of Dollyology Vintage Dolls.*

Ideal Novelty and Toy Co.

17".................. $275.00 – 300.00
20".................. $325.00 – 350.00

Snoozie, 1933 on, composition head, painted hair, hard rubber hands and feet, cloth body, open yawning mouth, molded tongue, sleep eyes, designed by Bernard Lipfert, marks: "©B. Lipfert//Made for Ideal Doll & Toy Corp. 1933" or "©by B. Lipfert" or "IDEAL SNOOZIE//B. LIPFERT" on head

14".................. $175.00 – 200.00
16".................. $275.00 – 325.00
18".................. $325.00 – 350.00
20".................. $350.00 – 375.00

Princess Beatrix, 1938 – 1943, represents Princess Beatrix of the Netherlands, composition head, arms, legs, cloth body, flirty sleep eyes, fingers molded into fists, original organdy dress and bonnet

14".................. $250.00 – 300.00
16".................. $350.00 – 400.00
22".................. $425.00 – 475.00
26".................. $475.00 – 525.00

Soozie Smiles, 1923, two-faced composition doll with smiling face, sleep or painted eyes, and crying face with tears, molded and painted hair, cloth body and legs, composition arms, original clothes, tag, also in gingham checked romper

15" – 17"........ $375.00 – 425.00

Composition Child, 1920s – 1940s

Buster Brown, 1929, composition head, hands, legs, cloth body, tin eyes, red outfit, mark: "IDEAL" (in a diamond)

17" .... $325.00 – 375.00

Charlie McCarthy, 1938 – 1939, hand puppet, composition head, felt hands, molded hat, molded features, wire monocle, cloth body, painted tuxedo, mark: "Edgar Bergen's//©CHARLIE MCCARTHY//MADE IN U.S.A."

8"........................ 450.00 – 60.00

Cinderella, 1938 – 1939, all-composition,

13½" Flexy dolls Mortimer Snerd and Baby Snooks, $400.00 each. *Photo courtesy of Joan & Lynette Antique Dolls and Accessories.*

brown, blond, or red human hair wig, flirty brown sleep eyes, open mouth, six teeth, same head mold as Ginger, Snow White, and Mary Jane with dimple in chin, some wore formal evening gowns of organdy and taffeta, velvet cape, had rhinestone tiara, silver snap shoes, Sears catalog version has Celanese rayon gown, marks: none on head; "SHIRLEY TEMPLE//13" on body

13".................. $300.00 – 325.00
16".................. $325.00 – 350.00
20".................. $350.00 – 375.00
22".................. $375.00 – 400.00
25".................. $400.00 – 425.00
27".................. $425.00 – 450.00

Deanna Durbin, 1938 – 1941, all-composition, fully jointed, dark brown human hair wig, brown sleep eyes, open mouth, six teeth, felt tongue, original clothes, pin reads: "DEANNA DURBIN//A UNIVERSAL STAR," more for fancy outfits, marks: "DEANNA DURBIN//IDEAL DOLL" on head; "IDEAL DOLL//21" on body

15".................. $600.00 – 700.00
18".................. $750.00 – 850.00
21"........... $1,000.00 – 1,500.00
24"........... $1,200.00 – 1,500.00

Flexy, 1938 – 1942, composition head, gauntlet hands, molded and painted hair, painted eyes, wooden torso and feet, flexible wire tubing for arms and legs, original clothes, paper tag, marks: "IDEAL DOLL// Made in U.S.A." or just "IDEAL DOLL" on head

Black Flexy, closed smiling mouth, tweed patched pants, felt suspenders

13½".............. $275.00 – 300.00

Baby Snooks (Fannie Brice), open/closed mouth with teeth

13½".............. $325.00 – 400.00

Clown Flexy, looks like Mortimer Snerd, painted white as clown

13½".............. $175.00 – 200.00

Mortimer Snerd, Edgar Bergen's dummy, smiling closed mouth, showing two teeth

13½".............. $325.00 – 400.00

Soldier, closed smiling mouth, in khaki uniform

13½".............. $200.00 – 225.00

Sunny Sam and Sunny Sue, girl with bobbed hair, pouty mouth, boy with smiling mouth

13½".............. $250.00 – 300.00

Judy Garland

1939 – 1940, as Dorothy from *The Wizard of Oz*, all-composition, jointed, wig with braids, brown sleep eyes, open mouth, six teeth, designed by Bernard Lipfert, blue or red checked rayon jumper, white blouse,

16" Judy Garland, $1,700.00. *Photo courtesy of Morphy Auctions.*

marks: "IDEAL" on head plus size number, and "USA" on body

13"........... $1,100.00 – 1,200.00

15½"........ $1,600.00 – 1,800.00

18"........... $1,900.00 – 2,200.00

1940 – 1942, teen, all-composition, wig, sleep eyes, open mouth, four teeth, original long dress, hang tag reads: "Judy Garland// A Metro Goldwyn Mayer//Star//in//'Little Nellie'//Kelly," original pin reads "JUDY GARLAND METRO GOLDWYN MAYER STAR," marks: "IN U.S.A." on head, "IDEAL DOLLS," a backwards "21" on body

15"................. $650.00 – 750.00

21".............. $900.00 – 1,000.00

Seven Dwarfs, 1938 on, composition head and cloth body, head turns, removable clothes, each dwarf has name on cap, pick, and lantern

12"................. $175.00 – 200.00

Dopey, 1938, one of Seven Dwarfs, a ventriloquist doll, composition head and hands, cloth body, arms, and legs, hinged mouth with drawstring, molded tongue, painted eyes, large ears, long coat, cotton pants, felt shoes sewn to leg, felt cap with name, can stand alone, mark: "IDEAL DOLL" on neck

20"................. $700.00 – 800.00

Snow White, 1938 on, all-composition, jointed body, black mohair wig, flirty glass eyes, open mouth, four teeth, dimple in chin, used Shirley Temple body, red velvet bodice, rayon taffeta skirt pictures seven Dwarfs, velvet cape, some unmarked, marks: "Shirley Temple/18" or other size number on back

11½".............. $400.00 – 450.00

13" – 14"........ $425.00 – 475.00

19" – 21"........ $550.00 – 650.00

Snow White, 1938 – 1939, as above, but with molded and painted bow and black hair, painted side-glancing eyes, add 50 percent more for black version, mark: "IDEAL DOLL" on head

9" Jiminy Cricket, $275.00. *Photo courtesy of Morphy Auctions.*

14½".............. $200.00 – 250.00
17½" – 19½".. $450.00 – 550.00
Shirley Temple, 1934 on: See Shirley Temple section.
Composition and wood dolls, 1940 on, segmented wooden body, strung with elastic
Ferdinand the Bull
9".................... $200.00 – 250.00
Gabby
10½".............. $325.00 – 400.00
Jiminy Cricket
9".................... $225.00 – 275.00
Pinocchio, 1939
8"..................... $200.00 – 275.00
11"................. $350.00 – 400.00
20"................. $575.00 – 650.00
Superman, 1940s, painted features
13"................. $800.00 – 900.00
Magic Skin Dolls, 1940 on, latex body, stuffed, original clothing. These doll bodies are prone to disintegration.
Baby Coos, 1948 – 1953, also Brother and Sister Coos, designed by Bernard Lipfert, hard plastic head, jointed arms, sleep eyes, molded and painted hair, closed mouth, squeeze box voice, later on cloth and vinyl body, marks on head, "16 IDEAL DOLL//

MADE IN U.S.A." or unmarked
14".................... $90.00 – 100.00
16" – 18"........ $125.00 – 135.00
20" – 22"........ $145.00 – 165.00
27" – 30"........ $195.00 – 215.00
Bonnie Braids, 1951 – 1953, comic strip character, daughter of Dick Tracy and Tess Trueheart, vinyl head, jointed arms, one-piece body, open mouth, one tooth, painted yellow hair, two yellow saran pigtails, painted blue eyes, coos when squeezed, long white gown, bed jacket, toothbrush, Ipana toothpaste, mark: "©1951//Chi. Tribune//IDEAL DOLL//U.S.A." on neck
Baby
11½".............. $150.00 – 200.00
14"................. $250.00 – 300.00
Toddler, 1953, vinyl head, jointed hard plastic body, open-closed mouth with two painted teeth, walker
11½".............. $100.00 – 125.00
13½".............. $150.00 – 175.00
Magic Skin Baby, 1940, 1946 – 1949, hard plastic head, one-piece body and legs, jointed arms, sleep eyes, molded and painted hair, some with fancy layettes or trunks, latex usually darkened
13" – 14"............ $40.00 – 65.00

11½" Bonnie Braids toddler, $100.00. *Doll courtesy of Pat Buckley.*

15" – 16"............ $65.00 – 80.00
17" – 18"........ $190.00 – 110.00
20".................. $110.00 – 125.00

Joan Palooka, 1953, daughter of comic strip character, Joe Palooka, vinyl, head, "Magic Skin" body, jointed arms and legs, yellow molded hair, topknot of yellow saran, blue painted eyes, open/closed mouth, smells like baby powder, original pink dress with blue ribbons, came with Johnson's baby powder and soap, mark: "©1952//HAM FISHER//IDEAL DOLL" on head

14"................. $175.00 – 200.00

Snoozie, 1951, open/closed mouth, vinyl head

11"................. $100.00 – 125.00
16"................. $125.00 – 150.00
20"................. $150.00 – 175.00

Sparkle Plenty, 1947 – 1950, hard plastic head, "Magic Skin" body may be dark, yarn hair, character from *Dick Tracy* comics

14"................. $275.00 – 350.00
MIB............................. $689.00*

Hard plastic and vinyl dolls, all in good condition with original clothing, mint-in-box can bring double the values listed

Baby

11"..................... $25.00 – 35.00
14"..................... $45.00 – 55.00
20"................................... $75.00

Child

14"..................... $25.00 – 35.00

Andy Gibb, 1979

7½"..................... $35.00 – 40.00

April Shower, 1969, vinyl, battery-operated, splashes hands, head turns

14"..................... $35.00 – 40.00

Baby Pebbles, 1963 – 1964, character from the *Flintstones* cartoons, Hanna Barbera Productions, vinyl head, arms, legs, soft body, side-glancing blue painted eyes, rooted hair with topknot and bone, leopard print nightie and trim on flannel blanket, also as an all-

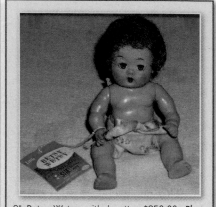

8" Betsy Wetsy with layette, $250.00. *Photo courtesy of Dollyology Vintage Dolls.*

vinyl toddler, jointed body, outfit with leopard print

14"................. $110.00 – 140.00

Tiny Pebbles, 1964 – 1966, hard vinyl body, came with plastic log cradle in 1965

8"....................... $75.00 – 85.00
12"................. $100.00 – 110.00
16"................. $130.00 – 150.00

Bamm-Bamm, 1964, character from *Flintstones* cartoon, Hanna Barbera Productions, all-vinyl head, jointed body, rooted blond saran hair, painted blue side-glancing eyes, leopard skin suit, cap, club

12"..................... $70.00 – 80.00
16".................... $95.00 – 125.00

Belly Button Babies, 1971, Me So Glad, Me So Silly, Me So Happy, vinyl head, rooted hair, painted eyes, press button in belly to move arms, head, and bent legs, boy and girl versions

White

9½" .... $20.00 – 30.00

Black

9½".................... $50.00 – 60.00

Betsy McCall, 1952 – 1953: See Betsy McCall section.

Betsy Wetsy, 1937 – 1938, 1954 – 1956, 1959 – 1962, 1982 – 1985, open mouth for

Ideal Novelty and Toy Co.

bottle, drinks, wets, came with bottle, some in layettes, marks: "IDEAL" on head, "IDEAL" on body

Hard rubber head, soft rubber body, sleep or painted eyes

11"	$95.00 – 125.00
13½"	$125.00 – 150.00
15"	$150.00 – 175.00
17"	$175.00 – 195.00
19"	$200.00 – 225.00

Hard plastic head, vinyl body

11½"	$300.00 – 325.00
13½"	$375.00 – 400.00
16"	$300.00 – 350.00
20"	$325.00 – 375.00

All-vinyl

8"	$60.00 – 80.00
11½"	$70.00 – 90.00
13½"	$80.00 – 100.00
16"	$120.00 – 150.00

Bizzie-Lizzie, 1971 – 1972, vinyl head, jointed body, rooted blond hair, sleep eyes, plugged into power pack, she irons, vacuums, uses feather duster, two D-cell batteries, doll without accessories will bring half the value listed

White

18" .... $65.00 – 75.00

Black

18" .... $75.00 – 85.00

Blessed Event, crying baby, vinyl head, squinting eyes

21" .... $150.00 – 200.00

Butterick Sew Easy Designing Set, 1953, hard vinyl mannequin of adult woman, molded blond hair, came with Butterick patterns and sewing accessories

14" .... $100.00 – 125.00

Captain Action® Superhero, 1966 – 1968, represents a fictional character who changes disguises to become a new identity, vinyl articulated figure, dark hair and eyes. MIB brings double values.

Action Boy

9"	$250.00
Robin Accessories	$150.00
Special Edition	$300.00

Captain Action

12" .... $140.00 – 160.00

Batman disguise .... $80.00 – 100.00

Silver Streak, box only $400.00

Too few in database for a reliable range.

Aquaman .... $100.00 – 125.00

Capt. Flash Gordon accessories . $150.00

Dr. Evil lab set .... $550.00 – 650.00

Lone Ranger, outfit only $150.00

Phantom set, MIB $1,009.00*

Spiderman .... $150.00 – 175.00

Steve Canyon disguise $200.00

Super Girl

11½" .... $350.00 – 400.00

Superman set w/dog $160.00

Tonto, outfit only $150.00

Clarabelle, 1954, clown from *Howdy Doody* TV show, mask face, cloth body, dressed in satin Clarabelle outfit with noise box and horn, later vinyl face

16"	$200.00 – 225.00
20"	$225.00 – 250.00

Crissy® Family of Dolls, 1969 – 1974, 1982, vinyl grow-hair dolls, all in good condition with original clothing, mint-in-box can bring double the values listed

Baby Crissy, 1973 – 1976, all-vinyl, jointed body, foam-filled legs and arms, rooted auburn grow hair, two painted teeth, brown sleep eyes, mark: "©1972//IDEAL TOY CORP.//2M 5511//B OR GHB-H-225" on back

White

24" .... $70.00 – 80.00

Black

24" .... $95.00 – 105.00

Beautiful Crissy, 1969 – 1974, all-vinyl, dark brown eyes, long hair, turn knob in back to make hair grow, some with swivel waist (1971), pull string to turn head (1972), pull

169

string to talk (1971), reissued ca. 1982 – 1983, first year hair grew to floor length

> White
> 18".................... $90.00 – 130.00
> Black
> 17½".................... $80.00 – 90.00
> *1982 doll* ....$35.00 – 40.00

Crissy's Friends, Brandi, 1972 – 1973; Kerry, 1971; Tressy, 1970 (Sears Exclusive), vinyl head, painted eyes, rooted growing hair, swivel waist

> White
> 18"..................... $65.00 – 70.00
> Black
> 18"..................... $70.00 – 80.00

Cinnamon, Velvet's Little Sister, 1972 – 1974, vinyl head, painted eyes, rooted auburn growing hair, orange polka dotted outfit, additional outfits sold separately, marks: "©1971//IDEAL TOY CORP.//G-H-12-H18//HONG KONG//IDEAL 1069-4 b" head; "©1972//IDEAL TOY CORP.// U.S. PAT-3-162-976//OTHER PAT. PEND.// HONG KONG" on back

> White
> 13½".................. $40.00 – 45.00
> Black
> 13½".................. $60.00 – 70.00

Cricket, 1971 – 1972 (Sears Exclusive); Dina, 1972 – 1973; Mia, 1971; vinyl, members of the Crissy® family, growing hair dolls, painted teeth, swivel waist

> 15"..............$65.00 – 75.00 each

Tara, 1976, all-vinyl black doll, long black rooted hair that "grows," sleep eyes, marked "©1975//IDEAL TOY CORP//H-250// HONG KONG" on head and "©1970// IDEAL TOY CORP//GH-15//M5169-01// MADE IN HONG KONG" on buttock

> 15½".................. $75.00 – 85.00

Velvet, Crissy's younger cousin, talker

> *1971 – 1973,*
> 15".................... $80.00 – 125.00

18" Giggles. $350.00. *Photo courtesy of Emmie's Antique Doll Castle.*

1974, non-talker, other accessories, grow hair

> White
> 15"..................... $55.00 – 60.00
> Black
> 15"..................... $60.00 – 65.00
> *Movin' Groovin' Velvet...* $75.00 – 95.00
> *Movin' Groovin' Dina.* $45.00 – 50.00
> *Movin' Groovin' Kerri.* $100.00 – 125.00
> *Movin' Groovin' Mia..* $75.00 – 95.00

Daddy's Girl, 1961, vinyl head and arms, plastic body, swivel waist, jointed ankles, rooted saran hair, blue sleep eyes, closed smiling mouth, preteen girl, label on dress reads "Daddy's Girl," marks: "IDEAL TOY CORP.//g-42-1" on head, "IDEAL TOY CORP.//G-42" on body

> 38"........... $1,300.00 – 1,400.00
> 42"........... $1,600.00 – 2,000.00

Davy Crockett and his horse, 1955 – 1956, all-plastic, can be removed from horse, fur cap, buckskin clothes

4¾" .... $40.00 – 50.00

Diana Ross, 1969, from the Supremes (singing group), all-vinyl, rooted black bouffant hairdo, gold sheath, feathers, gold shoes, or chartreuse mini-dress, print scarf, and black shoes

17½" .... $300.00 – 350.00

Dorothy Hamill, 1978, Olympic skating star, vinyl head, plastic posable body, rooted short brown hair, comes on ice rink stand with skates; also extra outfits available

11½" .... $20.00 – 25.00

Evel Knievel, 1974 – 1977, all-plastic stunt figure, helmet, more with stunt cycle

7" .... $30.00 – 40.00

Flatsy, 1969, flat vinyl doll with wire armature, rooted hair

6" .... $25.00 – 50.00

Giggles, 1960, vinyl head, giggling doll

18" .... $250.00 – 300.00

Harmony, 1972, vinyl, battery-operated, makes music with guitar

21" .... $110.00 – 140.00

Harriet Hubbard Ayer, 1953, cosmetic doll, vinyl stuffed head, hard plastic (Toni) body, wigged or rooted hair, came with eight-piece H. H. Ayer cosmetic kit, beauty table and booklet, marks: "MK 16//IDEAL DOLL" on head "IDEAL DOLL//P-91" on body

14" .... $100.00 – 125.00

16" .... $125.00 – 150.00

19" .... $150.00 – 175.00

21" .... $175.00 – 200.00

Honeybunch, 1956 – 1957, soft vinyl head, vinyl body and limbs are stuffed with cotton, curlable hair

15" – 23" .... $100.00 – 125.00

Hopalong Cassidy, 1949 – 1950, vinyl stuffed head, vinyl hands, molded and painted gray hair, painted blue eyes, one-piece body, dressed in black cowboy outfit, leatherette boots, guns, holster, black felt hat, marks: "Hopalong Cassidy" on buckle

20" .... $185.00 – 200.00

24" .... $200.00 – 225.00

Plastic, with horse, Topper

4½" .... $40.00 – 50.00

Howdy Doody, 1950 – 1953, television personality, hard plastic head, red molded and painted hair, freckles, ventriloquist doll, mouth operated by pull string, cloth body and limbs, dressed in cowboy outfit, scarf reads "HOWDY DOODY," mark: "IDEAL" on head

18" .... $450.00 – 500.00

20" .... $500.00 – 525.00

24" .... $525.00 – 550.00

1954, with vinyl hands, wears boots, jeans

20½" .... $250.00 – 275.00

25" .... $300.00 – 350.00

Jet Set Dolls, 1967, vinyl head, posable body, rooted straight hair, mod fashions, earrings, strap shoes, Chelsea, Stephanie, and Petula

24" .... $45.00 – 55.00

Jody, An Old Fashioned Girl, 1975, vinyl, long rooted red hair

9" .... $25.00 – 35.00

Judy Splinters, 1949 – 1950, vinylite, TV

9" Jody, ca. 1975, $30.00. *Photo courtesy of The Museum Doll Shop.*

character ventriloquist doll, open-closed mouth

18".................. $180.00 – 200.00
22".................. $225.00 – 250.00
36".................. $280.00 – 300.00

Baby

15".................. $275.00 – 300.00

Kissy, 1961 – 1964, vinyl head, rigid vinyl toddler body, rooted saran hair, sleep eyes, jointed wrists, press hands together and mouth puckers, makes kissing sound, original dress, panties, t-strap sandals, marks: "©IDEAL CORP.//K-21-L" on head "IDEAL TOY CORP.// K22//PAT. PEND." on body

White

22½".................. $75.00 – 90.00

Black

22½".............. $125.00 – 150.00

Kissy Baby, 1963 – 1964, all-vinyl, bent legs

22"..................... $45.00 – 65.00

Tiny Kissy, 1963 – 1968, smaller toddler, red outfit, white pinafore with hearts, marks: "IDEAL CORP.//K-16-1" on head "IDEAL TOY CORP./K-16-2" on body

White

16"..................... $50.00 – 60.00

Black

16"..................... $80.00 – 90.00

Lori Martin, 1961, character from *National Velvet* TV show, all-vinyl, swivel waist, jointed body, including ankles, blue sleep eyes, rooted dark hair, individual fingers, dressed shirt, jeans, black vinyl boots, felt hat, marks: "Metro Goldwyn Mayer Inc.//Mfg. by// IDEAL TOY CORP//38" on head, "©IDEAL TOY CORP.//38" on back

30".................. $500.00 – 600.00
38".................. $700.00 – 750.00

Little Lost Baby, 1968, three faced doll

22"..................... $75.00 – 100.00

Mary Hartline, 1952, from TV personality on *Super Circus* show, hard plastic, fully jointed, blond nylon wig, blue sleep eyes,

lashes, black eyeshadow over and under eye, red, white, or green drum majorette costume and baton, red heart paper hang tag, with original box, marks: "P-91//IDEAL DOLL//MADE IN U.S.A." on head, "IDEAL DOLL//P-91 or IDEAL//16" on body

7½" .... $80.00 – 110.00
16".................. $500.00 – 700.00
22½"........ $1,100.00 – 1,300.00

Mini Monsters, 1965, Wolfy, Vampy, Franky, others

8¼"..................... $65.00 – 85.00

Miss Clairol, Glamour Misty, 1965 – 1966, vinyl head and arms, rigid plastic legs, body, rooted platinum blond saran hair, side-glancing eyes, high-heeled feet, teen doll had cosmetics to change her hair, all original, marks: "©1965//IDEAL TOY CORP//W-12-3" on neck, "©1965 IDEAL" in oval on lower rear torso

12"..................... $55.00 – 65.00

Miss Curity, 1953, hard plastic, saran wig, sleep eyes, black eyeshadow, nurse's outfit, navy cape, white cap, Bauer & Black first aid kit and book, curlers, uses Toni body, mark: "P-90 IDEAL DOLL, MADE IN U.S.A." on head

14½".............. $300.00 – 325.00

14" Miss Curity, hard plastic, $325.00. *Photo courtesy of Alderfer Auction & Appraisal.*

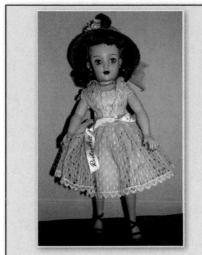

18" Miss Revlon, $325.00. *Photo courtesy of The Museum Doll Shop.*

Miss Ideal, 1961, all-vinyl, rooted nylon hair, jointed ankles, wrists, waist, arms, legs, closed smiling mouth, sleep eyes, original dress, with beauty kit and comb, marks: "©IDEAL TOY CORP.//SP-30-S" head, "©IDEAL TOY CORP.//G-30-S" back

    25" .... $200.00 – 235.00
    30" .... $300.00 – 350.00

Miss Revlon, 1956 – 1959, vinyl, hard plastic teenage body, jointed shoulders, waist, hips, and knees, high-heeled feet, rooted saran hair, sleep eyes, lashes, pierced ears, hang tag, original dress, some came with trunks, mark: "VT 20//IDEAL DOLL." Dolls listed are in good condition with original clothing, mint-in-box examples can bring double the values listed

    15" .... $225.00 – 275.00
    18" .... $300.00 – 325.00
    20" .... $200.00 – 250.00
    23" .... $250.00 – 400.00
    26", 1957 only . $300.00 – 350.00

Little Miss Revlon, 1958 – 1960, vinyl head and body, jointed head, arms, legs, swivel waist, high-heeled feet, rooted hair, sleep eyes, pierced ears with earrings, original clothes, with box, many extra boxed outfits available

    10¼" .... $125.00 – 200.00

Plassie, 1942, hard plastic head, molded and painted hair, composition shoulder plate, composition limbs, stuffed pink oilcloth body, blue sleep eyes, original dress, bonnet, mark: "IDEAL DOLL//MADE IN USA//PAT.NO. 225 2077" on head

    16" .... $160.00 – 200.00
    19" – 22" .... $120.00 – 145.00
    24" .... $160.00 – 180.00

Playpal Family of Dolls, 1959 – 1962

Patti, all-vinyl, jointed wrists, sleep eyes, curly or straight saran hair, bangs, closed mouth, blue or red and white checked dress with pinafore, three-year-old size, reissued in 1981 and 1982 from old molds, more for redheads, mark: "IDEAL TOY CORP.//G 35 OR B-19-1" on head

    35" .... $325.00 – 375.00
    Carrot red hair.. $700.00 – 800.00

Bonnie Playpal, 1959, Patti's three-month-old sister, made only one year, rooted blond hair, blue sleep eyes, blue and white checked outfit, white shoes and socks

    24" .... $375.00 – 400.00

Johnny Playpal, 1959, blue sleep eyes, molded hair, Patti's three-month-old brother

    24" .... $375.00 – 400.00

Pattite, 1960, rooted saran hair, sleep eyes, red and white checked dress, white pinafore with her name on it, looks like Patti Playpal

    18" .... $750.00 – 800.00
    18" ....$1,060.00* MIB

Penny Playpal, 1959, rooted blond or brown curly hair, blue sleep eyes, wears organdy dress, vinyl shoes, socks, Patti's two-year-old sister, made only one year, marks: "IDEAL DOLL//32-E-L" or "B-32-B PAT. PEND." on head, "IDEAL" on back

    32" .... $300.00 – 350.00

Peter Playpal, 1960 – 1961, gold sleep eyes,

23" Posie walker, vinyl and hard plastic, $250.00. *Photo courtesy of Alderfer Auction & Appraisal.*

freckles, pug nose, rooted blond or brunette hair, original clothes, black plastic shoes, marks: "©IDEAL TOY CORP.// BE-35-38" on head, "©IDEAL TOY CORP.//W-38//PAT. PEND." on body

    38".................. $700.00 – 750.00
    Walker
    38".................. $850.00 – 875.00
Suzy Playpal, 1959, rooted curly short blond saran hair, blue sleep eyes, wears purple dotted dress, Patti's one-year-old sister
    28".................. $375.00 – 400.00
Reissue Patti............. $200.00 – 225.00
Posie walker, 1954 – 1956
    17".................... $50.00 – 75.00
    23".................. $100.00 – 125.00
    25".................. $125.00 – 150.00
Rub-A-Dub Dolly, 1989
    15" – 18"............ $15.00 – 20.00
Samantha, 1965 – 1966, from TV show *Bewitched,* vinyl head, body, rooted saran hair, posable arms and legs, wearing red witch's costume, with broom, painted side-glancing eyes, other costume included negligee, mark: "IDEAL DOLL//M-12-E-2" on head

    12".................. $150.00 – 200.00
All original, with broom ..$550.00 – 600.00
Saucy walker, 1951 – 1955, all hard plastic, walks, turns head from side to side, flirty blue eyes, crier, open-closed mouth, teeth, holes in body for crier, saran wig, plastic curlers, came as toddler, boy, and "Big Sister"
    14".................. $130.00 – 155.00
    16".................. $160.00 – 190.00
    22".................. $175.00 – 200.00
Black
    16".................. $250.00 – 275.00
Big Sister, 1954
    25".................. $425.00 – 475.00
Snoozie
1958 – 1965, all-vinyl, rooted saran hair, blue sleep eyes, open-closed mouth, cry voice, knob makes doll wiggle, closed eyes, crier, in flannel pajamas
    14".................. $150.00 – 175.00
1964 – 1965, vinyl head, arms, legs, soft body, rooted saran hair, sleep eyes, turn knob, she squirms, opens and closes eyes, and cries
    20".................... $70.00 – 80.00
Storybook dolls, 1985, all-vinyl, rooted hair
    8"...................... $10.00 – 15.00

18" Saucy walker, $180.00. *Photo courtesy of McMasters Harris Auction Co.*

Ideal Novelty and Toy Co.

9" Pepper, Tammy family, $50.00. *Photo courtesy of The Museum Doll Shop.*

Tabitha, 1966, baby from TV show *Bewitched,* vinyl head, body, rooted platinum hair, painted blue side-glancing eyes, closed mouth, came in pajamas, mark: "©1965// Screen Gems, Inc.//Ideal Toy Corp.//T.A. 18-6//H-25" on head

    12½" .... $260.00 – 300.00

    Mint-in-box $1,500.00

Tammy Family dolls, dolls listed are in good condition wearing original clothing, mint-in-box examples can bring double the values listed.

Tammy, 1962+, vinyl head, arms, plastic legs and torso, head joined at neck base, marks: "©IDEAL TOY CORP.//BS12" on head, "©IDEAL TOY CORP.//BS-12//1" on back

    White

    12" .... $65.00 – 90.00

    Black

    12" .... $55.00 – 100.00

    Pos'n

    12" .... $40.00 – 50.00

    Mom

    12½" .... $35.00 – 40.00

    Dad

    13" .... $35.00 – 40.00

Dodi

    9" .... $35.00 – 40.00

Ted

    12½" .... $20.00 – 30.00

Pepper

    9" .... $35.00 – 70.00

Pos'n Pepper

    9" .... $40.00 – 50.00

Salty

    9" .... $65.00 – 85.00

Clothing (MIP) .... $70.00 – 140.00

Tearie Dearie, 1964

    9" .... $25.00 – 35.00

Thumbelina

1961 – 1962, vinyl head and limbs, soft cloth body, painted eyes, rooted saran hair, open-closed mouth, wind knob on back to move body, crier in 1962

    16" .... $200.00 – 225.00

    20" .... $300.00 – 350.00

1982 – 1983, all-vinyl one-piece body, rooted hair, non-moving, comes in quilted carrier, also black

    7" .... $20.00 – 30.00

1982, 1985, reissue from 1960s mold, vinyl head, arms, legs, cloth body, painted eyes, crier, open mouth, molded or rooted hair, original with box

    18" .... $30.00 – 40.00

Thumbelina, Ltd. Production Collector's Doll, 1983 – 1985, porcelain, painted eyes, molded and painted hair, beige crocheted outfit with pillow booties, limited edition 1,000

    18" .... $65.00 – 75.00

Tiny Thumbelina, 1962 – 1968, vinyl head, limbs, cloth body, painted eyes, rooted saran hair, wind key in back to make body and head move, original tagged clothes, marks: "IDEAL TOY CORP.//OTT 14" on head, "U.S. PAT. #3029552" on body

    14" .... $150.00 – 225.00

Newborn Thumbelina, 1968, vinyl head and

14" Toni, $600.00. *Photo courtesy of Morphy Auctions.*

arms, foam-stuffed body, rooted hair, painted eyes, pull string to squirm

9".................... $60.00 – 110.00

Toddler Thumbelina, 1969 – 1971, vinyl head and arms, cloth body, rooted hair, painted eyes

9".................... $75.00 – 100.00

Tiffany Taylor, 1974 – 1976, all-vinyl, rooted hair, top of head turns to change color, painted eyes, teenage body, high-heeled, extra outfits available

19".................... $60.00 – 80.00

Black

19".................... $60.00 – 70.00

Tippy Tumbles, 1977

17".................... $25.00 – 30.00

Toni, 1949, designed by Bernard Lipfert, all-hard plastic, jointed body, DuPont nylon wig, usually blue eyes, rosy cheeks, closed mouth, came with Toni wave set and curlers in original dress, with hang tag, marks: "IDEAL DOLL//MADE IN U.S.A." on head, "IDEAL DOLL" and P-series number on body. MIB can bring double

P-90

14"................. $300.00 – 400.00

P-91

16"................. $250.00 – 325.00

P-92

19"................. $480.00 – 500.00

P-93

21"................. $350.00 – 400.00

P-94

22½".............. $900.00 – 950.00

Tubsy, 1967

18"................. $180.00 – 200.00

Tuesday Taylor, 1976 – 1977, vinyl, posable body, turn head to change color of hair, clothing tagged "IDEAL Tuesday Taylor"

11½".................. $22.00 – 35.00

Whoopsie, 1978 – 1981, vinyl, reissued in 1981, marked: "22//©IDEAL TOY CORP// HONG KONG//1978//H298"

13".................... $25.00 – 35.00

Wizard of Oz Series, 1984 – 1985, Tin Man, Lion, Scarecrow, Dorothy, and Toto, all-vinyl, six-piece posable bodies

9"................$15.00 – 20.00 each

Batgirl, Mera Queen of Atlantis, Wonder Woman, and Super Girl, 1967 – 1968, all-vinyl, posable body, rooted hair, painted side-glancing eyes, dressed in costume

11½".............. $350.00 – 400.00

JULLIEN

1827 – 1904, Paris, France. After 1904 became a part of S.F.B.J. Had a porcelain factory, won some awards, purchased bisque heads from Francois Gaultier. Dolls listed are in good condition, appropriately dressed.

Child, bisque socket head, wig, glass eyes, pierced ears, open mouth with teeth or closed mouth, on jointed composition body

Closed mouth

17" – 19".. $3,600.00 – 4,100.00
24" – 26".. $4,600.00 – 5,000.00

Open mouth

18" – 20".. $1,900.00 – 2,400.00
29" – 30".. $2,300.00 – 2,500.00

JUMEAU

1842 – 1899, Paris and Montreuil-sous-Bois; in 1899 joined in S.F.B.J. which continued to make dolls marked Jumeau through 1958. Founder Pierre Francois Jumeau made fashion dolls with kid or wood bodies, head marked with size number, bodies stamped "JUMEAU//MEDAILLE D'OR//PARIS." Early Jumeau heads were pressed pre-1890. By 1878, son Emile Jumeau was head of the company and made Bébé Jumeau, marked on back of head, on chemise, band on arm of dress. Tête Jumeaux have poured heads. Bébé Protige and Bébé Jumeau registered trademarks in 1886, Bee mark in 1891, Bébé Marcheur in 1895, Bébé Francaise in 1896. Mold numbers of marked EJs and Têtes approximate the following heights: 1 – 10", 2 – 11", 3 – 12", 4 – 13", 5 – 14", 6 – 16", 7 – 17", 8 – 18", 9 – 20", 10 – 21", 11 – 24", 12 – 26", 13 – 30". Dolls listed are in good condition, nicely wigged, and with appropriate clothing. Exceptional dolls may be much more.

Poupée Jumeau (so-called French Fashion-type), 1860s on, marked with size number on swivel head, closed mouth, paperweight eyes, pierced ears, stamped kid body, add more for original clothes

Poupée Peau (kid body)

11" – 13".. $2,500.00 – 3,000.00
15" – 16".. $3,500.00 – 4,500.00
17" – 18".. $5,000.00 – 6,000.00
20"........... $6,000.00 – 6,100.00

Poupée Bois (wood body), bisque lower arms

10" – 11".$10,000.00 – 10,500.00
14" – 16".$13,00.00 – 14,000.00

So-called Portrait face

17" – 19". $7,500.00 – 8,000.00
21" – 23". $9,000.00 – 10,000.00

Wood body

19" – 21"..$10,000.00 – 12,000.00

Mature face with wooden body

25" $50,000.00*

Child doll

Portrait, 1877 – 1883, closed mouth, paperweight eyes, pierced ears, wigged (sometimes skin wig), straight-wristed composition body with separate balls at joints, head marked with size number only.

First series, almond eye

12" – 14½"
$24,000.00 – 30,000.00

21" Portrait poupée, $9,000.00. *Photo courtesy of Morphy Auctions.*

23" Portrait, second series, $19,000.00. *Photo courtesy of Skinner, Inc.*

16" – 18½"
$30,000.00 – 35,000.00
19" – 20".. $27,000.00 – 32,000.00
23"....... $39,000.00 – 41,000.00
25"....... $53,000.00 – 58,000.00
Second series
11" – 12".. $6,000.00 – 7,000.00
13" – 15".. $8,000.00 – 9,000.00
18" – 20".. $13,000.00 – 15,000.00
22"....... $17,000.00 – 19,000.00
25"....... $20,000.00 – 22,000.00
Long Face Triste Bébé, 1879 – 1886, head marked with number only, pierced applied ears, closed mouth, paperweight eyes, straight wrists on Jumeau marked body
20" – 23".. $25,000.00 – 30,000.00
26" – 27".. $26,000.00 – 33,000.00
31" – 33".. $29,000.00 – 35,000.00
Premiere, 1880, unmarked bébé, allow more for exceptional couturier outfit
9" – 12" .. $8,000.00 –12,000.00
15" – 16".. $13,000.00 – 14,000.00
17" – 19" . $14,000.00 – 17,000.00
E.J. Bébé, 1881 – 1886, earliest "EJ" mark above with number over initials, pressed bisque socket head, wig, paperweight eyes, pierced ears, closed mouth, jointed body with straight wrists
12" – 16". $10,000.00 – 11,000.00
17" – 18".. $12,000.00 – 16,000.00
19" – 21".. $16,000.00 – 23,000.00
23" – 24".. $23,000.00 – 27,000.00
EJ/A marked Bébé
25"....... $32,000.00 – 36,000.00
Mid "EJ," mark has size number centered between E and J (E 8 J), later with Déposé above
10" – 14" . $11,000.00 – 14,000.00
16" – 20".. $14,000.00 – 18,000.00
23" – 26".. $17,000.00 – 19,000.00
Déposé Jumeau, 1886 – 1889, poured bisque head marked "Déposé Jumeau" and size number, pierced ears, closed mouth, paperweight eyes, composition and wood body with straight wrists marked "Medaille d'Or Paris"
10" .... $9,000.00 – 10,000.00
12" – 14" .. $6,000.00 – 7,000.00
16" – 18" .. $8,000.00 – 10,000.00
20" – 23" . $11,000.00 – 13,000.00
25" – 26".. $14,000.00 – 15,000.00
Tête Jumeau, 1885 on, poured bisque socket head, red stamp on head, stamp or sticker on body, wig, glass eyes, pierced ears, closed

22" closed mouth tête, $8,200.00. *Photo courtesy of Morphy Auctions.*

27" open mouth tête, $2,900.00. *Photo courtesy of Sweetbriar Auctions.*

mouth, jointed composition body with straight wrists, may also be marked E.D. with size number when Douillet ran factory, uses tête face. The following sizes were used for têtes: 0 – 9", 1 – 10", 2 – 11", 3 – 12", 4 – 13", 5 – 14½", 6 – 16", 7 – 17", 8 – 19", 10 – 21½", 11 – 24", 12 – 26", 13 – 29", 14 – 31", 15 – 33", 16 – 34" – 35"

Bébé (Child), closed mouth

    9" – 10" , $9,000.00 – 10,000.00
    12" – 13" ... $6,000.00 – 8,000.00
    16" – 17".. $7,000.00 – 8,000.00
    19" – 22" ..... $7,500.00 – 8,500.00
    24" – 26".. $8,000.00 – 9,000.00
    29" – 31"..$12,000.00 – 15,000.00

Lady body

    14" – 16".. $3,700.00 – 4,500.00
    18" – 22".. $5,000.00 – 7,800.00

Open mouth, child

    12".......... $2,500.00 – 3,000.00
    17" – 22".. $3,000.00 – 3,200.00
    24" – 25".. $2,500.00 – 3,200.00
    27" – 29".. $2,900.00 – 3,400.00
    32" – 35".. $3,100.00 – 4,000.00

B. L. Bébé, 1892 on, marked "B. L." for the Louvre department store, socket head, wig, pierced ears, paperweight eyes, closed mouth, jointed composition body

    15" – 16".. $3,500.00 – 4,500.00
    18" – 23".. $4,700.00 – 5,100.00

Phonographe Jumeau, 1894 – 1899, bisque head, open mouth, phonograph in torso, working condition

    24" – 25"..$8,000.00 – 10,000.00

R.R. Bébé, 1892 on, wig, pierced ears, paperweight eyes, closed mouth, jointed composition body with straight wrists

    21" – 23".. $4,400.00 – 4,800.00
    Open mouth
    18"........... $3,000.00 – 3,100.00

Child, 1907 on, some with Tété Jumeau stamp, sleep or set eyes, open mouth, jointed French body

    14" – 16".. $1,200.00 – 1,500.00
    19" – 20".. $1,500.00 – 2,000.00
    23" – 26".. $2,500.00 – 2,600.00
    29" – 32".. $3,000.00 – 3,200.00
    35"........... $3,500.00 – 3,800.00

Character child

Mold 203, 208, and other 200 series, 1882 – 1899, glass eyes

    20" $70,000.00

Too few in database for a reliable range.

25", mold 1907, $2,600.00. *Photo courtesy of Dolls and Lace.*

Mold 217, crier
> 20".......................... $88,000.00
> 21"........................ $110,000.00

Too few in database for a reliable range.

Mold 230 child, 1910 on, open mouth socket head, glass eyes, wig, composition body
> 12" – 14"........ $650.00 – 700.00
> 20" – 23".. $1,100.00 – 1,300.00

Two-Faced Jumeau, crying and smiling
> 18"....... $15,000.00 – 16,000.00

Too few in database for a reliable range.

Princess Elizabeth, made after Jumeau joined SFBJ and adopted Unis label, mark will be "71 Unis//France 149//306//Jumeau//1938//Paris," bisque socket head with high color, closed mouth, flirty eyes, jointed composition body •
Mold 306
> 15"........... $1,500.00 – 1,800.00
> 18" – 19".. $2,000.00 – 2,200.00
> 32" – 33".. $4,500.00 – 5,000.00

Great Ladies of Fashion, Mold 221, 1940s – 1950s, bisque head, five-piece composition body with hole in one foot for stand, elaborate costumes and wigs representing Queen Victoria, Marie Antoinette, etc.
> 10"................. $400.00 – 600.00

10" Great Lady of Fashion, $500.00. *Photo courtesy of The Museum Doll Shop.*

Accessories
Marked Jumeau shoes
> 5" – 6"............ $300.00 – 400.00
> 7" – 10" .... $600.00 – 700.00

KAMKINS

1919 – 1928, Philadelphia, Pennsylvania, and Atlantic City, New Jersey. Cloth doll made by Louise R. Kampes Studio. Clothes made by cottage industry workers at home. All-cloth, molded mask face, painted features, swivel head, jointed shoulders and hips, mohair wig. Dolls listed are in good, clean, un-faded condition, allow 50% less for soiled or faded examples.
> 18" – 20".. $2,000.00 – 3,500.00

19" cloth boy, $3,000.00. *Photo courtesy of Skinner, Inc.*

KÄMMER & REINHARDT

1885 – 1933, Waltershausen, Germany. Registered trademark KAR, Majestic Doll, Mein Leibling, Die Kokette, Charakterpuppen (character dolls). Designed doll heads, most bisque were made by Simon & Halbig; in 1918, Schuetzmeister & Quendt also supplied heads; Rheinische Gummi und Celluloid Fabrik Co. made celluloid heads for Kämmer & Reinhardt. Kämmer & Reinhardt dolls were distributed by Bing, Borgfeldt, B. Illfelder, L. Rees & Co., Strobel & Wilken, and Louis Wolfe & Co. Also made heads of wood and composition, later cloth and rubber dolls. Mold numbers identify heads starting with 1) bisque socket heads; 2) shoulder heads, as well as socket heads of black or mulatto babies; 3) bisque socket heads or celluloid shoulder heads; 4) heads having eyelashes; 5) googlies, black heads, pincushion heads; 6) mulatto heads; 7) celluloid heads, bisque head walking dolls; 8) rubber heads; 9) composition heads, some rubber heads. Other letters refer to style or material of wig or clothing. All dolls listed are in good condition with appropriate clothing.

Child

Bisque socket head child

Mold 192 (possibly as early as 1892), jointed composition body, sleep eyes

    Closed mouth

    6" – 7"............ $600.00 – 700.00

    10" – 11" .... $900.00 – 1,000.00

    16" – 18".. $2,000.00 – 2,200.00

    22" – 24".. $2,400.00 – 2,600.00

    Open mouth

    7" – 8"............ $550.00 – 600.00

26" dolly-faced doll, no mold number, $1,100.00. *Photo courtesy of Morphy Auctions.*

15½", mold 101, flocked hair, $4,700.00. *Photo courtesy of Skinner, Inc.*

    12" – 14"........ $700.00 – 750.00

    16" – 18"........ $750.00 – 850.00

    20" – 22"........ $875.00 – 975.00

    26" – 28".. $1,100.00 – 1,300.00

Child, dolly face, 1910 to 1930s, bisque head with open mouth, jointed composition body, sleep eyes

No mold number or molds 191, 401, 402, 403

    On five-piece flapper style body

    5" – 6"............ $450.00 – 550.00

    7" – 8"............ $550.00 – 600.00

    Jointed composition body

    8" – 10" .... $400.00 – 500.00

    12" – 14"........ $450.00 – 550.00

    16" – 18"........ $600.00 – 750.00

    19" – 21"........ $800.00 – 900.00

    25" – 26".. $1,000.00 – 1,100.00

    28" – 30".. $1,200.00 – 1,500.00

Child shoulder head doll, kid body

    14"................. $325.00 – 375.00

    19" – 22" .... $400.00 – 425.00

Character dolls, 1909 on

Mold 100, baby often referred to by collectors as "Kaiser Baby," solid dome head, intaglio eyes, open-closed mouth, composition bent-limb body

    11" – 12"........ $425.00 – 475.00

    14" – 15"........ $575.00 – 600.00

    18" – 20"........ $700.00 – 800.00

Mold 101, Peter or Marie, painted eyes,

closed mouth, jointed body

    7" – 8"...... $1,700.00 – 1,900.00

    10" – 12".. $3,000.00 – 3,800.00

    14" – 15".. $4,200.00 – 4,500.00

    17" – 18".. $5,500.00 – 6,000.00

    19" – 20".. $5,500.00 – 6,000.00

Glass eyes

    18" – 20" . $9,000.00 – 12,500.00

Mold 102, Elsa or Walter, painted eyes, molded hair, closed mouth, very rare

    12"....... $19,000.00 – 22,000.00

Too few in database for a reliable range.

Mold 103, painted eyes, closed mouth

    19"......................... $80,000.00+

Too few in database for a reliable range.

Mold 104, ca. 1909, painted eyes, laughing closed mouth, very rare

    18"......................... $80,000.00+

Too few in database for a reliable range.

Mold 105, painted eyes, open-closed mouth, very rare

    21" $170,956.00

Too few in database for a reliable range.

Mold 106, painted intaglio eyes to side, closed mouth, very rare

    22"......................... $145,000.00

Too few in database for a reliable range.

Mold 107, Karl, painted intaglio eyes, closed mouth

    21" – 22" . $44,000.00 – 48,000.00

Mold 108, one example reported

                $275,000.00+

Too few in database for a reliable range.

Mold 109, Elise, painted eyes, closed mouth

    9" – 10".... $9,000.00 – 8,000.00

    12" – 14".. $14,000.00 – 18,000.00

    20" – 24".. $23,000.00 – 26,000.00

Mold 112, painted, open-closed mouth

    9"............................... $5,000.00

    13" – 15" . $9,000.00 – 10,000.00

    17" – 18".. $10,000.00 – 12,000.00

Glass eyes

    12" – 16" . $14,000.00 –18,000.00

22", mold 107, $48,000.00. *Photo courtesy of Skinner, Inc.*

Too few in database for a reliable range.

Mold 112X, flocked hair

    17"....... $13,000.00 – 15,000.00

Mold 114, Hans or Gretchen, painted eyes, closed mouth

    8" – 9"...... $2,000.00 – 2,200.00

21", mold 109, $24,000.00. *Photo courtesy of Skinner, Inc.*

13", mold 116A, open-closed mouth character baby, $1,200.00. *Photo courtesy of Morphy Auctions.*

12" – 13".. $3,000.00 – 4,000.00
18" – 20".. $7,000.00 – 8,000.00
23" – 25".. $8,000.00 – 9,000.00
Glass eyes
9"............. $5,900.00 – 6,200.00
15" .... $9,250.00 – 9,350.00
Mold 115, solid dome, painted hair, sleeping eyes, closed mouth, toddler
15"........... $4,250.00 – 5,750.00
Mold 115A, sleep eyes, closed mouth, wig
Baby, bent-leg body
10" – 12".. $2,200.00 – 2,400.00
14" – 16".. $2,900.00 – 3,300.00
19" – 22".. $3,300.00 – 3,500.00
Toddler, composition, jointed body
15" – 16".. $3,750.00 – 4,300.00
18" – 20".. $4,900.00 – 5,300.00
Mold 116, dome head, sleep eyes, open-closed mouth
10" – 13".. $1,500.00 – 1,800.00
Mold 116A, sleep eyes, open-closed mouth or open mouth, wigged, bent-leg
Baby
10" – 12".. $1,000.00 – 1,200.00
15" – 18".. $1,100.00 – 1,400.00
21" – 23".. $1,600.00 – 2,000.00
Toddler body

15" – 18".. $4,000.00 – 5,000.00
21" – 23".. $6,000.00 – 7,500.00
Mold 117, 117A Mein Liebling (My Darling), glass eyes, closed mouth
8" – 11".... $3,400.00 – 3,800.00
14" – 16".. $4,000.00 – 4,500.00
18" – 20".. $5,000.00 – 6,000.00
22" – 24".. $6,000.00 – 7,000.00
28" – 30".. $7,500.00 – 9,000.00
Flapper body
8".............................. $3,500.00
Too few in database for a reliable range.
Mold 117N, Mein Neuer Liebling (My New Darling), flirty eyes, open mouth
14" – 16" .. $1,100.00 – 1,300.00
20" – 22".. $1,400.00 – 1,600.00
28" – 30".. $2,200.00 – 2,400.00
Mold 117X, socket head, sleep eyes, open mouth
14" – 16"........ $850.00 – 950.00
22" – 24" ... $1,300.00 – 1,400.00
30" – 32" ... $1,600.00 – 1,800.00
Mold 118, 118A, sleep eyes, open mouth, baby body
11"........... $1,100.00 – 1,200.00
15"........... $1,300.00 – 1,500.00
18"........... $1,900.00 – 2,200.00

24", mold 121, open mouth character baby, $1,400.00. *Photo courtesy of Morphy Auctions.*

Mold 119, sleep eyes, open-closed mouth, marked "Baby," five-piece baby body

24" – 25".................. $16,000.00

Too few in database for a reliable range.

Mold 121, 122, sleep eyes, open mouth

Baby

10" – 11"........ $550.00 – 625.00

15" – 16"........ $850.00 – 950.00

20"........... $1,000.00 – 1,100.00

22" – 24".. $1,200.00 – 1,400.00

Toddler body

10".............. $900.00 – 1,000.00

13" – 14".. $1,150.00 – 1,250.00

18" – 20".. $1,300.00 – 1,500.00

Mold 123, Max, and Mold 124, Moritz, flirty sleep eyes, laughing/closed mouth, special body with molded shoes

16" . $48,000.00 – 55,000.00 pair

Mold 126 Mein Liebling Baby (My Darling Baby), sleep or flirty eyes, bent-leg

Baby

10" – 12"........ $450.00 – 500.00

14" – 16"........ $600.00 – 700.00

18" – 20"........ $500.00 – 600.00

22" – 24"........ $600.00 – 650.00

Toddler body

Five-piece body, with "starfish" hands

6" – 8"............ $700.00 – 800.00

9" – 10".......... $800.00 – 900.00

20" – 22", with flirty eyes

$1,200.00 – 1,300.00

Jointed composition body

15" – 17"........ $850.00 – 950.00

22" – 24".. $1,100.00 – 1,400.00

Mold 127, 127N, domed head-like mold 126, bent-leg body, add more for flirty eyes

Baby

10" – 11"........ $650.00 – 750.00

14" – 15"........ $800.00 – 900.00

18" – 22"..... $900.00 – 1,000.00

Toddler body

15" – 16".. $1,100.00 – 1,300.00

20" – 22".. $1,600.00 – 1,700.00

23", mold 717, celluloid socket head doll, $825.00. *Photo courtesy of Cybermogul Dolls.*

26"........... $1,900.00 – 2,000.00

Mold 128, sleep eyes, open mouth, baby body

10".................. $550.00 – 600.00

13" – 15"........ $700.00 – 800.00

20" – 24".. $1,200.00 – 1,600.00

Mold 131: See Googly section.

Mold 135, sleep eyes, open mouth, baby body

13" – 16"..... $950.00 – 1,100.00

Mold 171, Klein Mammi (Little Mammy), dome, open mouth

14" – 15".. $3,000.00 – 3,500.00

Too few in database for a reliable range.

Mold 214, shoulder head, painted eyes, closed mouth, similar to mold 114, muslin body

15"........... $3,100.00 – 3,400.00

Too few in database for a reliable range.

Mold 314, socket head, composition body, painted eyes, flocked hair

14" $6,250.00*

Puz, composition head, cloth body

16" – 17".. $1,000.00 – 1,300.00

25"........... $1,400.00 – 1,500.00

Cloth character dolls, 1927, wire armature body, needle-sculpted stockinette heads,

13" cloth caricature doll, $400.00. *Doll courtesy of Alfred Edward.*

painted features, wooden feet, all in good clean, unfaded condition

12" – 13"........ $300.00 – 400.00

Composition, 1930s on, sleep eyes, wigged

Baby, Mold 926

22"................. $150.00 – 200.00

Adult

Fat Character Man & Woman pair

8"................,,, $600.00 – 800.00

Too few in database for a reliable range.

Celluloid: See Celluloid section.

KENNER

1947 to 2000, Cincinnati, Ohio. Purchased by Tonka Toys in 1987 and then by Hasbro in 1991, run as a separate division by both. Dolls listed are in very good condition with all-original clothing and accessories. MIB can bring double valued listed.

Baby Alive, 1990, vinyl head, eats and drinks

16"..................... $18.00 – 24.00

Baby Bundles

16"..................... $10.00 – 15.00

Baby Yawnie, 1974, vinyl head, cloth body

15"..................... $15.00 – 20.00

Blythe, 1972, pull string to change color of eyes, mod clothes

11½"........... $900.00 – 1,300.00

Bob Scout, 1974

9"...................... $25.00 – 30.00

Butch Cassidy or Sundance Kid

4"...................... $10.00 – 15.00

Charlie Chaplin, 1973, all-cloth, walking mechanism

14"..................... $80.00 – 90.00

Cover Girls, 1978, posable elbows and knees, jointed hands

Dana, black

12½"................. $20.00 – 35.00

Darci, 1979

12½"................. $25.00 – 30.00

Erica, redhead

12½"................. $40.00 – 50.00

Crumpet, 1970, vinyl and plastic

18"..................... $45.00 – 50.00

Dusty, 1974, vinyl teenage doll

11"..................... $18.00 – 22.00

Skye, black, teenage friend of Dusty

11"..................... $15.00 – 20.00

Gabbigale, 1972

White

18"..................... $25.00 – 30.00

11½" Blythe, $1,000.00. *Photo courtesy of Withington Auction, Inc.*

Black

18".................... $30.00 – 35.00

Garden Gals, 1972, hand bent to hold watering can

6½"........................ $4.00 – 6.00

Hardy Boys, 1978, Shaun Cassidy, Parker Stevenson

12".................... $30.00 – 35.00

International Velvet, 1976, Tatum O'Neill

11½"................. $15.00 – 20.00

Jenny Jones and baby, 1973, all-vinyl, Jenny, 9"; Baby, 2½"

Set..................... $20.00 – 25.00

Nancy Nonsense, 1975, pull-string talker

17"..................... $50.00 – 60.00

Rose Petal, 1984, scented, various flowers and colors

7"....................... $12.00 – 25.00

Sea Wees, 1979 – 1984, mermaid dolls

7"....................... $10.00 – 15.00

Six Million Dollar Man figures, 1975 – 1977, TV show starring Lee Majors

Bionic Man, Big Foot

13".................... $20.00 – 25.00

Bionic Man, Masketron Robot

13"..................... $25.00 – 30.00

Bionic Woman, Robot

13"..................... $75.00 – 85.00

Jaime Sommers, Bionic Woman

13"..................... $30.00 – 45.00

Oscar Goldman, 1975 – 1977, with exploding briefcase

13"................... $90.00 – 100.00

Steve Austin, The Bionic Man

13" .... $75.00 – 90.00

Steve Austin, Bionic Grip, 1977

13"..................... $75.00 – 95.00

Star Wars figures, 1974 – 1978, large size action figures. Dolls listed are complete dolls in excellent condition. Never-removed-from-box would bring double the price or more.

Ben-Obi-Wan Kenobi

12"..................... $75.00 – 95.00

5" Cherry Cuddler, Strawberry Shortcake series, $65.00. *Photo courtesy of Emmie's Antique Doll Castle.*

Boba Fett

13"................. $155.00 – 175.00

16"................. $175.00 – 200.00

C-3PO

12".................... $90.00 – 100.00

Chewbacca

12"..................... $85.00 – 90.00

Darth Vader

12"................. $205.00 – 220.00

Han Solo

12"................. $400.00 – 500.00

IG-88

15"................. $450.00 – 550.00

Jawa

8½".................. $80.00 – 100.00

Leia Organa

11½".............. $225.00 – 275.00

Luke Skywalker

12"................. $225.00 – 275.00

R2-D2, robot

7½"................ $100.00 – 125.00

Stormtrooper

12"................. $200.00 – 235.00

Steve Scout, 1974, black

9"....................... $35.00 – 40.00

Strawberry Shortcake, ca. 1980 – 1986

5"....................... $45.00 – 50.00

Baby Strawberry Shortcake, blows kisses
    15".................... $20.00 – 25.00
Sweet Cookie, 1972
    18".................... $25.00 – 30.00
Terminator, Arnold Schwarzenegger, 1991, talks
    13½"................. $20.00 – 25.00

J.D. KESTNER

1805 – 1938, Waltershausen, Thüringia, Germany. Kestner was making dolls by the 1820s and was one of the first firms to make dressed dolls. Besides wooden dolls, papier-mâché, wax over composition, and Frozen Charlottes, Kestner made bisque dolls with leather or composition bodies, chinas, all-bisque dolls, and celluloid dolls. Supplied bisque heads to Catterfelder Puppenfabrik. Borgfeldt, Butler Bros., Century Doll Co., Horsman, R.H. Macy, Sears, Siegel Cooper, F.A.O. Schwarz, and others were distributors for Kestner. Early bisque heads with closed mouths marked X or XI, turned shoulder head, and swivel heads on shoulder plates are thought to be Kestners. After 1892, dolls were marked "made in Germany" with mold numbers.

Bisque heads with early mold numbers are stamped "Excelsior DRP No. 70 685," heads of 100 number series are marked "dep." Some early characters are unmarked or only marked with the mold number. After "211" on, it is believed all dolls were marked "JDK" or "JDK, Jr." Registered the "Crown Doll" (Kronen Puppe) in 1915, used crown on label on bodies and dolls.

The Kestner Alphabet was registered in 1897 as a design patent. It is possible to identify the sizes of doll heads by this key. Letter and number always go together: B/6, C/7, D/8, E/9, F/10, G/11, H/12, H¾ /12¾ , J/13, J¾ /13¾ , K/14, K½ /14½ , L/15, L½ /15½ , M/16, N/17.

Dolls listed are in good condition with original clothes or appropriately dressed. Exceptional dolls may be more.

Early socket head child, bisque socket head, 1880 on. Closed or open-closed mouth, plaster pate, may be marked with size numbers only, glass eyes, may sleep, composition ball-jointed body, sometimes with straight wrists, appropriate wig and dress, in good condition, more for original clothes.

Mold 128, 169, or no mold number, closed mouth, round or long face styles
    10" – 12".. $1,900.00 – 2,100.00
    14" – 16".. $2,900.00 – 3,200.00
    19" – 21".. $2,800.00 – 3,200.00
    24" – 25".. $3,100.00 – 3,400.00

Square face, closed mouth, some with white space between lips, no mold number
    14" – 16".. $2,000.00 – 2,600.00
    19" – 21".. $2,800.00 – 3,000.00
    24" – 25".. $3,200.00 – 3,400.00

A.T. look, closed mouth, glass eyes, marked only with size number such as 15 for 24"
    12" – 15" . $8,500.00 – 10,000.00
    21" ...... $11,000.00 – 14,000.00
    26"....... $15,000.00 – 16,000.00

16" early socket head child, closed mouth, $3,000.00. *Photo courtesy of Morphy Auctions.*

12" round face, $2,500.00. *Photo courtesy of Gloria's Antique Dolls.*

19" Bru-type, $5,500.00. *Photo courtesy of Gloria's Antique Dolls.*

Bru look, closed mouth with space between lips, glass eyes, resembles circle dot Bru
19" – 22".. $5,000.00 – 6,500.00
Mold X
15"........... $3,900.00 – 4,200.00
Mold XI
16"........... $4,000.00 – 4,200.00
Mold XII
17"........... $4,400.00 – 4,600.00
Mold 102, open mouth with square-cut teeth
9".............. $2,200.00 – 2,400.00
12" – 14".. $2,200.00 – 2,600.00
16" – 18".. $2,800.00 – 3,000.00
24" – 25".. $3,400.00 – 3,500.00

21" long face style doll, closed mouth, $3,200.00. *Photo courtesy of Dolls and Lace.*

Mold 103, pouty closed mouth
20"........... $2,200.00 – 2,500.00
23"........... $3,300.00 – 3,400.00
Pouty, no mold mark, closed mouth
10" – 12".. $1,300.00 – 1,500.00
22" – 24".. $3,500.00 – 4,000.00
Early shoulder head child, 1880 on, bisque shoulder head, glass eyes, plaster pate, wig, kid body with bisque lower arms, marked with size numbers or letter only
Closed mouth
12"................. $475.00 – 525.00
14" – 16"........ $700.00 – 800.00
20" – 22"........ $750.00 – 850.00
25" – 26"..... $900.00 – 1,000.00
A.T. look, closed mouth
11"........... $2,300.00 – 2,700.00
21" – 25".. $7,000.00 – 7,500.00
Open mouth
16" – 18"........ $350.00 – 400.00
22" – 24"........ $500.00 – 550.00
Turned shoulder head, closed mouth
16" – 18"........ $800.00 – 900.00
22" – 25".. $1,000.00 – 1,200.00
28"........... $1,500.00 – 1,700.00
Shoulder head child, 1892 on, bisque shoulder head with sleep eyes, open mouth, plaster pate, wigged, kid body

J.D. Kestner

26" turned shoulder head, $1,300.00. *Photo courtesy of Morphy Auctions.*

Mold 145, 147, 148, 154, 166, 195

10" – 14"........	$300.00 – 400.00
15" – 18"........	$400.00 – 500.00
20" – 22"........	$500.00 – 600.00
26" – 29"........	$650.00 – 700.00

Bisque socket head child, open mouth, glass eyes, Kestner ball-jointed body

Mold 142, 144, 146, 164, 167, 171, 214

8" – 12"..........	$700.00 – 800.00
14" – 16".....	$900.00 – 1,100.00
18" – 22"..	$1,100.00 – 1,200.00
24" – 26".....	$900.00 – 1,100.00
28" – 32"..	$1,200.00 – 1,500.00

Mold 171, 18" size only, called "Daisy"

18"...........	$1,500.00 – 1,800.00

Mold 129, 130, 149, 152, 160, 161, 168, 173, 174

10" – 12"........	$850.00 – 900.00
14" – 16"..	$1,200.00 – 1,500.00
18" – 22".....	$900.00 – 1,200.00
24" – 26"..	$1,000.00 – 1,400.00
28"..............	$900.00 –1,200.00

Mold 155, open mouth, glass eyes, five-piece or fully jointed body

11".................	$750.00 – 800.00

Molds 196, 215

18" – 20"........	$550.00 – 650.00
26" – 28"........	$700.00 – 750.00
32".................	$800.00 – 900.00

Character baby, 1910 on, socket head with wig or solid dome with painted hair, glass eyes, open mouth with bent-leg baby body, more for toddler body

Marked "JDK," solid dome bisque socket head, glass sleep eyes, molded and/or painted hair, composition bent-leg baby body, add more for body with crown label and/or original clothes

16" socket head, mold 167, $1,100.00. *Photo courtesy of Morphy Auctions.*

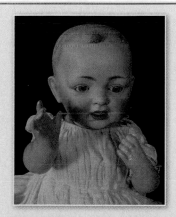

16" baby, incised JDK, $700.00. *Photo courtesy of Withington Auction, Inc.*

14", mold 245, Hilda, $2,200.00. *Photo courtesy of Morphy Auctions.*

12" – 14"........ $500.00 – 700.00
16" – 18"........ $700.00 – 900.00
21" – 25"..... $900.00 – 1,000.00
So-called Baby Jean, solid dome, fat cheeks, marked JDK
12" – 13".. $1,000.00 – 1,100.00
15" – 18".. $1,100.00 – 1,400.00
22" – 24".. $1,600.00 – 1,800.00
Mold 211, 226, 236, 257, 260, allow 25% more for toddler body
8" – 13".......... $400.00 – 600.00

11" character baby, mold 247, $1,100.00. *Photo courtesy of Morphy Auctions.*

16" – 18"........ $700.00 – 800.00
20" – 22"........ $800.00 – 900.00
24" – 26".. $1,000.00 – 1,200.00
Mold 210, 234, 235, 238, shoulder head, solid dome, sleep eyes, open-closed mouth or open mouth
12" – 14"........ $750.00 – 900.00
Mold 220, sleep eyes, open-closed mouth
14"........... $3,800.00 – 4,200.00
Toddler
19" – 20".. $5,000.00 – 5,500.00
26½"........ $8,000.00 – 9,000.00
Hilda, mold 237, 245, 1070 (bald solid dome), sleep eyes, open mouth
11" – 13".. $1,900.00 – 2,100.00
16" – 18".. $2,700.00 – 3,000.00
20" – 22" ..$3,500.00 – 4,500.00
25" – 26" .. $4,800.00 – 5,000.00
Mold 243, Asian baby, sleep eyes, open mouth
13" – 14" ..$5,000.00 – 5,500.00
16" – 18".. $6,000.00 – 6,500.00
Mold 247, socket head, open mouth, sleep eyes
14" – 16".. $1,500.00 – 1,800.00
Toddler
16" – 21".. $2,000.00 – 3,000.00
Mold 255, marked "O.I.C. made in

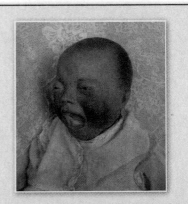

13" character baby, incised OIC, $3,100.00. *Photo courtesy of Dolls and Lace.*

12" character child, mold 206, $9,000.00. *Photo courtesy of James D. Julia, Inc.*

23½", mold 208, painted eyes, sold for $37,920.00 at auction. *Photo courtesy of Skinner, Inc.*

Germany," solid dome flange neck, glass eyes, large open-closed screamer mouth, cloth body

    11" – 13".. $2,800.00 – 3,100.00

Character child, 1910 on, socket head, wig, glass eyes, composition and wood jointed body

Mold 143 (1897 on, precursor to character dolls), open mouth, glass eyes, jointed body

    8" .... $950.00 – 1,000.00
    9" – 10".... $1,100.00 – 1,200.00
    12" – 14".. $1,300.00 – 1,500.00
    16" – 20".. $1,500.00 – 1,900.00

Mold 178, 179, 180, 181, 182, 184, 185, 186, 187, 189, 190, 191

Painted eyes

    9" – 12".... $2,000.00 – 3,000.00
    15" .... $3,500.00 – 4,000.00
    18" .... $7,500.00 – 9,000.00

Glass eyes

    12" .... $3,200.00 – 3,500.00
    15" .... $4,800.00 – 5,200.00
    18" .... $6,000.00 – 6,500.00

Mold 206, fat cheeks, closed mouth, glass eyes, child or toddler

    12" – 15" . $9,000.00 – 11,000.00
    19" .... $22,000.00 – 25,000.00

Too few in database for a reliable range.

Mold 208, for all-bisque, see that category

Painted eyes

    12" .... $9,500.00 – 10,500.00
    23½" $37,920.00*

Glass eyes

    16" .... $6,750.00 – 9,000.00

Too few in database for a reliable range.

Mold 239, socket head, open mouth, sleep eyes

Toddler, also comes as baby

    15" – 17".. $3,600.00 – 4,000.00

Mold 241, socket head, open mouth, sleep eyes

    17" – 18".. $6,000.00 – 7,000.00
    21" – 22".. $7,000.00 – 7,500.00
    25" .... $7,500.00 – 8,000.00
    28" – 30" . $8,000.00 – 10,000.00

Other character dolls

Mold 279 socket head with molded bobbed hairstyle, open mouth, glass eyes, on composition body

    15" .... $500.00 – 600.00

14" Moritz, $7,200.00. *Photo courtesy of Skinner, Inc.*

Max and Moritz, socket head on composition body
13" ...$6,700.00 – 7,200.00 each
Lady Doll, 1998 on, bisque socket head, open mouth, glass eyes, composition body, slender waist and molded breasts
Mold 162
16" – 22".. $1,500.00 – 2,000.00
Gibson Girl, Mold 172, shoulder head,

20" Gibson Girl, $2,100.00. *Photo courtesy of Withington Auction, Inc.*

closed mouth, glass eyes, kid body, bisque forearms
10"........... $1,000.00 – 1,100.00
15"........... $1,500.00 – 1,600.00
18" – 21".. $1,900.00 – 2,200.00
Wunderkind, set includes doll body with four interchangeable heads, some with extra apparel
With heads 174, 178, 184, or 185
11"........... $9,000.00 – 9,500.00
With heads 171, 179, 182, or 183
14½"........................ $12,650.00
Too few in database for a reliable range.
Celluloid shoulder head doll, sleep eyes, kid body, wigged
Mold 200, 201
16" – 20"........ $225.00 – 350.00

KEWPIE

1913 on, designed by Rose O'Neill. Manufactured by Borgfeldt, later Joseph Kallus, and then Jesco in 1984, and various companies with special license, as well as unlicensed companies. They were made of all-bisque, celluloid, cloth, composition, rubber, vinyl, zylonite, and other materials. Kewpie figurines (action Kewpies) have mold numbers 4843 through 4883. Kewpies were also marked with a round paper sticker on back, "KEWPIES DES. PAT. III, R. 1913; Germany; REG. US. PAT. OFF." On the front was a heart–shaped sticker marked "KEWPIE//REG. US.// PAT. OFF." May also be incised on the soles of the feet, "O'Neill." Dolls listed are in good condition, add more for label, accessories, original box, or exceptional doll.

All-bisque

Immobiles, standing, legs together, immobile, no joints, blue wings, molded and painted hair, painted side-glancing eyes
2" – 2½"........... $90.00 – 110.00

Kewpie

4"................... $110.00 – 125.00
5"................... $135.00 – 145.00
6"................... $200.00 – 225.00

Jointed shoulders

2" – 2½"......... $125.00 – 150.00
4"................... $225.00 – 275.00
5"................... $300.00 – 350.00
6"................... $350.00 – 400.00
7"................... $400.00 – 450.00
8"................... $475.00 – 500.00
10"................ $700.00 – 800.00
12"........... $1,000.00 – 1,100.00

Jointed hips and shoulders

4"................... $600.00 – 650.00
5" – 6"............ $700.00 – 850.00
7" – 8"......... $950.00 – 1,050.00
10"........... $1,150.00 – 1,250.00
12½"........ $1,300.00 – 1,350.00

Jointed shoulders with any article of molded clothing

2½"................ $500.00 – 600.00
4½".......... $1,100.00 – 2,100.00
6"............. $1,500.00 – 2,500.00
8"............. $1,800.00 – 2,800.00

With Mary Jane shoes

4½"................ $350.00 – 400.00
6½"................ $500.00 – 575.00

Bisque action figures

Arms folded

6"................... $525.00 – 600.00

Aviator

8½"................ $775.00 – 850.00

Back, laying down, kicking one foot

4"................... $250.00 – 300.00

Basket and ladybug, Kewpie seated

4"............. $1,400.00 – 1,700.00

"Blunderboo," Kewpie falling down

4½"................ $400.00 – 425.00

Bottle, green beverage, Kewpie standing, kicking out

2½"................ $525.00 – 575.00

Bottle stopper

2"................... $100.00 – 150.00

Box, heart shaped, with Kewpie kicker atop

4"................... $650.00 – 750.00

Bride and groom

3½"........$300.00 – 350.00 each
5"............$400.00 – 450.00 each

Boutonnière

1½"................. $85.00 – 110.00
2"................... $110.00 – 130.00

Bunny, in lap of seated Kewpie

2"................... $425.00 – 475.00

Candy container

4"................... $400.00 – 500.00

Carpenter, wearing tool apron

5" bride and groom, jointed shoulders, $700.00 pair. *Photo courtesy of Morphy Auctions.*

8½"............. $975.00 – 1,100.00

Cat, on lap of seated Kewpie
3" – 3½"......... $525.00 – 575.00

Chick, with seated Kewpie
2"................... $525.00 – 575.00

Christmas ornament, molded bisque clip on back
2"................... $500.00 – 550.00

Cowboy
10"................. $700.00 – 800.00

Dog, with Red Cross Kewpie
4"................... $250.00 – 300.00

Doodle Dog, alone
1½"............. $900.00 – 1,000.00
3"............. $1,400.00 – 2,000.00

Doodle Dog, with Kewpie
2½"......... $1,000.00 – 1,500.00

Drum, on brown stool, with Kewpie
3½"......... $2,000.00 – 2,200.00

Farmer
6½"................ $800.00 – 900.00

Flowers, Kewpie with bouquet in right hand
5"................... $825.00 – 925.00

Gardener
4"................... $475.00 – 525.00

Governor
2½"................ $325.00 – 375.00
3¼"................ $400.00 – 475.00

Guitar, standing Kewpie playing
3½"................ $300.00 – 350.00

Hatbox (turquoise), held by seated Kewpie
3"........... $1,500.00 – 1,600.00

Hottentot, black Kewpie
3½"................ $425.00 – 500.00
5"................... $575.00 – 675.00
9"................... $925.00 – 975.00

Huggers
2½"................ $150.00 – 175.00
3½"................ $225.00 – 250.00
4½"................ $300.00 – 325.00

Inkwell, with writing Kewpie
4½"................ $475.00 – 525.00

Jack-O-Lantern between legs of Kewpie

2"................... $450.00 – 500.00

Jester, with white hat on head
4½"................ $500.00 – 575.00

Kneeling
4"................... $475.00 – 550.00

Lying on Back
4" long............ $325.00 – 375.00

Lying on Tummy
3¼" long......... $275.00 – 325.00

Mailing label in hand
2¼"................ $550.00 – 650.00

Mandolin, green basket and seated Kewpie
2"................... $300.00 – 350.00

Mandolin, with Kewpie on placecard holder
2¾" long........ $150.00 – 200.00

Mayor, seated Kewpie in green wicker chair
4"................... $375.00 – 425.00

Minister
5"................... $200.00 – 250.00

Policeman
4½"........................... $1,100.00*

Reader Kewpie, seated, with book
2"................... $200.00 – 250.00
3½"................ $275.00 – 325.00
4"................... $450.00 – 500.00
2¾" long, on placecard holder
$150.00 – 175.00

Reader Kewpie in green armchair, seated with book
5½"........................... $1,350.00*

Rose in hand, on placecard holder
2"........................ $60.00 – 75.00

Salt shaker
2"................... $150.00 – 175.00

Seated with fly on hand
4"............. $1,000.00 – 1,400.00

Sailor
5"............................. $2,900.00*

Soldier, Confederate
4"................... $225.00 – 250.00

Soldier, Confederate, lying on stomach, aiming rifle
3"................... $450.00 – 500.00

Kewpie

12" composition, $190.00. *Photo courtesy of Withington Auction, Inc.*

Soldier, in Prussian helmet
5½"............... $800.00 – 850.00
Soldier, in Prussian helmet with rifle and saber
3¾"............. $900.00 – 1,000.00
Soldier, lying on stomach aiming rifle
3"................... $400.00 – 450.00
Soldier, vase, vase looks like tree
6½"............... $850.00 – 900.00
Soldier
2¾"............... $450.00 – 500.00
4½"............... $500.00 – 550.00
Stomach, Kewpie laying flat, arms and legs out
4" .... $375.00 – 450.00
Sweeper, with dust bin by leg
3½" – 4"......... $300.00 – 400.00
Teddy Bear held in arm of Kewpie
3¾" .... $625.00 – 650.00
Thinker
4" – 5"............ $200.00 – 300.00
6"................... $300.00 – 350.00
Traveler, with dog and umbrella
3½".......... $1,300.00 – 1,550.00
Traveler, with umbrella and bag
4"................... $350.00 – 400.00
5"................... $500.00 – 550.00

Vase, kewpie wearing pith helmet
6½"............... $475.00 – 525.00
Vase, with huggers
3¾"............... $575.00 – 650.00
Writer, seated Kewpie with pen in hand
2"................... $425.00 – 475.00
4"................... $500.00 – 550.00
Writer, seated Kewpie with pen in hand on bisque tray with note written on it
2½" X 4½" ..... $175.00 – 225.00
Bisque shoulder head, on cloth body
Painted eyes
7"............... $875.00 – 1,000.00
Glass eyes
12"........... $2,500.00 – 2,800.00
Bisque socket head, made by Kestner, glass eyes, composition body
12"........... $1,600.00 – 2,000.00
Carnival chalk, Kewpie with jointed shoulders
13"................... $75.00 – 125.00
Celluloid
Bride and Groom
4"....................... $15.00 – 40.00
Jointed arms, heart label on chest
5"................... $80.00 – 100.00
8"................... $165.00 – 185.00
12"................. $275.00 – 325.00
China
Perfume holder, one-piece, with opening at back of head
4½" .... $550.00 – 1,100.00
Salt Shaker
1¼"................... $85.00 – 125.00
Hatpin holder, Blue Jasperware with Kewpie figures
4½" .... $225.00 – 300.00
Dishes
Service for four......... $850.00 – 900.00
Service for six .... $1,000.00 – 1,200.00
German jasperware plaque, oval, 6" diameter
$200.00 – 250.00
Cloth
Richard Krueger "Kuddle Kewpie," silk-

14" Kuddle Kewpie, by R. Krueger, $325.00.
Photo courtesy of The Museum Doll Shop.

screened face, stockinette or sateen body, tagged

8" – 10".......... $250.00 – 300.00
13" – 14"........ $325.00 – 375.00
18" – 23"........ $575.00 – 650.00

Plush, with stockinette face, tagged

8"................... $195.00 – 225.00

Composition, made by Cameo Doll Co., Mutual Doll Co., and Rex Doll Co.

Hottentot, all-composition, heart decal to chest, jointed arms, red wings, ca. 1946

11" – 13"........ $400.00 – 450.00

All-composition, jointed body, blue wings

8"................... $125.00 – 150.00
11"................. $175.00 – 225.00
13"................. $225.00 – 275.00

Composition head, cloth body, flange neck, composition forearms, tagged floral dress

11"................. $250.00 – 300.00

Talcum container

One-piece composition talcum shaker with heart label on chest

11"................. $200.00 – 225.00

Hard plastic

Original box, 1950s, Kewpie design

8½"................ $275.00 – 300.00

Sleep eyes, five-piece body with starfish hands

14"................ $400.00 – 475.00

Metal

Figurine, cast steel on square base, excellent condition

5½"..................... $40.00 – 55.00

Sitting on a stamp box

4"................... $300.00 – 400.00

Soap

Kewpie soap figure with cotton batting, colored label with rhyme, marked "R.O. Wilson, 1917"

4"..................... $90.00 – 110.00

Vinyl

Cameo Dolls, 1960s, in very good condition with original clothing

12"..................... $65.00 – 75.00
14" – 16"............ $80.00 – 90.00
27"................. $125.00 – 175.00

Jesco Dolls, 1980s, mint, all-original condition

8"....................... $50.00 – 60.00
12"..................... $55.00 – 65.00
18"..................... $70.00 – 80.00
24"................. $140.00 – 200.00

Knickerbocker, late 1950s on, vinyl mask face on plush body

8" – 10" seated ... $60.00 – 70.00

Bunny Kuddles, Kewpie mask faced bunny wearing vinyl hat

11" seated........... $30.00 – 35.00

R. John Wright, 1999 on, molded felt, jointed shoulders, values listed are for secondary market dolls, dolls also available at retail

6"................... $400.00 – 500.00

KLEY & HAHN

1902 – 1930s, Ohrdruf, Thüringia, Germany. Bisque heads, jointed composition or leather bodies, composition and celluloid head dolls. Was an assembler and exporter; bought heads from Bähr & Pröschild, Kestner (Walkure), Hertel, Schwab & Co, and Rheinische Gummi. Dolls listed are in good

Kley & Hahn

condition, appropriately dressed.

Character baby, bisque socket head, bent-limb composition body, molds such as 133, 135, 138, 158, 160, 161, 167, 176, 525, 571, 680, and others

    11" – 13"........ $725.00 – 775.00
    16" – 18"........ $675.00 – 825.00
    20" – 22"........ $800.00 – 900.00
    24" – 26".. $1,000.00 – 1,100.00

Toddler body

    14" – 16".. $1,200.00 – 1,500.00
    18" – 21".. $1,700.00 – 2,000.00
    26"........... $2,200.00 – 2,300.00

Mold 567 (made by Bähr & Pröschild) character multi-face, laughing face, glass eyes, open mouth; crying face, painted eyes, open-closed mouth

    11"........... $1,000.00 – 1,400.00
    15"........... $1,950.00 – 2,100.00
    17"........... $2,200.00 – 2,400.00
    19"........... $2,400.00 – 2,600.00

Child, 1920, dolly face, sleep eyes, open mouth, molds 250, 282, or Walkure

    12" – 13"........ $475.00 – 550.00
    16" – 18"........ $550.00 – 750.00
    22" – 24"........ $600.00 – 700.00
    28" – 30"........ $700.00 – 800.00

23", mold 520, $4,500.00. *Photo courtesy of Skinner, Inc.*

    33" – 34"........ $800.00 – 900.00

Mold 325, "Dollar Princess," open mouth

    18" – 20"........ $425.00 – 475.00
    23" – 25"........ $400.00 – 450.00

Character child, 1912, bisque socket head, jointed composition body

Mold numbers 154, 166, 169

Closed mouth

    14" – 16" . $1,700.00 – 2,100.00
    19" – 20".. $2,400.00 – 2,700.00
    27"........... $3,000.00 – 3,300.00

Open mouth

    17" – 20".. $1,000.00 – 1,200.00

Painted-eye character, mold 520, 525, 526, 531

    14" – 16".. $2,100.00 – 2,700.00
    17" – 19".. $3,000.00 – 3,500.00
    20" – 23".. $4,000.00 – 4,500.00

Mold 336, open-closed mouth, intaglio eyes

    11" – 16".. $4,000.00 – 5,000.00

Mold 546, 549, ca. 1912, character face

    12" – 14".. $3,000.00 – 3,500.00
    15" – 16".. $4,100.00 – 4,700.00

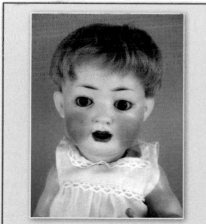

16", mold 167 Baby, $675.00. *Photo courtesy of McMasters Harris Auction Co.*

18" – 21".. $5,000.00 – 6,000.00
Mold 554, 568, ca. 1912, character face
21"............................. $1,400.00
Too few in database for a reliable range.

C.F. KLING & CO.

1834 – 1940s, Ohrdruf, Thüringia, Germany. Porcelain factory that began making doll heads in 1879, made china, bisque, and all-bisque dolls, and snow babies. Often mold number marks are followed by size number. Dolls listed are in good condition, appropriately dressed, more for exceptional doll with elaborate molded hair or bodice.

Bisque shoulder head, 1880 on
Painted eyes, molded hair, cloth or kid body, molds such as 123, 124, 131, 167, 178, 182, 186, 189, and others
7" – 8"............. $225.00 – 275.00
12" – 14"........ $300.00 – 400.00
15" – 16"........ $475.00 – 550.00
18" – 20"........ $625.00 – 700.00

22", mold 144, $2,200.00. *Photo courtesy of Withington Auction, Inc.*

23" – 25"........ $800.00 – 900.00
Glass eyes, molded hair, cloth or kid body, molds such as 190, 203, 204, 214, 217, 247, 254, and others
15" – 16"..... $800.00 – 1,300.00
22" – 23".. $1,000.00 – 1,400.00
Bisque lady, molded bodices, fancy hair, molds such as 135,144, 170, and others
15" – 17".. $1,500.00 – 2,000.00
19" – 21".. $1,900.00 – 2,200.00
China shoulder head, 1880 on, molded hair, painted eyes, closed mouth, molds such as 131, 188, 189, 202, 220, 285, and others
13" – 15"........ $250.00 – 300.00
18" – 20"........ $400.00 – 550.00
24" – 25"........ $700.00 – 775.00
Mold 188, glass eyes
18" – 20"........ $450.00 – 500.00
Bisque socket head, 1900 on, open mouth, sleep eyes, jointed body, molds such as 182, 370, 372, 373, 377
13" – 15"........ $225.00 – 350.00
17" – 22"........ $375.00 – 500.00
All-Bisque: See All-Bisque German section.

KLUMPE

1952 – 1970s, Barcelona, Spain. Caricature figures made of felt over wire armature with painted mask faces. Figures represent professionals, hobbyists, Spanish dancers, historical characters, and contemporary males and females performing a wide variety of tasks. Of the 200 or more different figures, the most common are Spanish dancers, bullfighters, and doctors. Some Klumpes were imported by Effanbee in the early 1950s. Originally the figures had two sewn-on identifying cardboard tags. Dolls listed are in good condition.
Average figure

10½" Klumpe lace maker, $100.00. *Photo courtesy of The Museum Doll Shop.*

10½".............. $90.00 – 110.00
Elaborate figure, with tags and accessories
    10½"... $200.00 – 275.00 and up

KNICKERBOCKER DOLL & TOY CO.

1927 – 1980s, New York, New York. Made dolls of cloth, composition, hard plastic, and vinyl.
Cloth
Clown
    17" .... $18.00 – 25.00
Disney characters
Donald Duck, Mickey Mouse, etc., all-cloth
    10½" – 12"..... $675.00 – 800.00
Matador from Ferdinand the Bull, all-cloth
    23"......................... $1,600.00*
Mickey Mouse, ca. 1930s, oilcloth eyes
    10" – 12".. $2,500.00 – 3,000.00
Cowboy Mickey
    12" – 17".. $3,000.00 – 4,000.00
Pinocchio, cloth and plush

13"................. $200.00 – 250.00
Seven Dwarfs, 1939 on, mask face, mohair beard, up-turned toes
    14".........$200.00 – 225.00 each
Snow White, all-cloth, mask face
    16"................. $325.00 – 375.00
Flintstones characters
    6½"..................... $12.00 – 16.00
Holly Hobbie, 1970s, cloth, later vinyl
Cloth
    7" – 9"................ $15.00 – 20.00
    14" – 16"............ $25.00 – 35.00
    26" – 28"............ $30.00 – 35.00
Vinyl
    11" .... $20.00 – 30.00
Levi's Big E Jeans dolls, 1973
    10" – 16"............ $40.00 – 50.00
Little Orphan Annie, 1977
    16"...................... $20.00 – 25.00
Composition
Blondie comic strip characters, painted features, hair
Alexander Bumstead, molded hair
    9"................... $375.00 – 425.00

14" cloth mask-face dwarf, Doc, $225.00. *Photo courtesy of The Museum Doll Shop.*

Blondie Bumstead, mohair wig
11"................. $725.00 – 800.00
Dagwood Bumstead, molded hair
14".............. $950.00 – 1,050.00
Child, 1938 on, mohair wig, sleep eyes
15"................. $220.00 – 265.00
18"................. $275.00 – 300.00
Disney, 1930s – 1940s, Mickey Mouse composition, cloth body
18".............. $900.00 – 1,100.00
Jiminy Cricket, all-composition
10"................. $500.00 – 550.00
Pinocchio, all-composition
14"................. $300.00 – 450.00
Seven Dwarfs, 1939+
9" ....$175.00 – 200.00 each
Sleeping Beauty, 1939+, bent right arm
15"................. $325.00 – 375.00
18"................. $400.00 – 450.00
Snow White, 1937+, all-composition, bent right arm, black wig
15"................. $395.00 – 425.00
20"................. $425.00 – 475.00
Molded hair and ribbon, mark: "WALT DISNEY//1937//KNICKERBOCKER"
13"................. $200.00 – 225.00

15"................. $225.00 – 275.00
Plastic and vinyl mask face dolls, 1950s – 1960s
Plush body
Pinocchio
13"..................... $40.00 – 60.00
Santa Claus, 1955 on
14"..................... $30.00 – 40.00
Sleepy Head
23"..................... $30.00 – 35.00
Cloth body
Lovely Lori
15"..................... $65.00 – 75.00
Vinyl head on cloth body
Soupy Sales
13"..................... $50.00 – 55.00
Quick Draw McGraw
16½"................. $80.00 – 90.00
Winnie Witch
13"..................... $45.00 – 50.00
Hard plastic and vinyl
Bozo the Clown
14"..................... $18.00 – 25.00
17" – 24"............ $40.00 – 60.00
Cinderella, two faces, one sad, one with tiara
16"..................... $15.00 – 20.00

3½" Dolly Pops, 1979 on, $12.00 – 15.00 each. *Photo courtesy of Memories of Things Past.*

Flintstones characters
17"..................... $36.00 – 43.00
Kewpies: See Kewpie section.
Little House on the Prairie, 1978
12"..................... $20.00 – 30.00
Little Orphan Annie comic strip characters, 1982
Daddy Warbucks
7"....................... $15.00 – 18.00
Little Orphan Annie, vinyl
6"....................... $14.00 – 18.00
11"..................... $20.00 – 30.00
Miss Hannigan
7"....................... $10.00 – 15.00
Molly
5½"..................... $8.00 – 12.00
Punjab
7" .... $12.00 – 15.00
Rattle dolls, hard plastic, jointed shoulders, painted side-glancing eyes
6"....................... $15.00 – 20.00
Snoopy, Charles Schulz character, 1965
8"....................... $40.00 – 50.00
Outfits, MOC.............. $10.00 – 30.00
Two-faced dolls, 1960s, vinyl face masks, one crying, one smiling
12"..................... $14.00 – 18.00
Dolly Pops, 1979 on, molded vinyl with synthetic hair, molded changeable vinyl clothing
2½"..................... $15.00 – 20.00
Dolly Pops playhouse
1982 .... $40.00 – 60.00

GEBRUDER KNOCH

1887 – 1919, Neustadt, Thüringia, Germany. Porcelain factory that made bisque doll heads with cloth or kid body.

Shoulder head
Dolly face
12" – 15"........ $125.00 – 195.00
Mold 203, 205, ca. 1910

Mold 203, character face, painted eyes, closed mouth, stuffed cloth body
Mold 205, "GKN" character face, intaglio eyes, open-closed mouth, molded tongue
12" – 13"........ $500.00 – 600.00
14" – 15"........ $675.00 – 725.00
Too few in database for a reliable range.
Socket head
Mold 179, 181, 190, 192, 193, 201, ca. 1900, mold 201 also came as black, dolly face, glass eyes, open mouth, ball jointed composition body
7" – 8" on five-piece body
$100.00 – 150.00
10" – 13"........ $175.00 – 250.00
18" – 25"........ $400.00 – 700.00
Mold 204, 205, ca. 1910, character face
15"............. $865.00 – 1,150.00
Mold 216, ca. 1912, "GKN" solid dome, intaglio eyes, laughing, open-closed mouth
11" – 13"........ $300.00 – 350.00
Too few in database for a reliable range.
Mold 229: See All-Bisque German category.
Mold 230, ca. 1912, molded bonnet, character shoulder head, painted eyes, open-closed mouth laughing, mold 232, ca. 1912, molded bonnet, character shoulder head
13"................ $675.00 – 900.00

15"........... $1,200.00 – 1,600.00

KÖNIG & WERNICKE GMBH

1912 – 1930s, Waltershausen, Germany. Had doll factory, made bisque or celluloid dolls with composition bodies, later dolls with hard rubber heads. Bought bisque heads from Bähr & Pröschild, Hertel, Schwab & Co., and Armand Marseille. Made "My Playmate" for Borgfeldt. Dolls listed are in good condition, appropriately dressed.

Bisque baby

Mold 98, 99, ca. 1910, *Mold 1070,* ca. 1915 "made in Germany" (made by Hertel, Schwab & Co.), character, socket head, sleep eyes, open mouth, teeth, tremble tongue, wigged, composition bent-leg baby body

    9" – 12".......... $325.00 – 450.00
    15" – 16"........ $500.00 – 600.00
    18" – 22"........ $600.00 – 800.00
    24" – 27"....... $900.00 – 1,100.0

Toddler

    11" – 13" .... $850.00 – 900.00
    15" – 17"........ $900.00 – 950.00
    19" – 20".. $1,000.00 – 1,200.00

14", mold 1070, $1,000.00. *Photo courtesy of Alderfer Auction & Appraisal.*

Child, socket head, composition body
Dolly face

    15"............... $475.00 – 525.00
    26" – 29"..... $950.00 – 1,000.00
    36"........... $1,100.00 – 1,200.00

Mold 1070, character child, sleep eyes

    15" .... $1,100.00 – 1,300.00
    20"........... $1,700.00 – 1,900.00
    30"........... $2,500.00 – 2,600.00

Painted bisque child, regional dress

    18"................. $125.00 – 175.00

Composition child, composition head on five-piece or fully jointed body, open mouth, sleep eyes, add more for flirty eyes

    14"................. $225.00 – 300.00
    16"................. $350.00 – 450.00

Celluloid child, mold 777, celluloid socket head, glass eyes, wigged

    13" – 15"........ $125.00 – 150.00
    17" – 21"........ $175.00 – 200.00

RICHARD KRUEGER

1907 – 1950s, New York City. Made cloth mask-faced dolls.

Child, 1930 on
Cloth body

    10"..................... $65.00 – 85.00
    12"................... $95.00 – 115.00
    16"................. $125.00 – 150.00
    20"................. $200.00 – 225.00

Oilcloth body

    10"..................... $65.00 – 80.00
    14" – 16".......... $85.00 – 100.00

Walt Disney and other characters
Dwarf, plush beard

    12½".............. $200.00 – 250.00

Pinocchio

    16"................. $500.00 – 600.00

Snow White

    18"................. $350.00 – 400.00

Three Little Pigs

    7"................$50.00 – 65.00 each

13" Krueger cloth mask-faced doll, $90.00. *Photo courtesy of Memories of Things Past.*

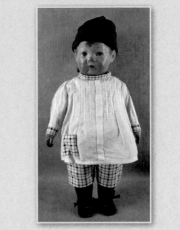

16", Doll I series, $3,000.00. *Photo courtesy of Joy's Antique Dolls.*

Kuddle Kewpie: See Kewpie section.
Scootles, 1935, designed by Rose O'Neill, yarn hair

10"................. $750.00 – 800.00
18"................. $825.00 – 875.00

KÄTHE KRUSE

1910 to present, Prussia, after WWII, Bavaria. Made cloth dolls with molded stockinette heads and waterproof muslin bodies, heads, hair, and hands oil painted. Early dolls are stuffed with deer hair. Early thumbs are part of the hand; after 1914 they are attached separately, later they're again part of the hand. Marked on the bottom of the left foot with number and name "Käthe Kruse," in black, red, or purple ink. After 1929, dolls had wigs, but some still had painted hair. Later dolls have plastic and vinyl heads. Original doll modeled after bust sculpture "Fiamingo" by Francois Duquesnois. Dolls listed are in good condition, appropriately dressed, allow significantly less for dirty or faded examples.
Cloth

Doll I Series, 1910 – 1929, all-cloth, jointed shoulders, wide hips, painted eyes and hair, three vertical seams in back of head, marked on left foot

16"........... $6,000.00 – 7,000.00
Ball-jointed knees, 1911 variant produced by Kämmer & Reinhardt

17"....... $12,000.00 – 14,000.00
Later model, 1929+, now with slim hips

17"........... $5,000.00 – 6,000.00
Doll IH Series, wigged version, 1930+

17"........... $3,200.00 – 3,500.00
Bambino, a doll for a doll, circa 1915 – 1925

8"................................. $500.00
Too few in database for a reliable range.
Doll II Series, "Schlenkerchen," ca. 1922 – 1936, smiling baby, open-closed mouth, stockinette covered body and limbs, one seam head

13"........... $8,500.00 – 9,500.00
Doll V, VI, Sandbabies Series, 1920s+, "Traumerchen" (closed eyes) and "Du Mein" (open eyes) were cloth dolls with painted hair, weighted with sand or unweighted, with or without belly buttons, in 19⅝" and 23⅝" sizes, one- or three-seam heads or cloth

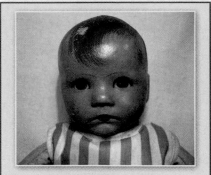

14" VII with "Du Mein," $3,500.00. *Photo courtesy of Joan & Lynette Antique Dolls and Accessories.*

14", marked "Made in US Zone," $500.00. *Photo courtesy of McMasters Harris Auction Co.*

over cardboard, later heads were made in the 1930s from a heavy composition called magnesit

19⅝" – 23½"
$6,000.00 – 8,000.00
Magnesit head, circa 1930s+
20"........... $1,500.00 – 1,600.00
Doll VII Series, circa 1927 – 1952, two versions were offered
Smaller 14" Du Mein open-eye baby, painted hair or wigged, three-seam head, wide hips, sewn-on thumbs, 1927 – 1930
14"........... $4,000.00 – 4,500.00
Doll I version, with wide hips, separately sewn-on thumbs, painted hair or wigged, after 1930 – 1950s slimmer hips and with thumbs formed with hand
14"........... $2,200.00 – 2,500.00
Doll VIII Series
Deutsche Kind, the "German child," 1929 on, modeled after Kruse's son, Friedebald, hollow head, swivels, one vertical seam in back of head, wigged, disk-jointed legs, later made in plastic during the 1950s
20"........... $2,500.00 – 3,000.00
Doll IX Series
"The Little German Child," 1929 on, wigged, one seam head, a smaller version of Doll VIII
14"........... $1,400.00 – 1,600.00

Doll X Series, 1935 on, smaller Doll I with one-seam head that turns
14"........... $2,500.00 – 2,800.00
Doll XII Series, 1930s, Hampelchen with loose legs, three vertical seams on back of head, painted hair, button and band on back to make legs stand. The 14" variation has head of Doll I; the 16" variation also has the head of Doll I, and is known after 1940s as Hempelschatz, Doll XIIB
14"........... $2,500.00 – 3,500.00
18"........... $4,000.00 – 5,000.00
Hard plastic, 1948 – 1975, celluloid and other synthetics
US Zone mark
14" – 19"........ $500.00 – 800.00
Turtle Mark Dolls, 1955 – 1961, synthetic bodies
14"................. $225.00 – 275.00
16"................. $300.00 – 350.00
18"................. $400.00 – 450.00
1975 to date, marked with size number in centimeters, B for baby, H for hair, and G for painted hair
10"................. $150.00 – 200.00
13"................. $175.00 – 225.00

GEBRUDER KUHNLENZ

1884 – 1935, Kronach, Bavaria, Germany. Porcelain factory made dolls, doll heads, movable children, and swimmers. Butler Bros. and Marshall Field distributed their dolls.

Closed-mouth child

Mold 22, bisque solid dome socket head, closed mouth, glass eyes, pierced ears, wig, wood and composition jointed body

    10" – 12"........ $525.00 – 575.00

Mold 28, 31, 32, 39, ca. 1890, bisque socket head, closed mouth, glass eyes, pierced ears, wig, wood and composition jointed body

    8" – 10"....... $800.00 – 1,000.00
    15" – 16".. $1,500.00 – 1,700.00
    21" – 23".. $2,200.00 – 2,500.00

Mold 34, Bru type, paperweight eyes, closed mouth, pierced ears, composition jointed body

    12½" – 15".. $2,900.00 – 4,000.00
    18" – 20".. $4,500.00 – 6,300.00

Mold 38, solid dome turned shoulder head, closed mouth, pierced ears, kid body

    12" – 15"........ $450.00 – 525.00
    17" – 20"........ $700.00 – 800.00

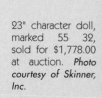

23" character doll, marked 55 32, sold for $1,778.00 at auction. *Photo courtesy of Skinner, Inc.*

Open-mouth child

Mold 41, 44, socket head, glass eyes, open mouth, composition body

    6" – 8"............ $250.00 – 300.00
    9" – 10" .... $575.00 – 675.00
    15" – 19"........ $725.00 – 800.00
    24" – 26" . $1,000.00 – 1,200.00
    30" – 31".. $1,300.00 – 1,400.00

Mold 165, ca. 1900, socket head, sleep eyes, open mouth, teeth

    16" – 18"........ $400.00 – 450.00
    22" – 24"........ $500.00 – 600.00
    30" – 33"........ $725.00 – 800.00

Mold 47, 61, 170, shoulder head

    14" – 16"........ $375.00 – 450.00
    18" – 20"........ $425.00 – 500.00

Character dolls

Mold 205, shoulder head, open-closed mouth, intaglio eyes, molded painted hair

    20".................. $550.00 – 600.00

No mold #, open-closed laughing mouth, glass eyes

    15"........... $1,000.00 – 1,200.00

Small dolls, 44 marked "Gbr. K" in sunburst, socket head, glass eyes, open mouth, five-piece composition body

    7" – 8"............ $250.00 – 325.00

All-bisque, swivel neck, molds 31, 41, 44, 56, others, glass eyes

    5" – 7"......... $650.00 – 1,000.00

A. LANTERNIER & CIE.

1915 – 1924, Limoges, France. Porcelain factory, made dolls and heads. Lady dolls were dressed in French provincial costumes, bodies by Ortyz; dolls were produced for Association to Aid War Widows.

Adult, ca. 1915

Marked "Caprice," "Lorraine," "Favorite," bisque socket head, open-closed mouth with

18" open-mouth child, $575.00. *Doll courtesy of Lucy DiTerlizzi.*

teeth, composition adult body

13"................. $800.00 – 900.00
16" – 18"..... $900.00 – 1,000.00
22"........... $1,000.00 – 1,200.00

Painted eyes

12½"........ $1,000.00 – 1,975.00

Child, dolly face no mold name or "Cherie," "Favorite," "La Georgienne," bisque socket head, open mouth with teeth, wig, composition jointed body

12" – 14"........ $400.00 – 450.00

17" Toto, $1,000.00. *Photo courtesy of Joan & Lynette Antique Dolls and Accessories.*

16" – 20"........ $550.00 – 600.00
22" – 24"........ $600.00 – 700.00
25" – 26"........ $700.00 – 900.00

Character child, marked "Toto"

15" – 18"..... $800.00 – 1,000.00

LAWTON DOLL CO.

1979 to present, Turlock, California. Founded by Wendy Lawton. Dolls listed are mint-in-box; dolls missing accessories or with flaws would be priced less.

Connoisseur Collections

Best Friends

Bianca & Bratwurst, 2003
$250.00 – 300.00

Gigi & Gigot, 2003
$375.00 – 400.00

Cherished Customs

The Blessing, 1990
13½" .... $165.00 – 195.00

Childhood Classics

Bobbsey Twins, 1991
$135.00 – 175.00 each

Hans Brinker, 1985
14"................. $300.00 – 350.00

Heidi, 1984
14"................. $150.00 – 200.00

Li'l Princess, 1989
14"................. $400.00 – 450.00

Marcella & Raggedy Ann, 1988
$350.00 – 400.00

Pollyanna,1986
14"................. $350.00 – 400.00

Children's Literature

Mirette, LE 750, 1998, porcelain and wood
14" .... $250.00 – 300.00

Christmas Collection

Christmas Joy, 1988
$650.00 – 700.00

Christmas Angel, 1990
$100.00 – 150.00

Yuletide Carole, 1991

Lawton Doll Co.

9" Mary Lennox, Library Collection, ca. 2000, $500.00. *Doll courtesy of Dominique Perrin.*

$150.00 – 200.00
Victorian Christmas, 1997
$175.00 – 200.00
Music of Christmas, 2001
$215.00 – 265.00
Classic Literature
Scarlet Letter, 1996
$325.00 – 350.00
Daughters of Faith
Ransom's Mark, 2003
$350.00 – 400.00
Hallelujah Lass, 2004
$350.00 – 400.00
Library Collection
Secret Garden, 2000
9".................. $450.00 – 500.00
Alice in Wonderland, 2002
9".................. $425.00 – 450.00
Rebecca of Sunnybrook Farm, 2004
9".................. $425.00 – 475.00
Gallery Editions
Story Book Collection
Polly Put the Kettle On, porcelain doll, 2000
14"..................... $25.00 – 30.00
Toy's 'n' Treasures Collection
Sarah's Sock Monkey, porcelain doll, 2000
12"..................... $55.00 – 65.00
Ashton-Drake Collection

Lawton's Nursery Rhymes
Little Bo Peep, Miss Muffet, Mary Mary, Mary
Had a little Lamb
$25.00 – 35.00
Little Women Collection, 1994
Set of four .... $275.00 – 300.00
Walt Disney Collection
Main Street, 1989 (250)
$200.00 – 300.00
Liberty Square, 1990 (250)
$250.00 – 350.00
Tish, 1991 (250)...... $250.00 – 350.00
Melissa & Her Mickey, 1994 (100)
$600.00 – 700.00
Passionate Pursuits
The Bookworm, 2002
9".................. $250.00 – 275.00
Guild Doll Collection
Ba Ba Black Sheep, 1989, porcelain
14"................. $200.00 – 300.00
Lavender Blue, 1990.. $300.00 – 400.00
Travel Doll, 1997, with trunk and accessories
$900.00 – 1,000.00
Haute Couture, 2002
14"................. $275.00 – 300.00
Bon Voyage, 2003 ... $350.00 – 400.00
Exclusive Editions Collection
Convention/event dolls

1ˢᵗ WL Convention, Lotta Crabtree, 1992
$1,300.00
Too few in database for a reliable range.
Beatrice Louise, UFDC, 1998 Luncheon
$890.00 – 975.00
Josephine, UFDC Regional
12"................. $700.00 – 750.00
Katrena, UFDC Convention, 2002
9½"..................... $50.00 – 75.00
Store Specials
Little Colonel, Dolly Dears, Birmingham, Alabama................. $375.00 – 425.00

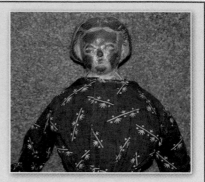

16" leather doll by Darrow, $400.00. *Photo courtesy of The Museum Doll Shop.*

LEATHER

Leather was an available resource for Native Americans to use for making doll heads, bodies, or entire dolls. It was also used by American doll makers such as Darrow and by French and Moroccan doll makers, as well as others. Some examples of Gussie Decker's dolls were advertised as "impossible for child to hurt itself" and leather was fine for teething babies.

Darrow, American, molded rawhide. These dolls are almost always found with very little original paint remaining, values listed reflect this condition
12"................. $300.00 – 350.00
18" – 22"........ $550.00 – 650.00
French, all-leather baby, molded head, jointed body, painted eyes
4" – 4½"... $2,400.00 – 2,600.00
French boudoir-type doll, 1960s, appliquéd mouth, fur eyelashes
23"..................... $75.00 – 85.00
Moroccan leather dolls, 1900 – 1940s, souvenir-type dolls depicting regional characters
9" – 11".............. $25.00 – 45.00
Native American dolls
Plains tribes, various, 1900 on
5" – 8"............ $130.00 – 225.00

13" – 15"........ $400.00 – 650.00
23"................. $700.00 – 850.00
Eskimo, ca. 1940
10"...............................$110.00
12"...............................$125.00
Todhunter, M. 1926 on, England, leather over molded clay face, wire armature body wrapped with suede
10" – 12"........ $120.00 – 150.00

LENCI

1919 to 2003, Turino, Italy. Lenci was the trademark and name of firm started by Enrico and Elena di Scavini that made felt dolls with pressed faces, also made composition head dolls, wooden dolls, and porcelain figurines and dolls. Early Lenci dolls have tiny metal button hang tags with "Lenci//Torino//Made in Italy." Ribbon strips marked "Lenci//Made in Italy" were found in the clothes ca. 1925 – 1950. Some, but not all dolls have "Lenci" marked in purple or black ink on the sole of the foot. Some with original paper tags may be marked with a model number in pencil. Dolls have felt swivel heads, oil-painted features, often side-glancing eyes, jointed shoulders and hips, third and fourth fingers are often sewn together, sewn-on double felt ears, often

Lenci

dressed in felt and organdy original clothes, excellent condition. May have scalloped socks.

The most sought after are the well constructed early dolls from the 1920s and 1930s, when Madame Lenci had control of the design and they were more elaborate with fanciful, well-made accessories. They carried animals of wood or felt, baskets, felt vegetables, purses, or bouquets of felt flowers. This era of dolls had eyeshadow, dots in corner of eye, two-tone lips, with lower lip highlighted and, depending on condition, will command higher prices.

After WWII the company was purchased by the Garella Brothers. The later dolls of the 1940s and 1950s have hard cardboard-like felt faces, with less intricate details, like less elaborate appliqués, fewer accessories, and other types of fabrics such as taffeta, cotton, and rayon, all showing a decline in quality and should not be priced as earlier dolls. The later dolls may have fabric covered cardboard torsos. Model numbers changed over the years, so what was a certain model number early, later became another letter or number.

Lenci characteristics include double layer ears, scalloped cotton socks. Early dolls may have rooted mohair wig, 1930s dolls may have "frizzed" played-with wigs. Later dolls are less elaborate with hard cardboard-type felt faces. Dolls listed are in clean condition and wearing original clothing. Soiled, faded examples will bring significantly less. Add more for tags, boxes, or accessories. Exceptional dolls and rare examples may go much higher.

Baby
    13" – 15".. $1,700.00 – 1,900.00
    18" – 22".. $2,700.00 – 3,000.00
    1930s, Bambino, felt over metal baby
    16"........... $5,000.00 – 6,500.00

19" 300 Series in regional costume, $3,000.00. *Photo courtesy of Morphy Auctions.*

Too few in database for a reliable range.

Child
1920s – 1930s, softer face, more elaborate costume, face model numbers 300, 109, 149, 159, 111
    12" – 14".. $1,200.00 – 1,500.00
    16" – 18".. $2,100.00 – 3,000.00
Model 1500, scowling face
    17" – 19".. $2,200.00 – 2,700.00

10" Funghetto, $200.00. *Photo courtesy of Lucy DiTerlizzi.*

Lenci

Model 500

    21".......... $1,600.00 – 1,800.00

1940s – 1950s+, hard face, less intricate costume

    13"................ $300.00 – 400.00

    15"................ $400.00 – 500.00

    17"................ $500.00 – 600.00

Small dolls

Mascottes and miniatures, 9"

Child .... $300.00 – 475.00

Regional costume...... $300.00 – 450.00

Long-limbed lady dolls, with adult face, flapper or boudoir body with long slim limbs

    17" – 20".. $3,000.00 – 3,500.00

    24" – 28".. $4,000.00 – 6,000.00

    32".......... $5,200.00 – 6,200.00

Rarities

Celebrities

Bach

    17".......... $2,500.00 – 2,850.00

Mendel

    22".......... $3,400.00 – 3,700.00

Mozart

    11".......... $2,300.00 – 2,400.00

    14".......... $3,000.00 – 3,200.00

Pastorelle

    14".......... $2,900.00 – 3,100.00

Tom Mix

    18".......... $3,000.00 – 3,500.00

Valentino

    30"........................ $15,099.00*

Characters

Aladdin

    14".......... $7,000.00 – 7,750.00

Aviator, girl with felt helmet

    18".......... $2,900.00 – 3,200.00

Becassine

    11"................ $925.00 – 975.00

    20" glass eyes

             $2,900.00 – 3,100.00

Benedetta

    19".......... $1,000.00 – 1,100.00

Black child, in native garb

    15".......... $3,200.00 – 4,000.00

Cowboy

    14".......... $1,000.00 – 1,100.00

Cupid

    17".......... $4,900.00 – 5,200.00

Elf, ca. 1926, black

    7"............................. $3,000.00*

Fascist Boy, rare

    14".......... $1,500.00 – 2,000.00

Flower Girl, ca. 1930

    20".......... $1,200.00 – 1,400.00

9" Mascottes, $300.00 – 475.00 each. *Dolls courtesy of Carol Barboza.*

Henriette
26".......... $1,800.00 – 2,100.00
Indian
17".......... $3,200.00 – 3,600.00
Laura
16".............. $950.00 – 1,100.00
Pierrot
21".......... $2,100.00 – 2,900.00
Pinocchio
11"...................... $1,100.00 MIB
Salome, ca. 1920, brown felt, ball at waist allows doll to swivel
17".......... $3,000.00 – 3,500.00
Smoker
Glass eyes
24".......... $4,000.00 – 4,200.00
Painted eyes
28".......... $2,500.00 – 3,000.00
Solider, in Italian uniform
17".......... $2,500.00 – 3,000.00
Sport Series
16" – 18".. $3,000.00 – 6,000.00
Polo Player
16" – 17" . $9,000.00 – 12,000.00
Val Gardena
19"................. $800.00 – 900.00
Winking Boy
11".............. $950.00 – 1,050.00
Ethnic or Regional Costume
Asian boy with lantern
25".......... $4,500.00 – 5,000.00
Bali dancer
15".............. $950.00 – 1,500.00
Dutch boy
18".......... $4,750.00 – 6,000.00
Madame Butterfly, ca. 1926
17".......... $3,000.00 – 3,200.00
25".......... $4,300.00 – 4,800.00
Marenka, Russian girl, ca. 1930
19".......... $3,000.00 – 3,500.00
Scottish girl, ca. 1930
14"................. $600.00 – 700.00
Spanish girl, ca. 1930

14".......... $1,200.00 – 1,400.00
19".......... $2,500.00 – 3,000.00
Tyrol boy or girl, ca. 1935
18".......... $4,500.00 – 5,000.00
Eye variations
Glass eyes
16".......... $1,400.00 – 1,600.00
22".......... $2,800.00 – 3,000.00
Flirty glass eyes
15".......... $2,000.00 – 2,200.00
20".......... $2,600.00 – 2,800.00
Surprise eye, widow, "O" shaped eyes and mouth
19" – 20".. $3,000.00 – 3,500.00
Modern, 1979 on
12" – 14".......... $90.00 – 150.00
21" – 26"........ $100.00 – 300.00
Pinocchio, 1981
18"................. $100.00 – 120.00
Accessories
Lenci Dog................ $100.00 – 150.00
Purse .... $175.00 – 225.00

LENCI-TYPE

1920 – 1950. These were made by many English, French, or Italian firms like Anili, Gre-Poir, or Raynal from felt with painted features, mohair wig, original clothes. These must be in very good condition, tagged or unmarked. Usually Lenci-types have single felt ears or no ears.
Child
Low quality
15" – 17"........ $145.00 – 165.00
High quality
11" – 15" .... $500.00 – 600.00
17" – 20"........ $600.00 – 650.00
Regional costume, makers such as Alma, Vecchiotti, and others
8" – 9"............ $125.00 – 145.00
11" – 15"........ $150.00 – 200.00
Smoker
16"................. $350.00 – 400.00

Alma, dolls have elastic strung heads
Child
    11" .... $200.00 – 225.00
    15" – 17"..... $700.00 – 1,100.00
Anili, founded by the daughter of Elena Di Scavini (Lenci), molded felt dolls
Child
    16" – 21" .... $125.00 – 150.00
Gre-Poir, France, New York City, 1927 – 1930s, Eugenie Poir made felt or cloth mask face dolls, unmarked on body, no ears, white socks with three stripes, hang tag
    16" – 18"
    Cloth face .... $375.00 – 425.00
    Felt face .... $800.00 – 900.00
Messina-Vat, 1923 on, Turin, Italy
    20" .... $375.00 – 450.00

LIBERTY OF LONDON

1906 to 1950s, London, England. Liberty of London was founded in 1873. In

9" Queen Elizabeth II, $250.00. *Photo courtesy of Alderfer Auction & Appraisal.*

1920 they registered the name "Liberty" for their line of needle-sculpted cloth art dolls.
British characters and historical figures, such as Shakespeare, John Bull, Queen Victoria, and others
    9" – 10".......... $150.00 – 250.00
Beefeater................. $100.00 – 150.00
Coronation dolls
    9" – 10".......... $200.00 – 250.00
Princess Elizabeth or Margaret
    7" .... $300.00 – 350.00

A.G. LIMBACH

1772 – 1927 on, Limbach, Thüringia, Germany. This porcelain factory made bisque head dolls, china dolls, bathing dolls, and all-bisque dolls beginning in 1872. Usually marked with three-leaf clover.
All-bisque
Child, small doll, molded hair or wigged, painted eyes, molded and painted shoes and socks, may have mark "8661," and cloverleaf, more for exceptional dolls
    3½".................... $75.00 – 85.00
    4" – 5"............ $110.00 – 125.00
    6" – 7"............ $175.00 – 225.00
    11" – 12"........ $350.00 – 450.00
Paper sticker marked "Our Mary," all-bisque, glass sleep eyes, wigged
    6" – 8"............ $225.00 – 275.00
Baby, mold 8682, character face, bisque socket head, glass eyes, clover mark, bent-leg baby body, wig, open-closed mouth
    8½" – 11"....... $325.00 – 400.00
Child
Bisque socket head, may have name above mold mark, such as Norma, Rita, Wally, glass eyes, clover mark, wig, open mouth
    18" – 20"........ $400.00 – 500.00
    22" – 24"........ $600.00 – 675.00
Bisque shoulder head, open mouth, glass eyes, kid body

10" – 11"........... $80.00 – 110.00

Lady

Irish Queen: See Parian-type, Untinted Bisque section.

MAROTTES

1860 on and earlier. Doll's head on wooden or ivory stick, sometimes with whistle, when twirled some play music. Bisque head on stick made by various French and German companies.

Bisque

German head, open mouth dolly-face mold, various German makers such as Armand Marseille, Gebrüder Heubach, etc.

9" – 14"........... $500.00 – 800.00

16" – 18"..... $900.00 – 1,100.00

Character mold

9" – 14"....... $900.00 – 1,500.00

French head

14" – 16".. $1,000.00 – 1,400.00

Celluloid

11" – 15"........ $200.00 – 350.00

9", German bisque head, $600.00. *Photo courtesy of Dollsantique.*

ARMAND MARSEILLE

1884 – 1950s, Sonneberg, Köppelsdorf, Thüringia, Germany. One of the largest suppliers of bisque doll heads, ca. 1900 – 1930, to such companies as Amberg, Arranbee, Bergmann, Borgfeldt, Butler Bros., Dressel, Montgomery Ward, Sears, Steiner, Wiegand, Louis Wolfe, and others. Made some doll heads with no mold numbers, but names, such as Alma, Baby Betty, Baby Gloria, Baby Florence, Baby Phyllis, Beauty, Columbia, Duchess, Ellar, Florodora, Jubilee, Mabel, Majestic, Melitta, My Playmate, Nobbi Kid, Our Pet, Princess, Queen Louise, Rosebud, Superb, Sunshine, and Tiny Tot. Some Indian dolls had no mold numbers. Often used Superb kid bodies, with bisque hands. After WWII and into the 1950s the East German government continued to produce dolls marked "A.M." Dolls listed are in good condition, appropriately dressed.

Child doll, 1890 on, no mold number, or just marked "A.M.," and molds 390, Floradora, 1894, bisque socket head, open mouth, glass eyes, wig, composition fully jointed body. Dolls listed are in good condition, appropriately dressed, allow more for flirty eyes.

Composition body

9" – 10"........... $175.00 – 200.00

12" – 14"........ $220.00 – 300.00

16" – 18"........ $200.00 – 275.00

20" – 24"........ $300.00 – 400.00

28" – 30"........ $500.00 – 650.00

32" – 36"........ $725.00 – 750.00

40" – 42"........ $800.00 – 900.00

Five-piece flapper body, high quality

6" – 7"............. $225.00 – 350.00

10" – 13"........ $300.00 – 400.00

Five-piece body, low quality

10" – 12"........ $125.00 – 135.00

Armand Marseille

15", mold 390, MIB, $275.00. *Photo courtesy of Withington Auction, Inc.*

16" mold 370 shoulder head doll, $250.00. *Photo courtesy of Morphy Auctions.*

14" – 16"........ $150.00 – 175.00
Molds Queen Louise, Rosebud
    12" – 13"........ $225.00 – 275.00
    15" – 17"........ $250.00 – 300.00
    22" – 24"........ $300.00 – 375.00
    26" – 28"........ $400.00 – 450.00
    31" – 34"........ $500.00 – 650.00
Mold Baby Betty
    14" – 16"........ $325.00 – 375.00
    18" – 20"........ $350.00 – 400.00
Kid Body
Shoulder head molds 370, 1894, 3200, Alma, Beauty, Floradora, Lily, Mabel, My Playmate, Princess, Rosebud
    10" – 12"........ $125.00 – 150.00
    14" – 16"........ $200.00 – 250.00
    18" – 20"........ $325.00 – 375.00
    22" – 24"........ $350.00 – 400.00
Molds 1890, 1892, 1895, 1897, 1899, 1901, 1902, 1903, 1909
    10" – 12"........ $175.00 – 225.00
    14" – 16"........ $275.00 – 300.00
    18" – 20"........ $325.00 – 400.00
    22" – 24"........ $425.00 – 450.00
Character baby

Baby Betty, usually found on child composition body, some on bent-leg baby body
    16"............................ $500.00
Too few in database for a reliable range.
Molds Kiddiejoy, 256, 259, 326, 327, 328, 329, 360A, 750, 790, 900, 927, 970, 971, 975, 990, 991, 992 Our Pet, 995, 996, 1330, bisque solid-dome or wigged socket head, open mouth, glass eyes, composition bent-leg baby body, add more for toddler body or flirty eyes or exceptional doll

29" mold 980 character baby, $600.00. *Photo courtesy of Morphy Auctions.*

19" Kiddiejoy character baby, $425.00. *Photo courtesy of Morphy Auctions.*

16½" rare character girl, marked A4M, sold for $15,405.00 at auction. *Photo courtesy of Skinner, Inc.*

8" – 10".......... $250.00 – 300.00
12" – 15"........ $325.00 – 400.00
17" – 21"........ $425.00 – 450.00
24" – 26"........ $500.00 – 525.00
Mold 233
8".................... $425.00 – 475.00
12" – 13"........ $500.00 – 600.00
15"................. $600.00 – 650.00
Mold 250, open-closed mouth with two lower teeth, molded hair, intaglio eyes
9".................... $275.00 – 325.00
Mold 251/248
Closed mouth
12"................. $425.00 – 450.00
Open-closed mouth
10" – 12"........ $500.00 – 600.00
Mold 410, two rows of retractable teeth
12".............. $900.00 – 1,100.00
Mold 500, intaglio eye, bent-limb composition body
13" – 15"........ $575.00 – 700.00
Mold 518
16" – 18"........ $400.00 – 600.00
Mold 560A
8" – 9"............ $225.00 – 275.00
15" – 16"........ $475.00 – 500.00
Mold 580, 590

15" – 16"........ $750.00 – 900.00
19"........... $1,000.00 – 1,100.00
Mold 920
21"................................ $650.00
Too few in database for a reliable range.
Melitta, toddler
16"................. $800.00 – 900.00
Character child
No mold #, marked A (size #) M, bisque socket head, Intaglio eyes, closed mouth,

19" A6M character boy, $17,000.00. *Photo courtesy of Skinner, Inc.*

wigged, composition jointed body

    15" – 19" . $16,000.00 – 17,000.00

Too few In database for a reliable range.

Mold 225, ca. 1920, bisque socket head, glass eyes, open mouth, two rows of teeth, composition jointed body

    14"........... $3,000.00 – 3,600.00

    19"........... $4,000.00 – 4,650.00

Fany, ca. 1912, can be child, toddler, or baby

230, molded hair

    15" – 16" . $8,000.00 – 9,000.00

    17" – 18"..$10,000.00 – 11,500.00

231 (wigged)

    13" – 14".. $4,500.00 – 5,000.00

    16"........... $6,500.00 – 7,000.00

Mold 250, ca. 1912, domed

    9" – 13".......... $575.00 – 600.00

    15"................. $600.00 – 650.00

    18"................. $750.00 – 875.00

Mold 251, ca. 1912, socket head, open-closed mouth

    12" – 13".. $1,100.00 – 1,250.00

    17" – 18".. $2,000.00 – 2,200.00

Mold 253: See Googly section.

Mold 310, Just Me, ca. 1929, bisque socket head, wig, flirty eyes, closed mouth,

9" bisque Just Me, $1,600.00. *Photo courtesy of Morphy Auctions.*

composition body

    7½" – 8"... $1,400.00 – 1,500.00

    9" – 10".... $1,600.00 – 1,900.00

    11"........... $2,100.00 – 2,300.00

    13"........... $2,400.00 – 2,800.00

Painted bisque, with Vogue labeled outfits

    7" – 8"...... $1,000.00 – 1,200.00

    10"........... $1,500.00 – 1,800.00

Mold 345, pouty

Painted intaglio eyes

    10" – 11".. $6,500.00 – 7,000.00

Too few in database for a reliable range.

Glass eyes

    10"................. $825.00 – 900.00

Mold 350, ca. 1926, glass eyes, closed mouth

    16"........... $1,950.00 – 2,250.00

    20"........... $2,500.00 – 2,850.00

Mold 360A, ca. 1913, open mouth

    12"................. $350.00 – 400.00

Mold 400, 401, ca. 1926, glass eyes, closed mouth

    13" – 15".. $1,500.00 – 1,600.00

    20" – 24".. $1,800.00 – 1,900.00

Mold 449, ca. 1930, painted eyes, closed mouth

    13"................. $575.00 – 625.00

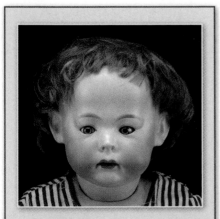

18" Fanny, ca. 1912, $8,000.00. *Photo courtesy of James D. Julia, Inc.*

Armand Marseille

18".............. $900.00 – 1,000.00
Painted bisque
 11"................. $200.00 – 250.00
 15"................. $375.00 – 450.00
Mold 450, glass eyes, closed mouth
 14"................. $575.00 – 700.00
Mold 500, 600, ca. 1910, domed shoulder head, molded/painted hair, painted intaglio eyes, closed mouth
 10" – 12" .... $800.00 – 1,000.00
 17"................. $800.00 – 950.00
Painted bisque
 21"................. $175.00 – 200.00
Mold 520, ca. 1910, domed head, glass eyes, open mouth
Composition body
 12"................. $675.00 – 750.00
 19"........... $1,800.00 – 2,000.00
Kid body
 16"................. $800.00 – 900.00
 20"........... $1,200.00 – 1,400.00
Mold 550, ca. 1926, domed, glass eyes, closed mouth
 14" – 15".. $1,600.00 – 1,900.00
Mold 560, ca. 1910, character, domed, painted eyes, open-closed mouth or 560A, ca. 1926, wigged, glass eyes, open mouth
 14"................. $850.00 – 900.00

13" Dream Baby, newborn baby on composition body, $300.00. *Photo courtesy of Emmie's Antique Doll Castle.*

22"........... $1,200.00 – 1,300.00
Mold 570, ca. 1910, domed, closed mouth
 12"........... $1,600.00 – 1,750.00
Mold 590, ca. 1926, sleep eyes, open-closed mouth
 9".................... $450.00 – 500.00
 16".............. $900.00 – 1,000.00
 18" – 20".. $1,000.00 – 1,100.00
Mold 600, shoulder head, solid dome with molded hair, closed mouth, intaglio eyes
 12" – 15"........ $450.00 – 600.00
Mold 690, socket head, open mouth
 18"................. $800.00 – 850.00
Mold 700, ca. 1920, closed mouth
Painted eyes
 12½"........ $1,800.00 – 2,000.00
Glass eyes
 14"........... $3,800.00 – 4,200.00
Mold 701, 711, ca. 1920, socket or shoulder head, sleep eyes, closed mouth
 16"..........., $2,000.00 – 2,250.00
Mold 800, ca. 1910, socket head, 840 shoulder head
 18"........... $2,000.00 – 2,200.00
Lady, 1910 on, bisque head, wigged, sleep eyes, open or closed mouth, composition lady body
Mold 400, 401, 14"
Closed mouth ..... $2,100.00 – 2,400.00
Open mouth ...... $1,100.00 – 1,300.00
Painted bisque ...... $900.00 – 1,000.00
Newborn Baby, 1924 on, bisque solid-dome socket head or flange neck, may have wig, glass eyes, closed mouth, cloth body with celluloid or composition hands
Mold 341, My Dream Baby, 351, 345, 352, Rock-A-Bye Baby, marked "AM."
 8".................... $175.00 – 225.00
 10" – 12"........ $250.00 – 300.00
 14" – 16"........ $325.00 – 400.00
 22" – 24"........ $375.00 – 425.00
Bent-limb composition body
 11" – 12"........ $275.00 – 325.00

16" .... $350.00 – 375.00

Toddler body

    28" .... $900.00 – 1,200.00

Pillow puppet

    10" .... $175.00 – 200.00

Baby Gloria, solid dome, open mouth, painted hair

    12" .... $350.00 – 375.00

    15" .... $475.00 – 525.00

Baby Phyllis, head circumference:

    9" – 10" .... $275.00 – 350.00

    13" – 15" .... $375.00 – 425.00

Composition child, 1940s – 1950s, mold 2966 and others, sleep eyes, synthetic wig, five-piece composition body (very thin cardboard-like composition)

    22" .... $165.00 – 175.00

MARX TOY CORP.

1919 to present, Sebring, Ohio. Founded in 1919 as Louis Marx & Co. in New York City. Dolls listed are in perfect condition with original clothing.

Archie and Friends, characters from comics, vinyl, molded hair or wigged, painted eyes, in package

Archie, Betty, Jughead, Veronica

    8½" .... $12.00 – 18.00

Freddy Krueger, 1989, vinyl, pull-string talker from horror movie *Nightmare on Elm Street,* character played by Robert Englund

11½" Jane West, $40.00. *Photo courtesy of Morphy Auctions.*

Johnny West Family of action figures, 1965 – 1976, Adventure or Best of the West Series, rigid vinyl, articulated figures, molded clothes, came in box with vinyl accessories and extra clothes, had horses, dogs, and other accessories available, dolls listed are complete with box and all accessories, allow more if never removed from box or special sets

Bill Buck, brown molded-on clothing, 13 pieces, coonskin cap

    11½" .... $175.00 – 250.00

Captain Tom Maddox, blue molded-on clothing, brown hair, 23 pieces

    11½" .... $30.00 – 40.00

Chief Cherokee, tan or light colored molded-on clothing, 37 pieces

    11½" .... $50.00 – 70.00

Daniel Boone, tan molded-on clothing, coonskin cap

    11½" .... $125.00 – 150.00

Dangerous Dan, blue figure, flocked hair and beard

    11½" .... $225.00 – 250.00

Fighting Eagle, tan molded-on clothes, with mohawk hair, 37 pieces

    11½" .... $100.00 – 150.00

General Custer, dark blue molded-on clothing, yellow hair, 23 pieces

    11½" .... $25.00 – 30.00

Geronimo, light colored molded-on clothing

    11½" .... $35.00 – 55.00

Orange body

    11½" .... $90.00 – 110.00

Jamie West, dark hair, molded-on tan clothing, 13 accessories

    9" .... $20.00 – 25.00

Jane West, blond hair, turquoise molded-on clothing, 37 pieces

    11½" .... $30.00 – 40.00

Janice West, dark hair, turquoise molded-on clothing, 14 pieces

    9" .... $30.00 – 35.00

Marx Toy Corp.

Jay West, blond hair, tan molded-on clothing, 13 accessories, later brighter body colors

9" .... $35.00 – 45.00

Jed Gibson, c. 1973, black figure, molded-on green clothing

12" .... $150.00 – 175.00

Johnny West, brown hair, molded-on brown clothing, 25 pieces

12" .... $35.00 – 45.00

Johnny West, with quick-draw arm, blue clothing

12" .... $90.00 – 115.00

Josie West, blond, turquoise molded-on clothing, later with bright green body

9" .... $20.00 – 25.00

Princess Wildflower, off-white molded-on clothing, with papoose in vinyl cradle, 22 accessories

11½" .... $60.00 – 80.00

Sam Cobra, outlaw, 26 accessories

11½" .... $30.00 – 40.00

Sheriff Pat Garrett (Sheriff Goode in Canada), molded-on blue clothing, 25 accessories

11½" .... $25.00 – 35.00

Zeb Zachary, dark hair, blue molded-on clothing, 23 pieces

11½" .... $40.00 – 60.00

Mike Hazard Double Agent, 1967, vinyl, trench coat, accessories

12" .... $40.00 – 50.00

Knight and Viking Series, ca. 1960s, action figures with accessories

Gordon, the Gold Knight, molded-on gold clothing, brown hair, beard, mustache

11½" .... $100.00 – 125.00

Sir Brandon, blue molded-on clothing, gray hair, mustache

11½" .... $20.00 – 25.00

Sir Stuart, Silver Knight, molded-on silver clothing, black hair, mustache, goatee

11½" .... $30.00 – 35.00

Brave Erik, Viking, with horse, ca. 1967,
molded-on green clothing, blond hair, blue eyes

11½" .... $25.00 – 40.00

Odin, the Viking, ca. 1967, brown molded-on clothing, brown eyes, brown hair, beard

11½" .... $30.00 – 40.00

Miss Marlene, hard plastic, high heeled, Barbie-type, ca. 1960s, blond rooted wig

11" .... $125.00 – 150.00

Miss Seventeen, 1961, hard plastic, high-heeled, fashion-type doll, modeled like the German Bild Lilli (Barbie doll's predecessor), came in black swimsuit, black box, fashion brochure pictures 12 costumes, she was advertised as "A Beauty Queen"

18" .... $125.00 – 150.00

Miss Toddler, also know as Miss Marx, vinyl, molded hair, ribbons, battery-operated walker, molded clothing

18" .... $65.00 – 85.00

Pee-Wee Herman, 1987 TV character, vinyl and cloth, ventriloquist doll in gray suit, red bowtie

18" .... $18.00 – 25.00

Pull-string talker, 18" ..... $20.00 – 30.00

Sindy, ca. 1963+, in England by Pedigree, a fashion-type doll, rooted hair, painted eyes, wires in limbs allow her to pose, distributed in U.S. by Marx, c. 1978 – 1982

11" .... $30.00 – 40.00

Pedigree .... $100.00 – 120.00

Gayle, Sindy's friend, black vinyl

11" .... $120.00 – 140.00

Outfits .... $75.00 – 95.00

Soldiers, ca. 1960s, articulated action figures with accessories

Buddy Charlie, Montgomery Ward exclusive, a buddy for G.I. Joe, molded-on military uniform, brown hair

11½" .... $80.00 – 100.00

Stony "Stonewall" Smith, molded-on army fatigues, blond hair, 36 accessories

11½"................ $80.00 – 100.00
Twinkie, doll with vinyl clothing and wigs
    4½".................... $70.00 – 80.00

MATTEL

1959 to present, founded by Ruth and Elliot Handler. Many dolls of the 1960s and 1970s designed by Martha Armstrong Hand. Dolls listed are in excellent condition with all-original clothing and accessories. Allow double for mint-in-box examples.

Baby Beans, 1971 – 1975, vinyl head, bean bag dolls, terrycloth or tricot bodies filled with plastic and foam
    12"..................... $30.00 – 35.00
Talking
    12"..................... $35.00 – 40.00
Baby Come Back, 1976, battery-operated walker, rooted hair
    16"..................... $20.00 – 25.00
Baby First Step, 1965 – 1967, battery-operated walker, rooted hair, sleep eyes, pink dress
    18"..................... $50.00 – 60.00
Talking
    18"..................... $60.00 – 70.00
Longer hair, pink outfit... $75.00 – 85.00
Baby Go Bye-Bye and Her Bumpety Buggy, 1970, doll sits in car, battery-operated, 12 maneuvers

10" Baby Beans and Baby Booful, ca. 1970, $35.00 each. *Photo courtesy of My Dear Dolly.*

18" Baby First Step, ca. 1964, $50.00. *Photo courtesy of The Museum Doll Shop.*

    11"................ $120.00 – 140.00
Baby Pattaburp, 1964 – 1966, vinyl, drinks milk, burps when patted, pink jacket, lace trim
    16"..................... $70.00 – 85.00
Baby Play-A-Lot, 1972 – 1973, posable arms, fingers can hold things, comes with 20 toys, moves arm to brush teeth, moves head, no batteries, has pull string and switch
    16"..................... $18.00 – 22.00
Baby Say 'n See, 1967 – 1968, eyes and lips move while talking, white dress, pink yoke
    17"................... $95.00 – 125.00
Baby Secret, 1966 – 1967, vinyl face and hands, stuffed body, limbs, red hair, blue eyes, whispers 11 phrases, moves lips
    18"..................... $75.00 – 85.00
Baby Skates, 1982, vinyl face and hands, rooted blond hair, battery-operated rollerskating doll
    15"..................... $20.00 – 25.00
Baby Small Talk, 1968 – 1969, says eight phrases, infant voice, additional outfits available
    10¾".................. $35.00 – 40.00
Black
    10¾".................. $50.00 – 60.00
In Nursery Rhyme outfit
    10¾".................. $55.00 – 65.00
Baby Tender Love, 1970 – 1973, baby doll, realistic skin, wets, can be bathed
Newborn
    13"..................... $55.00 – 65.00

Mattel

Talking
    16".................... $30.00 – 45.00
Bless You, 1974
    13" black .... $20.00 – 25.00
Molded hairpiece, 1972
    11½".................. $20.00 – 25.00
Brother, sexed
    11½".................. $40.00 – 50.00
Baby Walk 'n Play, 1968
    11"...................... $8.00 – 12.00
Baby Walk 'n See
    18".................... $12.00 – 18.00
Barbie®: See Barbie® section.
Big Jim Series, vinyl action figures, many boxed accessory sets available
Big Jim, black hair, muscular torso
    9½".................... $35.00 – 50.00
Big Jim with Talking Field Radio
    9½".................. $90.00 – 110.00
Big Jack, African American
    9½".................... $35.00 – 40.00
Big Josh, dark hair, beard
    9½".................... $25.00 – 35.00
Dr. Steele, bald head, silver tips on right hand
    9½".................... $30.00 – 35.00
Sports Camper set
    MIB............................. $125.00*
Beany, from *Beany and Cecil* TV show, 1962, vinyl head, hands, feet, cloth body, pull-string talker........................ $75.00 – 100.00
Bozo, 1964
    18"...................... $75.00 – 90.00
Buffy and Mrs. Beasley, 1967 and 1974, characters from TV sitcom *Family Affair*
Buffy, vinyl, rooted hair, painted features, holds small Mrs. Beasley, vinyl head, on cloth body
    6½".................. $75.00 – 100.00
Talking Buffy, vinyl, 1969 – 1971, holds tiny 6" rag Mrs. Beasley
    10¾"................ $80.00 – 100.00
Mrs. Beasley
1965, vinyl head, cloth body
    16"................ $200.00 – 275.00

1973, non-talker
    15½".............. $125.00 – 150.00
Captain Kangaroo, 1967, Sears only, talking character, host for TV kids' program
    19".................... $80.00 – 100.00
Captain Laser, 1967, vinyl, painted features, blue uniform, silver accessories, batteries operate laser gun, light-up eyes
    12".................... $75.00 – 100.00
Casper, the Friendly Ghost
ca. 1964
    16"................. $100.00 – 150.00
1971
    5"........................ $50.00 – 60.00
Chatty Cathy Series
Chatty Cathy, 1960 – 1963, vinyl head, hard plastic body, pull-string activates voice, dressed in pink and white checked or blue party dresses, 1963 – 1965, says 18 new phrases, red velvet and white lace dress, extra outfits available
Blond
    20"................. $150.00 – 200.00
Black
    20"................. $500.00 – 550.00
Canadian version ..... $450.00 – 550.00
1995 reissue.............. $75.00 – 100.00
Charmin' Chatty, 1963 – 1964, talking doll, soft vinyl head, closed smiling mouth, hard

24" Charmin' Chatty, $150.00. *Photo courtesy of The Museum Doll Shop.*

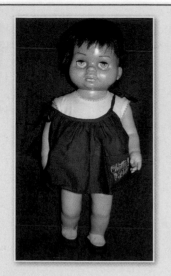

18" Chatty Baby, $90.00. *Photo courtesy of The Museum Doll Shop.*

vinyl body, long rooted hair, long legs, five records placed in left side slot, one-piece navy skirt, white middy blouse with red sailor collar, red socks, and saddle shoes, glasses, five disks; extra outfits and 14 more disks available

24".................. $120.00 – 150.00
Chatty Baby, 1962 – 1964, red pinafore over rompers

18".................... $90.00 – 100.00
Tiny Chatty Baby, 1963 – 1964, smaller version of Chatty Baby, blue rompers, blue and white striped panties, bib with name, talks, other outfits available

15½".................. $55.00 – 80.00
Black

15½".............. $100.00 – 125.00
Tiny Chatty Brother, 1963 – 1964, boy version of Tiny Chatty Baby, blue and white suit and cap, hair parted on side

15½".................. $55.00 – 65.00
Cheerful Tearful, 1966 – 1967, vinyl, blond hair, face changes from smile to pout as arm is lowered, feed her bottle, wets and cries real tears

13"..................... $65.00 – 75.00
Tiny Cheerful Tearful

7"....................... $60.00 – 80.00
Dancerella, 1978 battery-operated

19"................... $75.00 – 100.00
Dancerina, 1969 – 1971, battery-operated, posable arms and legs, turns, dances with control knob on head, pink ballet outfit

24"................. $120.00 – 140.00
Baby Dancerina, 1970, smaller version, no batteries, turn-knob on head, white ballet outfit

16"..................... $85.00 – 95.00
Black

16"............... $125.00 – 150.00
Teeny Dancerina

12"..................... $25.00 – 35.00
Debbie Boone, 1978

11½"................. $45.00 – 55.00
Dick Van Dyke, 1969, as Mr. Potts in movie *Chitty Chitty Bang Bang,* all-cloth, flat features, talks in actor's voice, mark: "©

15½" Drowsy, $75.00. *Photo courtesy of The Museum Doll Shop.*

Mattel

Mattel 1969" on cloth tag

    24"................ $100.00 – 120.00

Drowsy, 1965 – 1974, vinyl head, stuffed body, sleepers, pull-string talker

    15½"................ $50.00 – 100.00

Reissue, 2001

    15"..................... $25.00 – 35.00

Dr. Dolittle, 1968, character patterned after Rex Harrison in movie version, talker, vinyl with cloth body

    24"..................... $40.00 – 50.00

All-vinyl

    6"....................... $15.00 – 20.00

Gramma Doll, 1970 – 1973, Sears only, cloth, painted face, gray yarn hair, says ten phrases, talker, foam-filled cotton

    11"..................... $15.00 – 20.00

Grizzly Adams, 1971

    10"..................... $40.00 – 50.00

Guardian Goddesses, 1979

    11½"................. $45.00 – 50.00

Herman Munster, 1965, cloth doll, talking TV character, *The Munsters*

    21"................ $150.00 – 175.00

Liddle Kiddles, 1966 on, small dolls of vinyl over wire frame, posable, painted features, rooted hair and came with bright costumes and accessories, packaged on 8½" x 9½" cards, mark: "1965//Mattel Inc.//Japan" on back, dolls listed are in excellent condition with all accessories, add double for mint-in-package (or card) and never-removed-from-package, less for worn dolls with missing accessories

1966, First Series

3501, Bunson Bernie

    3"....................... $60.00 – 80.00

3502, Howard "Biff" Boodle

    3½"................. $95.00 – 105.00

3503, Liddle Diddle

    2¾"................ $125.00 – 150.00

3504, Lola Liddle

    3½"..................... $75.00 – 80.00

3505, Babe Biddle

    3½"..................... $65.00 – 80.00

3506, Calamity Jiddle

    3"....................... $60.00 – 70.00

3507, Florence Niddle

    2¾"................. $85.00 – 100.00

3508, Greta Griddle

    3"....................... $55.00 – 75.00

3509, Millie Middle

    2¾"............... $120.00 – 150.00

3510, Beat A Diddle

    3½"................. $75.00 – 100.00

1967, Second Series

3513, Sizzly Friddle

    3"..................... $80.00 – 100.00

3514, Windy Fliddle

    2½"............... $125.00 – 150.00

3515, Trikey Triddle

    2¾"............... $125.00 – 150.00

3516, Freezy Sliddle

    3½"................. $90.00 – 120.00

3517, Surfy Skiddle

    3"....................... $60.00 – 70.00

3518, Soapy Siddle

    3½"................. $75.00 – 90.00

3519, Rolly Twiddle

    3½"................. $90.00 – 100.00

3548, Beddy-Bye Biddle (with robe)

    $70.00 – 90.00

3549, Pretty Priddle

    3½"................. $75.00 – 100.00

1968, Third Series

3587, Baby Liddle

    2¾"............... $100.00 – 120.00

3751, Telly Viddle

    3½"................. $80.00 – 110.00

3752, Lemons Stiddle

    3½"................. $60.00 – 75.00

3753, Kampy Kiddle

    3½"................. $80.00 – 100.00

3754, Slipsy Sliddle

    3½"................. $75.00 – 100.00

4" Skediddle Kiddle, $40.00. *Photo courtesy of The Museum Doll Shop.*

Doug from the Rock Flowers series, $20.00. *Photo courtesy of The Museum Doll Shop.*

Storybook Kiddles, 1967 – 1968
$75.00 – 150.00
Skediddle Kiddles, 1968 – 1970
4".......................... $35.00 – 50.00
Kiddles 'n Kars, 1969 – 1970
2¾"................... $80.00 – 100.00
Tea Party Kiddles, 1970 – 1971
3½"..................,.... $50.00 – 60.00
Lucky Locket Kiddles, 1967 – 1970
2".......................... $20.00 – 40.00
Kiddle Kolognes, 1968 – 1970
2".......................... $30.00 – 40.00
Kiddle Kones, 1968 – 1969
2".......................... $65.00 – 85.00
Kola Kiddles, 1968 – 1969
2".......................... $30.00 – 40.00
Kosmic Kiddle, 1968 – 1969
2½"................ $120.00 – 160.00
Sweet Treat Kiddles, 1969 – 1970
2"..................... $80.00 – 100.00
Liddle Kiddle Playhouses, 1966 – 1968
$65.00 – 75.00

Matty Mattel
16"..................... $50.00 – 60.00
Mork & Mindy, 1979
9"...............$20.00 – 30.00 each
My Child, 1986, cloth over vinyl head, cloth body, synthetic wig
13".................... $75.00 – 100.00

Osmond Family
Donny or Marie Osmond, 1978
12"..................... $25.00 – 35.00
Jimmy Osmond, 1979
10"..................... $40.00 – 50.00
Rainbow Brite, 1983 vinyl head, cloth body, orange yarn hair
18½"................. $60.00 – 70.00
Rock Flowers, 1970, vinyl mod dolls
6"......................... $20.00 – 25.00
Scooba Doo, 1964, vinyl head, rooted hair, cloth body, talks in Beatnik phrases, blond or black hair, striped dress
23".................... $75.00 – 100.00
Shogun Warrior, all plastic, battery-operated
23½".............. $100.00 – 225.00
Shrinkin' Violette, 1964 – 1965, cloth, yarn hair, pull-string talker, eyes close, mouth moves
16"................. $200.00 – 300.00
Sister Belle, 1961 – 1963, vinyl, pull-string talker, cloth body
16"..................... $55.00 – 65.00
Star Spangled dolls, uses Sunshine Family adults, marked "1973"

Pioneer Daughter.......... $30.00 – 40.00
Sunshine Family, vinyl, posable, come with Idea Book, Father, Mother, Baby
Family of three............. $45.00 – 55.00
Steve
    9".................... $10.00 – 15.00
Stephie
    7½".................. $10.00 – 15.00
Swingy, 1968, mechanical dancing doll
    18".................. $60.00 – 75.00
Tatters, 1965 – 1967, talking cloth doll, wears rag clothes
    19"................ $95.00 – 110.00
Teachy Keen, 1966 – 1970, Sears only, vinyl head, cloth body, ponytail, talker, tells child to use accessories included, buttons, zippers, comb
    16".................. $30.00 – 40.00
Timey Tell 1969, talking
    17".................. $40.00 – 50.00
Tippee Toes, 1968 – 1970, battery-operated, legs move, rides accessory horse, tricycle, knit sweater, pants
    17".................. $40.00 – 50.00
Truly Scrumptious, character from movie *Chitty Chitty Bang Bang*
    11½"............... $160.00 – 200.00
    Talking................. $300.00 – 350.00
Welcome Back, Kotter, 1973, characters from TV sitcom
Freddie "Boom Boom" Washington, Arnold Horshack
    9".................... $30.00 – 40.00
Vinnie Barbarino (John Travolta)
    9".................... $30.00 – 35.00
Gabe Kotter
    9".................... $15.00 – 25.00
Zython, 1977, has glow-in-the-dark head, Enemy in *Space: 1999 series*
    $80.00 – 90.00

MAWAPHIL

1920 – 1942, Atlanta, Georgia.

14½" Mawaphil Mistress Mary, $250.00. *Photo courtesy of The Museum Doll Shop.*

Dolls designed by Mary Waterman Philips, manufactured by the Rushton Co. Stockinette crib dolls and cloth mask face dolls.
Crib doll, all-cloth, stockinette or velveteen
    8" – 12"............. $60.00 – 90.00
Cloth mask face doll, cloth body, appropriately dressed
    15"................ $200.00 – 250.00

MEGO CORPORATION

1954 to 1982. Made many vinyl "action figure" dolls during the 1970s. Prices shown are for excellent condition dolls with all appropriate clothes and accessories, allow double values listed for mint-in-box examples.

Action Jackson, 1971 – 1972, vinyl head, plastic body, molded hair, painted black eyes, action figure, many accessory outfits, mark: "©Mego Corp//Reg. U.S. Pat. Off.// Pat. Pend.//Hong Kong//MCMLXXI"
    8"...................... $25.00 – 30.00

18" Baby Sez So, 1970s, $40.00. *Photo courtesy of Emmie's Antique Doll Castle.*

Black
    8".......................$45.00 – 55.00
Dinah-mite, black ....$30.00 – 35.00
Baby Sez So, 1976
    16".....................$20.00 – 25.00
Bubble Yum Baby, 1978, blows up "gum"
    14".....................$15.00 – 20.00
Candy, 1979, fashion doll
    11½"..................$10.00 – 12.00
    18".....................$40.00 – 50.00
Captain and Tennille, Daryl Dragon and Toni Tennille, 1977, recording and TV personalities, Toni Tennille doll has no molded ears
    12½"...........$30.00 – 40.00 each
Charlie's Angels, 1977, TV show dolls based on characters played by Farrah Fawcett, Jaclyn Smith, Kate Jackson, and Cheryl Ladd, vinyl dolls, rooted hair
    9".......................$10.00 – 15.00
    12½"...............$50.00 – 100.00
    Jaclyn Smith, MIB..............$177.00*
Cher, 1976, TV and recording personality, husband Sonny Bono, all-vinyl, fully jointed, rooted long black hair, also as grow-hair doll
Cher
    12"....................$40.00 – 50.00
Growing Hair Cher, 1976
    12"....................$75.00 – 90.00
Sonny Bono
    12"....................$25.00 – 35.00
Sonny & Cher's roadster car
    Excellent condition, no box
                       $400.00*
CHiPs, 1977, California Highway Patrol TV show, Jon Baker (Larry Wilcox), Frank "Ponch" Poncherello (Erik Estrada)
    8".......................$30.00 – 40.00
Diana Ross, 1977, recording and movie personality, all-vinyl, fully jointed, rooted black hair, long lashes
    12½"..................$55.00 – 75.00
Dukes of Hazzard, 1982, from TV show, Bo, Luke, Boss Hogg, Cleatus, Rosco
    8" – 9"...............$35.00 – 80.00
Flash Gordon Series, ca. 1976, vinyl head, hard plastic articulated body
Dale Arden
    9"...................$100.00 – 125.00
Dr. Zarkov
    9½"..................$75.00 – 100.00
Flash Gordon
    9½"..................$75.00 – 100.00

12½" Diana Ross, ca. 1977, MIB, $150.00. *Doll from private collection.*

Mego Corporation

Ming, the Merciless
    9½".................... $55.00 – 65.00
Happy Days Series, 1976, characters from *Happy Days* TV sitcom, Henry Winkler starred as Fonzie, Ron Howard as Richie, Anson Williams as Potsie, and Don Most as Ralph Malph
Fonzie
    8"....................... $25.00 – 40.00
Richie, Potsie, Ralph, each
    8"....................... $50.00 – 60.00
Joe Namath, 1970, football player, actor, soft vinyl head, rigid vinyl body, painted hair and features
    12".................... $75.00 – 100.00
Outfit, MIP................................ $33.00
KISS, 1978, rock group, with Gene Simmons, Ace Frehley, Peter Cris, and Paul Stanley, all-vinyl, fully jointed, rooted hair, painted features and makeup
    12½"...........$65.00 – 75.00 each
Kristy McNichol, 1978, actress, starred in TV show *Family,* all-vinyl, rooted brown hair, painted eyes, marked on head: "©MEGO CORP.//MADE IN HONG KONG," marked on back: "©1977 MEGO CORP.//MADE IN HONG KONG"
    9"....................... $20.00 – 30.00
Laverne and Shirley, 1977, TV sitcom; Penny Marshall played Laverne, Cindy Williams played Shirley, also, from the same show, David Lander as Squiggy, and Michael McKean as Lenny, all-vinyl, rooted hair, painted eyes
    11½"...........$35.00 – 40.00 each
Marvel Super Heroes, 1974 on, vinyl head, rooted black hair, painted eyes, plastic body
    8"
Aquaman.................. $80.00 – 100.00
Batgirl..................... $200.00 – 250.00
Batman .... $150.00 – 200.00
Catwoman............... $100.00 – 125.00
Falcon...........................$40.00 – 45.00

Flash .... $100.00 – 125.00
Green Arrow .... $100.00 – 120.00
Iron Man ....$40.00 – 45.00
Joker .... $45.00 – 55.00
Mr. Fantastic............. $80.00 – 100.00
Mr. Mxyzptlk............... $75.00 – 90.00
The Riddler.................. $70.00 – 80.00
Robin........................ $80.00 – 100.00
Superman.....................$40.00 – 45.00
Supergirl................. $150.00 – 200.00
Wonder Woman........... $80.00 – 90.00
Our Gang, 1975, from *Our Gang* movie shorts that replayed on TV, included characters Alfalfa, Buckwheat, Darla, Mickey, Porky, and Spanky
    6"....................... $15.00 – 25.00
Planet of the Apes
Planet of the Apes movie series, ca. 1970s
Astronaut
    8"....................... $45.00 – 50.00
Cornelius
    8"....................... $50.00 – 70.00
Dr. Zaius
    8"....................... $40.00 – 50.00
Zira
    8"....................... $40.00 – 50.00
Planet of the Apes TV series, ca. 1974
Alan Verdon
    8"....................... $45.00 – 50.00
Galen
    8", Palitoy .... $60.00 – 70.00
General Urko
    8"....................... $60.00 – 75.00
General Ursus
    8".................. $200.00 – 250.00
Peter Burke
    8"....................... $40.00 – 50.00
Forbidden Zone Playset
    $125.00 – 150.00
Star Trek
TV series, ca. 1973 – 1975
Captain Kirk
    8"....................... $40.00 – 55.00

8" Star Trek's Dr. McCoy, $40.00. *Photo courtesy of The Museum Doll Shop.*

Dr. McCoy

 8"...................... $50.00 – 60.00

Klingon

 8"...................... $45.00 – 60.00

Lt. Uhura

 8"...................... $45.00 – 60.00

Mr. Scott

 8"...................... $50.00 – 70.00

Mr. Spock

 8"...................... $30.00 – 55.00

Star Trek Aliens, ca. 1975 – 1976

Andorian

 8".................... $120.00 – 150.00

Cheron

 8"...................... $40.00 – 55.00

The Gorn

 8"...................... $50.00 – 75.00

Mugato

 8".................... $125.00 – 150.00

The Romulan

 8".................... $225.00 – 250.00

Talos

 8".................... $100.00 – 125.00

Star Trek Movie series, ca. 1979, 12½" dolls

Acturian .... $80.00 – 100.00

Captain Kirk .... $45.00 – 60.00

Commander Decker ...... $45.00 – 60.00

Ilia .... $60.00 – 80.00

Klingon .... $65.00 – 75.00

Mr. Spock.................. $80.00 – 100.00

Starsky & Hutch, 1976, police TV series, Paul Michael Glaser as Starsky, David Soul as Hutch, Bernie Hamilton as Captain Dobey, Antonio Fargas as Huggy Bear, also included a villain, Chopper, all-vinyl, jointed waists

 7½"..................... $30.00 – 60.00

Suzanne Somers, 1978, actress, TV personality, starred as Chrissy in *Three's Company,* all-vinyl, fully jointed, rooted blond hair, painted blue eyes, long lashes

 12½"................... $35.00 – 40.00

Waltons, The, 1975, from TV drama series, set of two 8" dolls per package, all-vinyl

John Boy and Mary Ellen set

 $20.00 – 25.00

Mom and Pop set.......... $20.00 – 25.00

Grandma and Grandpa

 set .... $30.00 – 40.00

Wizard of Oz, 1974

Dorothy, Glinda, Cowardly Lion, Scarecrow, Tin Man .... $25.00 – 30.00

Munchkins .... $50.00 – 60.00

Wonder Woman Series, ca. 1976 – 1977, vinyl head, rooted black hair, painted eyes, plastic body

Lt. Diana Prince

 12½".............. $125.00 – 150.00

Nubia

 12½".................. $65.00 – 75.00

Nurse

 12½".................. $30.00 – 40.00

Queen Hippolyte

 12½"................ $75.00 – 100.00

Steve Trevor

 12½"................ $75.00 – 100.00

Wonder Woman

 12½"................ $90.00 – 125.00

METAL HEADS

1850 – 1930 on. Made in Germany,

15" metal head doll by Minerva, glass eyes, $225.00. *Photo courtesy of Morphy Auctions.*

Britain and America, by various manufacturers, including Buschow & Beck (Minerva), Alfred Heller (Diana), Karl Standfuss (Juno), and Art Metal Works. Various metals used were aluminum, brass, and others, and they might be marked with just a size and country of origin, or unmarked. Dolls listed are in good condition with original or appropriate clothing. Dolls with chipped paint will bring significantly less.

Metal shoulder head, cloth or kid body,

12" molded hair metal head doll, painted eyes, molded hair, $100.00. *Doll courtesy of Lucy DiTerlizzi.*

molded and painted hair, glass eyes, more for wigged

12" – 14"	$150.00 – 175.00
16" – 18"	$175.00 – 225.00
20" – 22"	$250.00 – 275.00

Painted eyes

12" –14"	$100.00 – 125.00
20" – 22"	$150.00 – 175.00

All metal or with composition body, metal limbs

Baby

11" – 15"	$125.00 – 150.00
16" – 20"	$150.00 – 200.00

Child

15"	$350.00 – 400.00
20" – 22"	$500.00 – 600.00

Mama doll, metal shoulder head, cloth body

18"	$200.00 – 250.00

Swiss: See Bucherer section.

MISSIONARY RAG BABY (BEECHER BABY)

1893 – 1910, Elmira, New York. Julia Jones Beecher, wife of Congregational Church pastor Thomas K. Beecher, sister-in-law of Harriet Beecher Stowe. Made Missionary rag babies with the help of the sewing circle of her church. The dolls were made from old silk or cotton jersey underwear, with hand-painted and needle-sculpted features. All proceeds used for missionary work. Sizes 16" to 23" and larger. Dolls listed are in good condition, appropriately dressed. Exceptional examples will bring more.

16"	$2,800.00 – 3,000.00
21" – 23"	$4,200.00 – 4,900.00

Black Beecher, same construction and appearance as the white babies but from brown fabric with black yarn hair. Please note, this is not the black stockinette doll often

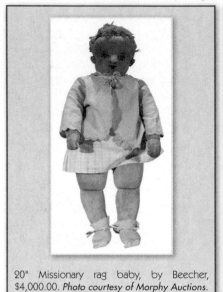

20" Missionary rag baby, by Beecher, $4,000.00. *Photo courtesy of Morphy Auctions.*

erroneously referred to as "a black Beecher," which is quite different in construction from a true black Beecher.

    21" – 23".. $6,000.00 – 6,500.00

MOLLY-'ES

    1920 to 1970s, Philadelphia, Pennsylvania. International Doll Co. was founded by Mollye Goldman. Molly-'es made cloth mask-faced dolls, doll clothing, briefly Raggedy Ann, as well as composition and vinyl dolls. Her mask-faced dolls had yarn or mohair hair, painted features, sewn joints at the shoulders and hips.

Cloth, fine line painted lashes, pouty mouth
Child
    12" baby............. $50.00 – 75.00
    15".................... $80.00 – 100.00
    18"................. $100.00 – 120.00
    24"................. $145.00 – 175.00
    29"................. $200.00 – 240.00
Internationals
    11"...................... $75.00 – 95.00

    15".................. $75.00 – 125.00
    27"................ $150.00 – 200.00
Lady
    16"................ $150.00 – 175.00
    21"................ $200.00 – 275.00
Princess, Thief of Baghdad
Prince, cloth
    23"................ $700.00 – 750.00
Princess
    Composition
    15"................ $575.00 – 625.00
    Cloth
    18"................ $600.00 – 650.00
Sabu, composition
    15"................ $550.00 – 650.00
Sultan, cloth
    19"................ $650.00 – 750.00
Composition
Baby
    15"................ $140.00 – 190.00
    21"................ $210.00 – 225.00
Cloth body
    18".................. $90.00 – 110.00
Toddler
    15"................ $170.00 – 200.00
    21"................ $200.00 – 250.00

14" cloth mask-faced International doll, Gyda of Norway, $100.00. *Photo courtesy of The Museum Doll Shop.*

Child

15"..............	$125.00 – 150.00
19"..............	$175.00 – 200.00

Lady, add more for ball gown

16"..............	$225.00 – 275.00
21"..............	$325.00 – 400.00

Hard plastic
Baby

14"..............	$65.00 – 85.00
20"..............	$100.00 – 135.00

Cloth body

17"..............	$55.00 – 75.00
25"..............	$100.00 – 125.00

Child

14"..............	$150.00 – 175.00
18"..............	$325.00 – 375.00
25"..............	$400.00 – 425.00

Lady

17"..............	$250.00 – 300.00
20"..............	$325.00 – 375.00
25"..............	$375.00 – 425.00

Vinyl
Baby

8½"..............	$12.00 – 20.00
12"..............	$18.00 – 25.00
15"..............	$28.00 – 40.00

Child

8"..............	$12.00 – 20.00
10"..............	$18.00 – 25.00
15"..............	$28.00 – 40.00

Little Women

9"..............	$45.00 – 55.00

MONICA DOLLS

1941 – 1951. Monica Dolls from Hollywood, designed by Mrs. Hansi Share, made composition and later hard plastic with long face and painted or sleep eyes, eyeshadow, unique feature is very durable rooted human hair, did not have high-heeled feet and unmarked, but wore paper wrist tag reading "Monica Doll, Hollywood,"

17" composition Monica, $550.00. *Photo courtesy of Withington Auction, Inc.*

composition dolls had pronounced widow's peak in center of forehead.

Composition, 1941 – 1949, painted eyes, Veronica, Jean, and Rosalind were names of 17" dolls produced in 1942

15"..............	$350.00 – 400.00
17"..............	$475.00 – 550.00
20"..............	$625.00 – 800.00
20" all-original mint condition wearing pesant costume..............	$2,750.00*

Hard plastic, 1949 – 1951, sleep eyes, Elizabeth, Marion, or Linda

14"..............	$400.00 – 500.00
18"..............	$500.00 – 600.00

MORAVIAN

1872 – present, Bethlehem, Pennsylvania. Cloth dolls made by the Ladies Sewing Society of the Moravian Church Guild. Fundraiser to support church work. Flat-faced rag doll with sewn joints at shoulders, elbows, hips, and knees, hand-painted faces, dressed in pink or blue gingham with apron and double bonnet, 18".

19th – early 20th century doll

$5,000.00 – 6,000.00

1920s – 1940s doll. $1,900.00 – 2,200.00
1950s to present....... $700.00 – 900.00

MULTI-FACE, MULTI-HEAD DOLLS

1866 – 1930 on. Various firms made dolls with two or more faces, or more than one head.

Bisque

French

Bru, Surprise poupée, awake/asleep faces

12"......................... $14,500.00*

Jumeau, crying, laughing faces, cap hides knob

18"....... $15,500.00 – 16,500.00

Too few in database for a reliable range.

German

Bartenstein, bisque socket head, papier-mâché hood and molded blouse shoulder plate, cloth over carton body with composition limbs, awake face with open mouth and glass eyes, crying face with open-closed mouth and glass eyes

20"............................ $2,750.00

Bergner, Carl, bisque socket head, two or three faces, sleeping, laughing, crying, molded tears, glass eyes, on composition jointed body, may have molded bonnet or hood, marked "C.B." or "Designed by Carl Bergner"

12".......... $1,200.00 – 1,400.00
15".......... $1,300.00 – 1,600.00
Black face/white face doll
13"............................ $3,650.00

Too few in database for a reliable range

Kestner, J. D., ca. 1900+, Wunderkind, bisque doll with set of several different mold number heads that could be attached to body, set of one doll and body with additional three heads and wardrobe

With heads 174, 178, 184, and 185
11"......... $9,000.00 – 10,000.00
With heads, 171, 179, 182, and 183
14½"....................... $12,650.00

Too few in database for a reliable range.

Kley & Hahn, solid-dome bisque socket head, painted hair, smiling baby and frowning baby, closed mouth, tongue, glass eyes, baby body

13".......... $1,500.00 – 1,700.00

Simon & Halbig, smiling, sleeping, crying, turn ring at top of head to change faces, glass/painted eyes, closed mouth

14½"........ $3,000.00 – 3,200.00

Hermann Steiner topsy-turvy baby

8".................. $500.00 – 600.00

18" two-faced doll by Jumeau, $16,500.00. *Doll courtesy of Dominique Perrin.*

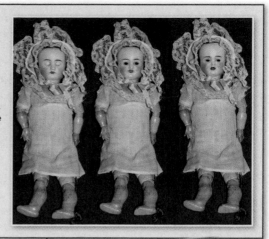

12" German multi-face doll, $1,400.00. *Photo courtesy of The Museum Doll Shop.*

Cloth

Topsy-Turvy: one black, one white head
Painted face
    13"................. $800.00 – 900.00
Lithographed face
    13"................. $650.00 – 700.00
Bruckner
    13"................. $500.00 – 600.00
China
Topsy-Turvy, white head and black head, mid-nineteeth century
    12"........... $1,200.00 – 1,600.00
Too few in database for a reliable range.

Composition
Berwick Doll Co., Famlee Dolls, 1926 on, composition head and limbs, cloth body with crier, neck with screw joint, allowing different heads to be screwed into the body, painted features, mohair wigs and/or molded and painted hair, came in sets of two to 12 heads, with different costumes for each head
Four-head set
    16"................. $550.00 – 600.00
Seven-head set
    16"................. $700.00 – 800.00
Effanbee, Johnny Tu-Face
    16"................. $375.00 – 425.00
Too few in database for a reliable range.

Ideal, 1923, Soozie Smiles, composition, sleep or painted eyes on happy face, two faces, smiling, crying, cloth body, composition hands, cloth legs, original romper and hat
    15½"............. $400.00 – 450.00
Three-in-One Doll Corp., 1946 on, Trudy, composition head with turning knob on top, cloth body and limbs, three faces, "Sleepy, Weepy, Smiley," dressed in felt or fleece snowsuit, or sheer dresses, more for exceptional doll
    15½"............. $175.00 – 225.00
Papier-mâché
Smiling/crying faces, glass eyes, cloth body, composition lower limbs
    19"................. $650.00 – 700.00
Wax
Bartenstein, glass eyes, carton body, crier
Black face/white face
    12"........... $1,100.00 – 1,200.00
Smiling/crying faces
    15"................. $750.00 – 800.00

MUNICH ART DOLLS

1908 – 1920s. Marion Kaulitz hand

painted heads designed by Marc-Schnur, Vogelsanger, and Wackerle, dressed in German or French regional costumes. Usually composition heads and bodies distributed by Cuno & Otto Dressel and Arnold Doll Co.

Composition, painted features, wig, composition body, unmarked

14" .... $12,000.00 – 13,000.00
17" – 18" .. $14,000.00 – 19,000.00

NANCY ANN STORYBOOK

1936 on, San Francisco, California. Started by Nancy Ann Abbott. Made small painted bisque and hard plastic dolls with elaborate costumes. Also made an 8" toddler doll to compete with Vogue's Ginny, 10" fashion dolls and larger size "style show" dolls. Painted bisque, mohair wig, painted eyes, head molded to torso, jointed limbs, either sticker on outfit or hang tag, in box, later made in hard plastic.

Dolls listed are in good condition with original clothing and wrist tags. Allow more for mint-in-box, add 30 percent or more for black dolls. Selected auction prices reflect once-only extreme high prices and should

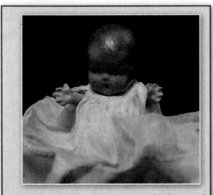

3½" baby, $225.00. *Photo courtesy of Cybermogul Dolls.*

be noted accordingly. Painted bisque baby prices vary with outfits.

Painted bisque

1936 – 1937, pink/blue mottled or sunburst box with gold label, gold foil sticker on clothes "Nancy Ann Dressed Dolls," marked "87," "88," or "93," "Made in Japan," no brochure

Baby

3½" – 4½" ...... $500.00 – 600.00

Child

5" .... $1,200.00 – 1,300.00

1938, early, marked "America" (baby marked "87," "88," or "93," "Made in Japan"), colored box, sunburst pattern with gold label, gold foil sticker on clothes: "Judy Ann," no brochure

Baby

3½" – 4½" ...... $475.00 – 525.00

Child

5" .... $800.00 – 1,000.00

1938, late, marked "Judy Ann USA" and "Story Book USA" (baby marked "Made in USA" and "88, 89, and 93 Made in Japan"), colored box, sunburst pattern with gold or silver label, gold foil sticker on clothes: "Storybook Dolls," no brochure

Judy Ann mold ...... $900.00 – 1,200.00
Storybook mold .... $550.00 – 750.00

1939, child, "Story Book Doll USA," molded socks and molded bangs (baby has star-shaped hands), colored box with small silver dots, silver label, gold foil sticker on clothes, "Storybook Dolls," no brochure

Baby

3½" – 4½" ...... $200.00 – 225.00

Child

5" .... $450.00 – 550.00

1940, child has molded socks only (baby has star-shaped bisque hands), colored box with white polka dots, silver label, gold foil sticker on clothes, "Storybook Dolls," has brochure

Baby

3½" – 4½" ...... $100.00 – 135.00

Child

5" .... $225.00 – 325.00

1941 – 1942, child has pudgy tummy or slim tummy, baby has star-shaped hands or fist, white box with colored polka dots, with silver label, gold foil bracelet with name of doll and brochure

Baby

3½" – 4½" ...... $100.00 – 125.00

Child

5" .... $200.00 – 250.00

1943 – 1947, child has one-piece head, body, and legs ("stiff" legs), baby has fist hands, white box with colored polka dots, silver label, ribbon tie or pin fastener, gold foil bracelet with name of doll, and brochure

Baby

3½" – 4½" .... $50.00 – 65.00

Child

5" .... $35.00 – 55.00

Hard plastic

1947 – 1949, child has hard plastic body, painted eyes, baby has bisque body, plastic arms and legs, white box with colored polka dots with "Nancy Ann Storybook Dolls" between dots, silver label, brass snap, gold foil bracelet with name of doll and brochure, more for special outfit

Baby

3½" – 4½" .... $55.00 – 70.00

Child

5½" .... $60.00 – 70.00

1949 on, hard plastic, both have black sleep eyes, white box with colored polka dots and "Nancy Ann Storybook Dolls" between dots, silver label, brass or painted snaps, gold foil bracelet with name of doll and brochure

Baby

3½" – 4½" .... $40.00 – 55.00

Child

5" .... $40.00 – 50.00

Special dolls

Mammy and Baby, marked "Japan 1146" or

Lot of four hard plastic Nancy Ann Storybook dolls, $60.00 – 70.00 each. *Photo courtesy of Alderfer Auction & Appraisal.*

America mold

5" .... $1,000.00 – 1,200.00

Storybook USA

5" .... $400.00 – 500.00

Topsy, bisque black doll, jointed legs

All-bisque .... $450.00 – 500.00

Plastic arms .... $150.00 – 200.00

All-plastic, painted or sleep eyes

$125.00 – 150.00

White boots, bisque jointed leg dolls

5" .... Add $50.00

Series dolls, depending on mold mark

All-Bisque

American Girl Series

Jointed legs ...... $175.00 – 250.00

Stiff legs .... $45.00 – 65.00

Around the World Series

$600.00 – 1,000.00

Masquerade Series

Ballet Dancer, Cowboy, Pirate

$750.00 – 900.00

Sports Series .... $1,000.00 – 1,300.00

Margie Ann Series

Margie Ann ...... $150.00 – 250.00

Powder & Crinoline Series

$75.00 – 100.00

Bisque or plastic
Operetta or Hit Parade Series
$140.00 – 175.00
Hard plastic
Big and Little Sister Series, or Commencement Series (except baby) ... $75.00 – 100.00
Bridal, Dolls of the Day, Dolls of the Month, Fairytale, Mother Goose, Nursery Rhyme, Religious, and Seasons Series, painted or sleep eyes .... $60.00 – 75.00
Other Dolls
Audrey Ann, toddler, marked "Nancy Ann Storybook 12"
6" .... $900.00 – 975.00
Nancy Ann Style Show, ca. 1954
Hard plastic, sleep eyes, long dress, unmarked
18" .... $800.00 – 1,200.00
Vinyl head, plastic body, all original, complete
18" .... $400.00 – 500.00
Muffie
1953, hard plastic, wig, sleep eyes, strung straight-leg, non-walker, painted lashes
8" .... $350.00 – 400.00
1954, hard plastic walker, molded eyelashes, brows
8" .... $200.00 – 250.00
1955 – 1956, vinyl head, molded or painted upper lashes, rooted saran wig, walker or bent-knee walker
8" .... $150.00 – 200.00
1968+, reissued, hard plastic
8" .... $90.00 – 105.00
Lori Ann
Vinyl
7½" .... $100.00 – 140.00
Tagged Lori Ann outfit.....$50.00 – 70.00
Debbie
Hard plastic in school dress, name on wrist tag/box
10" .... $150.00 – 200.00
Vinyl head, hard plastic body
10" .... $75.00 – 100.00

18" Style Show doll, $1,200.00. *Photo courtesy of Alderfer Auction & Appraisal.*

Hard plastic walker
10½" .... $125.00 – 150.00
Vinyl head, hard plastic walker
10½" .... $65.00 – 75.00
Little Miss Nancy Ann, 1959, high-heeled fashion doll
8½" .... $100.00 – 150.00
Miss Nancy Ann, 1959, marked "Nancy Ann," vinyl head, rooted hair, rigid vinyl

10½" Miss Nancy Ann, ca. 1959, MIB, $350.00. *Photo courtesy of Alderfer Auction & Appraisal.*

body, high-heeled feet, in undergarments or in day dress

10½" .... $150.00 – 200.00

Baby Sue Sue, 1960s, vinyl

Doll only................... $100.00 – 125.00

NESBIT

House of Nesbit, 1956 on, England. Historical costume and character dolls designed by Peggy Nesbit. Hard plastic heads on vinyl bodies.

7" – 10"

Simple costumes .... $25.00 – 40.00

Elaborate costumes ..... $75.00 – 150.00

GEBRUDER OHLHAVER

1913 – 1930, Sonneberg, Germany. Produced Revalo (Ohlhaver spelled backwards omitting the two H's) line; made bisque socket and shoulder head and composition dolls. Bought heads from Ernst Heubach, Gebrüder Heubach, and others.

25" Ohlhaver doll marked "Revalo," $850.00.
Photo courtesy of Morphy Auctions.

Dolls listed are in good condition with original or appropriate clothing.

Baby or toddler, character face, bisque socket head, glass eyes, open mouth, teeth, wig, composition and wood ball-jointed body (bent-leg for baby)

Baby

15" – 17"........ $375.00 – 425.00

21"................. $600.00 – 650.00

Toddler

14"................. $650.00 – 750.00

8" Peggy Nesbit limited edition set depicting Prince Charles and Princess Diana, 1986, $250.00 pair. *Photo courtesy of Alderfer Auction & Appraisal.*

22".................. $850.00 – 950.00
Child, Mold 150, or no mold number, bisque socket head, open mouth, sleep eyes, composition body

14" – 16"........ $425.00 – 500.00
18" – 20"........ $700.00 – 750.00
24" – 28"........ $800.00 – 900.00

Shoulder head, kid body

18" – 20"........ $350.00 – 400.00

Character, bisque solid dome with molded and painted hair, intaglio eyes, composition body

Molded bob, open-closed mouth, intaglio eyes, on five-piece body

12".................. $750.00 – 900.00

Too few in database for a reliable range.

Coquette-type, molded hair ribbon with bows
High quality bisque

11" – 12"........ $800.00 – 875.00

Low quality bisque

11" – 12"........ $375.00 – 450.00

OLD COTTAGE DOLLS

Late 1948 on, England. Dolls were designed by Greta and Susi Fleischmann. Made with hard rubber or plastic heads, felt body, some with wire armature, oval hang tag has trademark "Old Cottage Dolls," special characters may be more

8" – 9".............. $80.00 – 120.00
12" – 13"........ $200.00 – 250.00

ORIENTAL DOLLS

1850 to present. Dolls depicting Asian peoples. Made by companies in Germany, America, Japan, and others.

All-bisque

Heubach, Gebrüder, Chin-Chin

4"................... $250.00 – 300.00

5" all-bisque Oriental doll by Simon & Halbig, $800.00. *Photo courtesy of Withington Auction, Inc.*

Kestner

6"............. $1,100.00 – 1,500.00
8"............. $1,600.00 – 1,900.00

Simon & Halbig, mold 852, ca. 1880, all-bisque, swivel head, yellow tint bisque, glass eyes, closed mouth, wig, painted socks and curled pointed-toe shoes

4½"................ $650.00 – 700.00
5½"................ $875.00 – 950.00
7"................ $975.00 – 1,025.00

Unmarked or unknown maker, presumed German or French

6"................... $450.00 – 550.00

European bisque

Bisque head, jointed body

Barrois Poupée, swivel neck, glass eyes, kid body

15"............................$10,000.00

Too few in database for a reliable range.

Belton-type, mold 193, 206

10"........... $1,900.00 – 2,075.00
14"........... $2,500.00 – 2,700.00

Bru, pressed bisque swivel head, glass eyes,

closed mouth

    20" Bru Jne.............. $55,500.00*

Kestner, J. D., 1899 – 1930+, mold 243, bisque socket head, open mouth, wig, bent-leg baby body, add more for original clothing

    13" – 14" . $5,000.00 – 6,000.00

    16" – 18".. $6,000.00 – 8,000.00

    Solid dome, painted hair

    15"........... $4,500.00 – 5,000.00

König & Wernicke, mold 155, glass eyes, open mouth

    18"........... $1,700.00 – 1,800.00

Armand Marseille, 1925, mold 353, solid-dome bisque socket head, glass eyes, closed mouth

    Baby body

    7½".......... $1,000.00 – 1,100.00

    9" – 12"....... $900.00 – 1,000.00

    14" – 16".. $1,200.00 – 1,500.00

    Toddler

    16"........... $1,200.00 – 1,500.00

    Painted bisque

15" Simon & Halbig, mold 1329, $2,700.00. *Photo courtesy of Morphy Auctions.*

8" Schoenau & Hoffmeister, mold 4900, $700.00. *Photo courtesy of Morphy Auctions.*

    7"................................. $350.00

Too few in database for a reliable range.

Schmidt, Bruno, marked "BSW," mold 500, ca. 1905, glass eyes, open mouth

    13" – 14".. $1,600.00 – 2,000.00

Schoenau & Hoffmeister, mold 4900, bisque socket head, glass eyes, open mouth, tinted composition wood jointed body

    8" – 10".......... $700.00 – 800.00

Simon & Halbig, mold 1079, 1099, 1129, 1159, 1199,1329, bisque socket head, glass eyes, open mouth, pierced ears, composition wood jointed body

    8" – 10".... $1,200.00 – 1,400.00

    12" – 13".. $1,800.00 – 2,300.00

    16" – 18".. $2,800.00 – 3,400.00

    20" – 24".. $4,000.00 – 4,500.00

Unknown maker, socket head, jointed body, closed mouth, glass eyes

    4½"................ $550.00 – 650.00

    8" – 10".......... $700.00 – 900.00

    12" – 14".. $1,000.00 – 1,200.00

    20"........... $2,600.00 – 2,800.00

8" Ada Lum cloth doll, $40.00. *Photo courtesy of The Museum Doll Shop.*

Cloth

Ada Lum dolls, 1940s on, Shanghai, cloth dolls depicting Chinese people, embroidered features, black yarn hair

8" – 10".............. $50.00 – 65.00

14" – 18".......... $75.00 – 100.00

Shoasing Industrial Mission, Chekang Province, China, cloth dolls depicting Chinese people, painted features

1½" – 3"............. $20.00 – 40.00

Composition

Amusco, 1925, composition

17"........... $1,000.00 – 1,200.00

Effanbee

Butin-nose, in basket with wardrobe, painted Asian features including black bobbed hair, bangs, side-glancing eyes, excellent color and condition

8".................... $400.00 – 500.00

Patsy, painted Asian features, including black bangs straight across the forehead, brown side-glancing eyes, dressed in silk Chinese pajamas and matching shoes, excellent condition

14"................. $700.00 – 800.00

Horsman

Child, 1910 on, composition head and lower arms, cloth body, molded turban on head, painted eyes

11"................ $375.00 – 425.00

Jap Rose Kids, 1911 on, composition head, arms, cloth body, molded painted hair, painted eyes, advertising tie-in to Jap Rose soap

13" boy or 14" girl

$350.00 – 375.00

Baby Butterfly, 1914+, composition head, hands, cloth body, painted hair, and features

13"................ $250.00 – 300.00

15"................ $350.00 – 400.00

Quan-Quan Co., California, Ming Ming Baby, all-composition jointed baby, painted features, original costume, yarn queue, painted shoes

9".................. $125.00 – 150.00

11"................ $200.00 – 225.00

Traditional Chinese

Man or woman, composition-type head, cloth-wound bodies, may have carved arms and feet, in traditional costume

11"................ $150.00 – 225.00

14"................ $350.00 – 425.00

Traditional Japanese

Ichimatsu, 1870s on, a play doll made of papier-mâché-type material with gofun finish of crushed oyster shells, swivel head,

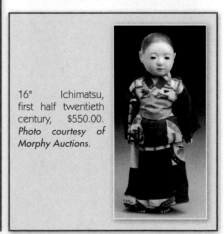

16" Ichimatsu, first half twentieth century, $550.00. *Photo courtesy of Morphy Auctions.*

shoulder plate, cloth midsection, upper arms, and legs, papier-mâché limbs and torso, glass eyes, pierced nostrils. Early dolls may have jointed wrists and ankles, in original dress. Later 1950s+ dolls imported by Kimport

Meiji era, ca. 1870s – 1912

10" – 12"	$600.00 – 750.00
16" – 18"	$850.00 – 950.00
22" – 24"	$1,800.00 – 2,200.00

Child

Painted hair, 1920s

12" – 15"	$450.00 – 550.00
17" – 18"	$575.00 – 625.00
24"	$825.00 – 875.00

1930s

12" – 15"	$350.00 – 425.00
17" – 18"	$550.00 – 600.00

1940s on

10" – 12"	$100.00 – 125.00
14" – 16"	$150.00 – 175.00

Lady

1920s – 1930s

12" – 14"	$200.00 – 250.00
16"	$250.00 – 275.00

1940s – 1950s

12" – 14"	$70.00 – 95.00
16"	$100.00 – 135.00

Hina Matsuri, Emperor or Empress, seated, Ca. 1890s

8"	$500.00 – 575.00

Ca. 1920s

4" – 6"	$150.00 – 175.00
10" – 12"	$250.00 – 300.00

Warrior

1880 – 1890s

16"	$750.00 – 850.00

Too few in database for a reliable range.

On horse

15"	$1,000.00 – 1,100.00

Too few in database for a reliable range.

1920s

15"	$350.00 – 400.00

Too few in database for a reliable range.

On horse

13"	$800.00 – 850.00

Japanese baby, ca. 1920s, bisque head, sleep eyes, closed mouth, papier-mâché body

8"	$50.00 – 70.00
14"	$65.00 – 90.00

Glass eyes

8"	$95.00 – 125.00
14"	$200.00 – 265.00

Gofun finish of crushed oyster-shell head, painted flesh color, papier-mâché body, glass eyes and original clothes

8" – 10"	$55.00 – 75.00
14" – 18"	$95.00 – 185.00

Wooden dolls

Door of Hope: See Door of Hope section.

PAPIER-MACHÉ

Pre-1600 on. Papier-mâché is an elastic substance made of paper pulp and a variety of additives. Dolls of papier-mâché were being made in France as early as the sixteenth century. In Germany and France papier-mâché dolls were being mass-produced in molds for heads after 1810. It reached heights of popularity by the mid-1850s and was also used for bodies. Papier-mâché shoulder head, glass or painted eyes, molded and painted hair, sometimes in fancy hairdos. Usually no marks. Dolls listed are in good condition, nicely dressed. More for exceptional examples, considerably less for dolls which have been repainted.

Molded hair papier-mâché, so-called Milliner's Models, German, 1820 – 1860s, molded hair, a shapely waist, kid body, and wooden limbs

Apollo topknot, side curls

8" – 10"	$1,400.00 – 1,700.00
12" – 14"	$2,500.00 – 3,000.00
16" – 18"	$3,500.00 – 4,000.00

9½" so-called milliner's model doll, 1840s, $1,200.00. *Photo courtesy of Skinner, Inc.*

20" – 23".. $4,000.00 – 5,000.00
Braided bun, side curls or long puffy side curls with simple bun
 7" – 11".... $1,200.00 – 1,800.00
 9" with applied curls
        $2,370.00*
 13" – 15".. $2,200.00 – 3,000.00
Braided coronet, 1840s style
 10" – 12".. $1,500.00 – 2,000.00

Center part, molded bun
 5" – 10"........ $900.00 –1,300.00
 13" – 15".. $1,400.00 – 1,700.00
 18" – 24".. $1,800.00 – 2,200.00
Center part, sausage curls
 11" – 14"..... $900.00 – 1,000.00
Coiled braids over ears, braided bun
 9" – 11".... $1,000.00 – 1,100.00
 20" – 21".. $2,100.00 – 2,300.00
Covered Wagon or flat top hairstyle
 6" – 10".......... $400.00 – 600.00
 14" – 16"........ $800.00 – 900.00
Empire-style short curls
 8".................... $750.00 – 850.00
 14" – 20".. $1,200.00 – 1,700.00
Long curls on shoulders
 7" – 14".... $1,200.00 – 2,000.00
Man, molded hat, mustache, beard or other feature
 6" – 10".... $1,200.00 – 2,200.00
 14" – 18".. $4,000.00 – 6,000.00
Molded comb, side curls, braided coronet
 20" – 25".. $3,200.00 – 3,800.00
Too few in database for a reliable range.
Early-type shoulder head, German, 1840s – 1860s, cloth body; wooden limbs, with topknots, buns, puff curls, or braids, dressed

18" so-called milliner's model, center part with curls, $1,500.00. *Photo courtesy of Withington Auction, Inc.*

24" man, 1840s, $8,000.00. *Photo courtesy of Skinner, Inc.*

13½" early-type shoulder head with molded bonnet, by Loenthal, sold for $4,444.00 at auction. *Photo courtesy of Skinner, Inc.*

10½" German glass-eyed child, $1,500.00. *Photo courtesy of Skinner, Inc.*

in original clothing or excellent copy, may have some wear; more for painted pate, elaborate hairstyle, or exceptional quality

Painted eyes

9" – 14".......	$900.00 – 1,400.00
16" – 18"..	$1,800.00 – 2,400.00
21" – 24"..	$2,200.00 – 2,800.00
26" – 30"..	$2,800.00 – 3,000.00

Glass eyes

16" – 18" ..	$1,500.00 – 2,000.00
20" – 24"..	$2,000.00 – 2,500.00
32" with applied hair loops in front of ear..........................	$11,850.00*

Long curls

14"...........	$1,100.00 – 1,500.00
16"...........	$2,000.00 – 2,200.00

20" with braided coronet hairstyle, 1840s, $3,500.00. *Photo courtesy of Skinner, Inc.*

30", German, with painted eyes, $3,000.00. *Photo courtesy of Skinner, Inc.*

18" French-type, all-original, $3,000.00. *Photo courtesy of Skinner, Inc.*

24"........... $3,200.00 – 3,500.00

Pre-Greiner-type, 1850s, German or American- made shoulder head, molded painted black hair, black glass eyes, cloth body

16" – 18" . $1,200.00 – 2,000.00
20" – 25" . $1,600.00 – 2,200.00
29" – 31".. $3,000.00 – 4,000.00

French-type, 1835 – 1850, made by German

33" German, with glass eyes, applied waxed human hair braids, ca. 1840, sold for $11,850.00 at auction. *Photo courtesy of Skinner, Inc.*

companies for the French trade, painted black hair, brush marks, solid-dome, shoulder head, some have nailed-on wigs, open mouth, bamboo teeth, kid or leather body, appropriately dressed

Glass eyes

13" – 14".. $1,000.00 – 1,400.00
18" – 20".. $1,800.00 – 2,000.00
24"........... $2,400.00 – 2,500.00
28" – 34".. $3,400.00 – 3,800.00

Painted eyes

8" – 12".......... $600.00 – 800.00
14" – 16".. $1,100.00 – 1,500.00
17" – 20".. $1,500.00 – 2,500.00

Papier-mâché, American, Greiner 1858 – 1883: See Ludwig Greiner section.

Poupard, French and German, all papier-mâché to represent a swaddled baby

12"................. $300.00 – 400.00

Sonneberg Taufling (so-called Motschmann): See Sonneberg Taufling section.

Patent washable, 1879 – 1910s, shoulder head with mohair wig, open or closed mouth, glass eyes, cloth body, composition limbs, made by companies such as F. M. Schilling and others

Better quality

12" – 15"........ $800.00 – 900.00
18"................. $650.00 – 675.00
22" – 24" .... $725.00 – 800.00

11" patent washable-type, $600.00. *Photo courtesy of Morphy Auctions.*

23" Sonneberg-type, 1880 – 1910, $500.00.
Photo courtesy of Morphy Auctions.

Lesser quality
 10" – 12"........ $125.00 – 175.00
 14" – 16"........ $225.00 – 250.00
 23" – 25"........ $300.00 – 400.00
Sonneberg-type, 1880 – 1910, "M & S Superior," Muller & Strasburger, Cunno & Otto Dressel, and others shoulder head, with blond molded hair, painted blue or brown eyes, cloth body, with kid or leather arms and boots
 13" – 15"........ $350.00 – 400.00

18", with molded hairband, 1870s, $550.00.
Photo courtesy of Sweetbriar Auctions.

 18" – 20"........ $450.00 – 525.00
 24" – 29"........ $575.00 – 650.00
Glass eyes
 12"................. $400.00 – 500.00
 16" – 18"........ $550.00 – 650.00
Wigged
 18" – 25"........ $600.00 – 700.00
Papier-mâché Child, 1920 on, head has brighter coloring, wigged, child often in ethnic costume, stuffed cloth body and limbs, or papier-mâché arms
French
 9" – 13".......... $100.00 – 125.00
 13" – 15"........ $200.00 – 275.00
German
 10"..................... $70.00 – 80.00
 15"................. $150.00 – 165.00
Unknown maker
 8"....................... $50.00 – 60.00
 12"................... $90.00 – 115.00
 16"................. $150.00 – 175.00
Clowns, papier-mâché head, with painted clown features, open or closed mouth, molded hair or wigged, cloth body, composition or papier-mâché arms, or five-piece jointed body
High quality child body
 16"............... $800.00 – 1,000.00
 20"........... $1,200.00 – 1,300.00
Lower quality crude body type
 8"................... $200.00 – 235.00
 14"................. $450.00 – 485.00

PARIAN-TYPE, UNTINTED BISQUE

1850 – 1900 on, Germany. The term "parian" as used in doll collecting refers to dolls of untinted bisque, in other words the doll's skin tone is white rather than tinted. These dolls were at the height of their popularity from 1860 through the 1870s. They are often found with molded blond hair, some with fancy hair

Parian-Type, Untinted Bisque

17" so-called Parian-type of the 1860s, with a simple hairstyle, $500.00. *Photo courtesy of Morphy Auctions.*

arrangements and ornaments or bonnets, can have glass or painted eyes, pierced ears, may have molded jewelry or clothing, occasionally solid dome with wig, cloth body, nicely dressed in good condition. Dolls listed are in good condition, appropriately dressed. Exceptional examples may be much higher.

Lady

Common hairstyle

Painted eyes

    Undecorated, simple molded hair

8" – 12"	$200.00 – 350.00
14" – 16"	$400.00 – 450.00
18" – 25"	$500.00 – 600.00

Molded bodice, fancy trim

17" – 23"	$600.00 – 900.00

Wigged, bald head with period wig

10" – 12"	$1,400.00 – 1,600.00

Glass eyes

10"	$800.00 – 900.00
12" – 14"	$1,300.00 – 1,600.00
16" – 18"	$1,800.00 – 2,000.00

Fancy hairstyle, with molded combs, ribbons, flowers, bands, or snoods, cloth body, untinted bisque limbs, more for elaborate hairstyle

Painted eyes, pierced ears

7" – 10"	$800.00 – 1,500.00
14" – 16"	$1,000.00 – 1,400.00
18" – 22"	$1,600.00 – 1,800.00
24" – 30"	$1,500.00 – 1,800.00

Decorated shoulder plate

    Simple bodice or tie

8½"	$275.00 – 300.00
13" – 15"	$450.00 – 600.00
20" – 23"	$650.00 – 750.00

18", fancy hairstyle and pierced ears, 1870s, $1,600.00. *Photo courtesy of Morphy Auctions.*

24", molded bodice with ruffles, $3,000.00. *Photo courtesy of Withington Auction, Inc.*

More elaborate bodice and hair
12" – 16".. $2,000.00 – 2,400.00
17" – 21".. $2,400.00 – 2,800.00
Glass eyes, pierced ears
12" – 15".. $1,600.00 – 1,900.00
18" – 20".. $2,000.00 – 2,500.00
Swivel neck
14" – 15".. $2,400.00 – 2,700.00
Named hairstyles, painted eyes unless otherwise noted, names applied by modern collectors to describe style
Alice in Wonderland, molded headband or comb
14" – 16"........ $675.00 – 800.00
19" – 21".. $1,000.00 – 1,200.00
Glass-eyed, 17"............. $1,900.00*
Countess Dagmar, no mark, headband, cluster curls on forehead
12" – 15"........ $750.00 – 900.00
18" – 21".. $1,100.00 – 1,600.00
Currier & Ives
7"............. $1,500.00 – 2,000.00
Dolley Madison
18" – 22"..... $750.00 – 1,200.00
Empress Eugenie, headpiece snood
12" – 15".. $1,500.00 – 1,700.00
25"........... $1,200.00 – 1,500.00
Irish Queen, Limbach, clover mark, #8552
14" – 16"........ $700.00 – 800.00
Molded hat, See Bonnet Head section.
Necklace, jewels, or standing ruffles
17" – 20".. $1,800.00 – 2,800.00
Princess Augusta Victoria, molded shoulder plate with cross necklace, glass eyes
13" – 15".. $1,100.00 – 1,300.00
22"........... $1,000.00 – 1,400.00
Men or boys, center or side-part hairstyles, cloth body, decorated shirts and ties
Painted eyes
13"................. $700.00 – 800.00
16" – 17"..... $900.00 – 1,100.00
Glass eyes
16"........... $2,400.00 – 2,825.00

RONNAUG PETTERSEN

1901 – 1980, Norway. Made cloth dolls, pressed felt head, usually painted side-glancing eyes, cloth bodies, intricate costumes, paper tags
7" – 8"............ $150.00 – 200.00
14½" .... $550.00 – 700.00
Nissa, gnome
11"................. $300.00 – 350.00

Group of 7½" Ronnaug Pettersen dolls, $150.00 – 200.00 each. *Dolls courtesy of Carol Barboza.*

DORA PETZOLD

Germany, 1919 – 1930+. Made and dressed dolls, molded composition head, painted features, wig, stockinette body, sawdust-filled, short torso, free-formed thumbs, stitched fingers, shaped legs

19" doll, $1,600.00. *Photo courtesy of Withington Auction, Inc.*

18"........... $1,000.00 – 1,500.00
20" – 22".. $1,600.00 – 2,000.00

PHILADELPHIA BABY (SHEPPARD BABY)

1900, Philadelphia, Pennsylvania. Rag baby sold by the J.B. Sheppard & Co. store. Molded stockinette, painted features, sewn joints at shoulders, hips, and knees. Dolls

21" Philadelphia Baby, $5,500.00. *Photo courtesy of Skinner, Inc.*

listed are in good condition, appropriately dressed. Allow more for exceptional condition.

18" – 22" .. $4,500.00 – 5,500.00
Doll in somewhat worn condition
18" – 22".. $1,600.00 – 2,700.00

PLEASANT COMPANY

1985 – present. Middleton, Wisconsin, founded by Pleasant T. Rowland. In 1998 the company was purchased by Mattel, Inc. Values listed are for good condition secondary market dolls in appropriate clothing, many dolls are still available at retail as well.

18" Rebecca by American Girl, $95.00. *Doll courtesy of Shirley Fisher.*

American Girl®, vinyl dolls with wigs
18"..................... $70.00 – 95.00
Nellie, retired... $150.00 – 175.00

POLISH RELIEF DOLLS

1914 on, Paris, France. Polish Relief dolls were created in the workshop of Madame Lazarski during and shortly after WWI. This project provided work for war refugees and the money raised from the sale of the dolls aided Polish widows and orphans. Cloth dolls with embroidered features and floss hair.

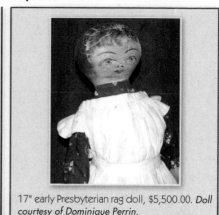

17" early Presbyterian rag doll, $5,500.00. *Doll courtesy of Dominique Perrin.*

1950s – 1980s .... $400.00 – 450.00

RABERY & DELPHIEU

1856 – 1930 and later, Paris. Became part of S.F.B.J. in 1899. Some heads pressed (pre-1890) and some poured, purchased some heads from Francois Gaultier. Dolls listed are in good condition, appropriately dressed. Exceptional dolls may be more.

17" doll, $400.00. *Doll courtesy of Elaine Holda.*

Adult
19" .... $400.00 – 500.00
Child
11" – 17" .... $300.00 – 400.00

PRESBYTERIAN RAG DOLLS

1885 on, Bucyrus, Ohio. The First Presbyterian Church made cloth dolls as a fundraiser, cloth doll with "pie-shaped gusseted" piece across top of head, flat face, painted hair and features, mitten hands, 17". 1880s – 1930s .. $4,500.00 – 5,500.00

20" bébé, $5,000.00. *Photo courtesy of Alderfer Auction & Appraisal.*

Child

Closed mouth, bisque socket head, paperweight eyes, pierced ears, mohair wig, cork pate, French composition and wood jointed body

    9" – 10".... $2,400.00 – 2,600.00
    13" – 15" . $3,000.00 – 4,500.00
    20" – 24".. $5,000.00 – 6,000.00
    28"........... $8,000.00 – 9,000.00

Open mouth, row of upper teeth

    18" – 21".. $1,400.00 – 1,600.00
    24" – 26".. $1,700.00 – 2,000.00

RAGGEDY ANN & ANDY

1915 to present. Rag doll designed by Johnny Gruelle in 1915, made by various companies. Ann wears dress with apron; Andy, shirt and pants with matching hat.
P.J. Volland, 1918 – 1934, early dolls marked "Patented Sept. 7, 1915," all-cloth, tin or wooden button eyes, painted features, some have sewn knee or arm joints, sparse brown or auburn yarn hair, oversize hands, feet turned outward. Dolls listed are in clean un-faded condition, appropriately dressed.
Raggedy Ann & Andy, 15" – 18"

16" Volland Raggedy Ann, $1,800.00. *Photo courtesy of Withington Auction, Inc.*

20" Exposition Raggedy Ann, ca. 1935, $7,000.00. *Photo courtesy of James D. Julia, Inc.*

Painted face....... $1,600.00 – 2,200.00
Printed face .... $1,000.00 – 1,600.00
Beloved Belindy, 1926 – 1930 painted face, 1931 – 1934 print face

    15"........... $3,000.00 – 3,500.00

Pirate Chieftain and other characters

    18"........... $2,200.00 – 2,400.00

Exposition, 1935

Raggedy Ann, no eyelashes, no eyebrows, outline nose, no heart, satin label on hem of dress

    18"........... $5,800.00 – 7,000.00

Too few in database for a reliable range.

Mollye Goldman, 1935 – 1937, marked on chest "Raggedy Ann and Andy Dolls Manufactured by Molly'es Doll Outfitters," nose outlined in black, red heart on chest, reddish-orange hair, multicolored legs, blue feet, some have oilcloth faces

    15"................. $850.00 – 950.00
    17" – 21".. $1,100.00 – 1,300.00

Baby Ann

    14"................. $700.00 – 800.00

Georgene Novelties, 1938 – 1962, Ann has orange hair and a topknot, six different mouth styles, early ones had tin eyes, later ones had plastic, six different noses, seams in middle of legs and arms to represent knees and elbows, feet turn forward, red and white striped legs, all have hearts that say "I love you" printed on chest, tag sewn to left side seam, several variations, all say "Georgene Novelties, Inc."

Raggedy Ann or Andy, 1930s – 1960s

Nose outlined with black, 1938 – 1944

    15" – 17"........ $450.00 – 500.00

    19" – 21"........ $600.00 – 700.00

Awake/Asleep, 1940s

    Nose outlined in black

    14"................. $400.00 – 500.00

Long nose face, 1944 – 1946

    19"................. $800.00 – 900.00

Curved nose edges, 1946 on

    15" – 19"........ $275.00 – 300.00

    20" – 23" .... $500.00 – 600.00

    32"................. $300.00 – 350.00

Beloved Belindy, 1940 – 1944

    14" – 18".. $1,700.00 – 2,100.00

Knickerbocker, 1962 – 1982, printed features, hair color change from orange to red, there were five mouth and five eyelash variations, tags were located on clothing back or pants seam

Raggedy Ann or Andy

1964, cloud box

    15"................. $200.00 – 275.00

Later examples

    6"....................... $20.00 – 30.00

    15".................... $75.00 – 100.00

18" Raggedy Ann by Molly'es, $1,000.00.
Photo courtesy of Withington Auction, Inc.

    19"................. $120.00 – 150.00

    30" – 36"........ $120.00 – 175.00

Musical Ann

    15"................. $100.00 – 150.00

Raggedy Ann, Talking, 1972

    19"................. $180.00 – 225.00

Beloved Belindy, ca. 1965

    15"............. $900.00 – 1,000.00

Camel with Wrinkled Knees

    15"................. $275.00 – 350.00

Nasco/Bobbs-Merrill, 1972, cloth head, hard plastic doll body, printed features, apron marked "Raggedy Ann"

    24"................. $125.00 – 150.00

Bobbs-Merrill Co., 1974, ventriloquist dummy, hard plastic head, hands, foam body, printed face

    30"................. $125.00 – 175.00

Applause Toy Company, 1981 – present, owned by Hasbro which also markets Raggedy Ann through its Playskool line

    8"....................... $10.00 – 15.00

    17"..................... $30.00 – 35.00

    48"................. $100.00 – 125.00

Limited Editions, Applause marketed as part of their Dakin line

75th anniversary Ann or Andy, 1992

    19"..................... $75.00 – 85.00

Molly-E Raggedy Ann, 1993

    18"..................... $40.00 – 50.00

Georgene reissues, 1996

    15"..................... $30.00 – 40.00

Ann or Andy, 1994

    13"..................... $80.00 – 90.00

US Patent Ann, 1995

    17"..................... $65.00 – 85.00

Stamp Ann, 1997

    17"..................... $45.00 – 55.00

R. John Wright, present, molded felt doll, secondary market values, dolls still available at retail

Ann or Andy

    17"................. $650.00 – 900.00

Ann, Andy, and the Camel with the Wrinkled Knees .... $1,800.00 – 2,000.00
Brass Key Productions, 1993 on, porcelain
7" .... $8.00 – 15.00

JESSIE McCUTCHEON RALEIGH

1916 – 1920, Chicago, Illinois. McCutcheon was a businesswoman who developed a line of dolls. These were distributed by Butler Brothers and perhaps others. She produced dolls of cloth and composition.
Shoebutton Sue, flat face, painted spit curls, mitten hands, sewn on red shoes, shown in 1921 Sears catalog
15" $1,900.00
Too few in database for a reliable range.
Baby, composition head on composition body
10" – 12" .... $300.00 – 450.00
18" .... $475.00 – 600.00
Child
Composition head on composition body, wigged
11" .... $425.00 – 500.00
13" .... $525.00 – 575.00
18" .... $775.00 – 975.00
Molded hair
11" – 13" .... $800.00 – 950.00
18" .... $1,400.00 – 1,600.00
Composition head on cloth body with composition lower arms and legs
22" – 24" .... $325.00 – 400.00

RAYNAL

1922 – 1930 on, Paris. Edouard Raynal made dolls of felt, cloth, or with celluloid heads with widely spaced eyebrows. Dressed, some resemble Lenci, except fingers were together or their hands were of celluloid, marked "Raynal" on soles of shoes and/or pendant
Cloth, 1922, molded head, cloth body, sometimes celluloid hands
14" – 16" .... $600.00 – 800.00
17" – 22" .. $1,600.00 – 2,200.00
Baby Shirley type
18" .... $1,500.00 – 2,000.00
Pressed felt child
14" .... $3,000.00 – 3,500.00
Celluloid, 1936, then Rhodoid
Baby
18" – 24" .... $575.00 – 675.00
Vinyl, 1960s – 1970s
Margaret
14" .... $50.00 – 60.00

THEODOR RECKNAGEL

1886 – 1930, Alexandrienthal, Coburg, Germany. Made bisque and composition doll heads of varying quality, incised or raised mark, wigged or molded hair, glass or painted eyes, open or closed mouth, flange neck or socket head. Dolls listed are in good condition, appropriately dressed.

11½", mold 1917, all-original, $190.00. *Photo courtesy of Cybermogul Dolls.*

Baby

Mold 121, 126, 127, 1924, bent-limb baby body, painted or glass eyes

6" – 7"............ $150.00 – 200.00
8" – 9"............ $200.00 – 225.00

Bonnet head baby, Mold 22, 23, 28, 44: See Bonnet Head section.

Child

Dolly face, 1890s – 1914

Mold 1907, 1909, 1914, open mouth, glass eyes

7" – 9"............ $100.00 – 160.00
10" – 12"........ $150.00 – 180.00
15" – 18"........ $225.00 – 300.00
22" – 24" .... $300.00 – 350.00

Character face, ca. 1910+, may have crossed hammer mark

7" – 8"............ $350.00 – 375.00
12" – 14"........ $700.00 – 775.00

Mold 57, open-closed mouth with teeth, molded hair

9" – 10".......... $875.00 – 975.00

Mold 58, open-closed mouth with teeth, molded hair with molded ribbon and three flowers

7".................... $300.00 – 325.00

Mold 31, 32, Max and Moritz

8"............$800.00 – 900.00 each
12"....$1,700.00 – 1,900.00 each

Googly molds 43, 45, 46, 50, no mold number: See Googly section.

REGIONAL DRESS DOLLS

This category describes dolls costumed in regional dress to show different nationalities, facial characteristics, or cultural backgrounds. Examples are dolls in regional costumes that are commonly sold as souvenirs to tourists. These dolls became popular about 1875 and continue to be made today. A

7" Goebel, mold 120, in regional costume, $200.00. *Photo courtesy of Cybermogul Dolls.*

well-made beautiful doll with accessories or wardrobe may be more.

Bisque, German

6" – 9"............ $200.00 – 300.00
10" – 13"....... $300.00 – 400.00

French Fisherfolk, bisque heads

8" – 12".......... $300.00 – 600.00

Painted bisque

4"....................... $45.00 – 65.00
10" .... $95.00 – 130.00

Celluloid

8"....................... $40.00 – 50.00
15"................. $100.00 – 125.00

Cloth

8"................... $100.00 – 155.00
13"................. $125.00 – 175.00

*Russian,*1920 on, all-cloth, molded and painted stockinette head, hands, in regional costumes

7"....................... $55.00 – 70.00
15"................. $125.00 – 150.00
18"................. $160.00 – 180.00

Composition child

8"................... $150.00 – 185.00
13" – 16"........ $200.00 – 250.00

Walker in Dutch costume, post-WWII era

22" .... $125.00 – 150.00

Jay Dolls, Dublin, Ireland, molded heads, cloth wrapped bodies

5" .... $35.00 – 40.00

7½" .... $50.00 – 60.00

11" .... $55.00 – 65.00

Native American Indian, cloth, leather, natural fibers, etc., nineteenth and early twentieth centuries

5" – 8" .... $130.00 – 225.00

13" – 15" .... $400.00 – 650.00

23" .... $700.00 – 850.00

Seminole, woven fiber

4½" – 6" .... $28.00 – 35.00

Skookum, 1913 on, designed by Mary McAboy, painted features, with side-glancing eyes, mohair wigs, cloth figure wrapped in Indian blanket, with folds representing arms, wooden feet, later plastic, label on bottom of foot, box marked "Skookum Bully Good"

4½" papoose on mailer card

$25.00 – 35.00

6" – 9" .... $65.00 – 100.00

10 – 12" .... $200.00 – 300.00

14" – 16" .... $325.00 – 425.00

18" – 20" .... $550.00 – 700.00

27" – 33" .. $1,000.00 – 1,350.00

Hard plastic, regional dress, unmarked or unknown maker

7" .... $8.00 – 15.00

12" .... $20.00 – 30.00

Baitz, Austria, 1970s, painted hard plastic, painted side-glancing eyes, open "o" mouth, excellent quality, tagged and dressed in regional dress

8½" – 9½" .... $45.00 – 55.00

Vinyl

6" .... $20.00 – 25.00

12" .... $40.00 – 45.00

Wood

Polish, painted features, 1930s on

7" .... $4.00 – 6.00

RELIABLE TOY CO.

1920 on, Toronto, Canada. Made composition, hard plastic, and vinyl dolls. Composition, all-composition or composition shoulder head and arms on cloth body, some with composition legs. Dolls listed are in good condition, appropriately dressed.

Baby, 1930s

20" .... $200.00 – 250.00

Baby Precious, 1947, Mama-style doll, sleep eyes, mohair wig

20" .... $100.00 – 175.00

Barbara Scott Ice Skating Doll

15" .... $300.00 – 425.00

Her Highness

15" .... $275.00 – 325.00

Hiawatha or Indian child

10½" .... $50.00 – 75.00

13" .... $100.00 – 135.00

16" .... $155.00 – 185.00

Military Man

14" .... $175.00 – 225.00

Mountie

17" .... $300.00 – 350.00

Nurse, painted eyes, mohair wig

18" .... $200.00 – 250.00

Scottish child

14" .... $75.00 – 100.00

17" .... $150.00 – 165.00

Shirley Temple

18" – 22" .. $1,000.00 – 1,200.00

Toddler

13" .... $150.00 – 200.00

Hard plastic

Baby, 1958, sleep eyes, open mouth

8" .... $40.00 – 50.00

Indian child, all hard plastic

8" .... $20.00 – 30.00

Toni, P-90

14" .... $300.00 – 350.00

Vinyl

Cindy Lou, 1961, vinyl head, rooted ponytail, sleep eyes

14".................... $20.00 – 30.00

Majorette, 1960s, vinyl head, rooted hair, sleep eyes

16".................... $60.00 – 75.00

Suzy Steps, walker, 1950, Canadian version of Ideal's Saucy Walker

35"................. $200.00 – 300.00

Tammy, Canadian version of Ideal's Tammy

12"................... $75.00 – 100.00

REMCO INDUSTRIES

1959 – 1974, Harrison, New Jersey. One of the first companies to market with television ads. Dolls listed are in good condition with original clothing and accessories, allow more for MIB.

Addams Family, 1964

Lurch

5½".................... $45.00 – 55.00

Morticia

4¾"................ $100.00 – 128.00

Uncle Fester

4½".................... $40.00 – 50.00

Baby Crawl-Along, 1967

20".................... $15.00 – 20.00

Baby Glad 'n Sad, 1967, vinyl and hard plastic, rooted blond hair, painted blue eyes

14".................... $12.00 – 18.00

Baby Grow a Tooth, 1968, vinyl and hard plastic, rooted hair, blue sleep eyes, open-closed mouth, one tooth, grows her own tooth, battery-operated

15".................... $18.00 – 22.00

Black

14".................... $20.00 – 25.00

Baby Know It All, 1969

17".................... $15.00 – 20.00

Baby Laugh a Lot, 1970, rooted long hair, painted eyes, open-closed mouth, teeth, vinyl head, hands, plush body, push button, she laughs, battery-operated

16".................... $55.00 – 75.00

Beatles, 1964, vinyl and plastic, Paul McCartney, Ringo Starr, George Harrison, and John Lennon, Paul 4⅞", all others 4½" with guitars bearing their names

Set of four .... $700.00 – 800.00

Individual Beatles ..... $120.00 – 150.00

Daniel Boone, 1964, Fess Parker from TV show

4½"................ $125.00 – 150.00

Dave Clark Five, 1964, set of five musical group, vinyl heads, rigid plastic bodies

Set .... $60.00 – 65.00

Dave Clark

5"...................... $10.00 – 15.00

Other band members have name attached to leg

3"........................ $6.00 – 10.00

Finger Dings, 1969 on, finger puppets, vinyl head

6"...................... $10.00 – 20.00

The Monkees, musical group

$25.00 – 35.00 each

Growing Sally, 1968, doll "grows" ¾", has extra clothes and additional wig

6"...................... $20.00 – 30.00

4¾" Dave Clark, $15.00. *Photo courtesy of Fourty Fifty Sixty.*

Black .... $30.00 – 40.00

Heidi and friends, 1967, in plastic case, rooted hair, painted side-glancing eyes, open-closed mouth, all-vinyl, press buttons and dolls wave

Heidi

    5½" .... $35.00 – 40.00

Herby

    4½" .... $35.00 – 40.00

Hildy

    4½" .... $30.00 – 40.00

Jan, Asian

    5½" .... $35.00 – 45.00

Pip

    5½" .... $35.00 – 45.00

Winking Heidi, 1968

    5½" .... $20.00 – 30.00

Heidi's Jeep set, pink jeep. $35.00 – 40.00

Hello Dolly, 1978, doll talks on phone

    13" .... $12.00 – 16.00

Jeannie, I Dream of

    6" .... $45.00 – 55.00

Plastic Bottle Playset, 6", Jeannie doll and accessories .... $100.00 – 115.00

Jumpsy, 1970, vinyl and hard plastic, jumps rope, rooted blond hair, painted blue eyes, closed mouth, molded-on shoes and socks

    14" .... $30.00 – 35.00

Black

    14" .... $35.00 – 40.00

Kitty Karry All, 1969, featured on the TV show *The Brady Bunch*

    20" .... $150.00 – 200.00

Laurie Partridge, 1973

    19" .... $120.00 – 140.00

Littlechap Family, 1963+, vinyl head, arms, jointed hips, shoulders, neck, black molded and painted hair, black eyes, box

Dr. John Littlechap

    14½" .... $35.00 – 40.00

Judy Littlechap

    12" .... $30.00 – 45.00

Libby Littlechap

    10½" .... $40.00 – 50.00

Lisa Littlechap

    13½" .... $30.00 – 50.00

Littlechap Accessories

Dr. John's Office .... $275.00 – 325.00

Bedroom .... $75.00 – 110.00

Family room................ $45.00 – 75.00

Dr. John Littlechap's outfits

Golf outfit .... $30.00 MIP

Medical .... $65.00 MIP

Suit .... $50.00 MIP

Tuxedo .... $70.00 MIP

Libby's, Judy's outfits

Jeans/sweater .... $30.00 MIP

Dance dress .... $45.00 MIP

Lisa's outfits

Evening dress .... $90.00 MIP

Coat, fur trim .... $50.00 MIP

Mimi, 1973, vinyl and hard plastic, battery-operated singer, rooted long blond hair, painted blue eyes, open-closed mouth, record player in body, sings "I'd Like to Teach the World to Sing," song used for Coca-Cola® commercial, sings in different languages

    19" .... $55.00 – 65.00

Black

    19" .... $75.00 – 85.00

Monsters, 1976, Dracula, Frankenstein, others, jointed hard vinyl

    9" .... $40.00 – 50.00

Munsters

Herman, pull-string talker

    20" .... $200.00 – 275.00

Lily, #1822, 1964, vinyl, one-piece body, played by Yvonne DeCarl

    4¾" .... $90.00 – 105.00

Grandpa, #1821, 1964, vinyl head, one-piece plastic body

    4¾" .... $95.00 – 110.00

Orphan Annie, 1967

    15" .... $95.00 – 120.00

Polly Puff, 1970, vinyl, came with inflatable furniture

12".................... $30.00 – 35.00
Ronald McDonald, 1976, vinyl
8"...................... $15.00 – 20.00
Snuggle Bun, 1969, vinyl, push button makes head turn while doll cries
16".................... $75.00 – 85.00
Sweet April,1971, vinyl
5½".................... $40.00 – 45.00
Black
5½".................... $45.00 – 50.00
Tippy Tumbles, 1968, vinyl, rooted red hair, stationary blue eyes, does somersaults, batteries in pocketbook
16".................... $40.00 – 55.00
Tumbling Tomboy, 1969, rooted blond braids, closed smiling mouth, vinyl and hard plastic, battery-operated
17".................... $30.00 – 45.00

RICHWOOD TOYS, INC.

1950s – 1960s, Annapolis, Maryland. Produced hard plastic dolls.

Sandra Sue, 1940s, 1950s, hard plastic, walker, head does not turn, slim body, saran wigs, sleep eyes, some with high-heeled feet, only marks are number under arm or leg, all prices reflect outfits with original socks, shoes, panties, and accessories, 8". Dolls listed are in good condition with appropriate clothing and tags, naked, played-with dolls will bring one-fourth to one-third the values listed.

Flat feet
In camisole, slip, panties, shoes, and socks
                    $100.00 – 150.00
In school dress.......... $125.00 – 150.00
In party/Sunday dress
                    $150.00 – 200.00
Special coat, hat, and dress, limited editions, Brides, Heidi, Little Women, Majorette
                    $175.00 – 225.00

Sport or play clothes . $100.00 – 150.00
High-heeled feet
Camisole, slip, panties, shoes, socks
                    $95.00 – 125.00
In school dress.......... $100.00 – 150.00
In party/Sunday dress . $125.00 – 175.00
Special coat, hat and dress, limited editions, Brides, Heidi, Little Women, Majorette
                    $125.00 – 175.00
Sport or play clothes ... $95.00 – 125.00
Sandra Sue outfits, mint, including all accessories
School dress .... $50.00 – 75.00
Party dress.................... $60.00 – 85.00
Specials .... $75.00 – 100.00
Sport sets .... $75.00 – 85.00
Cindy Lou, 14", hard plastic, jointed dolls were purchased in bulk from New York distributor, fitted with double-stitched wigs by Richwood
In camisole, slip, panties, shoes, and socks
                    $200.00 – 250.00
In school dress......... $200.00 – 250.00
In party dress........... $225.00 – 250.00
In special outfits........ $225.00 – 275.00
In sports outfits .... $200.00 – 250.00
Cindy Lou outfits, mint, including all accessories
School dress .... $75.00 – 100.00
Party dress................. $95.00 – 125.00

8" Sandra Sue dolls, flat feet, $175.00 each.
Photo courtesy of Alderfer Auction & Appraisal.

Special outfit .... $1250.00 – 200.00
Sports clothes .... $100.00 – 150.00

GRACE CORRY ROCKWELL

1926 – 1928, USA. Artist who designed dolls. Her bisque doll heads were made in Germany and were distributed by Borgfeldt. Her composition-head dolls were made by Averill.

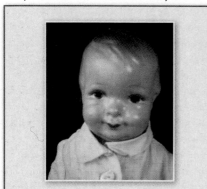

13" Little Brother, $350.00. *Photo courtesy of Withington Auction, Inc.*

Pretty Peggy, bisque socket head, open mouth
12" – 14" .. $2,600.00 – 3,500.00
16" – 19" . $4,200.00 – 5,200.00
Little Sister and Brother, composition, smiling mouth, molded hair
14" .... $300.00 – 350.00

ROHMER

1857 – 1880, Paris, France. Mme. Rohmer held patents for doll bodies, made dolls of various materials. Dolls listed are in good condition, appropriately dressed, may be much more for exceptional dolls.
Poupée (so-called fashion-type), bisque or china glazed shoulder or swivel head on shoulder plate, closed mouth, kid body with green oval

stamp, bisque or wooden lower arms
Glass eyes
13" – 16".. $6,000.00 – 6,500.00
17" – 19" . $9,000.00 – 11,000.00
Painted eyes
13" – 18".. $3,500.00 – 5,800.00

ROLDAN

1960s – 1970s, Barcelona, Spain. Roldan characters are similar to Klumpe figures in many respects. They are made of felt over a wire armature with painted mask faces. Like Klumpe, Roldan figures represent professionals, hobbyists, dancers, historical characters, and contemporary males and females performing a wide variety of tasks. Some, but not all Roldans, were imported by Rosenfeld Imports and Leora Dolores of Hollywood. Figures originally came with two sewn-on identifying cardboard tags. Roldan characters most commonly found are doctors, Spanish dancers, and bullfighters. Roldan characters tend to have somewhat smaller heads, longer necks, and more defined facial features than Klumpe. Dolls listed are all in good, clean, un-faded condition, allow more for elaborate figure with many accessories.
9" – 11" .... $75.00 – 200.00

GERTRUDE F. ROLLINSON

1916 – 1929, Holyoke, Massachusetts. Designed and made cloth dolls with molded faces, painted over the cloth on head and limbs, treated to be washable. Painted hair or wigged, some closed mouth, others had open-closed mouths with painted teeth. Some dolls closely resemble the dolls of the Chase Company while others are heavily sanded between coats of paint giving them a look of composition. Rollinson had her dolls made by the Utley Co. (later called New England Doll Company), and distributed by G. Borgfeldt, L. Wolfe, and Strobel & Wilken.

Chase-look doll with painted hair or wig

13" – 17".. $1,100.00 – 1,600.00
22" – 26".. $1,800.00 – 2,000.00

Composition-look doll with painted hair or wig

16".............. $800.00 – 1,200.00
22" – 24".. $1,500.00 – 2,000.00

RUBBER

1860s on, various European and American makers produced rubber dolls.

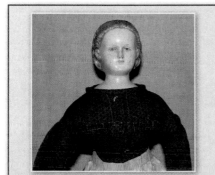

20" doll, $1,200.00. *Doll courtesy of Jean Grout.*

Goodyear Doll, molded shoulder head in the style of the china and papier-mâché dolls of the era.

10" – 18"..... $800.00 – 1,200.00
20" – 28".. $1,200.00 – 1,600.00

American rubber doll, 1920s on

Baby

12" – 15"............ $65.00 – 75.00

SANTONS

Santons (little Saints) France, 1930 on. Character figures depicting elderly peasants. Earthenware heads, hand, and legs on wire armature bodies. Dressed in regional or occupational costume.

7" – 8"................ $30.00 – 45.00
10" – 12" .... $65.00 – 100.00

SASHA

1945 – 2001. Sasha dolls were created by Swiss artist Sasha Morgenthaler, who handcrafted 20" children and 13" babies in Zurich, Switzerland, from the 1940s until her death in 1975. Her handmade studio dolls had cloth or molded bodies, five different head molds, and were hand painted by Sasha Morgenthaler. To make her dolls affordable as children's playthings, she licensed Götz Puppenfabrik (1964 – 1970 and 1995 – 2001) in Germany and Frido Trendon Ltd. (1965 – 1986) in England to manufacture 16" Sasha dolls in series. The manufactured dolls were made of rigid vinyl with painted features.

Price range reflects rarity, condition, and completeness of doll, outfit, and packaging, and varies with geographic location. Dolls listed are in good condition, with original clothing. Allow more for mint-in-box.

Original Studio Sasha Doll, ca. 1940s – 1974, made by Sasha Morgenthaler in Switzerland, some are signed on soles of feet, have wrist tags, or wear labeled clothing

20"......... $9,000.00 – 13,000.00

Götz Sasha Doll, 1964 – 1970, Germany, girls or boys, two face molds, marked "Sasha Series" in circle on neck and in three-circle logo on back, three different boxes were used, identified by wrist tag and/or booklet

16"........... $1,200.00 – 1,500.00

Frido-Trendon Ltd., 1965 – 1986, England, unmarked on body, wore wrist tags and current catalogs were packed with doll

Child

1965 – 1968, packaged in wide box

16".................. $500.00 – 600.00

1969 – 1972, packaged in crayon tubes

16".................. $550.00 – 700.00

Sexed Baby, 1970 – 1978, cradle, styrofoam cradles package or straw basket and box, white or black.......... $160.00 – 200.00

Unsexed Baby, 1978 – 1986, packaged in styrofoam wide or narrow cradles or straw basket and box......... $75.00 – 100.00

Child, 16"

1973 – 1975, packaged in shoebox-style box

1975 – 1980, white, shoebox-style box

1980 – 1986, white, packaged in photo box with flaps

Caleb .... $150.00 – 225.00

Cora .... $300.00 – 400.00

Gingham, 107......... $250.00 – 300.00

Gregor.................... $200.00 – 300.00

Marina.................... $275.00 – 325.00

Sasha, 101, 103, sailing$200.00 – 300.00

#1 Sasha Anniversary doll

16".................. $175.00 – 300.00

1986, Sasha "Sari" 117S, black hair, estimated only 400 produced before English factory closed January 1986

16".................. $700.00 – 800.00

130E Sasha "Wintersport," 1986, blond hair

16".................. $400.00 – 600.00

Limited Editions

Made by Trendon Sasha Ltd. in England, packaged in box with outer sleeve picturing individual doll, limited edition Sasha dolls marked on neck with date and number, number on certificate matches number on doll's neck

1981 "Velvet," girl, light brown wig, 5,000 production planned .. $200.00 – 225.00

1982 "Pintucks" girl, blond wig, 6,000 production planned .. $275.00 – 300.00

1983 "Kiltie" girl, red wig, 4,000 production planned .... $300.00 – 350.00

1984 "Harlequin" girl, rooted blond hair, 4,000 production planned

$300.00 – 375.00

1985 "Prince Gregor" boy, light brown wig, 4,000 production planned

$275.00 – 325.00

1986 "Princess Sasha" girl, blond wig, 3,500 production planned, but only 350 were made................ $1,000.00 – 1,500.00

Götz Dolls Inc., 1995+, Germany, they received the license in September 1994; dolls introduced in 1995

Child, 1995 – 1996, marked "Götz Sasha" on neck and "Sasha Series" in three-circle logo on back, about 1,500 of the dolls produced in 1995 did not have mold mark on back, earliest dolls packaged in generic Götz box, currently in tube, wear wrist tag, Götz tag, and have mini-catalog.

16½"............. $175.00 – 300.00

Baby, 1996, unmarked on neck, marked "Sasha Series" in three-circle logo on back, first babies were packaged in generic Götz box or large tube, currently packaged in small "Baby" tube, wears Sasha wrist tag, Götz booklet and current catalog.

12".................. $125.00 – 150.00

BRUNO SCHMIDT

1898 – 1930, Waltershausen, Germany. Made bisque, composition, and wooden head dolls, after 1913 also celluloid.

14" Wendy, glass eyes, $19,000.00. *Photo courtesy of Dollsantique.*

Acquired Bähr & Pröschild in 1918. Often used a heart-shaped tag. Dolls listed are in good condition, appropriately dressed.

Character baby, bisque socket head, glass eyes, composition bent-leg body
Mold 2092, 2094, 2095, 2097, ca. 1920, Mold 2097, ca. 1911

    13" – 15"........ $400.00 – 500.00
    18" – 20"........ $625.00 – 750.00
    33"................. $750.00 – 850.00

Mold 2097, toddler

    15"................. $750.00 – 800.00
    21"........... $1,100.00 – 1,300.00
    34"........... $1,600.00 – 1,700.00

Child, BSW, no mold numbers, bisque socket head, jointed body, sleep eyes, open mouth, add $50.00 more for flirty eyes

    14"................. $350.00 – 450.00
    18" – 20"........ $525.00 – 600.00
    22" – 24"........ $600.00 – 700.00

Character
Oriental, mold 500, ca. 1905, yellow-tint bisque socket head, glass eyes, open mouth, teeth, pierced ears, wig, yellow-tint composition jointed body

    11" – 14".. $1,375.00 – 1,600.00
    18"........... $1,800.00 – 2,000.00

Mold 529, "2052," ca. 1912, painted eyes, closed mouth

    20"........... $2,800.00 – 4,000.00

Mold 539, "2023," ca. 1912, solid dome or with wig, painted eyes, closed mouth

    24"........... $3,000.00 – 3,200.00

Mold 537, "2033" (Wendy), ca. 1912, sleep eyes, closed mouth

    11" – 13".. $12,000.00 – 18,000.00
    15" – 17".. $20,000.00 – 25,000.00
    20"....... $30,000.00 – 34,000.00

Mold 2025, closed mouth with slight smile, intaglio eyes, wigged

    21"......................... $10,073.00*

Mold 2048, ca. 1912, Tommy Tucker, 2094, 2096, ca. 1920, solid dome, molded and painted hair or wig, sleep eyes, open or closed mouth, composition jointed body
Open mouth

    12" – 14".. $1,000.00 – 1,300.00
    18" – 20".. $1,600.00 – 1,900.00
    26" – 28".. $1,800.00 – 2,100.00

Mold 2072, ca. 1920, sleep eyes, closed mouth

    16"........... $2,200.00 – 2,450.00
    19"........... $2,500.00 – 2,900.00

FRANZ SCHMIDT

1890 – 1937, Georgenthal, Thüringia, Germany. Made, produced, and exported dolls with bisque, composition, wood, and celluloid heads. Used bisque heads made by Simon & Halbig. Heads marked "S & C," mold 269, 293, 927, 1180, 1310. Heads marked "F.S. & C," mold 1250, 1253, 1259, 1262, 1263, 1266, 1267, 1270, 1271, 1272, 1274, 1293, 1295, 1296, 1297, 1298, 1310. Walkers: mold 1071, 1310. Dolls listed are in good condition, appropriately dressed.

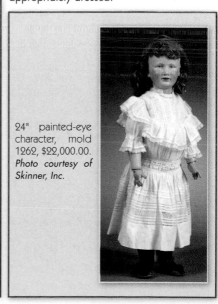

24" painted-eye character, mold 1262, $22,000.00.
Photo courtesy of Skinner, Inc.

Baby, bisque head, solid dome or cut out for wig, bent-leg body, sleep or set eyes, open mouth, some pierced nostrils, add more for flirty eyes

Mold 1271, 1272, 1295, 1296, 1297, 1310

    10" – 12"........ $350.00 – 400.00
    13" – 14"........ $450.00 – 525.00
    18" – 20"........ $600.00 – 700.00
    22" – 24"........ $750.00 – 825.00

Toddler

    10" – 12"........ $800.00 – 900.00
    16" – 20"..... $975.00 – 1,100.00
    22" – 24".. $1,600.00 – 2,000.00

Character face

Mold 1237, baby, open mouth, molded hair, breather, glass eyes

    13".......... $1,200.00 – 1,300.00

Mold 1257, baby, open mouth with wobble tongue, molded hair, breather, glass eyes

    13" toddler... $900.00 – 1,000.00

Mold 1266, 1267, ca. 1912, marked "F.S. & Co.," solid dome, painted eyes, closed mouth

    14".......... $2,750.00 – 2,850.00
    19" – 23".. $3,700.00 – 4,000.00

Mold 1270, ca. 1910, solid dome, painted eyes, open-closed mouth

    9".................. $575.00 – 650.00
    13".......... $1,500.00 – 1,800.00

Child

Dolly face, five-piece body, Mold 269, ca. 1890s, Mold 293, ca. 1900, marked "S & C," open mouth, glass eyes

    5" – 7"............ $300.00 – 375.00
    10" – 12"........ $475.00 – 550.00
    19" – 23"........ $550.00 – 650.00
    27" – 29".. $1,000.00 – 1,100.00

Character

Mold 1259, ca. 1912, marked "F.S. & Co." character, sleep eyes, pierced nostrils, open mouth

    15"................. $400.00 – 500.00

Mold 1262, 1263, ca. 1910, marked "F.S. & Co.," painted eyes, closed mouth

    17" – 24"..$19,000.00 – 22,000.00

Mold 1272, ca. 1910, marked "F.S. & Co.," solid dome or wig, sleep eyes, pierced nostrils, open mouth

    9½"................ $850.00 – 950.00

Mold 1286, ca. 1915, marked "F.S. & Co. 1286/40 Germany," molded hair side-glancing glass eyes

    14" – 16" . $8,000.00 – 12,000.00

SCHMITT & FILS

1854 – 1891, Noget-sur-Marne & Paris, France. Made bisque and wax-over-bisque or wax-over-composition dolls. Heads were pressed. Used neck socket-like on later composition Patsy dolls. Dolls listed are in good condition, appropriately dressed; more for exceptional doll with wardrobe or other attributes.

Child, pressed bisque head, closed mouth, glass eyes, pierced ears, mohair or human hair wig, French composition and wood eight ball-jointed body with straight wrists

15" closed mouth bébé, $17,000.00. *Photo courtesy of Withington Auction, Inc.*

Early round face
  12" – 14"..$16,000.00 – 18,000.00
  15" – 16"..$17,000.00 – 22,000.00
  18" – 24"..$24,500.00 – 28,000.00
Long face modeling
  16" – 18"..$20,000.00 – 25,000.00
  24" – 26"..$30,000.00 – 34,000.00
Wax over papier mâché, swivel head, cup-and-saucer-type neck, glass eyes, closed mouth, eight ball-jointed body
  16" – 17".. $5,000.00 – 6,000.00

SCHOENAU & HOFFMEISTER

1901 – 1939, Burggrub, Bavaria. Had a porcelain factory, produced bisque heads for dolls, also supplied other manufacturers, including Bruckner, Dressel, Eckhardt, E. Knoch, and others. Dolls listed are in good condition, appropriately dressed. More for exceptional dolls.

Baby, bisque solid-dome or wigged socket head, sleep eyes, teeth, composition bent-leg body, closed mouth, newborn, solid dome, painted hair, cloth body, may have celluloid hands, add more for original outfit
Solid dome infant
  10" – 12"........ $400.00 – 500.00
  13" – 15"........ $500.00 – 600.00
Mold 169, 170 (Porzellanfabrik Burggrub), bent-limb body
  13" – 15"........ $250.00 – 300.00
  18" – 20"........ $375.00 – 450.00
  23" – 25"........ $475.00 – 550.00
Hanna, sleep eyes, open-closed mouth, bent-leg baby body, $100.00 more for toddler
  13" – 15"........ $425.00 – 475.00
  18" – 20"........ $550.00 – 650.00
  22" – 24"........ $750.00 – 950.00
Princess Elizabeth, 1929, socket head, sleep eyes, smiling open mouth, chubby leg toddler body

27" dolly-face doll, mold 5500, $700.00.
Photo courtesy of Morphy Auctions.

  16" – 17".. $2,000.00 – 2,200.00
  20" – 22".. $2,500.00 – 3,000.00
  25"........... $3,500.00 – 4,000.00
Child, dolly face, bisque socket head, open mouth with teeth, sleep eyes, composition ball-jointed body
Mold 1906, 1909, 2500, 4000, 4600, 4700, 5000, 5500, 5700, 5800
  10" – 12"........ $150.00 – 200.00
  14" – 16"........ $350.00 – 450.00
  18" – 24"........ $450.00 – 550.00
  26" – 28"........ $600.00 – 800.00
Mold 914, ca. 1925, character
  24" – 25"........ $250.00 – 350.00
  27" – 28"........ $350.00 – 400.00
Mold 4900, ca. 1905, Asian, dolly-face
  8" – 10".......... $700.00 – 800.00
Shoulder head dolly, open mouth with teeth, sleep eyes, kid body
Mold 1800
  14"................. $225.00 – 275.00

A. SCHOENHUT & CO.

1872 – 1930 on, Philadelphia, Pennsylvania. Made all-wood dolls, using spring joints, had holes in bottoms of feet to fit

A. Schoenhut & Co.

into stands. Later made elastic strung with cloth bodies. Carved or molded and painted hair or wigged, intaglio or sleep eyes, open or closed mouth. Later made composition dolls. Dolls listed are in good condition, appropriately dressed; more for exceptional doll.

Babies
Graziano Infants, circa May 1911 – 1912
Schnickel-Fritz, carved hair, open-closed grinning mouth, four teeth, large ears, toddler

15".......... $3,600.00 – 4,000.00
Tootsie Wootsie, carved hair, open-closed mouth, two upper teeth, large ears on child body

15".......... $3,800.00 – 4,200.00
Too few in database for a reliable range.
Model 107, 107W (walker), 108, 108W (walker), 1913 – 1926, 109W, 110W, 1921 – 1923
Baby, nature (bent) limb

13" – 15"........ $400.00 – 550.00
Toddler

11" – 14"........ $600.00 – 700.00

17"................. $600.00 – 800.00
Elastic strung, 1924 – 1926

14"................. $675.00 – 750.00
Cloth body with crier

14"................. $750.00 – 825.00
Bye-Lo Baby, "Grace S. Putnam" stamp, cloth body, closed mouth, sleep eyes

13".............................$2,400.00
Too few in database for a reliable range.

Child
Graziano Period, 1911 – 1912, dolls may have heavily carved hair or wigs, painted intaglio eyes, outlined iris, all with wooden spring-jointed bodies and are 16" tall, designated with "16" before the model number, like "16/100"
Model 100, girl, carved hair, solemn face
Model 101, girl, carved hair, grinning, squinting eyes
Model 102, girl, carved hair, bun on top

Model 103, girl, carved hair, loose ringlets
Model 200, boy, carved hair, short curls
Model 201, boy, carved hair, based on K*R 114
Model 202, boy, carved hair, forelock
Model 203, boy, carved hair, grinning, some with comb marks
Model 300, girl, long curl wig, face of 102
Model 301, girl, bobbed wig with bangs, face of 300
Model 302, girl, wig, bases on K*R 101
Model 303, girl, short bob, no bangs, grinning, squinting eyes
Model 304, girl, wig in braids, ears stick out
Model 305, girl, snail braids, grinning, face of 303
Model 306, girl, wig, long curls, face of 304
Model 307, girl, short bob, no bangs, "dolly-type" smooth eye
Model 400, boy, short bob, K*R 101 face
Model 401, boy, side-part bob, face of 300/301
Model 402, boy, side-part bob, grin of 303
Model 403, boy, dimple in chin
Transition Period, 1911 – 1912, designs by Graziano and Leslie, dolls may no longer have outlined iris, some models have changed, dolls measure 16" – 17", now

15" Schnickel-Fritz, $3,600.00. *Photo courtesy of Morphy Auctions.*

have a groove above knee for stockings
Model 100, girl, same, no iris outline
Model 101, girl, short carved hair, bob/bow, round eyes/smile
Model 102, girl, braids carved around head
Model 103, girl, heavy carved hair in front/fine braids in back
Model 104, girl, fine carved hair in front/fine braids in back
Model 200, boy, carved hair, same, no iris outline
Model 201, boy, carved hair, same, iris outline, stocking groove
Model 202, boy, carved hair, same, smoother
Model 203, boy, smiling boy, round eyes, no iris outline
Model 204, boy, carved hair brushed forward, serious face
Model 300, girl, long curl wig, dimple in chin
Model 301, girl, bob wig, face of 102
Model 302, girl, wig, same like K*R 101
Model 303, girl, wig, similar to 303G, smiling, short bob, no bangs
Model 304, girl, wig, braids, based on K*R
Model 305, girl, wig, braids, face of 303
Model 306, girl, long curl wig, same face as 304
Model 307, girl, smooth eyeball
Model 400, boy, same (like K*R 101)
Model 401, boy, like K*R 114 (304)
Model 402, boy, smiling, round eyes
Model 403, boy, same as 300 with side-part bob
Model 404, boy, same as 301, side-part bob
Classic Period, 1912 – 1923, some models discontinued, some sizes added, those marked with[+] were reissued in 1930
Model 101, girl, short carved hair bob, no iris outline
    1912 – 1923[+], 14"
    1911 – 1916, 16"
Model 102, girl, heavy carved hair in front, fine braids in back

    1912 – 1923, 14"
    1911 – 1923, 16"
    1912 – 1916, 19" – 21"
Model 105, girl, short carved hair bob, carved ribbon around head
    1912 – 1923, 14" – 16"
    1912 – 1916, 19" – 21"
Model 106, girl, carved molded bonnet on short hair
    1912 – 1916, 14", 16", 19"
Model 203, 16" boy, same as transition
Model 204, 16" boy, same as transition[+]
Model 205, carved hair boy, covered ears
    1912 – 1923, 14" – 16"
    1912 – 1916, 19" – 21"
Model 206, 19" carved hair boy, covered ears
    1912 – 1916
Model 207, 14" carved short curly hair boy
    1912 – 1916
Model 300, 16" wigged girl, same as transition period
    1911 – 1923
Model 301, 16" wigged girl, same as transition
    1911 – 1924
Model 303, 16" wigged girl, same as transition 305
    1911 – 1916

16" Classic Period child with wig, $1,400.00.
Photo courtesy of Sweetbriar Auctions.

Model 307, 16" long curl wigged girl, smooth eye
    1911 – 1916
Model 308, 14" girl, braided wig
    1912 – 1916
    1912 – 1924
    19", bobbed hair
    1917 – 1924
    19" – 21", bob or curls
Model 309, 16", wigged girl, two teeth, long curls, bobbed hair, 1912 – 1913
    19" – 21"
Model 310, wigged girl, same as 105 face, long curls, 1912 – 1916
    14" – 16"
    19" – 21"
Model 311, wigged girl, heart shape 106 face, bobbed wig, no bangs, 1912 – 1916
    14" – 16"
    1912 – 1913
    19"
Model 312, 14", wigged girl, bobbed, 1912 – 1924, bobbed wig or curls, 1917 – 1924
Model 313, wigged girl, long curls, smooth eyeball, receding chin, 1912 – 1916
    14" – 16"
    19" – 21"
Model 314, 19", wigged girl, long curls, wide face, smooth eyeball, 1912 – 1916
    19"
Model 315, 21", wigged girl, long curls, four teeth, triangular mouth, 1912 – 1916
Model 403, 16", wigged boy, same as transition, bobbed hair, bangs, 1911 – 1924
Model 404, 16", wigged boy, same as transition, 1911 – 1916
Model 405, boy, face of 308, bobbed wig, 1912 – 1924
    14"
    19"
Model 407, 19" – 21", wigged boy, face of 310 girl, 1912 – 1916
Carved hair, allow more for earlier examples

and those in all-original condition
    14" – 16".. $2,200.00 – 3,800.00
    19" – 21".. $2,500.00 – 4,000.00
    15" woman, upswept hair with bun on top
        $3,700.00*
Wigged, allow more for earlier examples and those in all-original condition
    14"................. $700.00 – 900.00
    16"........... $1,000.00 – 1,400.00
    19" – 21".. $1,200.00 – 2,000.00
Miss Dolly
Model 316, open mouth, teeth, wigged girl, curls or bobbed wig, painted or decal eyes, all four sizes, circa 1915 – 1925
    15" – 21"........ $500.00 – 700.00
Model 317, sleep eyes, open mouth, teeth, wigged girl, long curls or bob, sleep eyes, four sizes, 1921 – 1928
    15" – 21"........ $600.00 – 800.00
Composition doll, 1924, molded curly hair, painted eyes, closed moth
    13".............,. $900.00 – 1,000.00
Manikin
Model 175, man with slim body, ball-jointed waist, circa 1914 – 1918
    19" .... $3,000.00 – 3,500.00
Small dolls, such as circus figures, storybook and comic characters
Circus performers, rare figures may be much higher
Bisque head
    Bareback Lady Rider or Ringmaster, all original
    9".................... $350.00 – 550.00
Wood heads
    Clowns
    8".................... $250.00 – 300.00
    Lion Tamer
    8½"................ $350.00 – 450.00
    Ringmaster, Acrobat Gent, Lady Bareback Rider
    8".................... $250.00 – 325.00
    Animals (some rare animals may be

much higher)

Camel

8".................................. $200.00

Giraffe

11"................................ $350.00

Horse

7"................................. $350.00

Tiger

7½"............................. $200.00

Cartoon Characters

Barney Google and Spark Plug, comic strip characters created by Billy de Beck

7½" – 8"...$700.00 – 800.00 pair

Maggie and Jiggs, from cartoon strip *Bringing up Father*

7" – 9"......$450.00 – 500.00 pair

Max & Moritz, carved figures, painted hair, carved shoes

8"............$500.00 – 550.00 each

Mary and her lamb... $650.00 – 750.00

Pinn Family, all wood, egg-shaped head, original costumes, names such as Bobby Pinn, Hattie Pinn, Ty Pinn, etc.

5" – 9" .... $75.00 – 150.00

Black Pinn dolls

9"................... $250.00 – 300.00

Rally-Dally figures

9" – 12"......... $350.00 – 850.00

Teddy Roosevelt

8"................ $800.00 – 1,600.00

SCHUETZMEISTER & QUENDT

1889 – 1930 on, Boilstadt, Gotha, Thüringia. A porcelain factory that made and exported bisque doll heads, all-bisque dolls, and Nankeen dolls. Used initials "S & Q," mold 301 was sometimes incised "Jeannette." Dolls listed are in good condition, appropriately dressed.

Baby, character face, bisque socket head, sleep eyes, open mouth, bent-leg body

Mold 201, 204, 300, 301, ca. 1920

10" – 12"....... $350.00 – 400.00

14" – 17"........ $475.00 – 550.00

19" – 25"........ $700.00 – 825.00

Mold 252, ca. 1920, character face, black baby

15"................. $550.00 – 600.00

Child

Mold 101, 102, ca. 1900, dolly face

16" – 17"........ $375.00 – 450.00

19" – 22"........ $550.00 – 625.00

Mold 1376, ca. 1900, character face

19"................. $475.00 – 550.00

S.F.B.J.

Société Francaise de Fabrication de Bébés & Jouets, 1899 – 1930+, Paris and Montreuil-sous-Bois. 1922 – 1930 on. Mark used by S.F.B.J. (Société Francaise de Fabrication de Bébés & Jouets) after 1922 is Union Nationale Inter-Syndicale. Competition with German manufacturers forced many French companies to join together including Bouchet, Fleischmann & Bloedel, Gaultier, Rabery & Delphieu, Bru, Jumeau, Pintel & Godchaux, Remignard and Wertheimer, and others. This alliance lasted until the 1950s. Fleischman owned controlling interest. 1922 – 1930 on. Mark used by S.F.B.J. (Société Francaise de Fabrication de Bébés & Jouets) after 1922 is Union Nationale Inter-Syndicale, UNIS FRANCE.

Dolls listed are in good condition, appropriately dressed; more for exceptional dolls.

Child, bisque head, glass eyes, open mouth, pierced ears, wig, composition jointed French body

Jumeau type, no mold number, open mouth

13" – 15".. $1,250.00 – 1,500.00

20" – 22".. $1,600.00 – 1,700.00

24" – 26".. $1,900.00 – 2,000.00
28"........... $2,200.00 – 2,300.00

Mold 301

6" – 8" on five-piece body
$250.00 – 300.00
8" – 10" .... $625.00 – 725.00
12" – 14" .... $725.00 – 900.00
18" – 20"..... $950.00 – 1,100.00
22" – 24".. $1,100.00 – 1,200.00
26" – 28".. $1,200.00 – 1,500.00

Bleuette: See Bleuette section.

Kiss Thrower

24"........... $1,650.00 – 1,750.00

Mold 60

6" – 8"............ $325.00 – 475.00
12" – 14"........ $650.00 – 775.00
18" – 21"........ $800.00 – 875.00
25" – 28"........ $850.00 – 875.00

Mold 301 or 60, papier-mâché head

8" – 10".......... $125.00 – 150.00
13" –16" .... $225.00 – 250.00
18" – 22"........, $300.00 – 400.00

Character faces, bisque socket head, wigged or molded hair, set or sleep eyes, composition body, some with bent baby limb, toddler or child body, mold number 227, 235, and 236 may have flocked hair, add $100.00 for toddler body

21", mold 301, $1,100.00. *Photo courtesy of Morphy Auctions.*

Mold 226, glass eyes, closed mouth
18" – 20".. $2,200.00 – 2,400.00

Mold 227, open mouth, teeth, glass eyes
14"........... $2,000.00 – 2,200.00
17"........... $2,700.00 – 3,000.00
19" – 21".. $3,000.00 – 3,100.00

Mold 230, glass eyes, open mouth, teeth
12" – 14"........ $650.00 – 700.00
20" – 23".. $1,100.00 – 1,300.00

Mold 233, ca. 1912, crying mouth, glass eyes
14" – 16".. $3,600.00 – 4,000.00

Mold 234
18"........... $2,800.00 – 3,050.00

Mold 235, glass eyes, open-closed mouth
14" – 15".. $1,400.00 – 1,600.00
18" .... $1,700.00 – 1,800.00

Mold 236, glass eyes, laughing open-closed mouth

Baby
12" – 13"........ $750.00 – 850.00
15" – 17"..... $900.00 – 1,100.00
20" – 22".. $1,300.00 – 1,500.00

Toddler
13"........... $1,100.00 – 1,300.00
15" – 18".. $1,400.00 – 1,500.00

Mold 237, glass eyes, open-closed mouth
13" – 14".. $2,500.00 – 2,700.00
16" – 17".. $3,000.00 – 3,300.00

Mold 238, small open mouth
18"........... $2,200.00 – 2,400.00

Mold 239, ca. 1913, designed by Poulbot
13"....... $12,000.00 – 15,000.00

Mold 242, ca. 1910, nursing baby
13" – 15".. $2,900.00 – 3,000.00

Mold 247, glass eyes, open-closed mouth

Baby body
6½"................ $550.00 – 650.00

Child or toddler
13"........... $1,900.00 – 2,100.00
16"........... $2,200.00 – 2,400.00
20"........... $2,900.00 – 3,100.00

Mold 248, ca. 1912, glass eyes, lowered

eyebrows, very pouty closed mouth

    10" – 12" . $7,500.00 – 8,000.00*

Mold 250, open mouth with teeth

    12", trousseau box $3,300.00*

    18" – 20".. $3,250.00 – 3,400.00

Mold 251, open-closed mouth, teeth, tongue

    15" – 18".. $1,700.00 – 1,900.00

    27" .... $3,000.00 – 3,200.00

Mold 252, closed pouty mouth, glass eyes

Baby

    8" .... $2,000.00 – 2,200.00

    10" .... $3,000.00 – 3,300.00

    13" – 15" toddler .$5,000.00 – 7,000.00

    19" .... $7,500.00 – 8,000.00

    26" $10,750.00*

Unis France, marked dolls, 1922 – 1930 on.

    Mold 60, 301, bisque head, fully jointed composition/wood body, wig, sleep eyes, open mouth

    5" – 6" .... $75.00 – 120.00

    8" – 10" .... $375.00 – 475.00

    13" – 16" .... $550.00 – 650.00

    21" – 23" .... $525.00 – 600.00

Five-piece composition body, glass eyes

    5" – 8" .... $250.00 – 300.00

    10" – 14" .... $300.00 – 350.00

    Mold 247, 251, toddler body

    15" .... $1,100.00 – 1,450.00

    27" .... $1,700.00 – 2,300.00

SHIRLEY TEMPLE

1934 on, Ideal Novelty Toy Corp., New York. Designed by Bernard Lipfert. Dolls listed are in very good condition, all-original. Add more for exceptional dolls or special outfits like Ranger or Wee Willie Winkie.

Composition, 1934 – 1940s, composition head and jointed body, dimples in cheeks, green sleep eyes, open mouth, teeth, mohair wig, tagged original dress, center-snap shoes, prototype dolls may have paper sticker inside head and bias trimmed wig

Shirley Temple

    11" .... $950.00 – 1,100.00

    13" .... $850.00 – 900.00

    16" .... $850.00 – 900.00

    17" .... $850.00 – 875.00

    18" .... $800.00 – 900.00

    18" all-original wearing fur hat and coat, MIB $3,500.00*

    20" .... $850.00 – 950.00

    22" .... $1,000.00 – 1,100.00

    27" .... $1,600.00 – 1,800.00

Baby Shirley

    15" .... $1,300.00 – 1,800.00

    18" .... $1,100.00 – 1,200.00

    21" .... $1,300.00 – 1,400.00

Hawaiian, "Marama," Ideal used the composition Shirley Temple mold for this doll representing a character from the movie *Hurricane,* black yarn hair, wears grass skirt, Hawaiian costume

    18" .... $875.00 – 950.00

Accessories:

Button, three types $125.00

Buggy, wicker or wood ..$500.00 – 575.00

Dress, tagged .... $125.00 – 575.00

Satin pajamas, tagged $670.00

Trunk .... $175.00 – 225.00

11" cowgirl, $1,100.00. *Photo courtesy of Morphy Auctions.*

Reliable Shirley Temple, composition, made in Canada

18" – 22".. $1,000.00 – 1,200.00

Japanese, unlicensed Shirley dolls

All-bisque

6".................. $195.00 – 225.00

Celluloid

5".................. $100.00 – 125.00

8".................. $100.00 – 125.00

Celluloid

Dutch Shirley Temple, ca. 1937+, all-celluloid, open crown, metal pate, sleep eyes, dimples in cheeks, marked: "Shirley Temple" on head, may have additional marks, dressed in Dutch costume

13"................. $295.00 – 320.00

15"................. $295.00 – 320.00

Cloth

Wacker Manufacturing Co., Chicago, painted features, side-glancing eyes, molded face, mohair wig

17"................. $300.00 – 400.00

Composition, Japanese, heavily molded brown curls, painted eyes, open-closed mouth with teeth, body stamped "Japan"

7½"................ $200.00 – 225.00

Vinyl, dolls listed are in excellent condition, original clothes, accessories, the newer the doll the more perfect it must be to command higher prices. MIB can bring double.

12", vinyl, MIB, $300.00. *Photo courtesy of McMasters Harris Auction Co.*

1957, all-vinyl, sleep eyes, synthetic rooted wig, open-closed mouth, teeth, came in two-piece slip and undies, tagged Shirley Temple, came with gold plastic script pin reading "Shirley Temple," marked on back of head: "ST//12"

12"................ $150.00 – 225.00

1958 – 1961, marked on back of head: "S.T.//15," "S.T.//17," or "S.T.//19," some had flirty ("Twinkle") eyes; add more for flirty eyes or 1961 Cinderella, Bo Peep, Heidi, and Red Riding Hood

15"................ $200.00 – 250.00

17"................ $225.00 – 250.00

19"................ $375.00 – 425.00

1960, jointed wrists, marked "ST–35–38–2"

35" – 36".. $1,000.00 – 1,600.00

1972, Montgomery Ward reissue, plain box

17"................ $125.00 – 150.00

1973, red dot "Stand Up and Cheer" outfit

16"..................... $45.00 – 75.00

1982 – 1983

8"....................... $20.00 – 55.00

12"..................... $20.00 – 40.00

1984, by Hank Garfinkle, marked "Doll Dreams & Love"

36".................. $90.00 – 125.00

Danbury Mint, reissue

36"................. $100.00 – 175.00

Porcelain

1987 on, Danbury Mint, various outfits

18"..................... $50.00 – 75.00

SIMON & HALBIG

1869 – 1930 on, Hildburghausen and Grafenhain, Germany. Porcelain factory, made heads for Jumeau (200 series), bathing dolls (300 series), porcelain figures (400 series), perhaps dollhouse or small dolls (500 – 600 series), bisque head dolls (700 series), bathing and small dolls (800 series), more bisque head dolls (900 – 1000 series). The earliest models of a series had the last digit of their model number ending with an 8, socket heads ended with 9, shoulder heads ended with 0, and models using a shoulder plate for swivel heads ended in 1.

Dolls listed are in good condition, appropriately dressed. All original or exceptional dolls may be more.

Molded hair lady, 1850s – 60s, molded hair, painted or glass eyes

12" – 18".. $1,000.00 – 3,000.00

Shoulder head child, 1870s, molded hair, painted or glass eyes, closed mouth, cloth body with bisque lower arms, appropriately dressed, marked "S&H," no mold number

13" – 15".. $1,100.00 – 1,200.00
17" – 19".. $1,400.00 – 1,600.00
21" – 23".. $1,900.00 – 2,100.00

Swivel neck

9" – 10".... $2,000.00 – 2,400.00
12" .... $2,000.00 – 2,200.00

Poupée (fashion-type doll), 1870s, bisque socket head with bisque shoulder plate on kid or twill over wood body, closed mouth, glass eyes, wigged

Kid body

15" – 18" .. $2,300.00 – 2,800.00

Twill covered wood body

10" – 11".. $6,000.00 – 9,000.00
15" – 16".$11,000.00 – 14,000.00

Closed-mouth child, 1879, socket head, most on composition and wood body, glass eyes, wigged, pierced ears, appropriately dressed

Mold 719

16" .... $5,900.00 – 6,100.00
18" – 22" . $7,500.00 – 8,000.00

Edison phonograph mechanism in torso

23" .... $4,900.00 – 5,400.00

Mold 739

15" – 20".. $1,700.00 – 2,600.00

Mold 749

22" .... $3,000.00 – 4,000.00

Mold 905, 908

15" – 17".. $2,000.00 – 3,300.00

Mold 919

15" .... $5,300.00 – 7,200.00
19" .... $6,000.00 – 8,150.00

Mold 929

14" .... $1,725.00 – 2,300.00
23" .... $2,450.00 – 3,400.00

Mold 939

14" – 16".. $1,800.00 – 2,000.00
18" – 20".. $2,200.00 – 2,500.00
26" – 27".. $2,700.00 – 2,800.00

Mold 949

10" – 12".. $2,000.00 – 2,400.00
14" – 16".. $2,800.00 – 3,200.00
21" – 23".. $4,200.00 – 4,600.00
31" .... $4,250.00 – 4,500.00

Mold 720, 740, 940, 950, dome shoulder head, kid body

8" – 10".......... $700.00 – 900.00
14" – 18".. $1,400.00 – 1,700.00
20" – 22".. $1,700.00 – 1,800.00

All-bisque child: See All-Bisque German section.

Open-mouth child, 1889 – 1930s, socket head on composition body (sometimes

26" mold 939 socket head, open mouth, $2,700.00. *Photo courtesy of Skinner, Inc.*

Simon & Halbig

16", mold 1079, $900.00. *Photo courtesy of Morphy Auctions.*

French), wigged, glass eyes may be stationary or sleep, appropriately dressed
Mold 530, 540, 550, 570, Baby Blanche
　　10"................. $500.00 – 600.00
　　20" – 22"........ $600.00 – 800.00
Mold 719, 739, 749, 759, 769, 939, 979
　　5½".............. $375.00 – 550.00
　　9" – 13".... $1,500.00 – 2,200.00
　　15" – 17".. $2,100.00 – 2,300.00
　　20" – 22".. $2,400.00 – 2,600.00
　　26" – 30".. $2,800.00 – 3,200.00
Mold 905, 908
　　18"........... $1,750.00 – 2,200.00
　　22"........... $1,425.00 – 2,600.00
Mold 929, 949
　　15" – 17".. $2,100.00 – 2,800.00
　　22" – 24".. $2,900.00 – 3,100.00
　　29"........... $2,900.00 – 3,000.00
Mold 1009
　　15" – 16"........ $725.00 – 800.00
　　19" – 21"........ $850.00 – 950.00
　　24" – 25".. $1,200.00 – 1,400.00
Mold 1029
　　16" – 18"........ $475.00 – 575.00
　　24" – 25"........ $700.00 – 800.00
　　28"................. $825.00 – 900.00
Mold 1039, 1049, 1059, 1069, 1078, 1079
Flapper body

　　8" – 10"......... $350.00 – 500.00
Child body
　　10" – 13" .... $775.00 – 900.00
　　16" – 18"..... $900.00 – 1,100.00
　　21" – 25"........ $650.00 – 750.00
　　27" – 28"........ $700.00 – 800.00
　　30" – 33"........ $700.00 – 900.00
Mold 1109
　　13"................ $750.00 – 800.00
　　18"........... $1,000.00 – 1,000.00
Mold 1248, 1249, Santa
　　6".................... $550.00 – 650.00
　　10" – 13"........ $850.00 – 950.00
　　15" – 18".. $1,000.00 – 1,200.00
　　20" – 24".. $1,300.00 – 1,800.00
　　26" – 28".. $1,900.00 – 2,000.00
　　38"........... $2,200.00 – 2.600.00
Open-mouth shoulder head child, 1889 – 1930s, kid body
Mold 1009, 1039
　　12" – 13" .... $950.00 – 1,000.00
　　19"................. $350.00 – 475.00
　　23"................. $750.00 – 900.00
Mold 1010, 1040, 1070, 1080
　　18"................. $425.00 – 525.00
　　23" – 25"........ $550.00 – 600.00
　　28" – 30"........ $625.00 – 700.00
Mold 1250, 1260
　　16"................. $500.00 – 625.00
　　18" – 19"........ $700.00 – 800.00
　　23" – 26"........ $750.00 – 900.00
Character face, 1909 on, bisque socket head, composition body, wig or molded hair, glass or painted eyes, open or closed mouth, appropriately dressed
Mold 111
　　18" – 22"..$16,000.00 – 18,000.00
Mold 150, ca. 1912, intaglio eyes, closed mouth
　　13" – 15" .$6,000.00 – 10,000.00
Too few in database for a reliable range.
Mold 151, ca. 1912, painted eyes, closed laughing mouth

Simon & Halbig

13" – 15".. $6,000.00 – 7,000.00
22" – 25" . $12,000.00 – 15,000.00
Too few in database for a reliable range.
Mold 152, lady, intaglio eyes
18" – 24".. $24,000.00 – 38,000.00
Mold 153, ca. 1912, molded hair, painted eyes, closed mouth
16" – 17" . $22,000.00 – 24,000.00
Too few in database for a reliable range.
Mold 600, ca. 1912, sleep eyes, open mouth
17"............................... $900.00
Too few in database for a reliable range.
Mold 611, solid dome
16"........... $4,000.00 – 5,000.00
Mold 729, ca. 1888, laughing face, glass eyes, open-closed mouth
16"........... $1,900.00 – 2,550.00
Mold 769, open mouth, paperweight eyes
17"........... $2,500.00 – 3,000.00
Too few in database for a reliable range.
Mold 969, ca. 1887, open smiling mouth
17" – 19".. $4,500.00 – 7,600.00
Too few in database for a reliable range.
Mold 1019, ca. 1890, laughing, open mouth
14"........... $4,275.00 – 5,700.00
Too few in database for a reliable range.
Mold 1269, 1279, sleep eyes, open mouth
14"........... $1,100.00 – 1,500.00
16"........................... $3,500.00
25"........... $4,500.00 – 5,500.00
Mold 1299, ca. 1912, marked "S&H"
13"........... $1,200.00 – 1,600.00
1300 Series, character faces
13" man with molded mustache
$7,800.00 – 9,000.00
Too few in database for a reliable range.
22" mold 1305 witch $14,000.00*
Mold 1448, ca. 1914, bisque socket head, sleep eyes, closed mouth, pierced ears, composition/wood ball-jointed body
16".......................... $17,500.00
20" – 24" . $25,500.00 – 27,500.00
Too few in database for a reliable range.

Little Women (so-called), 1909, mold 1160 shoulder head lady, fancy hairdo wig, closed mouth, glass eyes, cloth body with bisque lower limbs, appropriately dressed
6" – 7"............ $475.00 – 550.00
10" – 11"........ $625.00 – 700.00
14" .... $750.00 – 800.00
Baby, character face, 1910 on, molded hair or wig, painted or glass eyes, open or closed mouth, bent-leg baby body, appropriately dressed, add more for flirty eyes or toddler body
Mold 1294, ca. 1912, glass eyes, open mouth
16"................. $550.00 – 750.00
19".............. $800.00 – 1,100.00
Mold 1294, clockwork mechanism moves eyes
26" – 31".. $1,800.00 – 2,600.00
Mold 1428, ca. 1914, glass eyes, open-closed mouth
13" – 16".. $1,300.00 – 1,600.00
Toddler
12"........... $2,600.00 – 2,700.00
16"........... $2,100.00 – 2,300.00

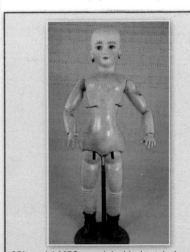

25", mold 1159 on original lady-style Jumeau body, $4,500.00. *Photo courtesy of McMasters Harris Auction Co.*

Mold 1488, ca. 1920, glass eyes, open-closed or open mouth

    19" – 20".. $4,600.00 – 5,100.00

Mold 1489, "Baby Erika," ca. 1925, glass eyes, open mouth, tongue

    20" – 23".. $4,200.00 – 6,000.00

Mold 1498, ca. 1920, solid dome, painted or sleep eyes, open-closed mouth

    24".............................. $3,700.00

Too few in database for a reliable range.

Lady doll, 1910 on, bisque socket head, composition lady body, sleep eyes, wigged, appropriately dressed

Mold 1079, open mouth, glass eyes

    24"........... $1,500.00 – 2,000.00

Mold 1159, ca.1894, glass eyes, open mouth, Gibson Girl

Flapper body

    12" – 15" . $1,900.00 – 2,100.00

Lady body

    18" – 20". $2,200.00 – 2,600.00

    22" – 24".. $2,200.00 – 3,200.00

    28"........... $3,800.00 – 4,000.00

Jumeau lady body

    20" – 25".. $3,000.00 – 4,500.00

Mold 1199, open mouth

    34"....... $17,500.00 – 18,000.00

Too few in database for a reliable range.

Mold 1303, ca. 1902, lady face, glass eyes, closed mouth

    14"............................ $5,815.00

Mold 1305, ca. 1902, old woman, glass eyes, open-closed laughing mouth

    18"........................... $10,035.00

Too few in database for a reliable range.

Mold 1308, ca. 1902, old man, molded mustache/dirty face, may be solid dome

    18"........... $4,200.00 – 5,600.00

Too few in database for a reliable range.

Mold 1329, Asian

    14" – 15".. $1,500.00 – 2,200.00

Too few in database for a reliable range.

Mold 1468, 1469, ca. 1920, flapper, glass eyes, closed mouth

    14" – 15".. $4,000.00 – 5,000.00

SNOW BABIES

    1901 – 1930 on. All-bisque dolls covered with ground porcelain slip to resemble snow, made by Bähr & Pröschild, Hertwig, C.F. Kling, Kley & Hahn, and others, Germany. Mostly unjointed, some jointed at shoulders and hips. The Eskimos named Admiral Robert E. Peary's daughter Marie, born in 1893, Snow Baby, and her mother published a book in which she called her daughter Snow Baby and showed a

2¼" X 1½" German bisque Snow Baby, $400.00. *Photo courtesy of The Doll Works.*

picture of a little girl in a white snowsuit. These little figures have painted features, various poses.

Figure listed are in good condition, allow more for exceptional figures.

New Snow Babies are being made today. Department 56 makes a line of larger scale figures (see below) and reproductions of earlier Snow Babies are being produced in Germany and by individual artisans.

Single Snow Baby, standing or sitting

1½" .... $45.00 – 60.00

3" – 4" .... $120.00 – 150.00

Snow Baby child with wire jointed limbs

3½" .... $150.00 – 175.00

Action babies

Baby with umbrella

2¾" .... $75.00 – 125.00

Bear on sled

3" .... $175.00 – 200.00

Child on skis

4½" .... $350.00 – 375.00

Riding on bear .... $300.00 – 350.00

Riding on sled

2" .... $150.00 – 180.00

Riding on reindeer

2½" .... $300.00 – 325.00

With broom

4½" .... $500.00 – 550.00

Melting snowman

1½" .... $75.00 – 95.00

Santa on igloo with baby inside

3½" .... $140.00 – 175.00

Santa riding camel, elephant, or polar bear

2½" .... $330.00 – 375.00

Two Snow Babies, molded together

1½" .... $125.00 – 155.00

3" .... $200.00 – 250.00

Two climbing an igloo

2½" .... $250.00 – 350.00

Three Snow Babies, molded together

3" .... $300.00 – 350.00

Three on sled

2½" .... $200.00 – 250.00

Snow Baby doll, jointed hips, shoulders

3" – 4" .... $275.00 – 350.00

5" .... $400.00 – 500.00

New Snow Babies, today's commercial reproductions are by Department 56 and are larger and the coloring is more like cream. Department 56 Snow Babies and their Village Collections are collectible on the secondary market. As with all newer collectibles, items must be mint to command higher prices. Values listed are for secondary market pieces, many are still available at retail.

Snow Baby winged clip ornament

1986 .... $35.00 – 50.00

Snow Baby Adrift

1987 .... $90.00 – 125.00

Polar Express

1988 .... $70.00 – 90.00

All Fall Down, set 4

1989 .... $30.00 – 45.00

Penguin Parade

1989 .... $50.00 – 70.00

1990 on, pieces, various

$15.00 – 50.00

Disney pieces, various ... $65.00 – 85.00

Eloise on the Polar Express

2002 .... $35.00 – 40.00

SONNEBERG TAUFLING

1851 – 1900 on, Sonneberg, Germany. Various companies made an infant doll with special separated body with bellows and voice mechanism. Motchmann is erroneously credited with the body style; but he did patent the voice mechanism. Some bodies stamped "Motchmann" refer to the voice mechanism. The Sonneberg Taufling was made with head, shoulder plate, pelvis, lower arms and lower legs

23" wax over papier-mâché, $3,000.00. *Photo courtesy of Joan & Lynette Antique Dolls and Accessories.*

of papier-mâché/composition, wax over papier-mâché, china, and bisque. Body parts put together with twill cloth in what are called "floating" joints. These dolls have glass eyes, closed or open mouth, painted hair or wigged. Dolls listed are in good condition.

Bisque: See also Jules Steiner section.

    7" – 12".... $2,700.00 – 4,500.00
    14" – 19" .. $5,500.00 – 6,500.00

China

    6" – 7"...... $4,500.00 – 5,500.00
    10" – 12".. $3,200.00 – 3,400.00
    14" – 16".. $3,700.00 – 4,000.00

Papier-mâché/composition or wax over papier-mâché

    8" – 12"....... $900.00 – 1,200.00
    13" – 15".. $1,500.00 – 1,700.00
    18" – 20".. $1,800.00 – 2,400.00
    22" – 24".. $2,600.00 – 3,000.00

Wood

Bébé tout en Bois, carved wooden socket head, closed mouth, painted hair, glass eyes. twill and wood torso, nude

    9"............................. $1,100.00

Too few in database for a reliable range.

MARGARETE STEIFF

1877 to present, Giengen, Wurtemburg, Germany. Known today for their plush stuffed animals, Steiff made clothes for children, dolls with mask faces in 1889, clown dolls by 1898. Most Steiff dolls of felt, velvet, or plush have seam down the center of the face, but not all. Registered trademark button in ear in 1905. Button-type eyes, painted features, sewn-on ears, big feet/shoes enable them to stand alone, all in excellent condition.

Values given are for dolls in good condition; for soiled, ragged, or worn dolls, use 35% of price.

Adults

    14½" – 18" .. $2,000.00 – 2,800.00

Characters, center seam face, military men in uniform and conductors, firemen, English bobby, bellhop, etc.

    10½" – 15".. $1,900.00 – 3,000.00
    18" – 22" .$8,000.00 – 10,000.00

Children

Center seam face

    12" – 14".. $1,500.00 – 1,700.00
    16" – 18".. $2,100.00 – 2,900.00

Molded felt face

    13"................. $475.00 – 550.00

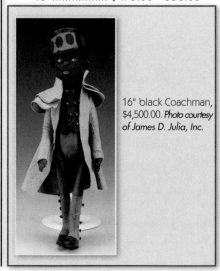

16" black Coachman, $4,500.00. *Photo courtesy of James D. Julia, Inc.*

Made in U.S. Zone, Germany, 1947 – 1953, glass eyes

    12".................. $550.00 – 650.00

Rubber head doll, cloth body

    12" – 13" .... $150.00 – 180.00

Vinyl characters, wire armature in body

Max or Moritz

    4".................... $125.00 – 175.00

Limited edition dolls, 1986 – 1987, felt, characters such as Tennis Lady, Gentleman in Morning Coat, Peasant Lady, Peasant Jorg

    MIB.................... $90.00 – 125.00

HERMANN STEINER

    1909 – 1930 on, near Coburg, Germany. Porcelain and doll factory. First made plush animals, then made bisque, composition, and celluloid head dolls. Patented the Steiner eye with moving pupils.

Baby

Mold 240, circa 1925, newborn, solid dome, closed mouth, sleep eyes

    6" – 8½"........... $95.00 – 125.00

    12" – 16",....... $300.00 – 350.00

Mold 246, circa 1926, character, solid dome, glass eyes, open-closed mouth, laughing baby, teeth, cloth or composition body

    15"................. $475.00 – 600.00

Topsy-Turvy baby doll

    8" .... $500.00 – 600.00

Child

Dolly face, no mold number, open mouth, glass eyes, jointed composition body

    6" – 10" .... $100.00 – 225.00

    6" on flapper body

              $280.00 – 300.00

    14" – 16"........ $500.00 – 600.00

    18" – 20"........ $350.00 – 400.00

Shoulder head child, no mold number, open mouth, glass eyes, kid body

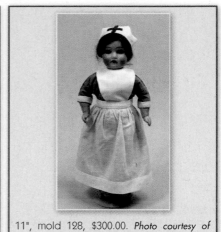

11", mold 128, $300.00. *Photo courtesy of Sharing My Dolls 'N Stuff.*

    18"................. $150.00 – 175.00

Living Steiner-eye doll, character with molded hair and Steiner patented eye

    9" – 10".......... $400.00 – 650.00

Mold 128, character bisque socket head, sleep eyes, open mouth, teeth, wig, composition/wood jointed body

    8" – 9"........... $175.00 – 225.00

    14"................. $650.00 – 700.00

Mold 401, shoulder head, solid dome, painted eyes, open-closed laughing mouth, teeth, molded tongue

    15"................. $350.00 – 475.00

JULES STEINER

    1855 – 1891 on, Paris. Made dolls with pressed heads, wigs, glass eyes, pierced ears on jointed composition bodies. Advertised talking, mechanical jointed dolls and bébés. Some sleep eyes were operated by a wire behind the ear, marked "J. Steiner." May also carry the Bourgoin mark.

    Dolls listed are in good condition, appropriately dressed. Add more for original clothes, rare mold numbers.

Baby with Taufling (Motchmann type) body,

Jules Steiner

20" Gigoteur, $2,500.00. *Photo courtesy of Dolls and Lace.*

solid dome bisque shoulder head, hips, lower arms and legs, with twill body in-between, closed mouth, glass eyes, wig

    12" – 14" .. $13,00.00 – 15,000.00

    20" – 22" . $10,000.00 – 12,500.00

Gigoteur, crying, kicking child, key-wound mechanism, solid dome head, glass eyes, open mouth, two rows of tiny teeth, pierced ears, mohair wig, papier-mâché torso

Earlier, paler doll head

    17" – 20" .. $3,500.00 – 4,500.00

Later, more highly colored head

    17" – 20".. $1,900.00 – 2,500.00

Round face Bébé, 1870s, early unmarked, pale pressed bisque socket head, rounded face, pierced ears, bulgy paperweight eyes, open mouth, two rows of teeth, pierced ears, wig, composition/wood jointed body

    16" – 18".. $5,500.00 – 6,800.00

Closed mouth, round face, dimples in chin

    16" – 18".....$10,000.00 – 11,500.00

Bébé with series marks, 1880 on, bourgoin red ink, Caduceus stamp on body, pressed bisque socket head, cardboard pate, wig, pierced ears, closed mouth, glass paperweight eyes, French composition/papier-mâché (purple) body with straight wrists or bisque hands, Series C and A more common, marked with series mark: Sie and letter and number, rare Series B, E, F, and G models may be valued much higher

Series A or C

    8" – 10" .. $9,000.00 – 15,000.00

    14" – 16"..$11,000.00 – 13,000.00

    21" – 23"..$12,000.00 – 15,000.00

    27" – 28"..$17,000.00 – 20,000.00

    38" ....$18,000.00 – 22,000.00

Series E

    12" – 15" .$15,000.00 – 20,000.00

Series F

    24" $48,000.00

Too few in database for a reliable range.

Series G

    19" .... $25,000.00 – 28,000.00

Too few in database for a reliable range.

Bébé with figure marks, 1887 on, bisque socket head, pierced ears, closed mouth, glass eyes, wig, composition/wood jointed French body, may use body marked "Le Parisien" or "Le Petit Parisien," head marked "Fire" and letter and number, and "J. Steiner," figure marks included A, B, C, D, and E; A and C are the most often found

Closed mouth

A or C

    8" – 10".... $4,000.00 – 6,250.00

    12" – 16".. $7,000.00 – 9,000.00

    18" – 24" ..$9,000.00 – 10,000.00

13", with figure mark A, $8,000.00. *Photo courtesy of Dollhappy.*

28" – 29" ... $8,000.00 – 9,000.00
Open mouth
Figure A
  18" – 23" .. $3,600.00 – 4,500.00
Figure B
  19" – 25".. $7,000.00 – 8,500.00
Figure E
  24" – 26" .$29,000.00 – 31,000.00
Phénix Baby, 1899 on, registered by Jules Mettais, successor of Jules Nicholas Steiner, bisque socket head, closed mouth, composition body
  17" – 22"..... $5,000.00 – 7,000.00

SUN RUBBER

1919 – 1950s, Barberton, Ohio. Made rubber and later vinyl dolls. Dolls listed are in excellent condition, allow less for faded, cracked dolls or dolls missing paint, MIB can bring double.
Psyllium, 1937, molded painted hard rubber, moving head, blue pants, white suspenders, black shoes and hat
  10"...................,, $10.00 – 15.00
One-piece Squeeze dolls, 1940s, designed by Ruth E. Newton, molded clothes, squeaker, names such as Bonnie Bear, Happy Kappy, Rompy, and others
  8".......,,,,,,,,,,,,, $20.00 – 30.00
So-Wee, 1941, molded hair, painted or sleep eyes
  10" – 12" .... $40.00 – 50.00
  Black .... $55.00 – 65.00
Sunbabe, 1950, drink and wet baby, painted eyes, molded hair
  8" – 13" .... $28.00 – 35.00
  Black................... $30.00 – 45.00
Betty Bows, 1953, molded hair with loop for ribbon, drink and wet baby, jointed body
  11"................... $75.00 – 100.00
Constance Bannister Baby, 1954, molded hair, drink and wet, sleep eyes

10" So-Wee, $35.00. *Photo courtesy of The Museum Doll Shop.*

  18"................... $85.00 – 105.00
Tod-L-Dee, 1950s, all vinyl soft stuffed one-piece body, molded underclothes and shoes, molded painted hair, sleep eyes, open mouth, there is also a Tod-L-Tee & Tod-L-Tim
  10"..................... $25.00 – 35.00
Peter Pan, 1950s, all vinyl soft stuffed one-piece body, molded outfit, molded painted hair, sleep eyes
  10"..................... $25.00 – 30.00
Amosandra: See Black or Brown Dolls section.
Gerber Baby: See Advertising Dolls section.

SWAINE & CO.

1910 – 1927, Huttensteinach, Thüringia, Germany. Made porcelain doll heads. Marked "S & Co.," with green stamp. May also be incised "DIP" or "Lori."
Baby
Baby Lori, marked "Lori," solid dome, open-closed mouth molded hair, sleep eyes
  16" – 18".. $1,200.00 – 1,400.00

11½", marked "DI," $675.00. *Photo courtesy of Morphy Auctions.*

23".......... $1,600.00 – 2,000.00
Mold 232, Lori variation, open mouth
    12" – 14" .... $800.00 – 1,000.00
    20" – 23".. $1,400.00 – 1,600.00
DI, solid dome, Intaglio eyes, closed mouth
    11" – 13"........ $650.00 – 700.00
DV, solid dome, sleep eyes, closed mouth
    13".............. $900.00 – 1,100.00
    15".......... $1,200.00 – 1,300.00
FP, S&C, socket head, sleep eyes, closed mouth
    8".................... $750.00 – 850.00
Too few in database for a reliable range.
Child
BP, socket head, open-closed smiling mouth, teeth, painted eyes
    14½ – 17".$5,000.00 – 6,500.00
Too few in database for a reliable range.
DIP, S&C, socket head, sleep eyes, closed mouth
    8" – 9"............ $800.00 – 900.00
    14".......... $1,000.00 – 1,200.00
Toddler body
    8".............. $1,000.00 – 1,300.00
    13" – 14".. $1,100.00 – 1,400.00

TERRI LEE

1946 – 1962, Lincoln, Nebraska, and Apple Valley, California. Company was founded by Violet Lee Gradwohl, the company went out of business in 1962. In 1997, Fritz Duda, Violet's nephew, was instrumental in founding Terri Lee Associates which is making Terri Lee dolls now. First dolls composition, then hard plastic and vinyl, the modern dolls are now being produced of a newer type of hard plastic. Closed pouty mouth, hand-painted features, wigged, jointed body. Values listed are for dolls in good condition and wearing original clothing. Allow significantly less for undressed, played-with dolls. Dolls in mint condition, with fancy costume, or additional wardrobe will bring more.

Terri Lee
Composition, 1946 – 1947
    16"................. $750.00 – 800.00
Painted hard plastic, 1947 – 1949
    16" .... $800.00 – 1,000.00
Flesh colored hard plastic, 1949 – 1952
    16"................. $750.00 – 800.00

16", hard plastic Terri Lee, $475.00. *Photo courtesy of Withington Auction, Inc.*

Hard plastic, 1952 – 1962
16"................ $475.00 – 600.00
Vinyl, less if sticky, 1950 – 1951
16"................ $500.00 – 600.00
Talking
16"................ $300.00 – 400.00
Hard plastic, 1997 – 2005, values listed are secondary market values, dolls are available at retail as well
16" .... $50.00 – 100.00
Benji, painted plastic, brown, 1946 – 1962, black lamb's wool wig
16"........... $1,800.00 – 2,000.00
Connie Lynn, 1955, hard plastic, sleep eyes, fur wig, bent-limb baby body
19"................ $350.00 – 400.00
Gene Autry, 1949 – 1950, painted plastic
16"........... $1,600.00 – 1,800.00
Jerri Lee, hard plastic, caracul wig
16"................ $600.00 – 700.00
Vinyl, 16"......... $1,200.00 – 1,500.00
Linda Lee, 1950 – 1951, vinyl
12"..................... $60.00 – 75.00
1952 – 1958, vinyl baby
10".................. $90.00 – 135.00

Mary Jane, Terri Lee look-alike, hard plastic walker
16"................ $225.00 – 275.00
Patty Jo, 1947 – 1949
16"........... $1,200.00 – 1,500.00
Bonnie Lou, black
16"........... $1,200.00 – 1,800.00
Tiny Terri Lee, 1955 – 1958
10"................ $200.00 – 250.00
Accessories
Terri Lee outfits:
Girl Scout/Brownie uniform......... $50.00
Heart Fund $325.00
School dress $150.00
Shoes...................................... $35.00
Tiny Terri Lee dresses ..... $20.00 – 50.00

A. THUILLIER

1875 – 1893, Paris. Made bisque head dolls with composition, kid, or wooden bodies. Some of the heads were reported made by Francoise Gaultier. Bisque socket head or swivel on shoulder plate, glass eyes, closed mouth with white space, pierced ears, cork pate, wig, nicely dressed, in good condition. Dolls listed are in good condition,

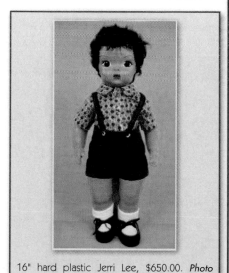

16" hard plastic Jerri Lee, $650.00. *Photo courtesy of McMasters Harris Auction Co.*

18" bébé, $68,000.00. *Doll courtesy of Dominique Perrin.*

appropriately dressed. Exceptionally beautiful dolls may run more.

Child

12" – 13"	$65,000.00 – 75,000.00
15" – 22"	$64,000.00 – 70,000.00

ROBERT TONNER

1991 to present, Hurley, New York. Robert Tonner is a fashion designer and sculptor who has created numerous dolls in porcelain and vinyl. Tonner Company also owns Effanbee dolls.

Values listed are for secondary market dolls, many of these dolls are still available retail as well.

American Models, 1993 on, vinyl, basic dolls at low end of value, dolls in elaborate costume at high end of value

16"	$75.00 – 100.00
19"	$200.00 – 300.00
22"	$150.00 – 300.00

Ann Estelle, 1999, a Mary Engelbreit character, hard plastic, blond wig, glasses

10"	$50.00 – 55.00

Sophie, 10" .... $65.00 – 75.00

10" Little Luxuries, limited edition for UFDC conference 2009, $85.00. *Photo courtesy of The Museum Doll Shop.*

Betsy McCall, see Betsy McCall section.

Kripplebush Kids, 1997, hard plastic, Marni, Eliza, Hannah

8"	$30.00 – 50.00

Tiny Kitty Collier, vinyl, basic dolls at low end of value, dolls in elaborate costume at high end of value

10"	$45.00 – 85.00

Tyler Wentworth, 1999, fashion-type, long, straight, brunette, blond, or red hair, allow more for special costumes

16"	$35.00 – 60.00

Cinderella, 2009, limited edition 100, 22" fashion doll body

$200.00 – 300.00

TROLLS

Trolls portray supernatural beings from Scandinavian folklore. They have been manufactured by various companies including Helena and Martii Kuuslkoski who made Fauni Trolls, ca. 1952+ (sawdust-filled cloth dolls); Thomas Dam, 1960+; and Scandia House, later Norfin®; Uneeda Doll and Toy Wishniks®; Russ Berrie; Ace Novelty; Treasure Trolls; Applause Toys; Magical Trolls; and many other companies who made lesser quality vinyl look-alikes, mostly unmarked, to take advantage of the fad. Most are all-vinyl or vinyl with stuffed cloth bodies.

Troll figures

1960s

2½"	$45.00 – 70.00
5"	$65.00 – 75.00
7"	$50.00 – 65.00
Bank, 8"	$18.00 – 22.00
10"	$40.00 – 50.00
12"	$60.00 – 70.00
15"	$75.00 – 85.00

1977

9"	$30.00 – 40.00
12"	$35.00 – 45.00

Thumb sucker, 18" $55.00
Too few in database for a reliable range.
Wishnik Trolls, by Uneeda
    3"....................... $23.00 – 29.00
1990s re-release
    6"....................... $12.00 – 18.00
Troll Animals, Thomas Dam, 1964
Cow
    6".................... $100.00 – 150.00
Elephant
    2½".................... $15.00 – 20.00
Giraffe
    12"..................... $60.00 – 75.00
Horse
    6"....................... $70.00 – 75.00

UNEEDA

1917 on, New York City. Made composition head dolls, including Mama dolls and made the transition to plastics and vinyl.

Composition
Rita Hayworth, as "Carmen," 1939, from *The Loves of Carmen* movie, all-composition, red mohair wig, unmarked, cardboard tag
    14"................. $350.00 – 400.00
Baby doll, 1930s, composition head, arms and legs on a cloth body
    14"................. $100.00 – 150.00
Hard plastic and vinyl
Baby Dollikins, 1960, vinyl head, hard plastic jointed body with jointed elbows, wrists, and knees, drink and wet
    21"................. $150.00 – 200.00
Baby Trix, 1965
    19"..................... $18.00 – 25.00
Bareskin Baby, 1968
    12½".................. $15.00 – 20.00
Blabby, 1962+
    14"..................... $20.00 – 28.00
Coquette, 1963+
    16"..................... $15.00 – 20.00

Black
    16"..................... $25.00 – 35.00
Dollikin, 1957 on, multi-joints, marked "Uneeda//2S," special costumes or outstanding condition will bring more
    19"................. $225.00 – 275.00
    21"................. $300.00 – 375.00
Dolly Walker, 1967
    36"................. $100.00 – 125.00
Fairy Princess, 1961
    32"................... $75.00 – 100.00
Freckles, 1960, vinyl head, rigid plastic body, marked "22" on head
    32"..................... $65.00 – 75.00
1973, ventriloquist doll, vinyl head, hands, rooted hair, cotton-stuffed cloth body
    30"..................... $45.00 – 60.00
Granny & Me, 1978
    11½" & 5½" ...$28.00 – 32.00 set
Jennifer, 1973, rooted side-parted hair, painted features, teen body, mod clothing
    18"..................... $15.00 – 20.00
Little Sophisticates, 1967, large mod-style head, closed eyes, painted smile, rooted hair

12½" Pir-thilla, ca. 1958, $15.00. *Photo courtesy of Judy Masters.*

8½"..................... $40.00 – 50.00

Magic Meg, w/Hair That Grows, vinyl and plastic, rooted hair, sleep eyes

16"..................... $30.00 – 45.00

Miss Dollikin, also called Action Girl, 1957 on, fashion doll

11½"................... $28.00 – 3800

Pee Wees, 1965 on, rooted hair, painted eyes

3½"...................... $8.00 – 15.00

Petal People, 1968, vinyl, rooted hair, came seated inside a vinyl flower in a pot (measured 12½")

2½" .... $18.00 – 25.00

Pir-thilla, 1958, blows up balloons, vinyl, rooted hair, sleep eyes

12½".................. $10.00 – 15.00

Priscilla, 1960s

12½".................. $15.00 – 18.00

Pollyanna, 1960, for Disney

11"..................... $25.00 – 35.00

17"..................... $50.00 – 70.00

31"................. $100.00 – 130.00

Purty, 1973, long rooted hair, vinyl, plastic, painted features

11"..................... $20.00 – 25.00

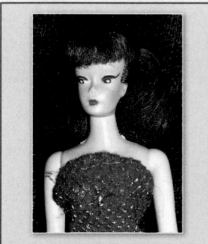

12" Suzette, $75.00. *Photo courtesy of The Museum Doll Shop.*

Saranade, 1962, vinyl head, hard plastic body, rooted blond hair, blue sleep eyes, red and white dress, speaker in tummy, phonograph and records came with doll, used battery

21"................... $75.00 – 100.00

Suzette (Carol Brent)

12"................. $100.00 – 125.00

Tiny Teen, 1957 – 1959, vinyl head, rooted hair, pierced ears, six-piece hard plastic body, high-heeled feet to compete with Little Miss Revlon, wrist tag

10½"............... $85.00 – 100.00

Tinyteens, 1968 on, vinyl doll, rooted hair, posable body, rooted lashes,12 dolls in series

5"...................... $35.00 – 35.00

Wendy, 1960s Barbie®-type, rooted hair, painted eyes

11½".................. $20.00 – 30.00

VINYL

1950s on. By the mid-1950s, vinyl (polyvinylchloride) was being used for dolls. Material that was soft to the touch and processing that allowed hair to be rooted were positive attractions. Vinyl became a desirable material and the market was soon deluged with dolls manufactured from this product. Many dolls of this period are by little known manufacturers, unmarked, or marked only with a number. With little history behind them, these dolls need to be mint-in-box and complete to warrant top prices. With special accessories or wardrobe values may be more.

Unknown maker

Baby, vinyl head, painted or sleep eyes, molded hair or wig, bent legs, cloth or vinyl body

12"...................... $8.00 – 10.00

16".................... $10.00 – 12.00

20".................... $16.00 – 20.00

Child, vinyl head, jointed body, painted or sleep eyes, molded hair or wig, straight legs

Vinyl

16", all-vinyl, unmarked, $75.00. *Photo courtesy of The Museum Doll Shop.*

14"..................... $10.00 – 14.00
22"..................... $18.00 – 25.00

Adult, vinyl head, painted or sleep eyes, jointed body, molded hair or wig, smaller waist with male or female modeling for torso

8"........................ $20.00 – 25.00
18"...................... $55.00 – 75.00

Known maker

Baby Barry

Alfred E. Neuman

20"................. $135.00 – 175.00

Captain Kangaroo

16"................. $100.00 – 130.00
19" – 24".......... $15.00 – 190.00

Christopher Robin

18"................. $100.00 – 135.00

Daisy Mae

14"................. $125.00 – 175.00

Emmett Kelly (Willie the Clown)

15"................... $85.00 – 100.00
21"................. $110.00 – 130.00

Li'l Abner

14"................. $120.00 – 160.00
21"................. $150.00 – 200.00

Mammy Yokum, 1957

Molded hair

14".................. $90.00 – 125.00
21"................. $195.00 – 225.00

Yarn hair

14"................. $125.00 – 150.00
21"................. $200.00 – 250.00

Nose lights up

23"................. $275.00 – 325.00

Pappy Yokum, 1957

14".................. $85.00 – 100.00
21"................. $195.00 – 225.00

Nose lights up

23"................. $275.00 – 325.00

Belle Doll & Toy Co., Brooklyn, New York, 1950s

Ballerina or Miss Revlon-type

18"..................... $50.00 – 60.00

Little Miss Margie, 1955 – 1957. Miss Revlon-type

10½"................... $26.00 – 40.00

Dee & Cee, Canada

Calypso Bill, 1961, black, vinyl, marked "DEE CEE"

16"................... $75.00 – 100.00

Flagg and Co., Brookline, Massachusetts, 1947 on, produced vinyl dolls with wire armatures

8"....................... $20.00 – 50.00

26½" Dick Clark by Juro Novelty Company, $90.00. *Photo courtesy of The Museum Doll Shop.*

Vinyl

19" Bride, $65.00. *Photo courtesy of The Museum Doll Shop.*

Glad Toy/BrookGlad
Poor Pitiful Pearl, 1955, vinyl, some with stuffed one-piece vinyl bodies, others jointed
    13" .... $175.00 – 225.00
    17" .... $275.00 – 325.00
Juro Novelty Co.
Dick Clark, 1958, vinyl head, hands, feet, cloth body
    26" .... $125.00 – 150.00
Libby
I Dream of Jeannie, 1966
    20" .... $350.00 – 400.00
Playmates, 1985 on, made animated talking dolls using a tape player in torso powered by batteries, extra costumes, tapes, and accessories available, more for black versions. Double values for MIB.
Amazing Amy, 1998, vinyl, cloth body, interactive
    20" .... $18.00 – 25.00
Corky, 1987 on
    25" .... $45.00 – 55.00
Cricket, 1986+ on
    25" .... $50.00 – 65.00
Jill, 1987, hard plastic, jointed body
    33" .... $125.00 – 200.00
Royal Doll Co.

Lonely Lisa, 1964, doll with large sad eyes, designed by Keane
    19" .... $80.00 – 100.00
1965
    11½" .... $40.00 – 50.00
Sayco, 1907 – 1950s, New York City, first made composition dolls, then hard plastic and vinyl dolls
Miss America Pageant, 1950s
    11" – 14" .... $150.00 – 200.00
    20" .... $200.00 – 225.00
Pouty girl, soft vinyl head, rooted hair, sleep eyes, soft stuffed vinyl body
    22" .... $40.00 – 45.00
Walker, costumed as a bride
    28" .... $75.00 – 85.00
Shindana, 1968 – 1983, Operation Bootstrap, Los Angeles, ethnic features
    14" .... $40.00 – 65.00
Talking Tamu, black, ethnic features
    16" .... $145.00 – 180.00
Susie Sad Eyes, maker unknown, vinyl doll, made in Hong Kong, large painted "sad" eyes, mod clothing
    8" .... $100.00 – 120.00

14" Sayco Miss America, $200.00. *Photo courtesy of My Dear Dolly.*

8" Susie Sad Eyes, $100.00.
Photo courtesy of The Museum Doll Shop.

Tomy
Kimberly, 1981 – 1985, closed mouth, more for black
17"..................... $25.00 – 45.00
Getting Fancy Kimberly, 1984, open mouth with teeth
17"..................... $35.00 – 55.00
Tristar
Poor Pitiful Pearl, circa 1955+, vinyl jointed doll came with extra party dress
11"..................... $90.00 – 125.00
Unique
Ellie Mae Clampett, 1964
11½"................. $30.00 – 35.00
Worlds of Wonder, circa 1985 – 1987+, Fremont, California, made talking dolls and Teddy Ruxpin powered by batteries, had extra accessories, voice cards
Pamela, The Living Doll, 1986+
21"..................... $75.00 – 100.00
Julie, 1987 on
24"..................... $85.00 – 100.00
Extra costume .... $20.00 – 30.00
Teddy Ruxpin, 1985+, animated talking bear

20"................... $75.00 – 100.00

VOGUE DOLL CO.

1930s on, Medford, Massachusetts, Jennie Graves started the company and dressed "Just Me" and Arranbee dolls in the early years, before Bernard Lipfert designed Ginny. After several changes of ownership, Vogue dolls was purchased in 1995 by Linda and Jim Smith.
Composition dolls
Dora Lee, sleep eyes, closed mouth
11"................. $400.00 – 475.00
Jennie, 1940s, sleep eyes, open mouth, mohair wig, five-piece composition body
13"................. $300.00 – 350.00
Cynthia, 1940s, sleep eyes, open mouth, mohair wig, five-piece composition body
13"................. $300.00 – 350.00
W.A.A.C. doll in Women's Army Auxiliary Corps uniform
13"................. $700.00 – 800.00

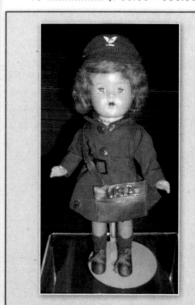

13" composition W.A.A.C., $800.00. *Photo courtesy of Withington Auction, Inc.*

Vogue Doll Co.

8" painted-eye Ginny Jack & Jill, $1,400.00 pair. *Photo courtesy of Withington Auction, Inc.*

Ginny Family

Toddles, composition, 1937 – 1948, name stamped in ink on bottom of shoe, some early dolls which have been identified as "Toodles" (spelled with two o's) are blank dolls from various companies used by Vogue, painted eyes, mohair wig, jointed body, some had gold foil labels reading "Vogue." Dolls listed are in good condition with original clothes, more for fancy outfits such as Red Riding Hood or Cowboy/Cowgirl or with accessories

    7½" – 8"......... $300.00 – 600.00

Painted-eye Ginny, 1948 – 1949, hard plastic, strung joints, marked "Vogue" on head, "Vogue Doll" on body, painted eyes, molded hair with mohair wig, clothing tagged "Vogue Dolls" or "Vogue Dolls, Inc. Medford Mass.," inkspot tag on white with blue letters

    8"................... $600.00 – 800.00

Crib Crowd, 1950, baby with curved legs, sleep eyes, poodle cut (caracul) wig

    8"................... $650.00 – 850.00

Strung Ginny, 1950 – 1953, hard plastic, sleep eyes, strung joints, marked "Vogue" on head, "Vogue Doll" on body, painted eyes, molded hair with mohair wig, clothing tagged "Vogue Dolls" or "Vogue Dolls, Inc.

Medford Mass.," inkspot tag on white with blue letters

    8"................... $400.00 – 650.00

Painted Lash Walker Ginny, 1954, sleep eyes, strung, dynel wigs, new mark on back torso: "GINNY//VOGUE DOLLS//INC.//PAT PEND.//MADE IN U.S.A."

    8"................... $300.00 – 400.00

Black Ginny, 1953 – 1954

    8"................... $500.00 – 600.00

Molded Lash Walker Ginny, 1955 – 1957, hard plastic, seven-piece body, sleep eyes, Dynel or saran wigs, marked: "VOGUE" on head, "GINNY//VOGUE DOLLS//INC.//PAT. NO. 2687594//MADE IN U.S.A." on back of torso

8" Molded Lash Walker Ginny, $300.00. *Photo courtesy of Withington Auction, Inc.*

Vogue Doll Co.

8".................. $225.00 – 300.00

Easter Bunny

8"............. $1,000.00 – 1,400.00

Bent-knee Molded Lash Walker Ginny, 1957 – 1962, hard plastic, jointed knees, sleep eyes, dynel or saran wigs, marked "VOGUE" on head, "GINNY//VOGUE DOLLS//INC.//PAT.NO.2687594//MADE IN U.S.A."

8".................. $275.00 – 325.00

Ginny, 1960, unmarked, big walker carried 8" doll dressed just like her

36"............................... $350.00

Too few in database for a reliable range.

Vinyl Walker Ginny, 1963 – 1965, soft vinyl head, hard plastic walker body, sleep eyes, molded lashes, rooted hair, marked: "GINNY," on head, "GINNY//VOGUE DOLLS, Inc.//PAT. NO.2687594//MADE IN U.S.A." on back

8"....................... $30.00 – 45.00

Ginny, 1965 – 1972, all-vinyl, straight legs, non-walker, rooted hair, sleep eyes, molded lashes, marked "Ginny" on head, "Ginny//VOGUE DOLLS, INC." on back

8"....................... $30.00 – 45.00

Ginny, 1972 – 1977, all-vinyl, non-walker, sleep eyes, molded lashes, rooted hair, some with painted lashes, marked "GINNY" on head, "VOGUE DOLLS©1972//MADE IN HONG KONG//3" on back, made in Hong Kong by Tonka

8"....................... $25.00 – 40.00

Ginny, 1977 – 1979, "Ginny from Far-Away Lands," made in Hong Kong by Lesney, all-vinyl, sleep eyes, jointed, non-walker, rooted hair, chubby body, same as Tonka doll overall, marked "GINNY" on head, "VOGUE DOLLS 1972//MADE IN HONG KONG//3", painted eyes, 1980 – 1981, marked "VOGUE DOLLS//©GINNYTIM//1977" on head, "VOGUE DOLLS©1977//MADE IN HONG KONG" on back

8"....................... $20.00 – 30.00

16" Ginny Baby, $45.00. *Photo courtesy of The Museum Doll Shop.*

Sasson Ginny, 1981 – 1982, made in Hong Kong by Lesney, all-vinyl, fully jointed, bendable knees, rooted Dynel hair, sleep eyes in 1981, painted eyes in 1982, slimmer body, marked "GINNY" on head, "1978 VOGUE DOLLS INC//MOONACHIE N.J.//MADE IN HONG KONG" on back

8"....................... $25.00 – 35.00

Ginny, 1984 – 1986, made by Meritus® In Hong Kong, vinyl, resembling Vogue's 1963 – 1971 Ginny, marked "GINNY®" on head, "VOGUE DOLLS//(a star logo)//M.I.I. 1984//Hong Kong" on back, porcelain marked: "GW//SCD//5184" on head, "GINNNY//®VOGUE DOLLS//INC//(a star logo) MII 1984//MADE IN TAIWAN"

8"....................... $35.00 – 55.00

Ginny, 1986 – 1995, vinyl, by Dakin, soft vinyl, marked "VOGUE®DOLLS//©1984 R. DAKIN INC.//MADE IN CHINA" on back; hard vinyl, marked "VOGUE//®//DOLLS//©1986 R. DAKIN and Co.//MADE IN CHINA"

8"....................... $18.00 – 25.00

Vogue Doll Co.

Ginny Baby, 1959 – 1982, vinyl, jointed, sleep eyes, rooted or molded hair, a drink and wet doll, some marked "GINNY BABY// VOGUE DOLLS INC."

    12"..................... $40.00 – 45.00
    18"..................... $50.00 – 60.00

Ginny outfits

Talon Zipper outfit MIB $250.00
Vinyl shoes MIB......................... $30.00

Ginnette

1955 – 1969, 1985 – 1986, vinyl, jointed, open mouth, 1955 – 1956 had painted eyes, 1956 – 1969 had sleep eyes, marked "VOGUE DOLLS INC"

    8".................... $175.00 – 225.00

1962 – 1963, rooted hair Ginnette

    8".................... $125.00 – 175.00

Jan, 1958 – 1960, 1963 – 1964, Jill's friend, vinyl head, six-piece rigid vinyl body, straight leg, swivel waist, rooted hair, marked "VOGUE," called Loveable Jan in 1963 and Sweetheart Jan in 1964

    10½"............. $100.00 – 125.00

Jeff, 1958 – 1960, vinyl head, five-piece rigid vinyl body, molded and painted hair, marked "VOGUE DOLLS"

    11"................. $100.00 – 150.00

Jill, 1957 – 1960, 1962 – 1963, 1965, seven-piece hard plastic teenage body, bent-

10½" Jill, $300.00. *Photo courtesy of Withington Auction, Inc.*

knee walker, high-heeled doll, big sister to Ginny (made in vinyl in 1965), extra wardrobe, marked "JILL//VOGUE DOLLS// MADE IN U.S.A.//©1957"

    10½"

Wearing leotard ....$125.00 – 175.00
Wearing a street dress
               $250.00 – 300.00
Wearing a formal .... $300.00 – 400.00

Jimmy, 1958, Ginny's baby brother, all-vinyl, open mouth, painted-eye Ginnette, marked "VOGUE DOLLS/INC."

    8"...................... $65.00 – 100.00

Little Miss Ginny, 1965 – 1971, all-vinyl, promoted as a pre-teen, one-piece hard plastic body and legs, soft vinyl head and arms, sleep eyes, head marked "VOGUE DOLL//19©67" or "©VOGUE DOLL//1968" and back, "VOGUE DOLL"

    12"..................... $30.00 – 40.00

Miss Ginny, 1962 – 1964, soft vinyl head could be tilted, jointed vinyl arms, two-piece hard plastic body, swivel waist, flat feet; 1965 – 1980, vinyl head and arms, one-piece plastic body

    15" – 16"............ $35.00 – 45.00

Hard plastic and vinyl

Baby Dear, 1959 – 1964, 18" vinyl baby

8" painted-eye Ginnette, 1955 – 1956, $225.00. *Photo courtesy of The Museum Doll Shop.*

designed by Eloise Wilkin, vinyl limbs, cloth body, rooted topknot or rooted hair, white tag on body "Vogue Dolls, Inc."; left leg stamped "1960/E.Wilkins," 12" size made in 1961

12"................... $90.00 – 130.00

18"................ $225.00 – 275.00

Baby Dear One, 1962, a one-year-old toddler version of Baby Dear, sleep eyes, two teeth, marked "C//1961//E.Wilkin//Vogue Dolls//Inc." on neck, tag on body, mark on right leg

25"................ $100.00 – 175.00

Baby Dear Musical, 1962 – 1963, 12" metal, 18" wooden shaft winds, plays tune, doll wiggles

12"................. $100.00 – 150.00

18"................ $200.00 – 250.00

Baby Too Dear, 1963 – 1965, two-year-old toddler version of Baby Dear, all-vinyl, open mouth, two teeth

17"................ $200.00 – 250.00

23"................ $300.00 – 350.00

Brikette, 1959 – 1961, 1979 – 1980, swivel waist joint, green flirty eyes in 22" size only, freckles, rooted straight orange hair, paper hang tag reads "I'm//Brikette//the//red headed//imp," marked on head "VOGUE INC.//19©60"

22"................. $225.00 – 250.00

1960, sleep eyes only, platinum, brunette, or orange hair

16"................ $100.00 – 125.00

1980, no swivel waist, curly pink, red, purple, or blond hair

16"..................... $45.00 – 60.00

Li'l Imp, 1959 – 1960, Brikette's little sister, vinyl head, bent-knee walker, green sleep eyes, orange hair, freckles, marked "R and B//44" on head and "R and B Doll Co." on back

10½"................ $75.00 – 125.00

Wee Imp, 1960, hard plastic body, orange saran wig, green eyes, freckles, marked

"GINNY//VOGUE DOLS//INC.//PAT.No. 2687594//MADE IN U.S.A."

8".................. $250.00 – 300.00

Littlest Angel, 1961 – 1963; 1967 – 1980

1961 – 1963, also called Saucy Littlest Angel, vinyl head, hard plastic bent-knee walker, sleep eyes, same doll as Arranbee's Littlest Angel, rooted hair, marked "R & B"

10½".............. $125.00 – 175.00

1967 – 1980, all-vinyl, jointed limbs, rooted red, blond, or brunette hair, looks older

11"................ $125.00 – 150.00

14".................. $75.00 – 100.00

Love Me Linda (Pretty as a Picture), 1965, vinyl, large painted eyes, rooted long straight hair, came with portrait, advertised as "Pretty as a Picture" in Sears and Montgomery Ward catalogs, marked "VOGUE DOLLS/©1965"

15"..................... $45.00 – 65.00

Welcome Home Baby, 1978 – 1980, newborn, designed by Eloise Wilkin, vinyl head and arms, painted eyes, molded hair, cloth body, crier, marked "Lesney"

18"..................... $40.00 – 60.00

Welcome Home Baby Turns Two, 1980, toddler, designed by Eloise Wilkin, vinyl head, arms, and legs, cloth body, sleep eyes, rooted hair, marked "42260 Lesney Prod. Corp.//1979//Vogue Doll"

22".................. $90.00 – 125.00

IZANNAH WALKER

1840s – 1888, Central Falls, Rhode Island. Made cloth stockinette dolls, with pressed mask face, oil-painted features, applied ears, brush-stroked or corkscrew curls, stitched hands and feet, some with painted boots. All in good condition with appropriate clothing.

Very good condition

17" – 19" . $20,000.00 – 26,000.00

Fair condition

18" Izannah Walker doll with wardrobe and provenance, sold for $41,000.00 at auction. *Photo courtesy of Withington Auction, Inc.*

17" – 19". $8,000.00 – 11,000.00

18", in good condition with wardrobe and provenance $41,000.00*

WAX

1850 – 1930. Made by English, German, French, and other firms, reaching heights of popularity ca. 1875. Seldom marked, wax dolls were poured, some reinforced with plaster, and less expensive, but more durable with wax over papier-mâché or composition. English makers included Montanari, Pierotti, and Peck. German makers included Heinrich Stier.

Dolls listed are in good condition with original clothes, or appropriately dressed. More for exceptional dolls; much less for dolls in poor condition.

Slit-head wax, English, 1830 – 1860s, wax over composition shoulder head, hair inserted into slit on center top of head, glass eyes may use wire closure

14" .... $875.00 – 950.00

37½" tall case with a slit-head wax doll in it, ca. 1860, $2,000.00. *Photo courtesy of Skinner, Inc.*

16" – 19".. $1,100.00 – 1,400.00
23" – 25".. $1,400.00 – 1,600.00

Poured wax, 1850s – 1900s

Baby, shoulder head, painted features, glass eyes, English Montanari type, closed mouth, cloth body, wig, or hair inserted into wax

10" – 13"..... $925.00 – 1,200.00
18" – 25".. $1,800.00 – 2,200.00

Child, shoulder head, inserted hair, glass eyes, wax limbs, cloth body

13" – 15"..... $900.00 – 1,100.00
18" – 22".. $1,700.00 – 2,200.00

14" poured wax, marked Peck, $1,100.00. *Photo courtesy of Withington Auction, Inc.*

Wax

25" – 27".. $3,000.00 – 4,000.00

Adult

Lady, elaborate costume brings high end of price range

    11" – 15".. $2,000.00 – 4,000.00

    23" – 27".. $2,500.00 – 5,000.00

Wax over composition or reinforced, 1860s – 1890s

Child

ca. 1860 – 1890, early poured wax shoulder head, reinforced with plaster, inserted hair, glass eyes, cloth body

    10" – 12"........ $700.00 – 900.00

    14" – 16"..... $950.00 – 1,000.00

    20" – 22".. $1,100.00 – 1,400.00

    25" – 29".. $1,050.00 – 1,600.00

25", socket head, glass eyes

    16" – 18".. $1,500.00 – 1,800.00

Later wax over composition shoulder head, open or closed mouth, glass eyes, wig, cloth body

    10" – 12"........ $250.00 – 300.00

    15" – 17"........ $350.00 – 400.00

    21" – 23"........ $525.00 – 675.00

Molded hair, wax over composition, shoulder head, glass eyes, cloth body, wooden limbs, molded shoes

21" wax over composition lady with sleep eyes, $1,500.00. *Photo courtesy of Morphy Auctions.*

    13" – 15"........ $200.00 – 400.00

    19" – 23"........ $400.00 – 500.00

Alice in Wonderland style, with molded headband

    16"................. $600.00 – 650.00

Lady

Wigged

    12" – 15" .... $700.00 – 900.00

    22" – 25"..... $900.00 – 1,200.00

Molded hair and gloves

    15" – 22".. $1,000.00 – 3,000.00

Bonnet Head: See Bonnet Head section.

24" wax over composition, $1,400.00. *Photo courtesy of Withington Auction, Inc.*

13" fashion figure, $500.00. *Photo courtesy of The Museum Doll Shop.*

Wax crèche figure, 1880 – 1910, poured wax Christ Child, inset hair, glass eyes

    6" .... $100.00 – 125.00
    13" – 23" .... $450.00 – 700.00

Wax fashion doll, 1910 – 1920, wax head, wire armature body, by makers such as LaFitte et Desirat and others, usually on wooden base

    11" – 14" .... $500.00 – 800.00

NORAH WELLINGS

1926 to 1960, Wellington, Shropshire, England. The Victoria Toy Works was founded by Norah Wellings and her brother Leonard. Norah had previously worked as chief designer for Chad Valley. They made cloth dolls with molded heads and bodies of velvet, velveteen, plush, and felt, specializing in sailor souvenir dolls for steamship lines. The line included children, adults, blacks, ethnic, and fantasy dolls.

Baby, molded face, oil-painted features, some papier-mâché covered by stockinette, stitched hip and shoulder joints

    10" .... $275.00 – 375.00
    15" .... $425.00 – 600.00

19" Indian with painted eyes, $275.00. *Photo courtesy of Withington Auction, Inc.*

    22" .... $775.00 – 900.00

Child

Painted eyes

    12" – 14" .... $400.00 – 500.00
    16" – 18" .... $500.00 – 575.00
    22" – 23" .... $600.00 – 700.00
    28" .... $750.00 – 900.00

Glass eyes

    15" –18" ...... $900.00 – 1,150.00
    22" – 26" .. $1,500.00 – 2,200.00

Characters in uniform, regional dress, Pixie People, floppy limbed, painted eyes, Mounties, sailors, policemen, Scots, Indians, others

    8" – 10" .... $100.00 – 160.00
    13" – 14" .... $200.00 – 250.00

Black or Asian

    8" – 13" .... $125.00 – 200.00
    16" – 18" .... $160.00 – 240.00

Black Islander, glass eyes

    13" .... $180.00 – 250.00
    16" .... $300.00 – 325.00

Jolly Toddlers

    11" .... $150.00 – 220.00

WOODEN

Wooden dolls have been made from the earliest recorded times. During the 1600s and 1700s they became the luxury play dolls of the era. They were made commercially in England, Germany, Switzerland, Russia, United States, and other countries. By the late 1700s and early 1800s inexpensive German wooden dolls were the affordable doll of the masses and were exported worldwide.

English

William & Mary period, 1690s – 1700, carved wooden head, tiny multi-stroke eyebrow and eyelashes, colored cheeks, human hair or flax wig, wooden body, fork-like carved wooden hands, jointed wooden legs, cloth upper arms, medium to fair condition

Wooden

17" English wooden, ca. 1735, $30,000.00.
Photo courtesy of Skinner, Inc.

18" – 22".. $36,350.00 – 46,000.00
Too few in database for a reliable range.
Queen Anne period, early 1700s, dotted eyebrows, eyelashes, painted or glass eyes, no pupils, carved oval-shaped head, flat wooden back and hips, nicely dressed, good condition

32" wooden doll, ca. 1790, from the Oberamagau region of Germany, sold for $16,590.00 at auction. *Photo courtesy of Skinner, Inc.*

7" 1820s wooden, German, $1,200.00. *Photo courtesy of Skinner, Inc.*

14"....... $15,000.00 – 25,000.00
Too few in database for a reliable range.
18"....... $30,000.00 – 45,000.00
Too few in database for a reliable range.
25"....... $36,000.00 – 51,000.00
Too few in database for a reliable range.
Georgian period, 1750s – 1800, round wooden head, gesso-coated, inset glass eyes, dotted eyelashes and eyebrows, human hair or flax wig, jointed wooden body, pointed torso, medium to fair condition
13" – 16" . $10,000.00 – 15,000.00
18" – 24" . $8,500.00 – 10,000.00
1800 – 1840, gesso-coated wooden head, painted eyes, human hair or flax wig, original clothing comes down below wooden legs
12" – 15" .. $1,500.00 – 3,000.00
18" – 22" .. $2,800.00 – 3,800.00
Continental European, eighteenth century, early nineteenth century, very fine details
5" – 6"...... $5,000.00 – 6,000.00
12" – 14"... $5,000.00 – 12,000.00
25" – 32" .. $20,000.00 – 25,000.00
39" $32,000.00*
German
1810 – 1850s, delicately carved painted hair style, spit curls, some with hair decorations such as "tuck comb," all wooden head and

32" German wooden with carved curls, $10,000.00. *Photo courtesy of Skinner, Inc.*

11" so-called Tuck Comb wooden, $1,500.00. *Photo courtesy of Withington Auction, Inc.*

body, pegged or ball-jointed limbs, allow more for exceptional original costume, wooden earrings, sideburn man, etc.

4½" .... $650.00 – 800.00
7" .... $850.00 – 1,200.00
12" – 13" .. $1,600.00 – 2,000.00
17" – 18" .. $2,100.00 – 2,400.00
1850s – 1900
All wood with painted plain hairstyle, may have split curls

1" .... $100.00 – 125.00
4" – 5" .... $150.00 – 175.00
6" – 8" .... $225.00 – 325.00

14" – 17" .... $475.00 – 625.00
23" .... $2,000.00 – 2,700.00
Wooden shoulder head, fancy carved hair style, wood limbs, cloth body

12" .... $375.00 – 500.00
23" .... $775.00 – 900.00
Bohemian, with red painted torso

8" – 10" .... $275.00 – 300.00
14" – 16" .... $350.00 – 500.00
1900 on, turned wooden head, carved nose, painted hair, lower legs with black shoes, peg jointed

11" .... $60.00 – 80.00
Bébé Tout en Bois, 1900 – 1914, all-wooden doll made by German firms such as Rudolf Schneider, Schilling, and others, made for the French trade, child or baby, fully jointed body, glass eyes or painted, open mouth. Glass eyes bring higher end of price range.

9" – 12" .... $350.00 – 675.00
15" .... $750.00 – 875.00
18" .... $875.00 – 975.00
23" .... $1,000.00 – 1,050.00
Kokeshi, 1900 on, Japan, traditional simple

Wooden

11" Bébé Tout en Bois, $650.00. *Photo courtesy of Withington Auction, Inc.*

turned wooden dolls made for native and foreign tourist trade, values can be higher for unusual design or known artists.

1850s – 1900

　　7" – 14"....... $900.00 – 1,000.00

1900 – 1930

　　7" – 9"............ $200.00 – 400.00

1950 to present

　　7" – 9"................ $35.00 – 90.00

Matryoshka, Russian nesting dolls, 1900, set of wooden canisters that separate in the middle, brightly painted with a glossy finish to represent adults, children, storybook or fairytale characters, and animals. These come in sets usually of five or more related characters, the larger doll opening to reveal a smaller doll nesting inside, and so on. Values can be much higher for unusual design or known artists.

Set, pre-1930s

　　4"..................... $70.00 – 100.00

　　7".................. $115.00 – 150.00

　　9".................. $175.00 – 230.00

³⁄₁₆" – 9" set of 13 in the Seminov style, $50.00. *Photo courtesy of The Museum Doll Shop.*

Set new

    5"...................... $12.00 – 20.00

    7"...................... $18.00 – 30.00

Political set: Gorbachev, Yeltsin

    5"...................... $20.00 – 35.00

    7"...................... $50.00 – 60.00

Swiss, 1900 on, carved wooden dolls with dowel jointed bodies, joined at elbow, hips, knees, some with elaborate hair

    8" – 10".......... $300.00 – 600.00

    12" – 16"........ $475.00 – 700.00

Springfield, Vermont Woodens

Cooperative Manufacturing Co., 1873 – 1874, Joel Ellis manufactured wooden dolls with pressed heads and mortise and double tennon joints, with metal hands and feet painted black or blue, painted black molded hair sometimes blond, similar type wooden dolls were made by Jointed Doll Co. under patents by Martin, Sanders, Johnson, Mason & Taylor, a variety of head and jointing styles were used on these dolls.

Ellis, Joel (Cooperative Manufacturing Co.)

    12"........... $1,100.00 – 1,500.00

    15"........... $1,700.00 – 2,000.00

Jointed Doll Co.

    11½"......... $600.00 – 1,000.00

Tynietoy, 1917 on, Providence, Rhode Island,

4¾" Wilson Walkie, $45.00. *Photo courtesy of The Doll Works.*

sold peg wooden type dolls called Peggity dolls.

    5"................... $500.00 – 600.00

Ramp Walker dolls, early to mid-twentieth century, such as Wilson Walkies, wooden body characters that walk down an incline

    4½"................... $30.00 – 45.00

    Santa, Easter bunny . $60.00 – 80.00

    Scary Ann, 1928, push lever raises

    hair $315.00*

Krahmer Dolls, Germany, wooden heads, cloth bodies, 1947 – 1960s

    10" – 13"........ $200.00 – 450.00

    1970 – 1980s

    10" – 13"........ $150.00 – 200.00

Hitty: See Artist Dolls.

Schoenhut: See Schoenhut section.

WPA, VARIOUS PROJECTS

1935 – 1943, Works Progress Administration project to provide work for

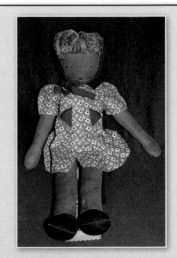

16" Milwaukee WPA doll, $600.00. *Photo courtesy of The Museum Doll Shop.*

artisans and home workers. Other states also ran doll-making projects under the WPA.

Milwaukee, Wisconsin project

Molded stockinette doll, cloth body, cotton yarn hair, painted features, tab-hinged joint and hips

    22".......... $1,200.00 – 1,600.00

    Black......... $2,500.00 – 3,500.00

Flat-face cloth doll, embroidered features, cotton yarn hair

11"................ $400.00 – 425.00

14"................ $450.00 – 500.00

16"................ $625.00 – 700.00

New York City project, cloth mask face

    14"................................$250.00

Too few in database for a reliable range.

Papier-mâché doll, project unknown, dressed in regional or historic costume

    14" – 16"...... $200.00 – 300.00

BIBLIOGRAPHY

Anderton, Johana Gast. *20th Century Dolls.* Des Moines, IA: Wallace-Homestead Book Co., 1971.

____. *More 20th Century Dolls, Vols. I and II.* Des Moines, IA: Wallace-Homestead Book Co., 1974.

____. *The Collector's Encyclopedia of Cloth Dolls.* Lombard, IL: Wallace-Homestead Book Co., 1984.

Angione, Genevieve, and Judith Whorton. *All Dolls Are Collectible.* New York, NY: Crown Publishers, Inc., 1977.

Bullard, Helen. *Crafts and Craftsmen of the Tennessee Mountains.* Falls Church, VA: The Summit Press Ltd., 1976.

____. *The American Doll Artist.* Boston, MA: the Charles T. Branford Co., 1965.

____. *The American Doll Artist.* Kansas City, MO: Athens Publishing Co., 1975.

Cieslik, Jurgen and Marianne. *German Doll Encyclopedia,* Grantsville, MD: Hobby House Press, 1985.

Coleman, Dorothy S., Elizabeth A., and Evelyn J. *The Collector's Encyclopedia of Dolls Vols. I & II.* New York, NY: Crown Publishers, Inc., 1968 and 1986.

____. *The Collector's Book of Dolls' Clothes.* New York, NY: Crown Publishers, Inc., 1975.

DeMillar, Suzanne L., and Dennis J. Brevik. *Arranbee Dolls.* Paducah, KY: Collector Books, 2004.

Edward, Linda. *Cloth Dolls from Ancient to Modern.* Atglen, PA: Schiffer Publishing, 1997.

Fawcett, Clara Hallard. *Dolls A Guide for Collectors.* New York, NY: H. L. Lindquist Publications, 1947.

____. *Dolls: A New Guide for Collectors.* Boston, MA: Charles T. Branford Co., 1964.

Foulke, Jan. *The Blue Book of Dolls and Values Vols. 2 through 14.* Grantsville, MD: Hobby House Press, 1976, 1978, 1980, 1982, 1984, 1986, 1987, 1989, 1991, 1993, 1995, 1997, 1999.

Grafnitz, Christiane. *German Papier-Mache Dolls, 1760 – 1860.* Germany: Verlag Puppen & Spielzeug, 1994.

Izen, Judith. *American Character Dolls.* Paducah, KY: Collector Books, 2004.

____. *Collector's Guide to Ideal Dolls.* Paducah, KY: Collector Books, 2005.

Izen, Judith, and Carol Stover. *Collector's Encyclopedia of Vogue Dolls.* Paducah, KY: Collector Books, 2005.

Bibliography

Jacobs, Flora Gill. *Dolls' Houses in America*. New York, NY: Charles Scribner's Sons, 1974.

____. *A History of Dolls' Houses*. New York, NY: Charles Scribner's Sons, 1953.

Jensen, Don. *Collector's Guide to Horsman Dolls*. Paducah, KY: Collector Books, 2002.

Johl, Janet Pagter. *The Fascinating Story of Dolls*. Watkins Glen, reissued Century House, 1970.

____. *More About Dolls*. New York, NY: H. L. Lindquist Publications, 1946.

____. *Still More About Dolls*. New York, NY: H. L. Lindquist Publications, 1950.

____. *Your Dolls and Mine*. New York, NY: H. L. Lindquist Publications, 1952.

Judd, Polly. *Cloth Dolls*. Grantsville, MD: Hobby House Press,1990.

Judd, Pam and Polly. *Americas, Australia & Pacific Islands Costumed Dolls*. Grantsville, MD: Hobby House Press, 1997.

King, Constance Eileen. *The Collector's History of Dolls*. New York, NY: Bonanza Books, 1981.

Lavitt, Wendy. *American Folk Dolls*. New York, NY: Alfred A. Knopf, Inc., 1982.

Lechler, Doris Anderson. *Bleuette her Gautier-Languereau Ads and Catalogues of Fashion 1905 – 1960*. Self published.

____. *Bleuette — Her Faces, Fashions and Family*. Self published.

McFadden, Sybill. *Fawn Zeller's Porcelain Dollmaking Techniques*. Grantsville, MD: Hobby House Press, 1984.

McGonagle, Dorothy. *A Celebration of American Dolls*. Grantsville, MD: Hobby House Press, 1997.

Merrill, Madeline Osborne. *The Art of Dolls*. Granstville, MD: Hobby House Press, 1985.

Merrill, Madeline O. and Nellie O. Perkins. *Handbook of Collectible Dolls Vol. I.,* 1969.

Mertz, Ursula. *Collector's Encyclopedia of Composition Dolls*. Paducah, KY: Collector Books, 1999.

____. *Collector's Encyclopedia of Composition Dolls, Vol. II*. Paducah, KY: Collector Books, 2004.

Mills, Winifred and Louise Dunn. *The Story of Old Dolls and How to Make New Ones*. New York, NY: Doubleday, Doran & Co., Inc., 1940.

Patino, Estelle. *American Rag Dolls*. Paducah, KY: Collector Books, 1988.

Pardee, Elaine, and Jackie Robertson. *Encyclopedia of Bisque Nancy Ann Storybook Dolls*. Paducah, KY: Collector Books, 2003.

Robinson, Julie Pelletier. *Celluloid Dolls, Toys & Playthings*. Paducah, KY: Collector Books, 2006.

Revi, Albert Christian. *Spinning Wheel's Complete Book of Dolls*. New York, NY: Galahad Books, 1975.

Richter, Lydia. *Treasury of German Dolls*. Tucson, AZ: HP Books, 1984.

____. *The Beloved Kathe Kruse Dolls*. Grantsville, MD: Hobby House Press, 1983.

Schiffer, Nancy. *Indian Dolls*. Atglen, PA: Schiffer Publishing Ltd., 1997.

Singleton, Esther. *Dolls*. New York, NY: Payson & Clark Ltd., 1927.

St. George, Eleanor. *The Dolls of Yesterday*. New York and London: Charles Scribner's Sons, 1948.

____. *Dolls of Three Centuries*. New York and London: Charles Scribner's Sons, 1951.

Smith, Patricia. *Antique Collector's Dolls Vol. 2*. Paducah, KY: Collector Books, 1976.

Sorensen, Lewis. *Lewis Sorensen's Doll Scrapbook*. Alhambra, CA: Thor Publications, 1976.

Sutton, Sydney Ann. *Scouting Dolls through the Years*. Paducah, KY: Collector Books, 2003.

Theiriault, Florence. *Catalog Reprint Series*. Annapolis, MD: Gold Horse Publishing, 1998.

Trotter, Gillian. *Norah Wellings Cloth Dolls and Soft Toys*. Grantsville, MD: Hobby House Press, 2003.

Van Patten, Joan, and Linda Lau. *Nippon Dolls & Playthings*. Paducah, KY: Collector Books, 2001.

Whitton, Blair. *Bliss Toys and Dollhouses*. New York, NY: Dover Publications.

COLLECTOR'S RESOURCES

Antique Doll Dealers

Ann Lloyd Dolls
5632 S. Deer Run Rd.
Doylestown, PA 18902
215-794-8164
www.rubylane.com/shops/anntiquedolls

American Beauty Dolls
Nancy Stronczek
26 Bouker Street
Greenfield, MA 01301
413-774-3260
njs@crocker.com
www.rubylane.com/shops/
    americanbeautydolls

Atlanta Antique Gallery
3550 Broad Street, Suite A
Chamblee, GA 30341
770-457-7444
Fax: 770-457-7445
info@atlantaantiquegallery.com
www.atlantaantiquegallery.com

Aunt Mary's Antique Dolls
P.O. Box 198
Hawleyville, CT 06440
203-426-9557
mfurse@earthlink.net
www.rubylane.com/shops
    /auntmarysantiquedolls

Zendelle Bouchard
zendelle@hotmail.com
www.vintagedollcollector.com

Connectibles
Maida Webster
47 Buttery Road
New Canaan, CT 06840
203-253-1162
www.connectibles.net or
www.buyconnectibles.com

Cybermogul Dolls
Marie Witherill
P.O. Box 762
Statesville, NC 28687-0762
704-450-5539

cybermogul@roadrunner.com
www.rubylane.com/shops/cybermogul

Dollhappy & Jean's Collection
Jean Johnson
2 Meadowbrook Lane
West Memphis, AR 72301
870-735-8159
Fax: 870-735-8159
triplejven@aol.com
www.rubylane.com/shops/dollhappy

Dollsantique
Patricia A. Vaillancourt
P.O. Box 326
Adamstown, PA 19501
717-484-2443
vaillsdoll@aol.com
www.dollsantique.com

Dolls and Lace
Susan Robison
P.O. Box 743
Lehi, UT 84043
susan@dollsandlace.com
www.dollsandlace.com

Dollyology Vintage Dolls & Antiques
Kate Gillen
Box 860
Lincoln, CA 95648
dollyology@hotmail.com
www.rubylane.com/shops/
    dollyologyvintagedolls

Emmie's Antique Doll Castle
Robbin Wilson
400 W. 32nd Court
Sand Springs, OK 74063
918-241-0269
www.rubylane.com/shops/emmiesgirl

Estate Auctions, Inc.
Norb and Marie Novocin
12221 Old Furnace Rd.
Seaford, DE 19973
1-800-573-3508
marie@estateauctionsinc.com
ebay@estateauctionsinc.com
www.estateauctionsinc.com

Collector's Resources

Fourty Fifty Sixty
Ben Cassara/Joe Bucchi
Rutherford NJ 07070
212-475-4015
bj4t5t6t@verizon.net
www.fourtyfiftysixty.com
www.rubylane.com/shops/fourtyfiftysixty

Glenda Antique Dolls & Collectables
Gray's Antique Market, 1-7 Davies Mews,
London W1K 5AB
020 8367 2441
Mobile 07970 722750
glenda@glenda-antiquedolls.co.uk
www.glenda-antiquedolls.co.uk

Gloria's Antique Dolls
Gloria Duddlesten
P.O. Box 5803
Texarkana, TX 75505
www.gloriasantiquedolls.com
dollstx@cableone.net

Hatton's Gallery of Dolls
90 Crow Hill Road
Stafford Springs, CT 06076
860-684-4156
www.hattonsgallery.com
info@hattonsgallery.com

Joan & Lynette Antique Dolls and Accessories
Joan Farrell or Lynette Gross
6551 Carrollton Avenue
Indianapolis, IN 46220
joanlynettedolls@sbcglobal.net
www.rubylane.com/shops/joan
   -lynetteantiquedolls

Joy's Antique Dolls
Joy Frizzell
P.O. Box 30
Westcliffe, CO 81252-0030
719-783-4500
www.joysantiquedolls.com

Linda Kellermann
11013 Treyburn Drive
Glen Allen, VA 23059
lindas-antiques@erols.com

Doris Lechler
949 E. Cooke Rd.

Columbus, OH 43224
614 -261-6659
dorislechler@aol.com

Joy Macielle
info@qualityvintagedollpatterns.com
www.qualityvintagedollpatterns.com

Memories of Things Past
Elizabeth Schmahl
520-664-0861
www.rubylane.com/shops/
   memoriesofthingspastantiques

Museum Doll Shop
104 Van Zandt Ave.
Newport, RI 02840
401-847-6866
www.dollmuseum.com

My Dear Dolly
Patricia Snyder
P.O. Box 303
Sparta, NJ 07871
mydeardollypat@yahoo.com
www.mydeardolly.com

My Dolly Dearest
P.O. Box 909
8 S. Village Circle
Adamstown, PA 19501
717-484-1137
sidneyjeffrey@mydollydearest.com
www.mydollydearest.com

N.A.D.D.A.
National Antique Doll Dealers Association
www.nadda.org

Roberta's Doll House
475 17th Avenue
Paterson, NJ 07504
800-569-9739
Fax: 973-523-7585
robertasdollhous@aol.com
www.robertasdollhouse.com

Sharing My Dolls 'N Stuff
Helen Welsh
799 Bent Creek Dr.
Lititz, PA 17543
helen1005@aol.com

Collector's Resources

www.rubylane.com/shops/
  sharingmydollsnstuff

Taecker House Antique Dolls
Thela Huffman
Brawley, CA 92227
760-455-3757
www.rubylane.com/shops/
  taeckerhouseantiquedolls

Tennessee Antique Dolls
Annalise Nohrudi
241 Park Ridge Ct.
Kingsport, TN 37664
423-323-7044
alnohrudie@charter.net
www.tennesseeantiquedolls.com

Trish's Treasures Antique Dolls
www.rubylane.com/shops/antiquedolls

The Doll Works
Judith Armitstead
P.O. Box 195
Lynnfield, MA 01940
www.TheDollWorks.net

Turn of the Century Antiques
1475 South Broadway
Denver, CO 80210
303-702-8700 or 303-778-7077
www.turnofthecenturyantiques.com

Useful Collectibles
Marsha Anderson
Liberty, MO
816-781-5598

Auction Houses

Alderfer Auction & Appraisal
501 Fairgrounds Rd.
Hatfield, PA 19440
215-393-3000
Fax: 215-368-9055
info@alderferauction.com
www.alderferauction.com

William J. Jenack Estate Appraisers &
  Auctioneers
62 Kings Highway Bypass
Chester, NY 10918

845-469-9095
Fax: 845-469-8445
www.jenack.com

James D. Julia, Inc.
203 Skowhegan Rd.
Fairfield, ME 04937
207-453-7125
Fax: 207-453-2502
info@jamesdjulia.com
www.jamesdjulia.com

McMasters Harris Auction Co.
Ohio & Kansas City
800-842-3526
info@mcmastersharris.com
www.mcmastersharris.com
www.mharrislive.com

Morphy Auctions
2000 N. Reading Rd.
Denver, PA 17517
717-335-3435
Fax: 717-336-7115
www.morphyauctions.com

Skinner, Inc.
274 Cedar Hill Street
Marlborough, MA 01752
508-970-3000
Fax: 508-970-3100
www.skinnerinc.com

Sweetbriar Auctions
P.O. Box 37
Earleville, MD 21919
410-275-2094
sweetbriar@live.com
www.sweetbriarauctions.com

Withington Auction, Inc.
17 Atwood Road
Hillsborough, NH 03244
603-478-3232
www.withingtonauction.com

Collector Clubs & Newsletters

Bleuette
Bleuette's World
Agnes J. Sura, Editor
489 Wilson Hill Rd

Collector's Resources

Hoosick Falls, NY 12090
518-686-5740
Quarterly publication

Chatty Cathy, Mattel
Chatty Cathy Collectors Club
Melissa Gilkey Mince, Editor
ChattynMe@aol.com
www.ttinet.com/chattycathy/

Chérie Amies de Bleuette Revue
Linda Justice, Editor
4143 Mercier
Kansas City, MO 64111
lindasruffles@yahoo.com
Quarterly publication

Cornerstones
Deanna Williams
733 de la Fuente
Monterey Park, CA 91754

Costuming
Doll Costumer's Guild™
Pat Gosh, Editor
P.O. Box 247
New Harmony, IN 47631
812-319-5300
Fax: 812-682-3815
patgosh@aol.com
www.dollcostumersguild.com
Quarterly publication

Dionne Quintuplets
Dionne Quintuplet Collectors Too Newsletter
Leonard Belsher & Dee Dee Backus, Editors
P.O. Box 468
Shawville, Quebec J0X 2Y0 Canada
819-647-1965
quintly2000@yahoo.ca
Quarterly newsletter

French Fashion Gazette
Adele Leurquin, Editor
1862 Sequoia SE
Port Orchard, WA 98366

Hitty
Friends of Hitty Newsletter
Virginia Ann Heyerdahl, Editor
2704 Belleview Ave.
Cheverly, MD 20785-3006

Four issues per subscription
vahhitty@aol.com

Mary Hoyer
T.H.E.L.M.A
(The Hoyer Enthusiastic Ladies Mail Association)
Thelma R. Bernard, Founder, Editor and Publisher
P.O. Box 42604
Las Vegas, NV 89114
starrlady@webtv.net
A by-mail doll group celebrating past and present Mary Hoyer dolls via newsletter format (quarterly).

Ideal
Ideal Collectors' Newsletter
Judith Izen, Editor
P.O. Box 623
Lexington, MA 02173
Jizen@aol.com
Quarterly

Kish Collectors Society
The Newsletter of the Kish Collectors Society
www.collectors@kishandcompany.com

Raggedy Ann
Rags Newsletter
Barbara Barth, Editor
P.O. Box 823
Atlanta, GA 30301

Sasha Friends
Sharon Sams, Editor and Publisher
304 12th Avenue NW
Altoona, IA 50009
sharon_sams_2000@yahoo.com
and
Chris Kading, Editor and Publisher
P.O. Box 104
Ames, IA 50010
kading@att.net
Quarterly newsletter

Shirley Temple
Australian Shirley Temple Collectors News
Victoria Horne, Editor
39 How Ave.
North Dandenong
Victoria, 3175, Australia

Collector's Resources

Quarterly newsletter

Publications

Antique Doll Collector Magazine
Keith Kaonis, Advertising & Creative Director
Donna Kaonis, Editor-in-Chief
P.O. Box 239
Northport, NY 11768
631-261-4100
1-888-800-2588
antiquedoll@gmail.com
www.antiquedollcollector.com
Monthly magazine

Collectors United
Dian or Gary Green, Publisher
P.O. Box 1160
Chatsworth, GA 30705
706-695-8242
Fax: 706-695-0770
diang@collectorsunited.com
www.collectorsunited.com
Monthly newspaper

Contemporary Doll Collector
2145 W. Sherman Blvd.
Muskegon, MI 49441
231-755-2200
Fax: 231-755-1003
www.contemporarydollcollector.com
Bi-monthly magazine

Doll Castle News
Barry Mueller, Publisher
P.O. Box 601
Broadway, NJ 08808
800-572-6607
info@dollcastlemagazine.com
www.dollcastlemagazine.com
Bi-monthly magazine

Doll Diary
Lauren Welker, Editor and Publisher
204 East Coover St.
Mechanicsburg, PA 17055-4221
717-691-8110
laurenwelker@laurenwelker.com
Quarterly publication

Doll News

Michael Canadas and David Robinson, Editors
P.O. Box 7198
Carmel, CA 93921
mnd@redshift.com
www.ufdc.org
Official publication of the United Federation of Doll Clubs, Inc.
Quarterly magazine

Doll One
The Newsletter for the Käthe Kruse Family
Quarterly newsletter
www.kaethekrusepuppen.de

Doll Reader
Susan Fitzgerald, Publisher
Kathryn Peck, Editor
Madavor Media, LLC
85 Quincy Ave., Suite B
Quincy, MA 02169
617-706-9110
Fax: 617-536-0102
Subscription information: 800-437-5828
www.dollreader.com
Published nine times a year

Dolls
Jones Publishing, Inc.
N7450 Aanstad Rd., P.O. Box 5000
Iola, WI 54945-5000
715-445-5000
800-331-0038
editor@dollsmagazine.com
www.dollsmagazine.com

Fashion Doll Quarterly
610 West 110th Street, Suite 5C
New York, NY 10025-2106
fdqmag@mac.com
www.fashiondollquarterly.net
212-961-0662
Quarterly magazine

Haute Doll
5711 Eighth Ave
Kenosha, WI 53140
262-658-1004
Fax: 262-658-0433
mcpub@hautedoll.com
www.hautedoll.com
Bi-monthly

Collector's Resources

Lollipop News
Shirley Temple Collectors by the Sea
P.O. Box 6203
Oxnard, CA 93031

Master Collector
Fun Publications, Inc.
225 Cattle Baron Parc Dr.
Fort Worth, TX 76108
817-448-9863
www.mastercollector.com

The Review
Manhattan Station
P.O. Box 2739
New York, NY 10027-9998
212-368-1047
info@madc.org
www.madc.org
Official publication of the Madame
Alexander Doll Club. Contact for club
information.

The United Federation of Doll Clubs, Inc.
10900 North Pomona Avenue
Kansas City, MO 64153
816-891-7040
Fax 816-891-8360
info@ufdc.org
www.ufdc.org

Doll Manufacturers

Adora Original Doll®
9 Goddard
Irvine, CA 92618
866-868-8698
info@adoradoll.com
www.adoradoll.com

Alexander Doll Company, Inc.
615 West 131st Street, 6th Floor
New York, NY 10027
212-283-5900
Fax: 212-283-4901
ma@alexdoll.com
www.madamealexander.com

American Girl
8400 Fairway Place
P.O. Box 620497
Middleton, WI 53562-0497

800-360-1861
www.americangirl.com

Bella! Studios
Christina Bougas, Artistic Director
16295 Highway 175, P.O. Box 1166
Cobb, CA 95426-1166
626-359-9097
info@cleabella.com
www.cleabella.com

Berdine Creedy Originals, Inc.
5015 NW 71st Place
Gainesville, FL 32653
352-336-2510
Fax: 352-336-7282
berdine@berdinecreedy.com
www.berdinecreedy.com

Charisma Brands, LLC
9 Goddard
Irvine, CA 92618
800-779-5335
Fax: 949-788-9911
info@charismabrands.com
www.charismabrands.com

D.A.E. Originals
835 N. 94th Place
Mesa, AZ 85207-5280
480-380-3119
miniquins@aol.com
www.daeoriginals.com

Heidi Plusczok Puppen Design
Heidi Plusczok Puppen
Erlenweg 5
D-61130 Nidderau, Germany
011-49-6187-23222
Fax: 011-49-6187-24608
plusdolls@aol.com
www.heidiplusczok.com

Horsman Ltd.
3 Park Plaza, Suite 1-118
Glen Head, NY 11545
516-504-0387
Fax: 516-504-0397
info@horsmanltd.com
www.horsmanltd.com

Collector's Resources

Kish & Company
1800 West 33rd Avenue
Denver, CO 80211
303-972-0053
Fax: 303-932-2405
www.kishandcompany.com

Käthe Kruse Puppen GmbH
Andrea-Kathrin Christenson, CEO
86609 Donauwörth
Alte Augsburger Str. 9, Germany
011-49-09-06-7-06-78-0
Fax: 011-49-09-06-78-70
mhohmann@kaethe-kruse.de
www.kaethekrusepuppen.de

The Lawton Doll Company
1651 Lander Ave, Ste. 125
Turlock, CA 95380
209-632-3655
Fax: 209-632-6788
info@lawtondolls.com
www.lawtondolls.com

Middleton Doll Company, Inc.
2400 Corporate Exchange Dr., Suite 220
Columbus, OH 43231
614-834-9750; 1-800-242-3285
www.leemiddleton.com

Nancy Ann Storybook Dolls, Inc.
P.O. Box 5072
El Dorado Hills, CA 95762
916-934-0726
www.nancyannstorybookdolls.com

Terri Lee Associates
www.terrilee.com

Tonner Doll Company, Inc.
Robert Tonner, CEO
14 Hurley Ave.
Kingston, NY 12401
845-339-2960
www.tonnerdoll.com
Tonner Doll Collectors Club
Quarterly newsletter

The Vogue Doll Company
P.O. Box 756
Oakdale, CA 95361-0756
209-848-0300

Fax: 209-848-4423
info@voguedolls.com
www.voguedolls.com

Internet

eBay auction site
www.ebay.com

Doll Collecting
Denise Van Patten
denise@dollymaker.com
www.collectdolls.about.com

Paper Doll Publications

Greetings
Louise Leek
10158 Land Catherine
Streetsboro, OH 44141

Now & Then
Arlene Del Fava
67-40 Yellowstone Blvd.
Forest Hills, NY 11375

O.P.D.A.G. (Original Paper Dolls Artists
Guild)/Paper Doll Studio Magazine
Jenny Taliadoros
P.O. Box 14
Kingfield, ME 04947
www.paperdollreview.com/catalog/Index/
php?main_page=index&cpath=

The Paper Doll Circle
Lorna Currie Thomopolous
28 Ferndown Gardens
Cobham, KT11 2BH
Surrey, England

Paper Doll Pal
Jim Faraone
19109 Silcott Springs Road
Purcellville, VA 20132

Paper Doll Review
Jenny Taliadoros
P.O. Box 14
Kingfield, ME 04947
800-290-2928
www.paperdollreview.com

Collector's Resources

Modern Doll Collectors Convention®

Modern Doll, Inc.
moddoll@yahoo.com
www.moderndollcollectors.com

Museums

Arizona
Arizona Doll & Toy Museum
602 E Adams Street, Phoenix, AZ
602-253-9337
Hours: Tue – Sat 10 – 4; Sun: 12 – 4
www.artcom.com/museums/nv/af/85004-
  23.htm

Colorado
Denver Museum of Miniatures, Dolls and
  Toys
1880 Gaylord St.
Denver, CO 80206
303-322-1053
director@dmmdt.org
Hours: Weds.– Sat. 10 – 4; Sun. 1 – 4
Closed all major holidays.
www.dmmdt.org

Louisiana
The Enchanted Mansion, A Doll Museum
190 Lee Drive
Baton Rouge, LA 70808
225-769-0005
Hours: Thurs – Sat. 10 – 5
www.enchantedmansion.org

The Lois Luftin Doll Museum
120 South Washington Avenue
DeRidder, LA 70634

Missouri
U.F.D.C.
10900 N. Pomona Avenue
Kansas City, MO 64153
www.ufdc.org

New Jersey
Princeton Doll & Toy Museum
8 Somerset St.
Hopewell, NJ 08525
609-333-8600
Hours: Mon., Fri. & Sat.10 – 5
www.princetondollandtoy.org

New York
Museum of the City of New York
1220 Fifth Avenue @ 103rd St.
New York, NY 10029
212-534-1672
Hours: Open daily.
www.mcny.org/toy.htm

Strong National Museum of Play
1 Manhattan Square
Rochester, NY 14607
585-263-2700
www.museumofplay.org

Ohio
Mid Ohio Historical Museum
Doll and Toy Museum
700 Winchester Pike
Canal Winchester, OH 43110
Hours: Wed. – Sat. 11 – 5
April - mid Dec.
www.dollmuseumohio.org
614-837-5573

The Children's Toy & Doll Museum
206 Gilman Avenue
Marietta, OH 45750
740-373-5178 or 740-373-0799
Hours: Sat. & Sun. 1 – 4, May – Oct.
www.toyanddollmuseum.com

Pennsylvania
Philadelphia Doll Museum
2253 North Broad Street
Philadelphia, PA 19132
215-787-0220
www.philadollmuseum.com

Texas
Museum of American Architecture &
  Decorative Arts
Houston Baptist University
7502 Fronden Rd
Houston, TX 77074-3298
281-649-3811

Vermont
Shelburne Museum
600 Shelburne Road, P.O. Box 10
Shelburne, VT 05482
802-985-3346

Collector's Resources

Hours: May – Oct.: 10 – 5 daily
www.shelburnemuseum.org

Washington
Rosalie Whyel Museum of Doll Art
1116 108th Avenue N.E.
Bellevue, WA 98004
425-455-1116
fax: 206-455-4793
dollart@dollart.com
www.dollart.com

Wisconsin
La Crosse Doll Museum
1213 Caledonia Street
La Crosse, WI 54603-2514
Hours: Mon. – Sat., 10 – 5, Sun. 11 – 4
608-785-0020

The Fennimore Doll & Toy Museum
1135 Sixth Street
Fennimore, WI 53809
608-822-4100
1-888-867-7935
Hours: May – Oct. 10 – 4 daily
dolltoy@fennimore.com
www.fennimore.com/dolltoy/

Doll Artists

NIADA
National Institute of American Doll Artists
www.niada.org

ODACA
Original Doll Artist Council of America
www.odaca.org

SYMBOL INDEX

LETTER INDEX

MOLD INDEX

Mold Index

Mold Index

Mold Index

Mold Index

Mold Index

Mold Index

Mold Index

Mold Index

Mold Index

MARKS INDEX

Alabama Baby

Alabama Indestructible Dolls Marks: "MRS. S.S. SMITH//MANUFACTURER AND DEALER IN// THE ALABAMA INDESTRUCTIBLE DOLL// ROANOKE, ALA.// PATENTED//SEPT. 26, 1905."

Henri Alexandre

Alt, Beck, & Gottschalck

Arranbee Doll Co.

ARRANBEE//DOLL Co. or R & B

Max Oscar Arnold

Art Fabric Mills

Art Fabric Mills Marks: *"ART FABRIC MILLS, NY, PAT. FEB. 13TH, 1900" on shoe or bottom of foot.*

Georgene Averill

Tag on original outfit reads: "BONNIE BABE COPYRIGHTED BY GEORGENE AVERILL MADE BY K AND K TOY CO."

COPR GEORGENE AVERILL 1005/3652 GERMANY

Bähr & Pröschild

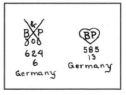

Barbie®

1959 – 1962
BARBIE™
PATS. PEND.
©MCMLVIII
BY//MATTEL, INC.
1963 – 1968
MIDGE™©1962
Barbie®/©1958
BY//MATTEL, INC.
1964 – 1966
©1958//MATTEL, IN.
U.S. PATENTED
U.S. PAT. PEND.
1966 – 1969
©1966//MATTEL, INC.
U.S. PATENTED//
U.S. PAT. PEND//
MADE IN JAPAN

E. Barrios

E 3 B
E. 8 DEPOSE B.

C.M. Bergmann

C. M. B
SIMON & HALBIG
Eleonore

Bru

Fashion-Type Mark:
Marked "A" through "M," "11" to "28," indicating size numbers only

Bru Jne Marks:
"BRU JNE," with size number on head, kid over wood body marked with rectangular paper label.

Bru Jne R. Marks:
"BRU. JNE R." with size number on head, body stamped in red, "Bébé Bru," and size number.

Bébé Breveté Marks:
"Bébé Breveté"
Head marked with size number only; kid body may have paper Bébé Breveté label.

Bye-Lo Baby

© 1923 by
Grace S. Putnam
MADE IN GERMANY
7372145

Catterfelder Puppenfabrik

Century Doll Co.

CENTURY DOLL C°.
Kestner Germany

Chuckles mark on back:
"CHUCKLES//A
CENTURY DOLL"

Chase Doll Company

"CHASE STOCKINET DOLL"
on left leg or under left arm.
Paper label, if there, reads
"CHASE//HOSPITAL DOLL//
TRADE MARK// PAWTUCKET,
RI// MADE IN U.S.A."

Chase doll mark,
1889 – 1894.

PAWTUCKET, R.I.

Chase doll mark,
1908 – 1945.

Columbian

"COLUMBIAN DOLL,
EMMA E. ADAMS,
OSWEGO, NY"

Danel & Cie

E. (Size number) D. on head.
Eiffel Tower "PARIS BEBE"
on body; shoes with "PARIS
BEBE" in star.

Cuno & Otto Dressel

E.D.

EDEN BEBE
PARIS

Eegee

Trademark, EEGEE,
or circle with the words,
"TRADEMARK //EEGEE//
Dolls//MADE IN USA"
Later changed to just
initials, E.G.

Effanbee

Some marked on shoulder
plate, "EFFANBEE //BABY
DAINTY"
or "EFFANBEE //DOLLS//
WALK, TALK, SLEEP"
in oval

Fulper Pottery Co.

Gans & Seyfarth Puppenbabrik

Germany
&. & S
3

Francois Gaultier

Gesland

E. GESLAND
B^{TE} S. G. D. G.
PARIS

Ruth Gibbs

RG on back shoulder blade
Box labeled:
"GODEY LITTLE LADY DOLLS"

Gladdie

Gladdie
Copyriht By
Helen W. Jensen
Germany

Wm. and F. & W. Goebel

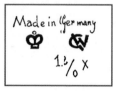

Ludwig Greiner

GREINER'S
PATENT HEADS.
No. 0.
Pat. March 30th, '58.

Gund

"A Gund Product, A Toy of Quality and Distinction." From World War II on: Stylized "G" with rabbit ears and whiskers. Mid 1960s – 1987: Bear's head above the letter "U." From 1987 on: "GUND."

Heinrich Handwerck

HANDWERCK
5
Germany

Max Handwerck

Max Handweik
Bebe Elite
286/3
Germany

283/28.5
MAJC.
HANDWERCK
GERMANY.
2¹/₄

Carl Hartmann

Globe Baby
DEP
Germany
C 3 H

Karl Hartmann

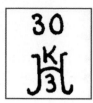

Hasbro

1964 – 1965
Marked on right
lower back:
G.I. Joe TM//COPYRIGHT 1964//
BY HASBRO ®//PATENT PENDING//
MADE IN U.S.A.//GIJoe®

1967
Slight change in marking:
COPYRIGHT 1964//BY HASBRO
®//PATENT PENDING// MADE IN
U.S.A.// GIJoe®
This mark appears on all four
armed service branches, excluding
the black action figures.

Hertel, Schwab & Co.

Ernst Heubach

Gebrüder Heubach

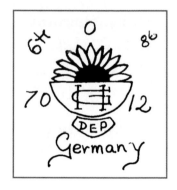

E.I. Horsman

"E.I. H.//CO."
and "CAN'T
BREAK 'EM"

Mary Hoyer Doll Mfg. Co.

"THE MARY HOYER DOLL" or "ORIGINAL MARY HOYER DOLL"

Adolph Hülss

Ideal Novelty and Toy Co.

"IDEAL" (in a diamond), "US of A: IDEAL NOVELTY," and "TOY CO. BROOKLYN, NEW YORK," and others.

Jumeau

E.J. Bébé
1881 – 86
6
E.J.

Jumeau, early EJ mark, 1881 – 1883.

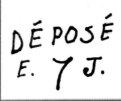

Jumeau, EJ Déposé mark, 1883 – 1886.

DÉPOSÉ
TETE JUMEAU
^{BTE} SGDG
6

Jumeau, mark used on body after 1887.

JUMEAU
MEDAILLE D'OR
PARIS

Tête Jumeau mark.

Kamkins

Heart-shaped sticker:
"KAMKINS// A DOLLY MADE TO LOVE // PATENTED//FROM// L.R. KAMPES//STUDIOS// ATLANTIC CITY//N.J."

Kämmer & Reinhardt

J.D. Kestner

Kewpie

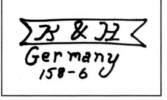

Kley & Hahn

C.F. Kling & Co.

Gebruder Knoch

König & Wernicke

Richard Krueger

"KRUEGER NY//REG. U.S. PAT. OFF/
/MADE IN U.S.A." on body or clothing seam.

Käthe Kruse

Gebruder Kuhnlenz

Lanternier

Lenci

A.G. Limbach

Marks Index

Armand Marseille

Armand Marseille
Germany
390
A. 4. M.

Queen Louise
Germany
7.

Made in Germany
Florodora
A 5 M

May Freres Cie

On head:
MASCOTTE
On body:
Bébé Mascotte Paris
Child marked:
Mascotte on head

Morimura Brothers

Mark for Morimura Brothers,
Japan 1915 on:

Gebruder Ohlhaver

Petite et Dumontier

P 3 D

Rabery & Delphieu

Mark: R.3. D

Theodor Recknagel

Rohmer

Bruno Schmidt

Franz Schmidt

or
S & C
ANVIL MARK

Schmitt & Fils

Shield on head, "SCH" in
shield on bottom of
flat cut derriere.

Schoenau & Hoffmeister

A. Schoenhut & Co.

Schuetzmeister & Quendt

Simon & Halbig

S.F.B.J.

Shirley Temple

Shirley Temple//
IDEAl Nov. & TOY on
back of head and
SHIRLEY TEMPLE on
body. Some marked
only on head and
with a size.

Margarete Steiff

Button in ear

Hermann Steiner

Swaine & Co.

Unis France

Unis France mark.

A. Thuillier

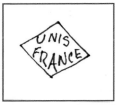

Unis France diamond mark.

Louis Wolfe & Co.

152
L. W. & Cº
12

INDEX

Index

Index

Index

Index

Index

Index

Index

Index

Index

Index

Index

Index

Index

Index

Index